DISCARDED

THE ARMENIAN FILE

THE
ARMENIAN FILE

THE MYTH OF INNOCENCE EXPOSED

Kamuran Gürün

Published by
Rustem

956.62
G

This book is copyrighted under the Bern Convention. All rights are reserved by the author. Apart from any fair dealing for the purpose of private study, research, criticism or review, as permitted under the Copyright Act, 1956, no part of this publication may be reproduced, stored in a retrieval system, or transmitted, in any form or by any means, electronic, electrical, chemical, mechanical, optical, photocopying, recording or otherwise, without the prior permission of the copyright owners. Enquiries should be addressed to the publisher: Rustem Bookshop, PO Box 239, Nicosia, Mersin10 Turkey.
e-mail:rustem@super-cyprus.com or rustemkitabevi@superonline.com

© *2001 Kamuran Gürün*

Turkish edition first published in 1983. Reprinted in 1984, 1985, 1988 and 2001
French edition first published in 1984. Reprinted in 1985.
This edition first published in 1985. Reprinted 2001.

Page setting by, Eylem Deliceırmak,
Cover designed by, Eylem Deliceırmak

We commemorate with respect our 41 diplomats
who were assasinated between the years 1973-1994,
and present our gratitude to the author of this book
retired Ambassador Kamuran Gürün

ISTANBUL TECHNICAL UNIVERSITY
FOUNDATION

We present this research to our readers which is based upon the tragedy lived between the Russian supported Armenians and the Turks during the First World War.

We hope that this book will assist the readers in finding out the true aspect of the issue.

ISTANBUL TECHNICAL UNIVERSITY
FOUNDATION

Sponsored by:
THE TEACHING STAFF AND THE GRADUATES OF THE
ISTANBUL THECNICAL UNIVERSITY

Contents

INTRODUCTION

"The Armenian File" which was completed in 1982 and published in 1983 for the first time was the second book that covered the subject with all of its aspects, after the late Esat Uras's book "Armenians in History and the Armenian Problem". The main difference of this book from Mr. Uras's book was that the performed research was mainly based on the Ottoman and foreign archives and documents, and all the available books of foreign authors who worked on this subject were througly incorporated into the book. The deficiency of this book as compared to Mr. Uras's book was that the texts written in Armenian were not directly referred to because the author was not competent in Armenian language. This deficiency was overcome by referring to Mr. Uras's book.

One might ask why it has been deemed necessary to write a new book when Mr. Uras's work was already present. Mr.Uras's book which was published in 1950 might be regarded as a reply to the Armenian allegations which have been exhumed after1945. The Armenian allegations posited at that time were such that the Ottomans had put an end to the Armenians independence by occupying their land and thus that the Armenians had to be returned their land allegedly invaded by the Ottomans. Besides these allegations,there were also allegations put forth by the Georgians. An other claim was that the Armenians had been exposed to a continuous massacre since 1877-78 Turkish-Russian war. These allegations were attempted to be raised again during the peace conference when Lausanne Peace Treaty was signed. Mr. Uras had mainly focused on these subjects and explained in detail how the Armenian historians changed and distorted these issues, also shedding light especially on the life of the Armenias under the Ottoman rule and the period of rebellions. Uras's book which briefly mentioned the First World War and The Turkish Independence War, was an important and objective book which served a vast source that could be referred to by those who would like to analyze the concerned subject in a scientific way.

At that time, the Armenians had not yet started their assaults on the Turkish Diplomats: Neither had they yet clung to the genocide claims by making up the story that 2 million Armenians were systematically massacred during the First World War, so as to justify their assaults which they were later to launch on the Turkish diplomats. Therefore, Mr. Uras was right in not thinking that these issues would also have to be examined.

By 1980, in addition to the previous claims which were also being posited, the main claim which was strongly at stake was the last allegation. Apart from this, the fabricated documents in Aram Andonian's, the inventor of Talat Pasha Telegrams, book had also been resurfaced even though these documents had been left aside for a long while as the Armenians also knew that these documents were all false. They must have thought that after a period of 50-60 years had elapsed, it would be impossible to prove that these documents were fake. Finally, in order to establish alikeness between the Armenians and the Jewish people who had been exposed to a systematic extermination plan, they claimed that the model for the Jewish genocide during the Second World War was taken from Turkey. Hence, obssessed with the attempt to secure support from the Jewish lobby, they alleged that while Hitler gave the "Endlosung" instruction, he had said:
"Who remembers the Armenians massacred in Turkey after all these years?".

I realised that remaining silent despite these new developments would be of no use. On the contrary, it would mean and was an acceptance. Therefore, as a scholar carrying out research in history, I decided to re-analyse the subject with all its aspects and write a book in short chapters which would adress the general reader rather than a researcher. This was why "The Armenian File" was written.

Following the publication of the book, I received various suggestions and criticism from my readers. Amongst these were that some chapters contained unnecessary information thus increasing the volume of the book, that some very interesting sources were not referred to, that the cruelty of the Armenian committee members towards the innocent Turkish people was not mentioned at all and that several important subjects were not covered.

All of them were right. Nevertheless, the book was shortly sold out for it had attracted an attention I had never thought of. Making the suggested changes, setting the book in type again and publishing it as a new addition would require a long time. Above all, it was necessary to wait for a certain period of time in order to be able to complete the parts which were missing. Because of this, the second and third editions were published with no changes made on the first copy of the book. It is only in the fourth eddition of the book that I have been able to fulfil some of the suggestions made. Although several suggestions were also correct, I have to explain why it is not possible for me to realize them.

While writing this book, I had to follow one of the two possible ways. The first one was to assume a typical Armenian authors style adressing merely the feelings and trying to speak ill of the Turkish nation, and instead of putting forth the truth, lay out the Armenian attacks and killings on the Turkish people with all the known disasters whose documents are abundant in the Ottoman archives or carry out an entirely objective and scientific research of the documents and analyze the issue with all its factual aspects,

Since I don't have the intention to insult the Armenian race and nation and to attribute actions of a small group to the whole Armenian people, I have chosen the second way. Therefore, I did not include in my book those observations and comments against the Armenian community which were evident in the texts and documents that I had analysed. Since there has been no change in my stance concerning this issue, I can not conform to these suggestions in this revised 2nd edition .

Suggestions stating that I have not referred to several vital sources well have their point. Nevertheless, the only reason for this is that I was either unaware of the presence of those sources while I was writing the book, or unable to find these sources no matter how much I tried to find them. In this edition, I intentionally was not involved in any attempt to abolish this deficiency since three or four new references would serve no other purpose than supporting the previous ones. Several sources which I have not been able to make use of, I leave to other authors. In my opinion, it is necessary to analyse each topic in The Armenian File very carefully. Especially the riots and the committee activities should be analysed as separate cases. I wish to hope that these issues would be analysed and documented by other authors.

These are the suggestions and criticism I could not fulfil. On the other hand, I accepted the suggestion that with the inclusion of unnecessary information such as the 1840 Lebanon Event, the discussion of several topics had increased the volume of the book and that this had to be re-evaluated. I removed those topics whose absence, according to me, would not violate the integrity of the structure of the book. Meanwhile, I also erased those sections in the first edition's foreword which I had taken down to state how the Armenian history is written. I thought that it would be of no use to analyse the method and system of the writings once it is determined and proven by documented evidence that what was written is wrong. Aram Andonian's book constitutes the only exception to this. This book, whose exclusion in the first edition has been a matter of criticism, has nothing to do with the Armenian history and contains merely fake documents that belong to the First World War. I added a 7th section at the end of chapter IV concerning this issue. The reason why I have not referred to this book in the first edition will be mentioned in this section.

Another issue which has been criticised for its absence in the first edition was the above mentioned statement that has been allegedly attributed to Hitler.

Since the Armenian File is a work dedicated to clarify the real aspects of historical events distortedly presented by the Armenians, and since these historical events happened before the Lausanne

Treaty, a discussion where we could analyse the stated allegation does not exist within the plan of our book. Therefore, I believe it would be useful to tackle and clarify this issue in this part of the book.

On November 24, 1945, Saturday, there was an unsigned article under the title of "The War Route of the Nazi Germany" in the *Times* newspaper published in London. In this article, one of Hitler's speeches, which he had made in his meeting with high ranking commanders on August 22, 1939, was quoted and it was declared that the minutes of this meeting was brought forward by the prosecutor on November, 23 1945, i.e., the previous day, as evidence at the Nurnberg Court of War Criminals. In the above mentioned article, Hitler is claimed to have uttered the following statement: "Who still talks nowadays of the extermination of the Armenians?"

In 1980's, this was the most frequently quoted statement by the Armenians who sought to prove their allegations. Especially on the occasion of April 24 in the American Congress, this statement was used in this or that way in speeches delivered by several senators and representatives.

When I started to write The Armenian File, this issue whose origin I tried to investigate was one of the matters which took most of my time. At that time, I was not aware of the above mentioned article that was published in the times. Naturally, I did not know on what occasion and when Hitler had used this sentence, if he of course had used it at all. The only thing which I had managed to find out especially following research carried out in Germany was that this sentence was claimed to have been uttered in Hitler's speech in Obersalzberg on August 22, 1939, when he was giving order for the invasion of Poland.

Because of another subject I was working on, I had a lot of documents concerning the attendees of the meeting and the instruction that was given the former by Hitler. Nevertheless, there was no sign in this documents attesting the utterance of such a statement by Hitler. In William Shirer's book[1] who has carried out a broad research about Nazi Germany, it was stated that three different minutes of the 22 August 1939 meeting were submitted to the Nuremberg Court of War Criminals, one of which had not been used as evidence by the prosecutor owing to the fact that it had been falsified. I must admit that I could not think the statement attributed to Hitler could have been in these allegedly falsified minutes, and hence it did not occur to my mind to refer to Nuremberg minutes. Because of this reason, no section was allocated in the first edition of the Armenian File concerning this issue.

In the meantime, an American researcher, Dr Heath Lowly, who has carried out research on the same subject, clarified this issue and published the results of his research.[2] In this way, it was revealed that the sentence attributed to Hitler had been never used

by Hitler, and this statement was added to the minutes of 22
August meeting that were fraudulently distorted. In this way,
I have found the opportunity in the fourth edition (Turkish
edition) to respond to and cover the criticism that was correctly put
forth in this direction. With the help of Lowry's article,
I summarise below the development of the subject.

In his book "What About Germany" published in 1942, Louis
Lochner, who served as the Chief of the Berlin Bureau of
Associated Press until the United States of America took part in the
war, revealed a document which he obtained from an unnamed
source titled The Contents of the Declaration made to the Army
and Force commanders in Obersalzberg on 22 August 1939. It is
understood from another book of Lochner, "Always the
Unexpected", published in 1956 that the concerned document was
given to him by a confidant of General Von Beck a short time
before USA entered the war. The name of this confidant was not
mentioned. In this document quoted in Lochner's book published
in 1942, the paragraph with the sentence attributed to Hitler is as
follows:

"*I have issued the command_I'll have anybody who utters on
word of criticism executed by a firing squad_that our war aim does
not consist in reaching certain lines, but in the physical destruction
of the enemy. Accordingly, I have placed my death-head formations
in readiness_for the present only in the East_with orders to them to
send to death mercilessly and without compassion, men,women, and
children of Polish derivation and language. Only thus shall we gain
the living space (Lebensraum) which we need. Who, after all, speaks
today of the annihilation of the Armenians ?*"

The paragraph included in the minutes of the same meeting
which was quoted in an unsigned article published in the *Times*
newspaper on 24 November 1945, and revealed on the grounds
that it was submitted to the court as evidence by the prosecutor in
Nuremberg, is as follows:

"*Accordingly* I have placed my death-head formations in
readiness_for the present only in the East_ with orders to them to
send to death *mercilessly and without compassion, men, women,
and children of Polish derivation and language. Only thus shall we
gain the living space (Lebensraum) which we need. Who, after all,
speaks today of the annihilation of the Armenians ?*"

Even though it was stated in the newspaper that the
prosecutor had submitted these minutes to the court the previous
day, this was not the case. On the contrary, on November 26 and
not on November 23 the prosecutor had declared at the court that
they possesed three different documents concerning Hitlers decision
to start the war one, of which was sent to them by an American
journalist. Nevertheless since the concerned document was given to
the journalist by another person and since there was no evidence
that the document was given to this person by the actual person

who took the records, he was of the opinion that this document was fraudulently distorted and would not hence submit this document to the court as evidence. On the defence attorneys' stating that the document which was not submitted to the court had been published in a newspaper, the prosecutor had regretfully admitted that this was the case. The conclusion arising out of these talks is that the journalist who sent the minutes to the court had his article published in the *Times* on November 24, believing that the minutes would anyway be submitted to the court on November 23 as evidence. However neither the issue was elaborated on November 23 nor the minutes were submitted to the court as evidence.

From his book, published in 1956, it became obvious that the above mentioned journalist was Lochner.

In the minutes submitted to the court as evidence by the prosecutor, there is not a single word concerning the Armenians. Furthermore, the issue of the massacre of the Jews is not mentioned in the text published by Lochner either. It is impossible, even if one bases his allegations on the distorted documents of Lochner, to claim that Hitler demonstrated the Armenians as an example when he was giving the orders for the mass destruction of the Jewish people. Inspite of this, as if there was such an expression in the minutes which was submitted to the court as evidence and accepted, the above mentioned sentence has been repetedly used for 40 years.

Here ends the summary of Dr. Lowry's research. We can add certain issues which we have found out during our own research.

After the removal of General von Fritsch as Chief of General Staff, acting upon a law which he passed on 4 February 1938, Hitler abolished the Ministry of War which then referred to the post of the Commander in Chief of the Armed Forces and, established 3 Force Commanderships which will be submit to the newly established Armed Forces Chief Commandership (OKW=Oberkommando Whermacht) and overtook the Chief Commandership post himself. He appointed General Keitel as the Chief of OKW and General von Brauchisch as the Land Forces Commander. Within this organisation, General von Beck was to serve as the Chief of Staff of the Land Forces.

Following the instructions of Hitler in the July of 1938 which was conveyed to lieutenant Generals and higher ranking Generals concerning his decision to operate against Checkoslavakia, von Beck withdrew from his post and was succeded by General Halder upon the former's objection to Hitler's decision. After this date General von Beck joined efforts to organise a resistance group against Hitler, later actively acting as the leader of this group, General Beck committed suicide after the unsuccesful assassination attempt against Hitler on July 20 1944.

It has been known that during the clandestine mission coordinated by General Beck the stated General had performed five secret contact with the western states. Efforts in these contacts were generally directed towards eliminating Hitler and establishing peace. I broadly explain these issues in my book "Waring World and Turkey".

I have not been able to find out who had given the document, to the journalist Lochner. General Beck, who was assigned no duties on 22 August 1939, had naturally not attended the above mentioned meeting. Information I have obtained from various sources shows that four persons took the minute of that meeting. Among them was General Halder, the successor of General Beck, who himself was also a member of the group working against Hitler. The minutes taken down by Halder have been aquired and published by the Americans. In these minutes which are the same with those submitted to the court as evidence, there is no record concerning the Armenians.

The second person who have taken the minutes of the above mentioned meeting was the Navy Commander Admiral Hermann Boehm. This document has been published too. It is also confirmed in the Memoirs of The Grand Admiral Reader, who was one of the attendees of the concerned meeting, that Admiral Boehm's notes are in conformity with the facts in the sense that these minutes in which there was not a single word concerning Armenians were the same with the ones submitted to the court as evidence.

The third minutes were the unsigned notes that were obtained at OKW Headquarters and submitted to the court by the prosecutor as evidence. It has not been possible to determine by whom these notes were taken. It is known that General Keitel did not take notes. Neither did his assistant General Jodle. Although it might be thought that these notes were taken by Rudolf Schbundt, Hitler's Chief of Staff, it is naturally not possible to say something certain on this issue. There is not a single word about the Armenians in these notes either.

It is known that the fourth person who took notes was the Military Intelligence Chief Admiral Canaris. The notes taken by Canaris have not been found. However H.B. Gisevius who was also a member of the resistance group but had survived after the unsuccessful assassination attempt against Hitler and published his memoirs, refers to Canaris's notes in his book.

Admiral Canaris who was also included in the resistance group was arrested after the assassination attempt on 20 July and was sent to Flossenburg concentration camp. He was executed there in 1945. It is said that Admiral Canaris had played a great role in peace efforts by trying to eliminate Hitler and in order to convince the western states that Hitler's personality was the source of all evil, he had recourse to various ways including making distorsions in official documents which would draw great attention in western states. From this stand point, it seemed quiet likely that the document which was delivered to Lochner had come out of this channel after going through several similar distortions. It might be thought that Admiral Canaris who owed his authority to his rather being known as a strong opponent had chosen to use General von Beck's name for he did not want his name to be revealed very often.

The only thing that is certain is that during the meeting held on 22 August 1939, Hitler did not utter the words attributed to him and no document containing this alleged statement was submitted to the court. There is no doubt that these issues are also known by the Armenian Historians who carry out broad research on this subject. Nevertheless they have seen no harm or disadvantage in spreading these words, which they know are not true as if these words were true.

This is the story behind those words which were attributed to Hitler.

I also have to say a few words on how I have prepared this book. During my study and research, I especially focused on official archives documents. But since several topics and issues such as those concerning the Armenian history did not bear the qualification to be included within the official archives documents, I tried to analyse these in the broadest sense possible. I naturally made use of the works written by Armenian historians. I was not interested whether the books which I made use of as the source of my study were for or against Turks. Most of these books were against Turks anyway.

As a principal, I did not use any book as reference which I did not read personally. The only exceptions are a few Armenian books, of which I could not find any translations in another language, since that language is not known by myself. Therefore, from some Armenian authors, such as Leo and Hadisyan, I included the quotations of Esat Uras who is perfectly fluent in the Armenian language.

Armenians during the First World War, declared that they had fought against Turkey and had attended the Sevres peace conference as belligerent. Since this was there claim and approved will, it is not possible to understand them refuse to accept the events as the relationship of two fighting parts. There behaviour to act as citizens in one circumstance and as an enemy in another one is difficult to explain.

If this book, which is based on objective research and study is read without any prejudice, the matter will be easliy understood. As a matter of fact, this is the reason why this book has been written.

Some readers may wonder why the book is titled 'The Armenian File'. Let me explain.

While the phrase, 'The Armenian Question' gained common acceptance in several languages during the second half of the nineteenth century, the Armenians were not viewed as a 'question' in the minds of the contemporary governments. The people who viewed the Armenians as a 'question' were the hierarchy of the Armenian Church, the Amenian terrorist organizations and those few Armenians who belonged to them.

There exists, however, among the Foreign Ministry records of every great power, an 'Armenian File'. From time to time, whenever it served their interests, these files were opened and examined. When their interest passed, the file was closed and returned to its spot on the shelf.

The Armenian organizations, labouring under the misapprehension that work towards a solution of their problems continued unabated, have never been able to see or comprehend the truth: that the only result of their actions is the addition of one more file to the files. They remain blithely unaware that the only place their dreams will bear fruit is in their own minds.

In one instance, Russia invaded Turkey's eastern provinces and promptly declared that it was illegal for Armenians to reside in the annexed areas. In the same way that they had decided that there was no Yakut problem in Russia, they now adopted the same attitude towards the Armenians. On another occasion when the French temporarily occupied the region of Cilicia in south-eastern Anatolia, they immediately announced that the question of the formation of an autonomous Armenian government in this region was not open for discussion. They even went so far as to prohibit Armenian immigration into the area.

These facts are well documented in the Foreign Ministry records of various governments. In point of fact, the place where they really belong is in the collective memory of the Armenian people.

In this book, we will open up these 'files'. It is for this reason, in keeping with the actual name of the files, that this book is entitled The Armenian File.

KAMURAN GÜRÜN
Ankara, 28 July 1982

CHAPTER ONE

Armenia and the Armenians

1. The origins of the terms Armenia and Armenian

There are countries which took their names from the people living on the land. There are also countries which took their names from their geographic locations or from their administrative divisions. The residents of these areas have often forgotten their original names and are remembered simply by the name of the region they inhabit. We may cite Turkey, Germany, and France as examples of countries, which took their names from the people living in them. In contrast, Italy and the United States of America are not the names of people, but rather geographical names, which were adopted by the people living in these areas, who consequently gave up their original names.

Likewise, in the ancient past of Anatolia there were geographical area names, and the people living in these regions were known by these 'geographical' names. As examples we may cite Cappadocia, Cilicia, Pamphilia, Pafloginya, etc. However, for those who once lived in these regions, these names were a means of identification, in the same way that today we say someone is from Istanbul, from Ankara, and so on.

Many sources claim that Armenia was also such a geographical region name. Armenians, however, call themselves 'Hai' and their country 'Haiastan' and there are no extant sources which clearly state the origin of the name Armenia. Some early Armenian historians, among whom we may name Moses of Khorene, claimed that the Armenians were Urartus and that the name 'Armenia' derived from that of an Urartu king named 'Aramu'. Contemporary Armenian historians have for the most part discarded this theory. As we shall establish shortly, there was in fact no relationship between the Urartus and their civilization on the one hand, and the Armenians on the other.

It is, however, possible to find a degree of truth in Moses of Khorene's theory if it is approached from another angle. Specifically, the use of the term Armenia to designate a geographical region may well have derived from the name Aramu and then its sources been forgotten. The result was that while 'Armenian' had originally meant 'from the region of Armenia' it lost this meaning. Today, the name Armenian is once again used in the sense of 'from Armenia', though this in fact has nothing to do with the present country of

Armenia. (In foreign languages there is no distinction made between 'from Armenia' and 'Armenian', and the word 'Armenian' is used for both meanings.)

Arnold Toynbee put forth the following ideas with regard to the origin of the name 'Armenian':

If the valley of the Teleboas had in fact thus been transferred from Urartu to Armenia at some date between the end of the Assyrian and the beginning of the Median Age, this might prove to be the explanation of two puzzling pieces of nomenclature. In the first place it might explain how the Mushkian (i.e. Phrygian) followers of Gurdi, who in their own language called themselves Haik, came to be known in the Achaemenian official terminology neither as Haik nor as Mushki nor as Gordians, but as 'Arminiya'. This old Persian ethnikon of a place name 'Arminiya' may represent the Urartian word Urmeniuhi-ni which occurs in Menuas' inscription found in the neighbourhood of Mush as the name of one of the conquered local cities which he had razed to the ground; and, in confirming the cession of this Urartian canton called Urmeniuhi-ni to the Mushki intruders who called themselves Haik, the Medes, and the Persians after them, may have labelled these new owners of this transferred piece of Urartian territory with the Urartian local place-name.[1]

Toynbee, while adding that this explanation is merely speculation, adds that it is possible that the term 'Armenia' may have been derived from the name of 'Erimena', who was the father of the last Urartian ruler, Russas III; alternatively, it might derive from 'Aruma-ni', which means the country of the Arameans, a people who came from the North Arabian steppes at the end of the 11th or beginning of the 10th century BC and conquered Nairi.

It is not our intention to introduce either historical or archaeological research on this topic. Our reasons for mentioning it at all are completely different. While it is accepted that the name 'Haiastan' has nothing to do with the name 'Armenia' or 'Haik' with 'Armenian', and while it is usual to find the residents of Armenia in ancient times referred to as 'Armenians', it is not usual for the word Armenian to be used as though it were synonymous with Haik. Thus it is not possible to ascertain whether the inhabitants of Armenia were the ancestors of the Armenians of today, or whether the region inhabited by those ancestors was identical with the region that was called Armenia in early times.

While the derivation of the name Armenia as a region thus remains an unanswered question, it is equally uncertain as to when the group known as 'Haik' first appeared in this area.

As this book is not designed as scholarly research into ancient Armenian history, we have not seen the necessity to delve into this subject further. We have been satisfied to repeat what appears in the books we have used as sources, and have followed the chronology which they present.

Early Armenian historians, such as Moses of Khorene, Toma Ardzouni and others, are content to write that the Armenians are the descendants of the Prophet Noah, and because they accept that Noah's Ark came to rest on Mount Ararat, they claim to have occupied this region throughout history. While there is no particular reason to respond to such mythical views of history, one point which has been overlooked by its proponents should be mentioned. Namely, if one wants to base understanding of history on religious books and mythology, one should be consistent. As these accounts tell how the entire human race increased from the children of the Prophet Noah, one must assume likewise that the Turkish people also increased in the vicinity of Mount Ararat and were successful in maintaining their hold on the lands of their origin.

Gatteyrias has this to say about the origins of the Armenians:

When the first tribes began to migrate out of the Pamir Plateau, one group settled in the Sind Valley to the South, while the remainder moved North and settled in the Iranian Plateau. As a result the only migratory path which remained open was that lying to the West. Correspondingly, subsequent migratory tribes were forced to settle in Europe. As they began the first steps of their migrations they encountered the Caucasus Mountains, and seeking a passageway they moved South to Asia Minor. . . .

These tribes who settled in various valleys of Armenia, developed and lived their own lives without contact with one another. Some of them became particularly strong, and on occasion formed confederations with other groups.

When the Assyrians conquered the country of Nairi in the year 1130 BC, up to the headwaters of the Tigris and Euphrates rivers, that is, during the period of the first Assyrian Dynasty, they found them in this state.

During the time of the Second Assyrian Dynasty, these wars of conquest continued in a more serious fashion and the people of Urartu of Ararat experienced a whole series of defeats. After the eighteenth or nineteenth campaign Armenia surrendered in 782-780 BC, and for a forty-year period the Assyrians remained the uncontested rulers of the Upper Tigris valley. Throughout this period they tried to expand their civilization.

During these attempts of the Semitic peoples to settle, the Armenian tribes of Urartu resisted these efforts and consequently they were able to preserve more effectively than the others their Aryan blood and spirits. . . .[2]

Without dwelling on its geographical and historical inconsistency, we understand that the author claims that during the period of the Great Migrations the Armenians migrated from the Pamir Plateau to this region. What is interesting here is that the Armenians were considered simply as one of the tribes which comprised the Urartu Empire, and that the word Armenian itself may have been used as a geographic term to indicate the Urartu borders.

The ideas of Jacques de Morgan on this point are as follows:

In any case according to the documents at our disposal the movement of the Armenians from Cappadocia to the Erzurum Plateau occurred between the VIII and VII centuries BC and this group of people had been occupying the Lake Van and Ararat regions for at least 600 years.[3]

Macler says

. . . .Armenia, or that geographical region known as Armenia since the earliest period of history, was not always occupied by those people whom we call Armenians . . . even if this region was not the home of another race *per se*, it certainly was the home of a people who spoke another language than Armenian.

The first recorded references to the Armenian people are inscriptions in stone found in Bissutun which date from 515 BC, that is from the Achemenid period of Darius. These inscriptions show that Armenia was a Satrap, or province of Darius' Empire.[4]

As we see, Macler's view was that Armenia was called Armenia long before the people we know as Armenians inhabited it. Later we shall return to a discussion of the Darius inscriptions.

Let us look at Pastermadjian's book:

. . . .The Armenians, who are an Indo-European people, first appear in the East in Urartu, that is Armenia, together with the Kimers who were another Indo-European group from the Caucasus; or alternatively, they may have come from the West via the Balkans and Asia Minor in the company of another Indo- European people, the Phrygians with whom they shared blood ties. They appear to have arrived in the VII or VI century BC. This second thesis, which is still accepted in the academic world, is that the Indo-European Armenians entered Anatolia from the Balkans.

According to legends the Chieftain of these Indo-European peoples was named Haik. According to the Armenians, Haik was the founder of their state and their first king. They gave themselves the name 'Hai,' that is, the sons of Haik.

The Armenian Chroniclers relate that Haik and his people came and settled in Armenia in the year 2200 BC, and in support of this they provide a list of Kings and Rulers who lived between 2200 BC and 800 BC. This is a legend which modern historical scholarship has rejected. Nations, unlike individuals, like to age. . . .[5]

As we read these lines, although it is not clear what theory Pastermadjian embraced, it is clear that he accepted the idea that Armenians came to the region called Armenia in the 7th or 6th century BC. As a result, Pastermadjian accepts the arrival of the Armenians as having occurred one hundred years later than does Jacques de Morgan.

Let us now examine Nalbandian:

. . . .The Urartu Kingdom was not only a powerful military state but it also had a highly developed civilization. Its people spoke a non-Aryan language, which has been deciphered and they believed in a single supreme god whom they named Khaldi. . . .

In the Eighth and Seventh centuries BC a new people invaded Urartu and conquered it. According to Herodotus, the people who overthrew Urartu were Phrygian colonists known as Armenians. As time passed, the Armeno-Phrygian tribes imposed their Indo-European language on the Urartians, and the amalgamation of the two peoples resulted in the formation of the Armenian nation.[6]

Let us first say that Herodotus in no way made the claims attributed to him by Nalbandian. (We shall prove this later.) On the other hand, it would be a unique process if a language which had its own script had been replaced by a language that did not have a script. Normal progress dictates just the reverse process. Nalbandian's contribution to the discussion is the idea that the Armenian people resulted from the combination of some Phrygian tribes who migrated to this region and the local populace: in other words, the idea that prior to this time there had been no such thing as the Armenian people.

Hovannisian's view is: 'They had moved on to the Plateau as Indo-European conquerors and extended their hegemony over the indigenous peoples whom they eventually assimilated. Then, after a period of submission to the Achaemenids and Seleucids, they regained independence under a dynasty that wielded authority throughout the two centuries before Christ.'[7]

From his style, it is not very clear from where and when Hovannisian thinks the Armenians arrived. His sense of scholarship prevents him from writing about points which have not been scientifically proved. What is clear is that he believes the Armenians to have migrated from another region to Armenia, and that this occurred prior to the Achaemenid invasion. In this respect it is worth recalling that the formation of the Achaemenid dynasty, that is the invasion of Armenia by the Medes, took place in the 6th century BC.

The following passages are quoted from Grousset, who was the author of a large work on Armenian history:

Towards the year 1200 BC one portion of the Thracian tribes passed over into Asia where they were assimilated into the Hittite Empire, under the name of Phrygians. These Phrygians settled on the Anatolian Plateau, and extended their sovereignty up to the Cilician Gates in the Southeast, and in the Northeast as far as Hoyuk (the former capital city of the Hittites, Bogazkoy), which lies to the North of Hattus. According to the Assyrians they must have been the same Phrygians who are mentioned in their sources under the name, 'Mouchki'. . . .

In the year 677 BC the Assyrian King, Assarhaddon, defeated a Cimmerian force which was commanded by one Teuchpa or Tiochpa.

This Cimmerian group then moved into Anatolia, where, between the years 676-675 BC they destroyed the remaining Phrygians and brought an end to their sovereignty, if not to their ethnic identity. . . .

These Cimmerians were unable to follow up their victory, but the Phrygian Empire was not reconstructed, and ultimately it was partially replaced by the Lydian Empire. Thus, one group of the defeated Phrygian tribes moved to the east in search of a new homeland. In all likelihood, this is the manner in which the people known as Armenians came into being.[8]

Grousset in this way accepts that the group of people whom we today call Armenians first entered the geographical region of Armenia after 675 BC.

Particularly today, when Urartian history is no longer a mystery, owing to the findings of various archaeological excavations, we have every right to expect that contemporary scholars will incorporate these new findings into their works. Those readers who feel this way will be disappointed by Professor Lang's study which makes the following statement in regard to Urartian history:

The founder of the unified Urartian kingdom was evidently King Arame or Aramu, mentioned in Assyrian inscriptions of King Salmanesar III under the years 860, 858 and 846 BC, and no doubt to be identified with the half-legendary Armenian king, Ara the Fair, loved by Queen Semiramis. . . . The Armenian chronicler Moses of Khorene regards the Urartian king Aramu as the eponymous ancestor of the Armenian Nation.[9]

Is it really possible that a professor of history has so failed to read the current research on Urartian history, that he can still accept myths written by Moses of Khorene (legends which are even rejected by many Armenian historians) as historical fact, and in this manner to find a connection between the Urartians and Armenians?

Professor Lang goes even further than this, and on page 114 of his work we read:

As mentioned, the Armenians term themselves 'Haik,' and their land 'Hayastan.' There seems good reason to connect this ethnic name with the old eastern Hittite province of Hayasa, in mountainous western Armenia, along the upper reaches of the River Euphrates or Kara-Su. The Hayasa people's language was evidently related to the ancient Indo-European languages.

After noting the fact that Professor Lang is not a linguist, let us answer him with Grousset's pen:

The name Hayasa does not go further than to draw attention to the Armenian name of Armenia. In reality, this is a fortuitous analogy. As for the location of this region, Louis Dalaporte placed it near Trebizond . . . Contrary to his opinion, N. Adontz feels that it was located in the Dersim Mountains on the upper Euphrates.[10]

The name of the country of Hayasa is also found in a Hittite inscription which belongs to the reign of Murshilish II, the Hittite ruler who reigned from 1345 to 1320 BC. Bedrich Hrozny, the famous Hittitologist and archaeologist, describes this period of Hittite history as follows:

The Hittite Empire comes to an end around the year 1200 BC. This catastrophe occurred in the reign of Tuthaliyash V (around 1200 BC), who was the son and successor of Arnuvantash. Groups of Phrygians, Thracians, and Mycinians, and other Balkan peoples including Armenians, were pushed into Asia Minor by the Illyrians. These 'migrations' were finally stopped by the Pharaoh Ramses III at the gateway of Egypt. When these waves of migrations ceased it becomes clear that the principal heirs of the Hittite Empire were the Phrygians in the west, and the Mouchkis in the east. Further to the south in the Toros and Anti-Toros mountain ranges a number of small Hittite states continued to exist right up until the year 717 BC when Sharruken (Sargon) the Assyrian king conquered the last great Hittite fortress of Kargemish, thereby bringing the political existence of the Hittites to an end.[11]

The first appearance of the word Armenia occurs in the Bissutun inscriptions from the reign of Darius. These inscriptions belong to the year 515 BC. After this date, the next appearance of the words Armenia and Armenian in historical texts are found in the work of Herodotus, who lived between the years 484 and 430 BC.

In Herodotus works the words 'Armenia' and 'Armenian' are mentioned on pp. 120, 244, 358, 360 and 468.[12] On p. 120, he mentions the area of 'Armenia'; on p. 244, while listing the various Iranian states, he writes: 'Pattyica, together with the Armenians and their neighbours as far as the Black Sea'; on p. 358, after mentioning the 'Ionians', 'Lydians', 'Phrygians', 'Cappadocians', and 'Cilicians', he adds: 'now the Armenians. . .'. On p. 360 he uses the word 'Armenia', writing: 'Leaving Armenia and entering Matiene. . . ,' On page 468 we find the following paragraph:

The dress of the Phrygians was, with a few small differences, like the Paphlagonian. This people, according to the Macedonian account, were known as the 'Briges' during the period when they lived in Macedonia, and changed their name at the same time as, by migrating to Asia, they changed their country. The Armenians, who are Phrygian colonists, were armed in the Phrygian fashion and both contingents were commanded by Artochmes, the husband of one of Darius' daughters.

Today, almost all serious scholars, relying on the combined testimony of the Darius inscriptions and Herodotus, accept that the Armenians migrated to and settled in the region of Armenia in 515 BC.

Yet in both the Darius inscriptions and in Herodotus' work the word 'Armenian' can also be understood as having the meaning of 'from Armenia'. Neither the Darius inscriptions nor Herodotus mention a particular race, but rather the people from a given region. As Armenia was known as such long before the people we call Armenians entered the region, it is hard to say that the documents cited prove that the Armenians came to this region prior to 515 BC.

The same comment may be made with regard to the relevant passages in Xenophon's *Return of the Ten Thousand*.[13] The third, fourth and fifth chapters of Book IV deal with the armies' journey through the region of Armenia in 401-400 BC. In these references it is also clear that 'Armenia' is used in the sense of a geographical region. The word 'Armenian' appears once in the third chapter, as 'These were Armenian, Mardian and Chaldean mercenaries in the service of Orontas and Artouchas', and once more at the end of the fifth chapter where we read: 'Armenian children in local clothes . . .' In both these instances it is possible to define his use of this term as meaning 'from' or 'of' Armenia. However, throughout his passage on the region of Armenia, he does not call the local villagers Armenian, and the language they used to communicate with the local people is defined as Persian. While there can be no doubt that the name of the region was in fact Armenia, there is no indication in this period that its residents were called 'Armenians' as a people.

On the last page of the French translation of the same book (Chapter 7, Book VII), there is a paragraph not written by Xenophon but supposedly added by Sophénète, which lists the names of the states through which the ten thousand passed, and of their governors.

From other sources we know that the Secretary of the Governor ruling the region of West Armenia through which the ten thousand passed was one Tribaz (Orantes was the Persian Governor of the whole region). In the above-mentioned paragraph by Sophénète, Tribaz is presented as being the head of the 'Phases' and 'Hesperites'; there is no mention of 'Armenians'.[14]

There are also a number of authors who have advanced some rather 'original' theories as to the origins of the Armenians. As an example of this type of writer we may mention Ruppen Courian, who makes the following claims:

The Armenians are the former inhabitants of today's Switzerland. The Romance language has many similarities to Armenian. While there are variations in the formation of words and expressions, the interpositioning of syllables, and loan-words, the background and the rhythm of both languages are the same. Some people will oppose this idea. To understand its basis we have only to examine the map of Switzerland. There, lying between the villages of Oberhalbstein, Muhlen, Piz Julien, and St. Moritz, we find a place called 'Piz Er'. What is the meaning of this name?

The Turks and other Asians say 'Ermeni' to indicate an Armenian. The meaning of 'er' is 'man', in other words, 'Ermeni' means the man who comes from the land.[15]

On page 31 of the same author's book we are told that the name of the province of Van is derived from the French word 'vent' meaning wind because Van in eastern Anatolia is a windy city.

If it were necessary to look for the meaning of the proper name of the Swiss village, Piz Er, in Turkish, surely a more logical explanation could be found. *Er* means man and *pis* means dirty, so we could define the 'Turkish' meaning of the proper name as 'Dirty Man'. But this kind of 'word-game' has no place in serious scholarship, and its only proper use is in humorous writings!

In conclusion, we may summarize the points we have discussed in the form of quotations from various books, as follows:

Since the very early days of history a particular region of Anatolia has been known as 'Armenia'. The people whom we now call 'Armenians' migrated to this region from the west. The earliest possible date at which they may have arrived in this region was in the course of the 6th century BC. It is equally plausible, however, to suggest that they may not have arrived in the region until the beginning of the 4th century BC. This whole question is shrouded in obscurity.

What we know for certain is that at the time of Alexander the Great's Anatolia campaign (331 BC), the Armenians were occupying the region in question. It is equally certain that there can be no question of their having existed as an independent state in this period, for they were simply living in one of the Persian provinces.

Let us now briefly summarize what has been written about Armenian history from the fourth century BC onward.

2. The earliest known history of the Armenians

At the end of September in the year 331 BC, Alexander the Great defeated Darius III, the last Achaemenid ruler. In so doing, he conquered this country, and the region known as Armenia, which had been part of a Persian province, now became part of the Macedonian Empire.

Following the death of Alexander the Great, his Empire was divided and redivided among his generals. In the year 301 BC, following the last such division, the geographical region of Armenia fell to the share of Seleucas, one of Alexander the Great's generals. The so-called Seleucid Empire, which was to rule in this region until it was defeated by the Romans in 198 BC, was named after him.

Various historical sources report that following the Roman victory over the Seleucid Empire at Manisa in 198 BC, the geographical region of Armenia was ruled by two governors, Artaksiyas and Zariadris (both these names are Persian), who were under the protection of the Roman state. In other words, they broke away from the Seleucid Empire.

This period coincided with that in which the Arsasids were beginning to establish their sovereignty in Persia by reassembling the pieces of what had been the great Persian Empire. We know that the Arsasids reached the height of their power during the reign of Mithridates IV, who ruled from 123 to 88 BC. It is also known that during this period of expansion the Arsasids invaded Armenia, and even took Tigran, the son of the Armenian ruler Artavzade II, as a hostage.

Following his father's death in 95 or 94 BC, Tigran purchased his freedom from Mithridates by relinquishing his claim to certain of his territories, and succeeded his father.

By taking advantage, on the one hand, of 'civil wars' which were sapping Roman strength, and on the other, of the fact that the Arsasids were more or less continuously defending themselves against the attacks of the Sakas, Tigran subsequently managed not only to unite several of the Armenian principalities, but also to gain their independence and expand the territories over which he ruled. While he was engaged in these activities, he signed a peace agreement with the King of Pontus, Mithridates IV, Jupiter. While initially he benefited from this agreement, when subsequently war broke out between Rome and the Pontus, it resulted in the loss of his freedom. In the year 66 BC the Roman General Pompey and his armies invaded Armenia. As a result, Tigran was forced to recognize Roman rule and surrender his own independence.

If we date Tigran's period of independence as beginning in 95 BC, we see that it only lasted for thirty years. After this date, Armenia was nothing but a pawn in the struggles between the Romans and Persians. As such it moved from one sphere of influence to the other.

In 53 BC when the Roman general Crassus was defeated and lost his life at the hands of the Persians, the Arsasids once again regained their hold over Armenia.

In 36 BC Antony, wishing to avenge this Persian victory over Rome, marched his armies to Persia via Armenia, where he too was defeated. He blamed his defeat on the Armenian Prince Artavzade III. Consequently, he allowed his soldiers to kill Artavzade and to loot Armenia: From this time on, the Romans appointed various individuals as governors of the region of Armenia.

Beginning in the year AD 11, the Persians began to interfere in the selection of the ruler of Armenia. From time to time Armenia was occupied by Rome or Persia, but overall Roman rule continued to prevail in the region.

This state of affairs continued until the year AD 63, when a *modus vivendi* was established by Rome and Persia. In accordance with this agreement, Armenia, while officially remaining 'Roman', was to be governed by members of the Arsasid dynasty. As a result of this treaty, Tiridates, the brother of Vologese, the Persian Emperor, became ruler of Armenia. In this manner the Arsasid dynasty was established in Armenia. Despite subsequent disputes between Rome and Persia, the status of Armenia remained unchanged,

In the year AD 224 the Arsasid dynasty in Persia came to an end, and was replaced by the Sassanids. From this date onward the Armenian branch of the Arsasids began a struggle aimed at restoring Arsasid rule in Persia. Armenia was again occupied on several occasions by either the Romans or the Sassanids. This struggle, which lasted until AD 297, did not affect the status quo, and Armenia remained under Roman sovereignty and Arsasid rule.

While it is generally understood that Armenia accepted Christianity after AD 301, it was in fact the Armenian Prince Tiridates III and not the Armenian people as a whole who accepted Christianity. It was many years before the other feudal princes and the Armenian people as a whole accepted Christianity. The Roman Emperor Constantine's acceptance of Christianity was to be an important factor contributing to the success of those peoples who began to gather round the newly formed Armenian Church after the bloody fighting which had occurred between the feudal princes.

In the same period the Zoroastrian religion was becoming firmly established in the Sassanian Empire. For this reason the Sassanids did not look with favour upon the establishment of Christianity in Armenia, and at the same time they viewed the advance of the Roman Empire as a danger to be overcome. For these reasons the long-standing series of wars between the Romans and the Sassanids were resumed. The end result of these events was the division of Armenia into two sections in the year 390. The eastern region's ruler, appointed by the Sassanids, was Husrev III who was a member of the Arsasid dynasty, while the western region was given to the Romans, who placed it under the control of Arshak III, a member of the former Arsasid dynasty in Armenia.

Following the death of Arshak III, Rome did not appoint a new prince to its region, but instead joined it directly to the Empire.

As for Husrev III, the Sassanid ruler soon became displeased with his actions, and in the year 392 he was replaced by his brother, Vram Chapouh. The development of the Armenian alphabet in the year 406 occurred during this prince's reign.

Following the death of the last Arsasid prince, Artakes, in the year 428, the then ruling Sassanid Emperor Vahram V, rather than assigning a new prince in his place, agreed to the request of the feudal lords that this region be annexed directly to the Persian crown.

It is known that under the reign of Emperor Yazdigirt II (438-457), a struggle against Christianity began, resulting in a rebellion in 451. Persia, having invaded Armenia, crushed the rebellion in the Avarian region on 2 June, 451.

The war undertaken by Emperor Firuz against the Eftalits in 484 and his death during the battle enabled Armenia to free herself from absolute Persian domination. A prince named Vahan Mamikonian was able to take the right to rule Armenia from the Persian Emperor. However, it is known that after Vahan's death the area was once again under the domination of the Sassanid throne.

These dates constitute the period in which relations between the Armenian Church and the Greek Church deteriorated. (We shall deal with this subject later in Chapter 2.) After these years, Byzantium, which replaced Rome, began a policy of expelling Armenians from Armenia which was under her rule. Byzantium not only expelled feudal heads of clans, replacing them with Byzantine officials, but deported the local inhabitants to Thrace, bringing in people from other regions and slaves obtained in wars and settling them there as well.

In 570, a war between Persia and Byzantium broke out, lasting until 591. During the reign of the Byzantine Emperor Maurice (582-602), the defeat of Persia resulted in Armenia being relinquished to Byzantium with the exception of the area beyond Dwin. The Zonga and the Garnicay rivers were established as the border between the two countries; the area west of these rivers was given to Byzantium and the eastern part including the city of Dwin was left to Persia. It is recorded that Emperor Maurice continued his policy of expelling Armenians from the areas which he occupied.

After the death of Emperor Maurice in 602, a new war lasting twenty-five years began between Byzantium and Persia (604-629). However, not only did Persia lose this war, but Persian Armenia came under Byzantine rule as well.

Under the feudal system of the geographical region called Armenia, during the Sassanid period, the nobility was divided into two groups, the feudal lords (Nakharark), and the lesser nobles or Azat class. Research done by Adontz shows that there were about fifty Nakhararks. These were the owners and rulers of a given land, where they were independent. The most famous of these big families, each of which was an independent principality, were the Kamsarakans, the Mamikonians, the Siunis, the Bagratunis, the Rektunis, the Arzdrunis, the Apahunis, the Vahevunis and the Gnunis. Each had different origins. For example, it is recorded that the Kamsarakans were originally from Persia, that the Mamikonians had come from Central Asia, and that the Siunis were pure Armenian.

These feudal lords would come together only in wartime, when they sent their soldiers to war along with the prince appointed to rule Armenia. It is impossible to say that all the feudal lords were united in every war.

The lesser nobles consisted of members of the old families who were independent on their own lands. They were also compelled to provide the feudal lords with cavalrymen. The common people who were living within the boundaries of feudalism were living as slaves.

While the Sassanids saw advantage in preserving this system in order to benefit from the conflicts between the feudal lords, Byzantium was inclined to destroy the feudal system and establish the power of the central government. Thus the feudal lords along with the local inhabitants (possibly those who were not slaves) were deported to other areas.

The first Arab invasion took place in 639 or 640.[16] It is said that the Arabs entered Dwin in 642, that 12,000 Armenians were killed and 35,000 people taken away as slaves. These raids continued, and in 653 Armenia came under the Arabs' sphere of influence.

The Byzantine Emperor Constantine II invaded Armenia in 654 and entered Dwin. However, because most of the Armenian feudal lords had preferred to cooperate with the Arabs, the previous situation was restored after the Emperor's death.

In 690 the Arabs assigned Achot Bagratuni to govern Armenia. In this period, raids were undertaken almost alternately by Byzantium from the west, the Khazars from the north and the Arabs from the south.

During the reign of Khalif Velid, it is said that Muhhamed Ibni Mervan, having defeated Byzantium in 705, invaded Armenia and had all the feudal lords killed.

After this date the city of Dwin became the capital of the Arab governors.

When the Abbasids replaced the Omayyads, the rule of Armenia was entrusted to the Khalif's brother, Mansur. After this, Armenia for many years was ruled by Arab governors. The Armenian feudal lords were constantly fighting one another during these years.

It is understood that, in 885, Achot from the Bagratid family came victorious out of these internal struggles, and upon the common wish of the others, the Khalif Al-Mutemed sent him the Khelaut, the robe of honour. Naturally the sending of the Khelaut had not ended Arab rule over Armenia. However, this was the first time since 430 that a new Armenian prince had been appointed to govern the whole of Armenia.

Although the Bagratid family was brought to the leadership of Armenia, it was never able to control the other big families. Moreover, the Arab governors were successful in preserving their *de facto* sovereignty, and in crushing revolts by the Bagratids.

From the 970s on, Byzantium regained its power, replacing the Abbasids and organizing campaigns to Armenia.

After 1020 Oguz raids started in the Vaspurakan principality around Van lake. It is recorded that its leader, Senegrin Hovhannes, chose to relinquish his lands to the Byzantine Emperor Basile II, and the Prince of Vaspurakan went to Sivas with 14,000 men followed by the women and children; they all became Byzantine subjects.

Basile II continued to invade the rest of Armenia. At the time of his death in 1025, he had invaded one third of Armenia. The Bagratid Prince in Ani, which was not yet invaded, had bequeathed his lands to the Emperor. The rest of the princes who seemed independent were the Bagratid Prince Abas, the Bagratid Prince of Tasir David and the Siuni Prince Grigor from the south of lake Sevan.

When the Ani Prince died, the Emperor Michael demanded that the land be handed over to him. When Gagik II, the son of the Prince, did not fulfil the will of his father, the Emperor sent an army. Constantine Monamak, who replaced the Emperor who had died in the meantime, took over Ani in 1045.

During the same year, Kutalmis Bey, the cousin of the Seljuk Emperor, defeated the Byzantine army at Gence, and the Emperor Constantine Monamak, disbanded the Armenian Militia Army of 50,000.

After this date, the Seljuk raids continued regularly, each raid resulting in a new conquest. Those who tried to resist the Turks were the Georgians and Byzantium. The Armenians, who were subdued and whose militia soldiers were disbanded by Byzantium, did not.

Finally, on 26 August 1071, the whole region of Armenia fell into the hands of the Seljuks, with the defeat of Romain Diogene at the battle of Malazgirt, and the gates of Anatolia were opened to the Oguz Turks.

The geographical area called Armenia stayed under the rule of the Seljuk Empire until 1157, the year of Sultan Sancar's death. From this date until 1194, it was under the Iraq Seljuks' rule, later under the Haresmshahs, and then under the Ilkhanids.

When the Ilkhanid dynasty dissolved, the area came under the rule of the Celayirs in 1334; under Timur's rule in 1383; after Timur's death, under the rule of the Karakoyunlus and the Akkoyunlus; and after the 1450's completely under the Akkoyunlus.

The last rulers of this region before the Ottomans took over were the Akkoyunlus and the Safavids. Conqueror Mehmet II defeated Uzun Hasan, the ruler of the Akkoyunlus, at Otluk Beli on 11 August 1473, but drew back instead of pursuing him. Uzun Hasan's country later fell under Safavid domination. In the year 1514, when Sultan Selim I began his Caldiran campaign, the frontier between the two states was the Enderes stream, an affluent of the Kelkit river between Sivas and Erzincan. On the way to Caldiran, Sultan Selim conquered Erzincan, Erzurum, Ahiska and Beyazit. After his victory in Caldiran on 23 August 1514, he entered Tabriz on 8 September, but returned without keeping the city. Kemah and Diyarbekir were conquered in 1515, and Mardin in 1517. The rest of the conquests in the east took place during the reign of Suleiman the Magnificent. The peace treaty with the Safavids was signed on 28 May 1555, and eastern Anatolia and Iraq came under the absolute sovereignty of the Ottomans.

We have not given any references for the history of Armenia from the 4th century BC, for the events which we have narrated are to be found in the works of Armenian historians, as well as every work written on the history of Byzantium and Persia. We have added nothing. On the contrary, we have omitted the various insults written by Armenian analists against Byzantium and the Byzantines, for we accepted them not as historical evidence, but rather as emotional expression. (These emotional statements are particularly abundant in the works of Matthew of Urfa.)

The conclusion we draw from the information provided to us by foreign historians is as follows.

From the 4th century BC, in the geographical area which is called Armenia, there was a community whom we call Armenians, but whose origins are not well known. There is no knowledge as to which part of the region they occupied and in what numbers. This region was a province under the administration of the Achaemenid dynasty until Alexander the Great defeated Darius in 331 BC. Later it became part of the Macedonian Empire. When the Empire was divided among the generals following Alexander's death, the region was allotted to Seleucos.

A feudal system prevailed in the region. Various feudal lords were the owners of several lands. It is not known which of these lords were Armenian, and which were of other origin. It is impossible to talk about the existence of Armenian nationalism or of Armenian consciousness in the region. From time to time a given feudal lord imposed his will on the others, but he never took their lands away from them.

The only period when these feudal lords were independent was between 94 and 66 BC, during Tigran's reign, when the Selucid Empire was dispersed and when the Iranian Arsasid family was not yet powerful. The region was under Roman administration from 66 BC to AD 63; we see that the Prince, a governor-general, was appointed by the Romans; that although Rome continued to rule from 63 BC to 390, the governor-general was selected first by the Arsasids, then by the Sassanids from the Arsasid dynasty; that Armenia was divided in 390 between Rome and the Sassanids, the area belonging to Iran being connected to the capital in 428; that after the Arab invasion Achot of the Bagratid family was appointed in 885 to govern Armenia, that his jurisdiction never extended outside the boundaries of his lands, that the other lands were governed by the rest of the princes and that at least four other principalities existed in Armenia; that towards the end of the 10th century Byzantium slowly began to invade the region, that by 1045 all the principalities had been dissolved, and that the Oguz raids started after this date.

In view of these historical facts, we see no possibility of talking about an independent Armenia, or the existence of a united Armenian nation. Nevertheless, under Tigran an independent Armenia did exist for about thirty years, but not all the feudal lords who preserved their autonomy within the state were Armenian, nor was the entire local population Armenian.

What can be said of Armenia under the feudal system is that the various feudal lords were constantly struggling to preserve their domination of various communities on their lands, whom they considered slaves.

The two factors which will enable Armenians today to prove themselves a nation are their religion and their language. However, religion is not a distinguishing characteristic of a nation. Not only are there different nations sharing the same faith, but there are nations having a common origin but different faiths. As for the language, this is a factor that is subject to change. Did the community which came from Phrygia to Armenia speak Armenian as it is spoken today? Or is present-day Armenian a combination of the languages of the various communities interacting with each other for centuries? It is impossible to give a definite answer to this question.

Consequently it will not be an error to accept the various books we read as Armenian history as the history of some feudal principalities whose backgrounds are very much unknown.

3. The Armenian kingdom of Cilicia

After having examined the history of the region which the Armenians claim as their homeland, before we go on to the Ottoman period it is necessary to mention the Armenian kingdom of Cilicia.

There are numerous sources available for us to use in summarizing the history of the Cilician Armenian state, for it was in reality a 'state' in the full meaning of the word. In the course of its history it had close relations with the Anatolian Seljuks, with Byzantium, with the Syrian and Iraqui Atabegs, with the Crusaders, and finally with the Ayyubids and Mamelukes. Consequently, it is possible to trace the history of the Cilician Armenian State, in the histories of these other states as well. However, as we have previously stated, it is not our intention to write Armenian history, we are only interested in summarizing its highlights until the time when the Armenians became subject to Ottoman rule. Therefore, to summarize this period of their history we will rely solely on one authority, Avedis Sanjian, who has not only summarized this period in an impeccable fashion, but also enjoys the respect of the entire Armenian community.[17]

Sanjian summarizes the establishment and political life of this state in the following terms. (Passages in square brackets in the following account are our additions.)

Henceforth, the Armenian church having seceded from the communion of the church of Byzantium became the stronghold of Armenian nationalism and the principal factor of national unity. Fully cognizant of this, the Byzantine emperors and the clergy sought, in pursuance of their assimilatory policies, to eliminate not only the feudal families of Armenia, but also the autonomy of the Armenian church. . . . In the furtherance of these objectives, they employed every means of persuasion, intimidation, and above all persecution. Mass deportations of the native population from Greek-held western Armenia to other Byzantine territories was but one of the measures. [p. 3]

The Arab occupation of Greater Armenia, which lasted from the close of the seventh to the middle of the ninth century, marked a new phase in Armeno-Syrian relations. During their early marauding expeditions, beginning in 639/640, the Arabs not only plundered several provinces, but also carried off thousands of native captives to the territories adjacent to the Euphrates, principally to Edessa, Antioch and Northern Syria. . . . [p. 6]

PUTNAM PUBLIC LIBRARY
PUTNAM, CT

In contrast to the policies of Byzantium, the Arabs during their occupation of Armenia showed a greater degree of tolerance toward Armenian Christianity, and unlike the Greeks they did not threaten Armenian national existence through a policy of assimilation. Indeed, the Arabs provided a haven in their territories for those Armenians who were victimized by the religious persecutions of Byzantium. For instance, when in 711-713 Emperor Philippicus expelled a large group of Armenians from Asia Minor for refusing to conform to the Greek Orthodox faith, the Arabs permitted these refugees to settle not only in Armenia proper, but also in the regions of Melitene and northern Syria. Many were enlisted in the Muslim frontier guards in the Taurus Mountains and in Mesopotamia to defend these lands against Byzantine attacks. [p. 6]

At the beginning of the eleventh century, Byzantium took advantage of Armenia's weakness to annex the country bit by bit. . . . [p. 7] They recompensed the Armenian rulers of these territories with lands in Sebastia (Sivas), Caesarea (Kayseri) and Tzamandos in Cappadocia. . . . When the Armenian nobility were dispossessed of their ancestral territories and were granted, in return, domains in Byzantine territories, a large wave of Armenian emigrants accompanied them to these regions which had already been settled by their fellow countrymen at an earlier period. [p. 8]

Certain Armenians in these regions had been appointed by the Byzantine emperors as governors of important cities and also as commanders of imperial armies. Gradually, however, a number of the Armenian officials took advantage of the weakening of the central authority to break off the ties that bound them to the empire.

The barony founded in Cilicia by the Armenian Prince Reuben, who declared his independence from Byzantium in 1080, proved to be the most important and enduring of the Armenian principalities established between the Byzantine and Arab domains. The emergence of this state, and its intimate associations with the Crusaders and the subsequently established Frankish principalities of Edessa, Antioch, and Tripoli and the Latin kingdom of Jerusalem, marked a significant turning point in the fortunes of the Armenians in historic Syria.

From its inception the Armenian barony, surrounded as it was by powerful neighbours, enjoyed only brief periods of peace. . . . .

Despite this delicate balance of power, the Christian barony was able to maintain its position as a vital Christian state even after the gradual disintegration of the Latin hegemony in the Levant. Indeed, the position of Prince Leon II (1187-1219) had become so strong that he succeeded in raising his barony to the status of a kingdom. In 1198 he received a royal crown from the German Emperor Henry VI and from Pope Celestine III. . . . Thus having lost their independence in historic Armenia, the Armenians were able not only to establish a new home on the shores of the Mediterranean, but to restore their ancient kingdom. The Cilician state, which reached its apogee under Leon who had extended its territories from Isauria [the region in which the Province of Antalya is located today] to the Amanus, attracted so many Armenians that the region could with justice be referred to as a 'Little Armenia'. [p. 10]

We have previously seen when and for just what period Armenia was an independent area. Further, it would hardly be an accurate historical concept to attempt to establish some continuity between the Cilician Armenian barony and the feudal Armenian principalities in the region of Armenia.

In the first half of the thirteenth century the Mongols swept through Armenia and far into Anatolia. Hence, with a view to protecting the integrity of Cilicia, King Het'um I concluded military alliances with the Mongol Goyuk Khan in 1247 and also with his successor Mangu Khan in 1253 [One cannot call these 'alliances'; in fact Het'um came under Mongol rule.] . . . Not only did the Armenians cooperate with the Mongols in the economic blockade of Egypt by witholding exports of Cilician timber, but Armenian contingents fought side by side with the Mongols in Anatolia as well as in Syria. The arrival of the Mongols in Syria had coincided with the disintegration of the Ayyubids and the rise of the Mamelukes in Egypt. [p. 14]

In the 1250's Het'um I and his Armenian contingents joined forces with Hulagu in the occupation of Aleppo, Hama, Homs, Heliopolis, Damascus, and other Syrian cities [The Mongols were defeated by the Mamelukes in 1260.] . . . The weakening of the Mongol power in Syria made the Cilician kingdom one of the principal targets of Mameluk attacks. In 1266 they invaded Cilicia, slaughtering the inhabitants or carrying them off as captives into Egypt. [p. 15]

The preceding passage has been written in such a way as to suggest that there was not a single living person left in Cilicia. At the same time it neglects to mention the activities of the Armenian forces in Syria. French sources contain interesting accounts of these activities.

In 1274/5 Baybars launched another expedition into Cilicia and also carried out raids into the Taurus. Especially hard hit was Tarsus, then capital of Cilicia, some ten thousand of whose inhabitants were carried off into Egypt. [p. 15]

When the Mongols renewed their Syrian expedition they, together with Het'um, scored temporary victories at Homs and Damascus in 1299; but another invasion in 1303 ended in the decisive defeat of the Mongols near Damascus. [p. 15]

Nevertheless, until 1342 the Cilician kingdom had been ruled by the Reubenian and Het'umian dynasties, which were of Armenian origin. Leon IV, the last of the Het'umian kings, having no male heir, named as successor his nearest kinsman, Guy de Luisignan, nephew of Henry II of Cyprus, both of whom were related by marriage to the Armenian ruling family. The crown of Cilicia thus passed from the Armenian princes to a French noble family, and the Armenian kingdom became a country under the Latin government. [p. 16]

With the fall of the capital of Sis and the capture of Leon v in the final expedition of 1375, the Armenian kingdom of Cilicia became incorporated into the Mameluke Empire. [p. 16]

Subsequent to the fall of Sis, the Mamelukes carried off some 40,000 Armenian captives, a number of whom settled at Aleppo. [p. 18]

It was in this manner that the Cilician Armenian State, which had existed for three hundred years, was brought to an end by the Mamelukes in 1375.

The transfer of these territories to the Ottomans occurred in 1516 after the Ottoman Sultan Selim, by defeating the Mamelukes in the battles of Mercidabik and Ridaniye, brought an end to their state.

The Armenian feudal principalities, which had been located in the geographical region of Armenia, were completely destroyed by Byzantium in the year 1045 and their populations were to a large extent moved and resettled in other territories. Then in 1071 the geographical region of Armenia was conquered by the Seljuks. Following various exchanges of rulers they were finally transferred to the Ottomans in 1514.

While the Armenian Kingdom of Cilicia had ceased to exist in 1375, its former territories came under Ottoman administration in 1516.

Consequently, when the Ottomans took over these territories, there had been neither an Armenian principality for 470 years in the east, nor an Armenian kingdom of Cilicia for the previous 150 years. No one then was mentioning the Armenians as being part of a nation. Thus, none of the contemporary sources written in the first half of the sixteenth century make any mention of an Armenian race or nation. The appearance of the Armenian *millet* within the framework of the Ottoman Empire is another matter.

In a work of this nature, which is designed solely to examine events which occurred at the end of the nineteenth and the beginning of the twentieth centuries, there is only one reason for us to have examined, even if in summary form, the former history of the Armenian people: that is, to show that the belief still current in certain Armenian circles, that the Ottomans conquered Armenian territory, thereby bringing to an end the existing Armenian state and enslaving the population, is false.

As the historical summary we have provided has been based solely on the writings of Armenian historians and their sympathizers (without benefit of any additions on our part) there may well be some people who are surprised at how these Armenian claims ever developed in the first place.

However, one should not be surprised, because the so-called 'Armenian Question' which passes from mouth to mouth is, just like the claims we have examined above, a figment of the imagination; in other words, an imaginary building whose only foundation is similar baseless claims.

CHAPTER TWO

The origins of the Armenian question

1. The Armenian Church

Toynbee says: 'a universal church is apt to come to birth during a Time of Troubles following the breakdown of a civilization, and to unfold itself within the political framework of a universal state which is the institutional manifestation of a temporary arrest in a broken-down civilization's decline and fall'.[1]

Our intention is not to examine theological theories. We will not analyse why and how Christianity came to be established. However, it is impossible not to agree with Toynbee that if a religion is to achieve universality, it will need the support of a universal state's legal framework. If the Roman Empire had not officially accepted Christianity, it might not have been possible for the religion of Jesus to spread in the world. If Abu-Bakr had not organized the first campaign to Syria and Iraq to ensure internal peace and quiet,[2] and thus started the Holy War, it might not have been possible for Islam to be a world religion.

At other times, various philosophies that did not rely upon such a framework were unable to spread, and, being in conflict with existing religions, were crushed.

In short, we can assume that all great religions, in order to be called such, must rely on the support of great states. It is also possible for a great state, or one that is potentially ready to expand, to use religion as a means of expansion. There follows an unavoidable struggle for power between church and State, as in the Middle Ages in Europe or in the world of Islam during periods when secular authority and spiritual authority were not embodied in one individual. The struggle between the Seljuk Sultans and the Abbasid Caliphs is the clearest example of this.

In the Ottoman Empire, after Sultan Selim I had conquered Egypt, as the sovereignty and the Caliphate had become unified in the person of the Sultan, such a danger disappeared. Nevertheless, because Shiites had not recognized the Sunni Caliph, the Ottoman-Iranian wars have been considered to be religious wars instead of wars of conquest.

When studying the Armenian Church it is essential to keep these points in mind.

Vazken I, Catholicos of Etchmiadzin, wrote his encylical dated 16 August 1964: 'The era of the national history of the Armenian people began in the Vth century with the invention of Armenian writing and the heroic battle of Avarayr.'[3]

This is correct. The battle of Avarayr ended on 2 June 451 with rebellious Armenians being crushed. At that time, it will be recalled, Armenia was divided between Byzantium and the Sassanids. The area belonging to Byzantium had been directly linked to Istanbul, and Byzantium had been trying to enable the Greek Church to dominate in this area. After the death of Artakes in 428, the Armenian feudal lords had wanted the Sassanid area to be directly linked to the Sassanid Crown, instead of having a new governor-general appointed, and the Sassanid ruler Vahram v had accepted this request.

Imagine a country which, instead of living as a relatively autonomous community, by having a prince or a governor-general appointed, prefers to be linked to the Sassanid throne. It is impossible to talk about the existence of a national consciousness in such a country. The Armenian Church, too, opposes this relative autonomy, for if a prince is to govern the land the Catholicos will have a secondary position. If there is no prince, he is the primary figure.

Vahram v was an emperor antagonistic to Christianity. But Yazdigirt who replaced him in 438 was hostile to Christians. He wanted to dissolve the Armenian Church and spread Masdeism, the religion of the Sassanids. The Church, seeing that its foundations were being shaken, called the feudal lords to rebel. Almost all of them were killed in the fight, and the country remained under absolute Sassanid rule; but, after this date, Yazdigirt gave the Armenian Church religious freedom.

This is the main point. Essentially one should not talk about the Armenian nation, the Armenian State or Armenian history, but about the Armenian Church, the Armenian Church State. The Armenian Church, in order to preserve its existence, needed a power, a state. It was not the Armenian nation that gave rise to the idea of an Armenian state, but the Armenian Church.

If there had been no rupture between the Byzantine Church and the Armenian Church, could the thought of an Armenian state have emerged? We do not think so, for if this were the case, then the Church would have kept the Armenian community within the Byzantine Church and Byzantine culture. Were the relations between the Byzantine Church and the Armenian Church severed because of differences in theological interpretations, or because the Armenian Church and those at its head had already decided to maintain their independence instead of becoming second-class clergy, and had thus adopted this theological difference as an excuse? This is the question to be examined and it seems that the second possibility is more likely, for the rupture between the two Churches had started long before, even before the invention of the Armenian alphabet, approximately in 387 or 388, when Sahak's consecration to the Catholicate was not performed by the Archbishop of Kayseri. We quote Boyajiyan and Sanjian:

'Hereditary succession to the Patriarchate continued for a century or more, with an interruption of about fifty years after the death of Nerses the Great, and in the year 387 or 388 the line of St. Gregory was restored by the Ascension of Sahag to the patriarchal throne. His ordination on Armenian soil put an end to the custom of going to Caesarea for ordination as Catholicos. The autonomy of the Armenian Church was thoroughly established.'[4]

'These harmonious relations between the Armenian and the Byzantine churches were disrupted at the beginning of the fifth century when the newly elected Armenian Catholicos was consecrated not by the archbishop of Caesarea but by the bishops of Armenia, a fact which was viewed by the Greeks as being tantamount to a schism!'[5]

Although the dates in these two quotations do not correspond, the date given by Boyajiyan seems to be more accurate because Sahak was Catholicos between the years 387 and 428.[6]

The important role of the Armenian Church is acknowledged by all Armenian historians.

Pastermadjian says: 'The Armenian Church has been the body where the soul of the Armenian people, revived by the church, lived, while waiting for the day of its resurrection.'[7] Nalbandian's view is: 'The most important role in these nationalistic efforts was played by the Armenian Church, which functioned both as a religious and as an intellectual force through certain distinguished leaders and in its major monasteries . . . In the absence of political independence, the Catholicos embodied the aspirations of its people and became the link between the Armenians in the Diaspora and those of the homeland.'[8]

Boyajiyan is more explicit: 'Any history of Armenia, no matter how comprehensive, will fail to depict the true life of the Armenians, without a comparable presentation on the Armenian Church. The Armenian Church and the Armenian nation have been so intertwined that the one could hardly have been conceived without the other.'[9]

I believe all these statements reflect in different ways the point we have attempted to present above. For this reason, when studying the Armenian question, it is necessary to look at the Armenian Church, which is its source.

Armenians, setting no limit to exaggeration in the history of their Church as well as in heir own history, would affirm that they were Christians even before Jesus without the slightest effort. Indeed, Samuel of Ani writes that

Sanatruk, who became an Armenian Prince in 37, had believed in Jesus through the teachings of apostle Thaddle, but after having lost his faith had him killed. [10] The same author has recorded that apostle Batholome had died in 50 in the city of Aseban. The Armenian Church recognizes these two disciples as its founders.

As we have stated above, Christianity was officially accepted by Tridat, Prince of Armenia in 301.

According to legend, Gregory Lussarovitch, who brought Christianity to Armenia, was from Iran (Persia). Born in 257, he belonged to the Arsasid family. His father Anak had killed Tridat II in a hunting party by order of the King of Persia. Before dying, Tridat had ordered that Anak and his whole family be killed. Before the order could be carried out, Gregory was able to flee and had come to Kayseri. He grew up there, with his sibling's Christian nurse. He also married an Armenian princess, had two children, and, as he returned to Armenia, had begun to spread Christianity. [11]

What follows this in the legend is even more interesting:

Tridat III, who was then Prince of Armenia, immediately reestablished the cult of the ancient gods . . . but when he tried to force his servant Gregory to offer sacrifices to the idols, this one refused obstinately and declared he was Christian. Tridat had him tortured for a long time; but when he learned Gregory was the son of his father's murderer, he had him thrown into a cellar of the Vaghashabad castle where he stayed for thirteen years. . . . A peculiar illness took over Tridat; he imagined he had turned into a beast . . . a divine revelation came in a dream to his sister, saying that Gregory could find a remedy to the sufferings of Tridat. . . . Gregory was taken out of the prison, was given clothing, and brought to Vaghashabad where the king, as soon as he saw him, regained his reason. . . . Gregory baptised the king and his family, the lords, all the people of the court, and 190,000 individuals. . . . Thus Christianity was definitely and officially established in Armenia. [12]

Gregory was placed at the head of the Armenian Church after this event, which occurred in 301, and went to Kayseri for consecration by Archbishop Leontius. It is written that Gregory, on his return, had many temples destroyed, had churches built, baptized thousands, and appointed many to the priesthood. [13]

In the early days of Christianity, different points of view emerged in various countries, especially with regard to the dual nature of Jesus. In order to end these doctrinal differences, Constantine, Emperor of Byzantium, called all the bishops in the world to a meeting in Iznik (Nicaea) in 318. This meeting, which lasted from 20 May to 25 July 325, is known as the first General Council of the Church. The Armenian Church was represented by Gregory's son Aristakes. Subsequent General Councils were held at Istanbul (Constantinople) in 381 and at Ephesus in 431.

Although theArmenian Church did not take part in these councils, it accepted all the decisions that were taken at them.

As mentioned above, the Armenian Catholicos did not go to Kayseri (Caesarea) for his consecration. It may be that his absence from the 431 Council is related to this.

The struggle with the Sassanids is given as the reason for not going to the 451 Council at Chalcedon, but it is obvious that this rebellion, which did not last long, would not have constituted an obstacle. The Armenian Church did not accept the decisions taken at the Council of Chalcedon. Thus it broke *de facto* with the Christian Church, with Rome and with the Byzantine Church.

At times, the various attempts of the Byzantine Church to unify the Church seemed to achieve positive results. For example, in 633 there was an agreement between Emperor Herachius and Catholicos Ezr. But each time, as in this case, the Armenian Church did not follow the agreement and furthered the process of dividing the two Churches.

It is possible to state that this schism was beneficial to the Armenian Church and not to the Armenian nation.

Under the Armenian Kingdom of Cilicia, there were attempts to unify, this line with the Roman Church. Although the Armenian King was in agreement, the Church was opposed once again and unification was not achieved.

The Armenian Church was established in Etchmiadzin. However, the Church found it useful to follow the secular governments as they changed their location. For this reason it moved to Dwin in 485, to Ani in 901, and, after frequently moving from one place to another, finally came to Rumkale (Cilicia) in 1147. In the meantime, as the Catholicate which had been transferred from Rumkale to Akdamar moved from there to Argina (a city near Ani), the Patriarch of Akdamar proclaimed himself Catholicos. Although the Armenian Church did not recognize him, this Catholicate continued until 1895, when the last Catholicos, Hatchatur Shiroyan, died and was not replaced. During the First World War the Catholicate was dissolved by the Ottoman Empire.

The Catholicate remained in Rumkale until 1292. When this city fell under Mameluke rule, it was transferred to Sis. After the Kingdom of Cilicia was dissolved in 1375, the Catholicate remained at Sis. A Synod met because they realized that they were now under the influence of the Roman Church. It was decided at the Synod that they should return to Etchmiadzin. The decision was acted upon in 1441, but this time the Catholicate in Sis remained. After the First World War the Catholicate was transferred from Sis to Antilyas, near Beirut.

Aside from these three Catholicates, two Patriarchates emerged, one in Istanbul, the other in Jerusalem.

Each Catholicos has the right to select the lower-ranking clergy in his area. The Patriarchs do not have this privilege.

The Istanbul Patriarchate was the most influential spiritual leader in the Empire, owing to its position of leadership within the Armenian community, although the Catholicates of Akdamar and Sis were in a higher position in the Church hierarchy.

According to the present-day Church structure, there are two Catholicates. The Catholicos of Etchmiadzin is considered the spiritual leader of all Armenians, and so is theoretically superior to the Catholicos of Antilyas, who in fact is totally independent.

A striking feature of the history of the Armenian Church is the attempt to avoid falling under the influence of the Byzantine or the Roman Church. Because we are not writing the history of the Church we have only attempted to describe the main outlines of this attempt. In many cases it has produced results which were politically against the interests of the Armenian community. However, this policy was not abandoned, maybe because the interest of the Church was given more weight than the interest of the community. Thus only initiatives that were to give more power to the Church were followed.

Other churches that were not successful in their attempts to bring the Armenian Church under their jurisdiction now tried to convert individuals. Those who joined the Greek Church, because they were living in Byzantium, were Hellenized and thus assimilated.

Those joining the Protestant and Catholic Churches became, especially in the Ottoman Empire, separate communities, and this gave rise to serious conflicts among the Armenians.

The conversion of individuals to other faiths was achieved, especially in the case of the Protestant Church, through missionaries. The role played by the missionaries in the emergence of the Armenian Question is quite close to that of the Gregorian Church. This missionary activity became apparent in the Ottoman Empire in the nineteenth century.

We have previously discussed Armenian history only up until the date when the land they occupied became subject to the Ottoman Empire. There is not much to discuss about Armenians in the Ottoman Empire until 1856, when the Armenian Question was to emerge, owing to the activities of the Church on the one hand, the activities of the missionaries on the other, and finally the policies of the great powers.

In order fully to understand and evaluate events, it is necessary first to establish their origins. For this reason we find it useful to examine the activities of the missionaries, the difference of religion, and the topic of propaganda separately, before looking at the life-style of Armenians from the sixteenth century on.

We shall return later to the subject of historical development.

2. The difference of religion

Their [the Armenians'] country is controlled by a rich and powerful potentate of another race, who with his court and army would be neither cruel nor revengeful except for their religion. They are Mohammedans and they have been taught for centuries that a Christian slain was the surest passport to the favor of God and the enjoyment of eternal happiness. Under the insane spell of this awful fanaticism, they have come down like wolves on the gentle Christian people under their sway, and within the last year have slaughtered men, women, and children without mercy, not for any wrong that they have done, but only because they are Christians.[14]

This passage is taken from the preface of Bliss's book. Bliss spent many years in Turkey, where he was a missionary.

If such a remark could be made in blind partiality in 1896 about Islam, which was established more than 1,270 years ago, and which more than 200 million people had chosen as their faith (a fact recorded by Bliss on pages 57-8 of his book), and about the 600-year-old Ottoman Empire whose religious tolerance is recognized by the entire world, then one can imagine, without reading the book, what could be said about events which had taken place a year earlier, in an area in which the world and especially Americans were almost uninterested.

It is true that the religious factor has always played an important role in relations between Turks and the Christian nations. One has always treated Turks differently, not because they were Turks, but because they were Muslims, and the Christian community has treated them as outcasts. This treatment was not restricted to Turks, but to other communities in Europe as well. Hungarians and Bulgarians were subjected to the same treatment until they accepted Christianity.

It is possible for this reason to explain the continuous antagonistic attitude of Europe towards the Ottoman Empire, solely because of the difference of religion. During the majestic period of the Empire this attitude was more reserved. As the decline of the Empire began, the hostility returned. Felix Valyi has written on this subject:

Truth to tell, European politicians have never been able to shake themselves free from theological bias, particularly in regard to Islam, and Christianity has always continued to prosecute the religious policy of preceding centuries, a policy infected with the prejudices which Byzantine chroniclers bequeathed to Western thought. These chroniclers were the great initiators of the anti-Moslim movement, and perverted European judgment regarding Oriental matters by such trumpery assertions as defeated nations usually make in order to wreak their vengeance upon their conquerors, and to comfort themselves in their humiliation. For a long while Byzantine sources of information constituted the basis of all European prejudices regarding the Near East, and the politicians of the Christian Powers

readily turned them to account, as long as Christianity was exposed to the
Turkish danger. One of the Popes, Pius II, the great humanist, known by
the name of Aeneas Sylvius, before organizing his crusade against the Turks,
thought of an exceedingly simple way of solving the Ottoman problem. In
a personal letter he invited Mohammed the Conqueror to become converted
to Christianity, together with all his people, and promised to reward him by
hailing him as the Supreme Head of Christianity and the protector
of European order. This letter is but the symbol of the real charge that
Europe brings against Turkey. Europe would have been prepared to forgive
her all her conquests, which were no worse than those of any other
conqueror, if only she had chosen to enter the Christian family.[15]

But the Turks, just as they did not consider conversion, did
not abandon religious tolerance either, as E. A. Powell noted:

The Turks are not, like their coreligionists, the Arabs, by nature
a fanatical people. As a matter of fact, the history of the Ottoman Empire
is less marred by religious intolerance and by massacres due to religious
hatreds than the history of European states from the thirteenth to the
sixteenth centuries. It is well to remember that when the Crusaders were
butchering their Moslem prisoners in Palestine, when the horrors of the
Spanish Inquisition were in full swing, when Cromwell's troopers were
massacring the Catholics of Ireland, when Protestants in' France were
being exterminated by order of the French king, when Jews were being
subjected to countless persecutions and barbarities in every European
country, Moslems, Christians and Jews were dwelling side by side, in
perfect amity, in Asia Minor.[16]

Ernest Jackh wrote:

Who but the infidel Turk opened up a Turkish haven, in the Middle
Ages, to the Jewish refugees of Christian Spain and Italy? Ottoman
sultans, Selim and Suleiman, early in the sixteenth century, invited them
to Constantinople and to Salonika. They offered the Jews the first Zionist
colonization in Palestine, around Lake Tiberias, and on Cyprus.[17]

Valyi added:

An important testimony to the toleration of Moslem rule is the fact
that persecuted Christian and other sects took refuge in Mohammedan
lands, to enjoy there the undisturbed exercise of their several cults.
Persecuted Spanish Jews at the end of the fifteenth century took refuge in
Turkey in great numbers. The Calvinists of Hungary and Transylvania and
the Unitarians of the latter country long preferred to submit to the Turks
rather than to fall into the hands of the fanatical House of Habsburg. The
Protestants of Silesia in the seventeenth century looked with longing eyes
towards Turkey, and would gladly have purchased religious freedom at
the price of submission to Moslem rule. The Cossacks, who belonged
to the 'Old Believers' and were persecuted by the Russian State Church

in 1736, found in Turkey the toleration which their Christian brethren denied them.[18]

Even Pastermadjian was not able to hide the tolerance and protection that the Ottoman Empire offered its non-Muslim subjects.

During the rule of the great Sultans, the limited rights of the Christian subjects were somewhat respected, and justice was quite impartially administered by the courts. Armenians often found an effective protection with them. Jorga states that Sultan Murad III energetically intervened in favor of Armenians from Walachia, who were persecuted for religious reasons by the orthodox, who wanted to convert them. It is likely that under the reign of Suleiman II, the condition of Christian peasants in the Ottoman Empire was not much worse than that of the serfs in Europe in the same period.[19]

It is of great significance that even Pastermadjian, whose book is filled with slanders against Turks, and whose father, a member of the Ottoman Assembly, had crossed over to Russia at the outbreak of the war to fight against the Ottomans under the nickname of Arman Garo, could not but accept this.

It is not possible to affirm that this religious tolerance has operated in favour of the Ottoman Empire. For one thing, this attitude was never appreciated. Some writers even go as far as to state that non-Muslims were regarded as a separate community, so that they could be charged more taxes. No book mentions the fact that the sum paid for exemption from military service, which lasted at times ten to twelve years, was also paid by Muslims, if they wished to be exempt. With regard to other taxes, whether a difference existed between Muslims and non-Muslims is never dwelled upon.

The important point, however, is not the fact that this practice was not appreciated, but the fact that it had a negative effect, as Talcott Williams noted:

The Christian races of Asiatic Turkey are the condemning indictment of Ottoman rule, both past and present. Their presence is a proof that the sultans of Turkey and the Moslems they ruled were not wise enough to see that, in the early stages of the development of a people, unity of faith must be secured or all union will be lost. The European races have understood this perfectly and acted upon it. Down to a time within the memory of men now living, nearly all European lands have placed heavy disabilities on any departure from the established religion. . . . Ottoman legislation and administration is legally more tolerant of the education and the religious association of alien creeds and hostile faiths than is Gallic liberty today in dealing with a creed and faith dominant in France for a thousand years.[20]

The Ottomans gave extensive cultural and legal rights, along with religious privileges, to the Orthodox Greeks and Gregorian Armenians. These rights, which almost amounted to their forming a state within a state, became a factor which was made use of by various powers during the decline of the Empire. While Russia claimed to be the protector of the Orthodox, and France of Catholics, the interest of the American public turned towards Turkey. This was due to the conversion of Armenians to Protestantism by American missionaries. This change of interest carried with it a negative attitude. Powell wrote:

The extent of American missionary effort in the old Ottoman Empire is quite generally known, but its effect on American public opinion is not, perhaps, so widely recognized. Very early in their work the American missionaries discovered that Moslems do not change their faith, so, debarred from proselytism among the Turks, they devoted their energies to religious, educational, and medical work among the Christian minorities, particularly the Armenians. For half a century or more, these missionaries provided our chief sources of information on conditions in the Near and Middle East; and by them public opinion in the United States on these subjects was largely molded. Having been rebuffed by the Moslem Turks and welcomed with open arms by the Christian Armenians, it is scarcely surprising that they espoused the cause of the latter and that the reports which they sent home and the addresses which they delivered, when in America on leave of absence, were filled with pleas for the oppressed Christians and with denunciations of their Turkish oppressors. The congregations which supported the missionaries accepted this point of view without question, and there was thus gradually developed, under the aegis of our churches, a powerful anti-Turkish opinion.[21]

On the missionaries, Clair Price recorded:

That the Armenians were grossly maladministered by the modern Sultans in Constantinople, there can be no manner of doubt. And so were their Turkish neighbours. It was in this very maladministration that the problem of the modern Ottoman Empire lay, and that problem was a Turkish problem as well as an Armenian problem. . . .

American missionaries established contact with the Armenian minorities nearly a century ago.... It was inevitable that the very real and undoubted wrongs which the Armenians were suffering under Hamidian administration should become known in the United States. This was in itself an entirely healthy process, but its tragedy lay in the fact that because the missionaries either could not or would not make it plain in the United States that the Hamidian regime in Constantinople was the oppressor and that Turks and Armenians alike were its victims, the result of American missionary endeavour was to focus American concern on the Armenians' sufferings alone.[22]

Just as Russia, France and the United States were interested in Turkey for religious reasons, Britain acted no differently, as Valyi explained:

After the Congress of Paris (1856) Russia invented a system which simply meant the suicide, limb by limb, of Turkey. The plan of fostering antagonism between Christianity and Islam, and of preventing by subterranean methods, the application of the principles of conciliation, professedly supported before public opinion in Europe, was an adroit policy all the more certain of success as the theocratic elements in Turkey were for a long time opposed to progress. If the Tanzimat, the first great attempt at reform in Turkey, ultimately failed, this was largely due to muddled foreign interference. To accustom the Christians of the Near East to constant interference from abroad and to a system of incessant meddling, amounting to a regular tutelage over Islam, was to give them carte blanche against the Turks. Beaconsfield thought the Musulmans as worthy of participating in the work of modern civilization as they had participated in the powerful civilizations that had preceded our own. He wished this country to preside in brotherly collaboration over the economical education of the Moslim peoples, and over the vast movements which have been agitating the minds of Musulmans for the last hundred years. Unfortunately England, which was soon to be absorbed in domestic troubles in which Gladstone was to play a high-handed part, did not understand Lord Beaconsfield. Hatred of Islam was, as everybody knows, one of the strongest actuating motives of Gladstone, deeply impregnated as he was by Christian theology. Under his ill-omened influence, the Eastern policy of Great Britain changed completely and she became, in fact, the unconscious ally of Tsarism against Islam.

It forms part of the programme of the Anglican Church to become unified sooner or later with Greek Orthodoxy, with whom she has been flirting for over thirty years; indeed, theological disputations worthy of the Middle Ages were arranged between the two Communions, the first of which took place in the episcopal palace of Archbishop Eulogus of Russia before the War, with the object of trying to reconcile the dogmas of the two Churches. Although the grand design of ecclesiastical union was not fulfilled, as neither of the two disputants would consent to sacrifice one iota of their dogmas, a tactical alliance, at least, was achieved in the shape of a common programme of religious policy uncompromisingly directed against Islam. To seize Constantinople and make it the seat of that future union of the two Churches which had always been flashed in the eyes of the English Episcopacy by the clever diplomatists of Greek Orthodoxy-such was the immediate political object of this interesting intercommunion. That is why Lord Robert Cecil and his brother, the militant protectors of this Orthodox-Anglican programme, were always to be found in the van of those who wished to exterminate the Turks. That is why the Archbishop of Canterbury and the Bishop of London, the Bishop of Manchester, and their brethren were always ready to preach a crusade against Turkey and Islam. And that is why Mr. Lloyd George and his Nonconformist brethren persisted in their efforts to kill the Turkish nation.[23]

This factor, the difference of religion, which functioned generally against Islam and also against the Turks because they were Muslims, played the largest role in the emergence of an Armenian question in the Ottoman Empire. There is no other explanation for the humane concern shown by the United States for the non-Muslims in Turkey, when they are not interested in the fate of Polish Christians suffering under Russian oppression.

Naturally the Armenian Church took advantage of this religious factor. The Armenian Church had been persuaded with the promise of an independent, or at least autonomous, Armenia. The fulfilment of such promise would mean the development of the power and authority of the Church. It is for this reason that the Church became a tool for schemes aimed at the Ottoman Empire.

3. The activities of missionaries

The first Protestant missionaries to come to Turkey were members of the British and Foreign Bible Society, which, soon after its foundation in 1804 started to send distributors of Bibles inland from Izmir (Smyrna).[24]

American missionaries started to arrive from 1819. In 1832 the station of Istanbul (Constantinople) was founded. At first, the activities of the missionaries were directed towards Muslims and the Oriental Churches. Work among the Jews was carried out chiefly by Scottish Presbyterians and members of the Church of England, but did not prove very successful.

After having realized that there was little opportunity of successful work among Muslims, the missionaries turned their attention towards the Oriental Churches, which included the Armenian, the Greek, the Bulgarian, the Jacobite, the Nestorian, the Chaldean, and the Maronite Churches.

Bliss explained the situation that the first missionaries encountered:

The first missionaries entered upon their work with no thought whatever of proselytising. They recognized the essential Christian character of the churches and their object was to set before them not a new creed, or a different form of church government, but simply a higher conception of what constituted Christian life. They found almost absolute ignorance of the Bible; complete domination by an ignorant and superstitious hierarchy; and a general feeling that their church life was so thoroughly identified with national life that to leave the church was to leave the nation, and that every heretic was also a traitor. [p. 303]

An Armenian or a Greek who incurred the hostility of a Bishop and was placed under the ban had no rights that any one was bound to respect. He could neither be baptized nor be buried; he could neither marry nor purchase; no baker would. furnish him with bread and no butcher with meat; no one would employ him and no court recognized his defence so as to give him the most ordinary protection [p. 304]

It is apparent that in this situation, the missionaries won the Armenian over to the Protestant Church. As for the Greeks, Bliss wrote: 'There were missionaries who sought to reach the Greeks, but their efforts met with very little success.

Their national and ecclesiastical pride was too strong, and their nearer relation to Western life made the new teaching appear less attractive than to those to whom it was in great degree a revelation. [p. 309]'

Naturally a question comes to mind. Since the situation of the Greeks was the same as that of the Armenians, and the reason why the Greeks were not interested in the new teaching was their close links with the Western world, then the Western world must have objected to the spreading of Protestantism. Indeed, Bliss writes (p. 312) that such an objection came not only from the Armenian and Greek Patriarchates, but from the Papal representative, as well as from the French and the Russian ambassadors.

These objections are more clearly expressed by Cyrus Hamlin: 'This democratic spirit of freedom was extravagantly attributed to the influence of the missionaries, who had nothing directly to do with it. But, above all, Russia pressed the Catholicos of Etchmiadzin to stop the progress of this heresy, and clear the empire of it. The decisive influence came from St. Petersburg through Etchmiadzin.' [25]

The decisive influence mentioned by Hamlin, who himself was a Protestant missionary who founded the Robert College in Istanbul, refers to the excommunication of those who had established contact with the Protestant Church.

In spite of this, the Ottoman administration officially gave permission to the Protestant Church, through the intervention of England, and thus a Protestant Armenian community was born.

In 1896, missionaries from seven separate churches from the United States and four churches from England were present in the Ottoman Empire. There were as many as 176 Americans and 869 local helpers who worked with them (Bliss p. 313). The main Anatolian cities where a mission was established were: Bursa, Izmir, Merzifon, Kayseri, Sivas, Trabzon, Erzurum, Harput, Bitlis, Van, Mardin, Antep, Maras, Adana, Hacin, Ankara, Yozgat, Arapkir, Malatya, Palu, Diyarbekir, Urfa, Birecik, Elbistan, and Tarsus.

Bliss wrote as follows about the activities of the missionaries:

The question is frequently asked, What are the relations between the missionaries and the Turkish government? Repeatedly the statement is made by that government that the influence of the missionaries is antagonistic, disturbing, and that they are the enemies of the present rule. This is in no sense true. American missionaries have invariably ranked themselves on the side of the law. They have taken the position that the Turkish Government is the government of the land and its law must be obeyed. If those laws are oppressive they will do their best to secure a change, but so long as the law is law it must be obeyed. In all the various attempts to stir up revolutionary feeling among the people, they have opposed such movements with all their influence. It is undoubtedly the fact that the general result of their instruction by stirring intellectual development, has

been to make men restive under oppression. Undoubtedly their preaching
has created an intense desire for true religious liberty. Undoubtedly they
have brought light into the empire, and light is always a disturbing
element where there is corruption; it creates fermentation, and such
fermentation as is not pleasant oppressors. [p. 321]

It is not easy to say whether this statement praises the
missionaries or condemns them. It is clear from Bliss's statement
that the Ottoman government was not pleased with the activities of
the missionaries, and saw them as enemies of the regime. If a
government accuses a foreigner in this manner, it may be expected
to expel him from the country. Because the missionaries remained
in the country, it is apparent that the government was not able to
expel them. Bliss says that the missionaries will do whatever they
can to change repressive laws, but will also respect the law. Is it the
people who decide whether the law is repressive, or the
missionaries? Bliss states that people, as their intellectual level rises,
become dissatisfied with repression. One is then led to assume that
missionaries gave rise dissatisfaction which did not previously
exist, and were the ones who decided that the laws were repressive.
Moreover, what is understood by true religious liberty' is not clear.
The Ottoman Government not being interested in the religion of
non-Muslims, and having allowed the establishment of the
Protestant Church, who will then be blamed for the lack
religious freedom'? Bliss asserts that missionaries oppose
revolutionary movements, yet he accepts that as a result of the
missionaries' activities of revolutionary climate was born, and that
the missionaries took it upon themselves to extinguish it. If they
had reported this climate to the government forces, then they could
indeed have prevented the rebellions.

For all these reasons it is difficult to understand whether the
statements made by Bliss are apologetic or accusatory. Other
writers have expressed their ideas more clearly. We quote from
Clair Price, Elie Kedourie and Sydney Whitman:

Moslems are usually hospitable to all foreigners and they frequently
respect missionaries personally. They use mission hospitals and
occasionally they avail themselves of the advantage of foreign schools. But
for missionaries as Christians engaged in spreading a gospel of peace while
their contemporaries at home invent poison gas, Moslems have neither
understanding nor respect. In their Christian capacities, missionaries are
tolerated as long as they do not offend.

The older missionaries know these things. They know that in their
effort spread Christianity, their greatest enemies have been the Christians,
and most their work in the Ottoman Empire has been an effort to convert
Eastern Christians to a Western interpretation of Christianity. But their
supporters in the United States have never understood this until now.
Americans at home have assumed that the word Christian is an
all-sufficing label, that the communicants of the Orthodox and Gregorian
Churches in the East are Christians as Western Protestants understand

the term, that Eastern Moslems are heathen in the Western meaning of the word; and on this assumption they have built up out of the mutual tragedies of racial and religious disentenglement in the Ottoman Empire, their Christian martyr-legend and the sorry butcher-legend which they have attached to the Turks.

The missionaries' supporters at home are firm believers in prohibition, but the missionaries themselves know that the liquor traffic in the Ottoman Empire has been in the hands of native and Western Christians, protected under the Capitulations by Christian Governments. Yet so habitual has the Christian attitude of superiority become, that American churchmen have actually gone to Constantinople within these last four years and have come away unhumbled.[26]

The religion of Armenians was their distinctive badge in an Ottoman society regulated and governed according to denominational distinctions. This religion was not only a matter for the individual conscience, for personal and private devotions; it was a rule of life regulating all social activities and all relations with the suzerain power, itself suzerain by virtue of professing the dominant religion. And the internal government of the community was similarly the prerogative of the religious hierarchy, which drew its civil power from the fact of its ecclesiastical authority.

Into these long standing and well understood arrangements the West, round about 1830, suddenly intruded. It came in the shape of American Protestant missionaries. They arrived with arguments and contracts and funds. Their purpose, they said, was to infuse vitality and spirit into the unprogressive and dormant eastern Christian communities. The established hierarchy resisted these encroachments. It exiled and imprisoned Armenian converts to Protestantism. It approached the Ottoman government with a request to forbid the activities of these missionaries.

What actually were the doctrines that the missionaries, arousing so much opposition and anger from so many different quarters, were teaching? Dwight defines them for us: 'The standard doctrine of the Reformation - salvation by grace alone, without the deeds of the law- was usually the great central truth, first apprehended by their awakened and inquiring minds, and made the ground of satisfactory repose.'

The introduction of these ideas, then, could not fail to affect the internal affairs of the Armenian community, as well as its relations with the Ottoman Power. To start with, a schism, encouraged by the missionaries, took place between the Orthodox majority and the converts to Protestantism, and a new Protestant Armenian community was formed. Then, within the Orthodox community itself, parties of 'Enlightened' and 'Reactionaries' were formed. After a while, the 'Enlightened', as is proper, won and reorganized the government of the Armenian community. Extensive powers were taken away from the ecclesiastical hierarchy and vested in a new elective Communal Council of Deputies.[27]

This is a large Moslem country. It is ruled by a sovereign whom International Law recognizes as the Sultan of Turkey. This country belonged to the Turks even before the discovery of America. Today it is honeycombed with Christian, and mostly Protestant missionary schools, the avowed object of which is to educate a small

Christian minority - be it admitted the most thrifty, shrewd, pushing, and intriguing of all Eastern races - in the Christian religion and at the same time modern European ideas, and to bid them look to the Western world outside Turkey as their natural protector. This was bound to make these Asiatics discontented with their Asiatic status. . . .

I willingly believe that they never really intended to provoke disturbances or encourage rebellion against the Turkish authorities. Still there cannot be a doubt that their teaching - not their doctines, perhaps - had the result, probably never intended, and one it has taken a couple of generations to attain-of fostering, the Armenian revolutionary movement throughout Asiatic Turkey. [28]

Henry Tozer, who was himself a Church member, wrote about his conversation with M. Wheeler, the President of the American College Harput:

Thus the missionaries, though they abstain on principle from taking any part in politics, exercise indirectly something of the influence of a European consul. Mr. Wheeler told me that he was frequently in communication with Sir Henry Layard (the British ambassador to Istanbul), who requested him to supply him with information about what was passing. In consequence of this, some time ago, a pasha, who openly manifested his ill-will towards them, received a sharp reprimand from Constantinople. [29]

These quotations show that the activities of missionaries, even if they did not buttress the Armenian rebellions, played an active part in laying the foundation of the rebellions.

The activities of the missionaries were covered extensively before and after the rebellions in reports coming from the provinces. We will return this subject in Chapter 4.

4. Propaganda

We can easily state that propaganda is one of the weakest points of Turks. This was so in the Ottoman Empire, as well as in the Turkish republic. The propaganda activity of Turks has been restricted to refuting articles a erroneous assertions; thus it has been nothing more than a passive effort to defend the Turkish position. This attitude enabled the opposite side to act freely in portraying Turks continuously as being guilty.

Anti-Turkish propaganda was most extensive in 1923, especially in the US. Powell wrote: 'The deep-seated hostility which exists in America against the Turk is traceable to several causes: chiefly, no doubt, to the atrocious treatment which he has accorded in the past to the Christian minorities, particularly the Armenians; secondly, to religious prejudice and political propaganda, of which it is difficult to say where one ends and the other begins; thirdly, to our disappointment and chagrin at the come-back of a supposedly vanquished and dismembered nation; and lastly to the Turk's persistent refusal to defend himself.' [30]

Powell mentions this last reason on page 32 of his book, and reports the following statement made by Sultan Vahdettin (Mohammed VI), during a conversation they had in the summer of 1922 in the Imperial Palace of Yildiz: 'If we sent one, your newspapers and periodicals would not publish an article written by a Turk, if they published it, your people would not read it, if they read it, they would not believe it. Even if we sent a qualified person to America, to convey to you in your language, the Turkish point of view, would he find an impartial audience ?'

What the Sultan said may be accurate. Indeed, on page 10 of his book Powell reports that an esteemed clergyman from New England stated: 'I don't want to hear the truth about the Turks, I have developed my opinion about them a long time ago.' The reason why things have come to this point is that Turks have remained silent, and that false propaganda spread by their opponents, with the addition of religious factors and political considerations, became established in people's minds. Consequently, the pessimistic 'it won't be published anyway, if it is published, it won't be read, if it is read, it won't be understood' mentality contributed to the development of an entirely hostile climate, and helped antagonistic propaganda to have a quick result

Generally, in almost every country, there is a tendency to believe that a newspaper article or a piece of news is naturally accurate.

We have stated above that the religious factor and political considerations have helped to establish an anti-Turkish climate. When conscious propaganda is added to this, then not only do we have biased news, but inaccurate news as well.

The following statements (by Powell and Whitman) confirming this assertion are worth reading:

Atrocity stories have been vastly overdone; some of the more recent massacres have been wholly nonexistent. One of the local (Constantinople) members of the press end of a relief organization told some friends openly that he could only send anti-Turkish despatches to America because that is what gets the money![31]

Shortly after the news had spread to Europe of the attack on the Ottoman Bank and the subsequent massacre of Armenians, a number of artists of illustrated newspapers arrived in Constantinople, commissioned to supply the demand for atrocities of the Million-headed Tyrant. Among these was the late Mr. Melton Prior, the renowned war correspondent. He was a man of a strenuous and determined temperament, one not accustomed to be the sport of circumstances, but to rise superior to them. Whether he was called upon to take part in a forced march or to face a mad Mullah, he invariably held his own and came off victorious.

But in this particular case, as he confided to me, he was in an awkward predicament. The public at home had heard of nameless atrocities, and was anxious to receive pictorial representations of these. The difficulty was how to supply them with what they wanted, as the dead Armenians had been buried and no women or children had suffered hurt, and no Armenian Church had been desecrated. As an old admirer of the Turks and as an honest man, he declined to invent what he had not witnessed. But others were not equally scrupulous. I subsequently saw an Italian illustrated newspaper containing harrowing pictures of women and children being massacred in a church.[32]

Among the men who were credited with a large share in the cruel measures of repression said to have been carried out by different Turkish high officials against the Armenians, the name of Marshal Chakir Pasha, Imperial Commissioner the introduction of reform in Anatolia, stood foremost. The story that the Marshal, who was at Erzeroum in the month of October 1895, at the time of Armenian rising, had, like a human bloodhound, stood, watch in hand, when asked for orders, and decided that the work of knocking the Armenians on the head was to continue for another hour and a half - some versions say two hours—went almost round the world. . . With the object of our journey in view we called successively upon Mr. Graves, the British Consul; Mohammed Sherif Raouf Pasha, the Governor-General (Vali); M. Roqueferrier, the French Consul; and M. V. Maximov, the Russian Consul-General. To each of these gentlemen we put the question whether he believed in the truth of the tale about Chakir Pasha, the watch-in-hand episode. M. Roqueferrier ridiculed the story. 'These are stories that have been invented ad lib', he said, and added a few words of high personal appreciation of Chakir Pasha.

The Russian Consul-General, M. Maximov, said: 'It is not my business to deny the truth of such tales. All I can tell you is, that Chakir Pasha is a worthy man very good natured man. I have known him for years, he is a friend of mine.' Mr. Graves, the British consul, said: 'I was not here at the time, nor have I spoken to Chakir Pasha about the matter, but the Vali assured me that it wasn't true, and that is quite sufficient for me, as I should believe implicitly any personal statement of Raouf Pasha.'

'Do you believe that any massacres would have taken place if no Armenian revolutionaries had come into the country and incited the Armenian population rebellion?' I asked Mr. Graves.

'Certainly not,' he replied. 'I do not believe that a single Armenian would have been killed.'[33]

These reports, however, have never been echoed in the Western press. The following report by Clair Price is another example:

By the end of October, the late Miss Annie T. Allen and Miss Florence Billings the Near East Relief's representative in Ankara (Angora), compiled a report on the state of the Turkish villages which the Greeks had burned during their retreat a forwarded it to the Near East Relief's headquarters in Constantinople. But the Near

East Relief has never published that report, just as Mr. Lloyd George never published the Bristol report on Greek misdeeds at Izmir (Smyrna).[34]

Indeed, Lloyd George had not allowed publication of the Bristol report, as Toynbee noted:

Their unwillingness to publish the report is not incomprehensible, and besides, Mr. Venizalos threw all his personal influence into the scale. He objected to the publication of evidence which had been taken by the Commission without the presence of a Greek assessor, and in which the names of the witnesses were withheld. There was, of course, a good reason for this, which reflected on the local Greek authorities and not on the Western Commissioners. The individuals giving damaging evidence against the Greeks were living under a Greek military occupation and could not safely be exposed to reprisals. There were the same legal flaws in the *Bryce Report on Alleged German Atrocities in Belgium and on The Treatment of Armenians in the Ottoman Empire*. But the Allied governments did not hesitate to publish these documents on that account.[35]

The Bryce Report mentioned by Toynbee is the Blue Book of the British, of which Toynbee was the editor. We shall return to this topic.

At times completely opposite situations could also arise.

In 1918 the British had been forced to set Baku free. Newspapers, while reporting this, had also mentioned the treachery of the Armenians. The British propaganda services were then alarmed, and they wanted to erase any effect such news would have. The following lines are taken from a memorandum prepared to that effect:

To lessen the credit of Armenians is to weaken the anti-Turkish action. It was difficult to eradicate the conviction that the Turk is a noble being always in trouble. This situation will revive this conviction and will harm the prestige not only of Armenians, but of Zionists and Arabs as well.

The treatment of Armenians by the Turks is the biggest asset of his Majesty's Government, to solve the Turkish problem in a radical manner, and to have it accepted by the public.[36]

The author of these sentences, A. J. Toynbee, was working for the British propaganda agency when he wrote this memorandum on 26 September 1919.

To understand the importance of propaganda, it is useful to take a look at Lucy Masterman's account of the agency founded for this purpose.

The earliest news that I personally had of a propaganda department was a conversation after a Sunday luncheon at Walton Golf Club during August 1914, when Mr. T. P. O'Connor pressed on Mr. Lloyd George the necessity for countering the propaganda already begun by the Germans in the United States in the form of leaflets given away in the streets, and thrust into the hands of passengers arriving by steamer. Mr. Lloyd George used the phrase: 'Will you look into it, Charlie, and see what can be done.' Masterman agreed.[37]

Mr. Masterman, a member of Parliament, was a former member of the cabinet.

It is known that, after this date, Mr. Masterman founded a bureau of propaganda, and directed it. The existence of the bureau was kept secret. Mr. Masterman having resigned from his office in the National Health Commission, 'Wellington House', where the Commission operated, was converted into the headquarters of the bureau, and the name of the bureau was entered in the registers as 'Wellington House'.

The object of Wellington House is stated in the following quotation '. . . . the dissemination of facts on "the Allied Cause, the British effort, the work of the Navy, the Army, the Mercantile marine and the munition factories, the economic and military resources of the Empire, the causes and aims of the war, the crimes and atrocities of Germany and her allies, the cause of Belgium, the submarine outrages". It is noticeable that "crimes and atrocities" come a long way down the list. The means used were "Book pamphlets, periodicals, diagrams, maps, posters, postcards, drawings photographs and exhibitions".[38]

It is reported that the bureau issued 17,000,000 copies of various publications in England alone, including fifteen daily illustrated magazine.

The British, instead of distributing these publications in the streets, as the Germans were doing, chose to find individuals and organizations which could influence public opinion, and distribute the publications through them. Moreover, by getting in touch with circles and publishing houses in neutral countries, they were able to issue their publications while remaining in the background.

The main goal of the bureau was to ensure, by making public the atrocious and inhuman actions of Germany and her allies, that neutral countries, and especially the United States, would enter the conflict on their side.

I remember at the end of the war I met Mr. Henry White, formerly American Ambassador in England and in Germany at the outbreak of the war. On hearing who I was he countered the observation of Lord Bryce, who was of the part stating that nothing had been done in propaganda, by saying: "I beg your pardon, it was the best thing done in the war. If it was your husband (turning to me) that did it, please give him my compliments. The Germans bothered and harassed us. You nursed us along till you got us just where you wanted us, and we never knew we were being brought there. We thought we were coming there of ourselves."[39]

I now refer to the third report concerning the activities of the Masterman bureau.[40] At the end of the 118—page report is a list of the books and pamphlets which were published.

At the end of the first half of 1916, 182 had been published. Among the authors were Max Aitken, William Archer, Balfour, James Bryce, E. T. Cook, Conan Doyle, Alexander Gray, Archibald Hurd, Rudyard Kipling, A. Lowenstein, C. F. G. Masterman, A. J. Toynbee and H. G. Wells. One of the books written by Toynbee was entitled *Armenian Atrocities, The murder of a nation.*

Although we shall deal later with the topic of propaganda against the Ottoman Empire throughout the war, we find it useful to include here a few passages from the report:

Within this development policy framework, we have ensured the possibility of publishing most of our publications in neutral or allied countries. Wellington House publications (in addition to those published in London), are at present being published and distributed in Paris, Madrid, Switzerland, Italy, Greece, Holland, Denmark, Sweden, and Russia. Many countries, especially small countries having a common border with Germany, are very sensitive to organized propaganda carried out by foreign states, and in some of them, especially in Sweden and Switzerland our publications have been censored, and have had difficulties in the customs. For this reason, the sale and the free distribution of our publications, their publication by the local publishing houses, without any apparent relationship to the British government's propaganda has been very useful. [p. 4]

One has witnessed the development of illustrated newspapers in this period. At the present time, 6 such newspapers are being published and distributed by Wellington House. [p. 5]. [One of these illustrated newspapers was *Al-Hakikat* (The Truth), published twice a month in Arabic, Turkish, Persian and Urdu.]

A former Turkish Consul distributes *Al-Hakikat* to local Moslems in Argentina. (P. 7]

Wellington House was an organization formed by eight different propaganda divisions: America, France, Spain and Portugal, Scandinavia, Italy and Switzerland, Greece and Rumania, Eastern, and Islamic countries. In addition there were the divisions of painting, photography and film, and the intelligence and distribution divisions. Although it had such a wide area of activity, only 74 people worked for the organization, including the president and the secretary. The organization worked in cooperation with the publishing houses.

Naturally there is no information as to how the propaganda material was gathered.

Lucy Masterman, who wrote her husband's biography, undoubtedly did not include anything that might be used against her husband. We even come across the following statement: 'What he objected to was the demand that his department should lose all integrity or sense as a condition of the work they were doing' (p. 275). This statement, however, does not tell us whether the bureau of propaganda conveyed only news that was accurate. Lucy

Masterman states that her husband had nothing to do with the unfounded news that appeared from time to time in certain newspapers.

Nevertheless, to show how propaganda was gathered, we may consider the preparations of the blue book on the Armenians published in 1916.

Apparently the first text of the blue book was the pamphlet entitled *Armenian Atrocities, The murder of a nation* by Toynbee, published, as mentioned above, by the Masterman bureau. We do not have this first text as a Wellington House publication. However, the book was reprinted 1975 by an Armenian publishing house in the United States.[41] It is impossible for us to know whether Toynbee, the author of *The Western Question in Greece and Turkey,* would have permitted this new edition of his book, if he had been alive in 1975.

The references given in this book are the Armenian newspapers *Horizon* published in Tiflis, the *Ararat* in London, the *Gotchnag* in New York, and the Armenian Atrocities Committee in the United States, which reported the information it had been given by the missionaries. What will be written in a book which relies on these sources is obvious. It may be mentioned that while the Armenians of Istanbul and Izmir were not deported, a map in the book indicates that they were. In the third report of the Masterman bureau it was stated that Toynbee's book aroused much interest.

The British documents describe the following situation (the numbers in brackets are those of the documents).

The British Consul in Batum, Stevens, writes in a telegram (F.O 371/2488/140259) to his Ministry on 10 September 1915 that he had his information from the Armenian newspapers in Tiflis, that Ottomans had destroyed Sasun and killed many people, that 10-15,000 refugees per day were coming to the region of Erivan, and that so far 160,000 refugees had come.

Lord Cromer writes in a memo dated 2 October 1915 that it is useful to publicize what the Turks have done, and thus prevent educated Muslims in India from associating the Islamic cause with the Turks. It is stated in subsequent memos that no other information was available, except that from newspapers.

These news items were made public in American newspapers on 4 October.

On 6 October, a question on this matter was directed to the Government in the House of Commons. (Records of Parliament, 6 October 1915 pp. 994-1004.) Spokesman for the government Lord Cromer states that they have heard of the massacre of 80,000, and repeats his opinion as stated in the memo.

Toynbee's book was published after this. We see that Toynbee, from February 1916 on, stating that he is acting on behalf of Lord Bryce, asks for information against Turkey from various countries and individuals, as well as from Armenian Committees (F.O. 96/205). These items of information were sent to Toynbee without details of their sources. All these writings are present in the above-mentioned dossier; among them was the following letter sent by Toynbee on 11 May 1916 to Lord Bryce:

Mr. Gowers from our office discussed with Montgomery from the Foreign Office how to publish the Armenian documents. They [the Foreign Office] claim that if you were to send these documents with an introductory note to Sir Edward Grey [Foreign Secretary] and state that they have been prepared under your supervision, that they are trustworthy, then your letter would be published by the Foreign Office as an official document, and the documents would constitute an appendix to your letter. The problem of publication would thus be solved. While giving the book an official character, it would free the Foreign Secretary from the obligation to take upon himself the proving of the accuracy of every matter mentioned in these documents.

Thus, the blue book was prepared by the Masterman bureau - by putting together documents without having checked their accuracy, documents exclusively collected from Armenian sources or from people sympathetic to Armenians from second or third hand - and was published with official status.

We would like to quote now from two authors who have studied how propaganda material was gathered.

The first is Arthur Ponsonby and the title of his book is *Falsehood in War-Time*.[42] Ponsonby was a member of the Liberal Party in the House of Commons from 1910 to 1918. He then transferred to the Labour Party and was opposed to war. He published his book in 1928. We quote hereunder some particularly interesting passages concerning the propaganda-gathering process.

A circular was issued by the War Office inviting reports on war incidents from officers with regard to the enemy and stating that strict accuracy was not essential so long as there was inherent probability [p. 20]

Atrocity lies were the most popular of all, especially in this country and America; no war can be without them. Slander of the enemy is esteemed a patriotic duty. [p. 22]

Even in inconsequential events the testimony of individuals is never absolutely convincing. But when prejudices, emotions, passions and nationalism are present, an individual's statement becomes worthless. It is impossible to describe all the types of atrocity stories. They were repeated for days in brochures, posters, letters and speeches. Renowned persons, who otherwise would be hesitant to condemn even their mortal enemies for lack of evidence, did not hesitate to accuse an entire nation of having committed every imaginable savagery and inhuman action. [p. 129]

For those who are unaccustomed, a photograph creates an inherent element of trust. For them there can be nothing more authentic than a snapshot. No one thinks of questioning the veracity of a photograph. For this reason even if they are subsequently shown to be fakes, the damage has already been done. During the war the faking of photographs became an industry. Every state engaged in this activity, but the French were the real experts. [p. 135]

During the massacres of 1905 many photographs were taken. One of these, a group of people surrounding a row of corpses, appeared on June 14, 1915 in le Miroir' with the headline: 'The Murders of the German Gangs in Poland.' Many other similar examples appeared in other newspapers. [p. 136]

The photograph of a German soldier leaning over his dead comrade was published on April 17, 1915 in 'War Illustrated' (published by the Masterman Bureau), as definite proof that the Huns were violating war regulations, 'a German savage robbing a dead Russian'. [p. 137]

The second author is Cate Haste and the title of her book is: *Keep the Home Fires Burning.*[43] A speech of US President Coolidge to the Association of Newspaper Editors is cited on the first page of the book: 'Propaganda seeks to present part of the facts, to distort their relations, and to force conclusions which could not be drawn from a complete and candid survey of all the facts.'

We quote some passages from the book:

The essence of propaganda is simplification. Through the methods adopted by the media and the organizations engaged in propaganda, a fabric of images about war was gradually built up, by endless repetition over a long period, to provide indisputable justification for the fighting. Propagandists create images with simple human content which are believable because they chime with what people have already been taught to believe. As Goebbels put it in a later war, the task is 'to provide the naively credulous with the arguments for what they think and wish, but which they are unable to formulate and verify themselves. [p. 3]

In wartime, this means firstly building up an image of 'the enemy' which accords with preconceived ideas of the behaviour which can be expected of 'enemies'. It entails constantly denigrating the enemy in such a way as to inspire hatred of him and excluding information which is sympathetic to his cause. [p. 3]

Atrocity stories have appeared in all wars, before and since. The intention is to create an image which acts as a repository for all the hatred and fear inspired by war. [p. 3]

The war is justified in the name of simple and universal ideals which everyone has learnt and with which nobody can be expected to disagree. Ideals like Freedom, Justice, Democracy and Christianity, which are the embodiment prevailing national virtues. [pp. 3-4]

The characteristic atrocity story came from 'a correspondent' some distance behind the scene of operations. It was invariably a supposedly verbatim account by an unidentified Belgian or French refugee. . . . Even these accounts were usually second-hand. [p. 84]

On page 87 an example of how a piece of news is transformed is given:

'When the fall of Antwerp got known the church bells were rung.' - *Kölnische Zeitung.*

'According to the *Kölnische Zeitung*, the clergy of Antwerp were compelled to ring the church bells when the fortress was taken.' - *Le Matin* (Paris).

'According to what *The Times* has learned from Cologne via Paris, the unfortunate Belgian priests who refused to ring the church bells when Antwerp was taken have been sentenced to hard labour.' - *Corriere della Sera* (Milan).

'According to information in the *Corriere della Sera*, from Cologne via London, it is confirmed that the barbaric conquerors of Antwerp punished the unfortunate Belgian priests for their heroic refusal to ring the church bells by hanging them as living clappers to the bells with their heads down.' - *Le Matin* (Paris).

The sixth chapter of this book reports the hostility shown by the people towards persons of German origin living in England, and their being gathered and sent to specific camps. We shall not dwell on this subject, for it has little to do with propaganda *per se*. We shall only cite the following sentence from p. 121 : 'Louis, Prince of Battenberg, son of Prince Alexander who has a high-ranking position in the Austrian army, has been forced to resign from his post as First Lord of the Admiralty.'

Propaganda during war was effective to this extent. But in the case of the Ottoman Empire, the propaganda had started long before the war, and continued, was even itensified, after the truce.

We shall conclude this subject by quoting C.F. Dixon-Johnson:

We have no hesitation in repeating that these stories of wholesale massacre have been circulated with the distinct object of influencing, detrimentally to Turkey, the future policy of the British Government when the time of settlement shall arrive. No apology, therefore, is needed for honestly endeavouring to show how a nation with whom we were closely allied for many years and which possesses the same faith as millions of our fellow-subjects, has been condemned for perpetrating horrible excesses against humanity on 'evidence' which, when not absolutely false, is grossly and shamefully exaggerated.[44]

CHAPTER THREE

The Armenians in the Ottoman Empire
and the policies of the great powers

1. The Ottoman Empire until the imperial reform edict

The history of the Ottoman Empire can be divided into four parts: its rise, its Golden Age, its decline and its fall. It is generaly accepted that the period of decline began in 1579, with the death of Sokullu Mehmet Pasha, and that the fall began in 1699 with the treaty of Karlowitz.

By the policies of the great powers we mean the policies followed during the decline and fall of the Ottoman Empire. During the Golden Age there was no state greater than the Ottoman Empire, and even in the period of decline, Britain and Russia were only in the background. Even after 1699 was another seventy-five years before the European powers became stronger than the Ottoman Empire, and were able to make their influence felt, when the treaty of Kuchuk Kaynarca was signed in 1774.

After this treaty, the Ottoman Empire bade farewell to its grandeur and might, replaced by Russia and Austria on the European scene. Initially only those two powers had a policy with regard to the Ottoman Empire, but after the French Revolution and the Napoleonic Wars, Britain and France followed suit. In 1870, immediately after its unification, Germany came to be included in this group, and the fate of the Ottoman Empire virtually depended on the decisions of these five powers.

Within this historical development, although its seeds were sown earlier the Armenian question was raised as a European issue at the Berlin Congress (1878).

Now we shall try to examine the condition of the Armenians within and without the frontiers of the Ottoman Empire.

We have previously stated that the Ottomans finally annexed in 1517 the area that had belonged to the old Cilicia kingdom, that although Sultan Selim I defeated Shah Ismail in Chaldiran in 1514 and entered Tabriz, the war having continued after his death, the truce was established only on May 1555. The occupation of Georgia occurred in 1578 under the reign Murat III. However, wars between the Ottomans and the Safavids continued after this date until the Kasri Sirin Treaty was signed under Murat IV in 1639.

Wars with Iran took place after 1639, in 1723-7, 1730-7, and 1743- 6. But ultimately the frontiers established by the Kasri Sirin Treaty remained.

This frontier was almost the present-day border between Turkey and Iran, with Erivan staying in Iran. In 1639, the Khanate of Crimea was legally under Ottoman rule, as well as the Black Sea shores and Georgia. The Russians had started to enter Caucasia towards the end of the 16th century by advancing towards the river Terek after dissolving the khanate of Astrakhan in 1556.

Theoretically the Caspian shores of Transcaucasia belonged to Iran, but the area of Azerbaijan was more in the sphere of influence of the Ottoman Empire.

Some of the Turco-Iranian wars took place in the geographical area called Armenia. However, Armenians living in the area are not mentioned, either in Ottoman or Iranian history. It is only recorded in Armenian history that during the 1603-4 wars, Shah Abbas transferred Armenians of Erivan and Julfa to the interior of Iran.[1]

As to the Ottoman Empire, it is known that Mehmet II, the Conqueror, brought the Armenian bishop Hovakim from Bursa to Istanbul and gave him the title of Armenian Patriarch. Earlier, in 1453, after the conquest of Istanbul, Gennadius II was brought to the Orthodox Patriarchate, whereby two Patriarchates were established in Istanbul. The Patriarchate was the sole authority in the Armenian community, not only in religious matters, but in personal and family matters as well. The Patriarch had the authority to inflict both ecclesiastical and civil penalties on his people; he could imprison or exile clergy at will, and though the consent of the government was necessary to imprison or exile laymen, such firmans (imperial decrees) were generally easily obtained.

Those who believed in the dual nature of Christ were under the Orthodox Patriarchate. The Monophysites, on the other hand, comprising the Armenian, Syrian Jacobite, Coptic, and Abyssinian communities, while retaining their own autocephalous hierarchies, were made subject to the jurisdiction of the Armenian Patriarchate.

Although the Catholicates of Sis and Akdamar were superior from the point of view of religious hierarchy, the Istanbul Patriarchate had considerably more authority from a legal point of view. The Catholicate of Etchmiadzin, in Iran, could not have its presence felt in the Ottoman Empire.

The Armenians were leading a normal life in the Ottoman Empire, without any reason to complain. 'From the day that the patriarchate and a strong Armenian colony were established at Constantinople, that city gradually became the real center of Armenian ecclesiastical and national life. By the beginning of the nineteenth century the Armenians of Constantinople were numbered upward of 150,000, the largest Armenian community in the world.'[2] And there was no state which was interested in this community.

Although the frontiers of Kasri Sirin were not changed despite the subsequent Turco-Iranian wars, and although there was no situation of interest for the Armenians living in Caucasia, the intention of the Russians to advance to southern Caucasia indicated that the future was ripe for new developments.

Russia for the first time invaded the khanate of Kuba, to the north of Baku, by transferring soldiers from the area of the Caspian Sea during the 1723-7 Ottoman-Iranian wars. However, the death of Peter the Great put an end to this.

In 1768 a war broke out between the Ottoman Empire and Russia, because of events in Poland. During this war, which ended with the defeat of the Turks on the western front and with the Kuchuk Kaynarca truce in 1774, Russians came to southern Caucasia for the first time through the Darial pass. In collaboration with the Georgian forces, they conquered Kutaisi besieged Poti. Another branch of the Russian army went on to Ahiska through the Koura pass.[3]

The Kuchuk Kaynarca Truce gave the area of Kabartay, to the south of Caucasia, to the Russians, and it also included a clause which gave the Russians the right to protect Christians living in Turkey. (We do not report the clauses concerning the western borders, as they are outside our topic of discussion.)

After this truce, Russia followed a policy of invading the Ottoman Empire piece by piece, and the aim of protecting Christians increasingly gained importance.

In 1783, Russia made a pact with the Eastern Georgian princes, and thus brought them under its patronage. In 1787, Catherine the Great and Joseph II, the Austrian Emperor, met in the city of Kerson in the Crimea, discussed the division of the Ottoman Empire between them. According to this plan, known as the `Greek Scheme', an independent Orthodox state, `Dacia', would be established in Moldavia Wallachia and Bessarabia; the area between the Dnieper and Bug rivers would be given to Russia; Serbia, Bosnia and Herzegovina would be given to Austria; the Mora peninsula Crete and Cyprus would be given to the Republic of Venice; in the event of the conquest of Istanbul, the Empire of Byzantium would be restored as an independent state.[4]

The Ottoman Empire declared war on Russia on 13 August 1787, because of this and similar events. Austria was allied with Russia. The war ended on 9 January 1792, with the truce of Yash, without any frontier changes.

After the Iranians attacked Tiflis in 1795, Russia invaded the south-eastern Caucasus, Kuba, Baku, Derbent, Shirvan, and the Karabagh principalities, but took its armies back after Catherine the Great died and Paul became Tsar.

Russia annexed Georgia in 1801.

In 1806 another war broke out between the Ottomans and the Russians, because of the Moldavia-Wallachia events. The Bucharest Pact in 1812 gave the area of Rion, to the west of Souram in the

Caucasus, to the Russians. In 1813, by the Treaty of Butistan between Iran and Russia, Russia annexed the coast of the Caspian Sea.

Abbas Mirza, Shah of Iran, wanted to annul this treaty. The subsequent war ended on 18 February 1828 with the Turkmenchai Pact, and Iran, in addition to the region she had lost in 1813, was forced to abandon the khanates of Erivan and Nahjivan to Russia. Thus, the present-day Russian-Iranian border was established. Armenian volunteers fought in this war with the Russians.

The Armenians living under Iranian rule in southern Caucasus were thus brought under Russian domination. The Catholicate of Etchmiadzin was also now part of the Russian Empire.

In 1828, Russia declared war on the Ottoman Empire, which was in difficulty because of the Greek rebellion, started with the instigation and help of the Russians. The war, which began on 26 April, was fought on two fronts; General Paskevitch's forces, which were freed of their engagement after the Turkmenchai Pact, attacked from the east. During this war, the Russian armies advanced up to Erzurum.

The Truce of Adrianople, signed on 14 September 1829, gave, on the eastern frontier, all the forts (Anapa, Poti), as well as Ahiska, Ahilkelek, and the areas of Akchur, to Russia, and the Ottoman Empire thus recognized that Georgia was now under Russian rule.

With this truce the entire Caucasus became part of the Russian Empire.

The Armenians living in the area, who were well incited and had welcomed the Russians with open arms in their advance towards Erzurum, opted for living under Russian rule when peace was established. The Muslims living in the area left to the Russians in turn opted for living under the Ottomans. Thus, about 100,000 Armenians went to Russia from Erzurum and Alashkird.[5] '. . . many thousands of Armenians . . . were settled in the newly incorporated regions of Erevan, Akhakkalaki and Akhaltzikhe. The Erevan province, later the core of S.S.R. Armenia, had at this period a majority of Turkish Muslims.'[6]

After the truce of Turkmenchai, the Tsar had proclaimed the khanates of Erivan and Nahjivan as an Armenian province, and the entire population as 'Russian'. At that time, the Armenians were hoping that the province would become independent, and that the Tsar would assume the title of 'King of Armenia' just as he was 'King of Poland'. These hopes did not last long. In 1849 Caucasia was divided in two, with an administrative reorganization. The province of Georgia and the Caspian province were established former province of Armenia was brought under the jurisdiction of the Georgian province. This arrangement lasted for only four years. Muslims of Caucasia did not want to live under Russian rule, and started a struggle under the leadership of Sheik Shamil. After this, Prince Vorontsov was appointed regent in 1844 to Caucasia, which waz reunited, to establish order in the region.

Vorontsov considered it more useful to form small provinces in Caucasia and formed first the provinces of Kutais, Tiflis, Shemakh and Derbent. These provinces were further subdivided. The majority of the Armenian community was within the province of Tiflis. After a while, Vorontsov formed the province of Erivan, which corresponded to the former province of Armenia. In later years, the borders and names of these provinces underwent some changes.[7]

After the Pact of Adrianople, the Ottoman Empire was struggling with the Mehmet Ali rebellion and could not contain it.

While this struggle was continuing, Sultan Mahmut II had died, and Abdulmejid ascended the throne on 1 July 1839. On 3 November 1839, Foreign Minister Reshid Pasha read a firman in Gulhane Park, in which various reforms were announced: '. . . It is necessary to formulate new laws for the satisfactory administration of our great state and country. The main points of these necessary laws are, to ensure the right to life, honour and property, to establish the collecting of taxes, to fix procedures for the recruiting of soldiers and the duration of military service.'

The Constitutional Reforms envisaged were aimed at establishing a just tax system, strongly punishing bribery, making the courts public, abolishing unjust punishment, and reducing military service to 4-5 years. In addition, the Sultan declared that the reorganization would be applied to all subjects of the state, without distinction between Muslims and non-Muslims.

It can be said that the first positive result of the Constitutional Reforms became apparent in Lebanon.

The Lebenon events having no relation to the Armenian question; we shall not deal with. The reason to mention it is that they constitute the first occasion on which France, Britain, Russia, and Austria interfered to promote reform for the religious minorities.

As the Lebanon topic was being taken temporarily off the agenda in 1846, the question of the `Holy Places' was appearing.

The 'Holy Places' are the church and the cave of Bethlehem in Jerusalem where Christ was born, Christ's tomb and its church, and other such places While various Christian sects had the right of worship here, the Catholics had been given the right, during the reign of Suleiman the Magnificent keep the keys, and to maintain the 'Holy Places'. Later, this right was given in 1634 to the Orthodox Church, as a result of some disagreements with France. From this date, the matter became a source of disputes between two Churches. These disputes had nothing to do with either Muslims or the Ottoman Empire, but because Jerusalem was within the Empire, the Empire was indirectly involved with them.

In 1853, Catholics had been granted a right to repair the Bethlehem Church. This provoked an objection by the Orthodox Church and consequently by Russia, its protector. France, too, had been requesting the return of the rights previously belonging to Catholics. The Babiali decided, after having had a Commission investigate the situation, to have Muslims perform the services which the two churches could not share between them.

At this point, the Tsar sent Admiral Prince Menchikov, Commander of the Baltic Fleet, General-Governor of Finland, Minister of Marine, to Istanbul on a special mission. Menchikov, who arrived at Istanbul on February 1853, gave an ultimatum to the Babiali, demanding that question of the 'Holy Places' be resolved as soon as possible to the advantage of Russia, and that a sound and irreversible guarantee be given to Russia on the privileges of the Orthodox Church. It is known that the real intention of Russia was to divide the Ottoman Empire, which she considered the Sick Man of Europe, and that she had proposed this scheme to Sir Hamilton Seymour, the British Ambassador in St. Petersburg. (The documents concerning this matter were later published by the British.)

The Babiali refused this demand, which would have meant the official acceptance of Russian protection of the Orthodox subjects. On 21 May, Menchikov left Istanbul, along with the Russian Embassy staff, and declared that diplomatic relations between the Ottoman Empire and Russia were broken off.

This incident eventually led to the Crimean War. We do not dwell on details irrelevant to our topic, but there is a subject which should be mentioned. It is reported in various Western sources that there were some clauses in the agreement signed by the Ottomans, the British, and the French against Russia on 12 March 1854, stating that Turkey would be granting certain rights to its Christian subjects. There is no such clause in the text of the agreement.

We want to mention only the eastern front of the war, which began with the entry of the Russians into Moldavia-Wallachia on 3 July 1853, and then moved to the Crimea.

After the Ottoman Empire declared war on 4 October 1853, Abdulkerim Pasha attacked, in the east, in the direction of Ahiska and Gumru, but, having been defeated at Gumru on 14 October, retreated to Arpachay. As he could not take a hold in the battle of Bashgedikler on 1 February, he retreated to Kars, which the Russians besieged.

Subsequently, the war offensives on the eastern front were limited to the siege of Kars. Alexander II, who ascended the throne after Nicholas I died on 2 March 1855, wanted to put an end to the war, especially after Sebastopol fell on 9 September. He declared a general attack on Kars on 29 September, in order to have won a victory. Although the 15,000 Turks inflicted over 7,000 losses on the 40,000 Russians, Kars surrendered on 28 November 1855, because of famine.

In order to put an end to the war, a protocol was signed on 1 February 1856. The fourth article of this protocol showed that the sovereignty of the Sultan and his state's administrative integrity would constitute one of the bases for peace. The Sultan would automatically confirm the guarantee he had given with regard to the legal equality with Muslims of Christians living as Ottoman subjects.

A ceasefire was declared after a decision to have the peace conference meeting in Paris in three weeks.

On 18 February 1856, the Babiali declared the Imperial Reform Edict, which confirmed the decrees of the Gulhane Edict. The main decrees of the Reform Edict are as follows.[8]

1. The inviolability of the right to life, property, and honour granted to every subject without discriminating on the basis of religion or sect, according to the Gulhane edict, is repeated and confirmed.

2. Privileges given since the reign of Mehmet II, the Conqueror, to non-Muslim communities, have been retained, along with spiritual immunities.

3. Special assemblies will be formed by the Patriarchates under the supervision of the government, to reconcile these privileges and immunities with the new conditions and needs. The decisions of these assemblies will be submitted to the Babiali, and will become definite by the approval of the government.

4. The election procedure of the Patriarchs will be revised, and spiritual leaders such as the patriarchs, the Catholic, Greek, and Armenian bishops, and the rabbis to be appointed for life will take an oath of loyalty to the State.

5. The favours and revenues given by the congregations to their spiritual leaders will be abolished, and they will receive salaries instead.

6. Congregational matters will be transferred to assemblies comprised spiritual and secular members.

7. In homogeneous areas inhabited by the congregation of one sect, outward and public worship will be permitted.

8. All sects, regardless of their size, will equally enjoy religious freedom.

9. No one will be forced to change his religion.

10. Every subject can be a government official, regardless of his race or sect.

11. Every individual having the necessary legal competence and qualifications will obtain the right to enter the Military and the Civil Servants' School, regardless of his religion.

12. The establishment of schools for non-Muslims will be permitted, on condition that they are supervised and inspected by an Education Assembly, a heterogeneous body, which would also supervise and establish their programme, and appoint their instructors.

13. Mixed courts will be established for commercial and murder cases occurring between Muslims and non-Muslims, or exclusively among non-Muslims, and the trials will be public.

14. Cases such as inheritance disagreements occurring among non-Muslims can be transferred, by request of the interested parties, to Patriarchs and spiritual assemblies.

15. Legal equality being dependent on equality of duties, non-Muslims will be obliged, like Muslims, to do their military service. They will have the right to actively perform their duty, as well as the right to acquit themselves of their duty by paying the necessary sum.

16. A corollary regulation with regard to the method of employment of non-Muslims in the army will be published as soon as possible. (Two main possibilities have been proposed. Although there were some who suggested establishing a battalion for every sect, it was ultimately preferred to form mixed batallions.)

17. In matters concerning all the subjects of the State, the spiritual leader of every congregation, along with its official appointed for one year by the government, will participate in the negotiations of `Meclis-i Valay-i Ahkam-i Adliyye', a law court established in 1837 to deal with cases of high officials.

18. The members of this court will speak freely during the discussions, and the content of their speech will never be used against them.

The Ottoman Empire wanted to prove that the Reform Edict was prepared with her own initiative, by publishing it before the Paris Conference. Moreover, it was explicitly stated in the Peace Agreement signed on 30 March 1856 that communicating this edict to foreign states by no means gave the right to those states to interfere with the internal affairs of the Ottoman Empire. But this was only to save appearances. In actuality the right to protect Christians was given to all the powers, instead of only Russia.

It cannot be stated that the Reform Edict satisfied non-Muslims.

The most important rights given to non-Muslims to please Europe, were the opportunity to enter civil and military schools, and to become civil servants, the possibility to transfer their inheritance cases to Patriarchates, the publishing of murder and commerce laws in the languages of the minorities, contrary to the official language principle, the representation of all congregations with two representatives from each, at the higher court, and finally, the extending of the right to property to foreigners. Among these, the right given to Patriarchates administer justice, even if limited, was an infringement of the judiciary sovereignty of the State.

There are many regulations in the Reform Edict, to the advantage, as well as the disadvantage of the non-Muslim minorities. The obligation to do one's military service, the reexamination of religious privileges and exemptions granted since the reign of Mehmet II, the Conqueror, the abolition of arbitrary fees exacted by priests all along from their congregations, and giving salaries, instead, to priests and the obligation of all spiritual leaders to take the oath of devotion, were to the disadvantage of non-Muslims.

For this reason, Muslims as well as non-Muslims were against the Reform Edict. The ones who were afflicted the most were the priests, who after having plundered for centuries, to use Engelhardt's term, now had their income reduced with the abolition of the favours and revenues demanded from the congregations. As for the common folk, who were now freed from being robbed, they were displeased by the military service obligation. For, from the beginning of Ottoman history, it had been the Muslims, and especially the Turks, who had shed their blood, while non-Muslims lived comfortably by themselves. For this reason, it is even said that, after the Babiali firman was read, and when it was being put into the satin pouch, the Bishop of Izmir said: 'Let us pray to God, that this firman is never taken out of that pouch.' The Orthodox Church attempted to portray the reexamination of privileges as interference by the Government in the affairs of the Patriarchate, even as its attempt to abolish them. Undoubtedly the 'favours and revenues question had a great deal to do with the Church's attempt to engage in negative propaganda through the newspapers, to open the way for possible European intervention.[9]

In this manner, after the Paris Truce, the four powers (Russia, Britain, France, Austria) began to intervene, on the pretext of protecting religious minorities.

The first such intervention took place because of new conflicts in Lebanon on 27 May 1860. Being irrelevant to our subject we shall not deal with.

These events occurring until 1856 show that, until then, Russia and other powers were not interested in the Armenian community within the Empire, that Russia aimed at having a say in the Empire by having the Ottoman Orthodox minority under her absolute protection, to ensure the superiority of the Greek Orthodox Church and consequently of the National Russian Church. French interest lay in the Catholics.

While these events were occurring, various changes were happening within the Armenian community, in the order established since 1461, and consequently some discontent was becoming apparent.

This community constitutes the very life of Turkey, for the Turks, long accustomed to rule rather than serve, have relinquished to them all branches of industry. Hence the Armenians are the bankers, merchants, mechanics, and traders of all sorts in Turkey.

Besides, there exists a congeniality and community of interest between them and the Musulmans. For, being originally from the same region, they were alike in their habits and feelings; therefore, easily assimilating themselves to their conquerors, they gained their confidence, and became and still are the most influential of all the rayahs. There is not a pasha, or a grandee, who is not indebted to them, either pecuniarily, or for his promotion, and the humblest peasant owes them the value of the very seed he sows; so that without them the Osmanlis could not survive a single day.

This is a fact so well attested, that Russia, with the design of undermining Turkey, always endeavoured to gain over this part of the population, and in 1828, when she took possession of Erzeroum, she enticed the Armenians of that place to acts of violence and revenge against the Turks, so that when the Russians retired, the Armenians were obliged to emigrate with them.[10]

These statements, attesting to the fact that the community had a certain place within Ottoman society, and that it led a normal life, were published in 1857.

It is nevertheless useful to examine in an overview how and why this discontent came about.

We have noted the attempts of the Vatican to bring the Gregorian Church under its sphere of influence during the rule of the Armenian Kingdom of Cilicia, and the transferring of the Catholicate from Sis to Etchmiadzin avoid failing under the influence of the Catholic Church.

While there was no organic link between the Churches, many Gregorian Armenians were being drawn, or went, into the Catholic religion. In the beginning, these individuals did not sever their links with the Gregorian Church, and were using a given church for specific reasons. For example, they were going to the Catholic Church to confess, while this practice was not accepted by the Gregorians. But as, in the course of time, the number of Catholics increased, the Armenian Patriarch felt it neccessary to take sides.

The Mekhitarists, who played an important role in the consciousness of Armenian nationalism, had been founded by a priest converted Catholicism.

Mekhitar was born towards the end of the 17th century, in Sivas.... became a monk at the early age of fifteen. . . . He became a priest when he was twenty years old. . . . Soon he was preoccupied by an idea which he later tried to resolve, and he began his attempt to unify the Roman Church and the Armenian Patriarchate. In 1700 he left his native land with a few disciples, with the aim of founding a congregation whose difficult task was to bring the education necessary to Armenia. After he stayed for a while in Constantinople, where he published first books, . . . was forced to leave, and chose as a meeting place with companians, the city of Modon, then under Venetian rule. . . . Because of an invasion by the Turks, the congregation was obliged to leave, and arrived Venice in 1715. In 1717, the Senate conceded forever the island of St. Lazarus to Mekhitar and his companions. . . . The conquest of Italy by general Bonaparte called in question once again the existence of the congregation, for a decree had abolished all the convents. Saint-Lazarus escaped this measure, by transfering itself into an Armenian Academy, which was facilitated by the scientific direction given to the works of the order's members. Since this period, the Armenian Academy of Saint Lazarus of Venice has continued to exist and to develop with the order itself.[11]

When the number of Catholic Armenians increased, despite the efforts the Armenian Patriarch, the Armenian Catholics were recognized as a separate community for the first time on 27 February 1830, through the efforts of the French Ambassador, and Hagopos Chukuryan was appointed Patriarch of this community on 22 December 1831 . The Patriarchate, which was established in the beginning at Adana, was later transferred to Istanbul.

We have mentioned the activities of the missionaries. Although missionaries claimed that they were not having anybody change their religion or sect, the number in the Ottoman Empire who were converting to the Protestant faith was increasing. This time, because of the insistence of the British Ambassador, despite the objections of the Russian Embassy and the Armenian Patriarchate, the Protestant Armenians became a separate community in 1859.

Another source of discontent of the Armenian Patriarchate, which witnessed the gradual erosion of its community, were developments, which appeared especially after the Constitutional Reforms, in the organization of the Gregorian Armenian community. We will approach this subject by summarizing an article by Migirdich B. Dadian, because, in our opinion, we can follow these developments best through the writings of an Armenian author.

This religious leader with the title of Patriarch is not only the spiritual leader of the community, but its secular leader as well. He was given this religious authority, like all the bishops and archbishops of the Armenian Church, by the Catholicos of Etchmiadzin. Approximately 50 regions were under the jurisdiction of the Istanbul Centre. Before the reorganization in 1860, the Patriarch could at will dismiss the Bishops he had appointed. He could annul their status as bishop, which they were given by the Catholicos, as well as take away their right to administer their areas. He even had the right to shave off their beards.

As the responsible chief, answerable to the Babiali, he was responsible to ensure the collection of the land tax. Among his duties was to resolve various disputes as a judge.

This dual authority could have produced useful, advantageous results in the absence of opposition by an adverse power. However, there was in Istanbul an Assembly, selected from among the Armenian aristocracy, called the `National Council'. This assembly was a constant source of intrigues and disputes.

This situation continued until 1839, without a major problem other than a few complaints.

In 1844, during the time of Patriarch Matheos Chuhajiyan, the structure of the National Council was transformed. It was decided that it should be comprised of 30 members, 16 of whom were to be selected from among the nobility and 14 from professional associations. The Patriarch would choose those representing the professional associations. Another change came about in 1847. It was decided that two councils should be formed, one dealing with religious matters, the other with remaining matters, and that the members of the Council should be elected. These principles became effective through a firman of the Sultan on March 9, 1847. This was a blow to the noble class.

When Matheos left the Patriarchate in 1848, Agob Serobian, who had previously been the Patriarch, replaced him despite the opposition of the nobility.

The Reform Edict of 1856 was decreed during Serobian's rule. Upon the declaration of the firman, the Armenians wanted to abolish oppression by the nobility, by drawing up a new 'National Regulation'. In 1859, as the Council dealing with religious matters was being reselected the majority of nobles were not included. The new Council formed a Commission to prepare a regulation. The activities of this Commission severed further the relations between the nobility and the other group. As a result of disputes, Gevorg Kerestejiyan, the Patriarch, was forced to resign. The election of Sergis Kuyumjiyan, who replaced him, gave rise to serious conflicts. Finally the Council accepted the draft regulation on May 24, 1860, and presented it to the Babiali. The Babiali ratified it with some minor changes, with a firman on March 17, 1863, and made it effective. [12]

This information, which we have summarized from Dadian, is in agreement with Ottoman records, and as a matter of fact was included in the same way in all the sources relating to this subject. The conclusion Dadian's article is of particular interest. We shall quote it below. The point to be emphasized is that the Armenians had no problem with the State, that they could administer their internal affairs almost independently, without the Government intervening in the decisions they took concerning themselves, and that all this was taking place without the interest or the support of any foreign country.

More than a hundred years have passed since the article was written in 1867. Today, in various countries in the world Armenian communities of varying size are living. Not one of these communities has freedom to this extent. It is obvious that the privileges present in the Ottoman Empire were nothing less than a landless autonomy. A landless nation's autonomy was a practice unheard of in international law, and these opportunities were officially given by the Babiali to the Armenian community, at a time when no state was interested in them, and there was no such subject as the 'Armenian Question'. As a matter of fact, these very privileges opened the way to the emergence of this question.

Dadian's article ends with the following statements:

We have thus reported the changes undergone by this important Armenian sector subject to the Sultan's laws. With the approval of the Government, this community was provided with a constitution, whose main principle was the sovereignty of the people, and favourable initiatives were taken to revive nation, education.

In these attempts at reform, the cooperation of the clergy was apparent, but was not extensive. In many cases it remained detached from, or stranger to, the developments which were strengthening the nation. While everything around it was in motion, it was motionless. Consequently, the influence it previously had without ever having to impose it, was now diminished. The new generation is not consenting to being directed by the clergy with the same docility, and does not go under under its authority of its own accord, as previous generations had done. . . Armenians . . . along with the Christian creeds, maintained their language customs, and traditions, and did not lose their identity within the society they were living in, as was the case with many other communities. . . . . East Asia commerce is in their hands, they travel continuously and have extensive contacts. They can well be an intermediary between Asia and Europe, if the expression is appropriate, they are the spreaders of Western civilization."

Such   is the opinion of an Armenian living outside the Ottoman Empire about the situation of Armenians in the Empire, an opinion published in 1867, in a newspaper in France. It is necessary to keep this in mind, while evaluating subsequent events.

The statement which calls for attention here is the observation that the Church was distant from, or stranger to, the developing thoughts and events. It is not difficult to consider this as a polite statement, and to recognize that the Church did not actually want these developments.

The 'Armenian National Regulation' made effective in 1863 had 99 paragraphs. An Assembly of 140 members was established; 20 members were to be selected from among the Istanbul priests, 40 members from the provinces, and 80 members from Istanbul.

The former 14-member religious assembly and the 20-member political assembly were maintained, but the regulation that their election is to be made by the national assembly was new.

The election of the Patriarch, too, had to be performed by the national assembly. While the Religious Assembly could nominate candidates, the National Assembly had the right to appoint a Patriarch from outside the candidates. The appointment of the Patriarch would be definitive with a firman.

The regulation also stated that the election of the Patriarch of Jerusalem was to be made by the National Assembly.

The 'Armenian National Regulation' constituted a change, not from the vantage point of the condition of Armenians within the state, but concerning the authority of the Patriarch. It did not consider this authority as absolute any more, but rather, meant the sharing of this authority between the Patriarch and the Armenian nation.

Dadian's statements concerning the subject of culture are also worth quoting:

The first newspaper written in Armenian was published in 1859. After the 'Armenian National Regulation' was published, the number of newspapers increased. We should nevertheless confess that, while the press gained in importance, it did not fulfill the duty expected of it. However, there was no obstacle to restrain it, or outside pressure to influence it. While some newspapers chose to defend the Church by giving priority to religious subjects, others began to shake the foundations of national faith, and did not hide any more their inclination towards Protestant ideas. . . , Between 1839 and 1866 the number of daily newspapers in Istanbul reached 14. Even in Van, which was the most remote province, a newspaper was published.

In Istanbul Armenian books were being printed during the 17th century. Mekhitar had printed his first books at the beginning of the 18th century in Istanbul. When an Armenian printing office in Marseilles was closed by Louis XIV,[13] Armenians had no complaint about the freedom of press in the Ottoman Empire, and this freedom was increasing.

These developments were laying the foundations of a serious problem for the Gregorian Church. On the one hand, the Armenian nation was converting to other churches, and Catholic and Protestant `Armenia nations' were emerging within the Empire, and on the other hand, part of the authority of the Gregorian Church was being transferred from the Patriarch to the Armenian nation. The Patriarch had no power to turn over to someone else the authority and privileges given to him through firmans While the Babiali did not object to this situation, if the climate of freedom developing in the country were to bring about a situation which would not require having different status because of belonging to different religions, then these rights transferred to the people would be abolished, and the Patriarch would remain only as a religious leader.

In addition, the ambition of Russia to destroy the Ottoman Empire, to restore Byzantium by taking Istanbul, had become apparent. If this possibility were to be realized, then the independent character and existence of the Gregorian Church might be abolished, and Russia, which was much more powerful than Byzantium, might achieve what Byzantium was unable to do, namely, to incorporate the Gregorian Church.

Under these circumstances, something had to be done for the Church to be able to exist, to maintain its influence, and to regain the privileges it has lost. Pastermadjian commented:

As far as the Armenian nation is concerned, its aspirations, as they were expressed by the national movement in the second half of the 19th century, could aim at neither the establishment of an independent Armenia, nor the annexation of Turkish Armenia by the Empire of the Czars. It was in fact evident that Czarist Russia was opposed to the creation of an Armenian State, because such a State would have been an inevitable attraction for the Armenian subjects of the Empire and would have reinforced, by its very existence, the aspirations of the peoples of Transcaucasia for greater autonomy. As for the annexation of Turkish Armenia by Russia, its result would have been the extending to this region of the policy of gradual rustication of the allogeneous peoples, which was the policy of the czarist government. Such an annexation would have therefore constituted a serious danger for preserving the Armenian cultural patrimony. [14]

The only hope for the survival of the Church was the establishment of an autonomous Armenia bound to the Ottoman Empire. The constitution of this autonomous Armenia was ready anyway. The only thing that remained to be done was to demarcate the borders of an area. From 1856 on, this idea became more and more onpressed. Patriarch Hrimyan was its most outspoken advocate.

Undoubtedly this idea was shared by the Church of Etchmiadzin, and was even spread by it. For, after the Turkmenchai Truce was signed, the Catholicos, who was hoping to become the ruler of an independent Armenia, had been disillusioned. To examine the developments in Russia will be useful in comparing the condition of Armenians in these two countries. We quote M. Varandian and E. Aknouni:

The secular yoke of Muslims (Turks and Persians) was a terrible burden for the Armenian populations. Nevertheless, these populations were not losing their hope of a future resurrection. And, besides, the whole of Armenia was not enslaved and condemned to a dismal and eternal silence. There were some mountainous regions, - Zeitoun, Sassoun, Karabagh, etc. - which had been able to keep a semi-independence and where the spirit of rebellion was manifesting itself from time to time through audacious unexpected attacks against the foreign despots. At the beginning of the 18th century, some insurrections broke out in the vast region of Karabagh, in Persian Armenia. An Armenian Prince endowed with rare fighting abilities, David-Bek, led the movement and won brilliant victories. The struggle continued for many years. It was a perpetual guerrilla-type action with the aim of driving the Muslims out of the country.

An important fact was encouraging the Armenians and was pushing them to the most brutal adventures. To the North, the great Christian Power, Russia, had expressed its project of descending towards Caucasia, and was assuming the role of protecting the small Christian communities. The despots of Turkey and Persia were beginning to tremble in front of the new colossus and Armenian expectations were growing.

It is only at the beginning of the 19th century that the armies of the Czar arrived at Transcaucasian Armenia, and little by little conquered vast regions there. In 1826-27, after a bloody war, Russia took two large Armenian provinces, Erivan and Nahjivan, from Persia. The entire Armenian population, headed by the Patriarch Nerses Ashtarak, participated actively in this liberation war.

A Russian Armenia was created. There is no need to dwell on the regime instituted by Czarist Russia. For approximately a century, Russian Armenians complained on many occasions of the crimes of this regime. Nevertheless, the changing of the yoke brought some relief to the Armenian populations, who, under the new regime, enjoyed a relative guarantee of their life and property. This minimum security was sufficient for the Armenians to engage in first-rate activity in Caucasia, to give free scope to their aptitudes in the field of commerce, industry, and intellectual life in the main centres : Tiflis, Baku, as well as in the provinces. Schools are being established here and there, books and periodicals are published. [15]

. . . . And when, at the beginning of the 19th century, the gigantic struggle against very powerful Mohammedanism began, the Armenian Church, although it had suffered so much, rushed into the conflict, relying upon Etchmiadzin.

And it is then that the Russian army, representing the Russian people's anger against Muslim domination, went towards Caucasia.

The Armenians took upon themselves to guide [them] in this country bathed with their sweat and which was unknown to the ruler of the future.

In Georgia, it was the nobility, bellicose by nature, which created the movement; in Armenia, it was the clergy. And it was the most valiant Armenian fighter of the time, Nerses Ashtarak, who was at the same time the most capable politican, who headed the movement. Regiments of Armenian volunteers appeared. Nerses, enraptured, made the following speech to his troops, in 1826:

'Armenians!

'The hour of the deliverance of the country of Ararat and of the Armenian people has come; Etchmiadzin can recover its former independence. Rise and rebel, brave Armenians! Shake off the Persian yoke, have old Ararat leap for joy, bathe your fatherland with blood, and you shall live forever free and independent!

'The time has come!

'Forward! Now or never!'

Nerses was enraptured by promises, either official, or secret, coming from Petersburg in regard to the independence of the Armenian provinces of Ararat, which were filling up with Armenian refugees coming from the neighbouring regions belonging to Persia. Independent Armenian provinces, a free Church Etchmiadzin saved from the Mohammedan yoke, how glorious all this appear how captivating was this delusion!

But as their domination was solidly established, when the monarchical government no more needed either the Armenian clergy or the popular forces to crush the Mohammedans, the wind changed and one started to hear completely different speeches, and soon even threats. [16]

It is mainly after 1863, after the insurrection of Poland, which was so audacious but so little successful - a new attempt of liberation by the generation which grew up after the movement of 1830 - that the policy of russification of the enslaved nations was born. . . . 500 Armenian schools in Caucasia were closed, and thus, 200,000 children from both sexes who were being educated, were thrown into street. . . . Acts of an inconceivable tyranny happened then: threats, the whip and the bastinado were begun. [17]

On page 72 of Aknouni's book, the following statement is made:

The obligatory study of the Armenian language had been for a long time abolished from Gymnasiums and state schools, for, according to Russian statesmen, an Armenian has only two obligations in this world: 1) to learn the Russian language; 2) to hate his mother tongue. And these two obligations are considered equally indispensable.

We have quoted above from two different books. The authors of the two books are Armenian. There is a difference of twelve years between the dates of publication.

In Russia, by the decree of the Tsar dated 11 March 1836, a regulation known as Polijenia, concerning the administration of the Catholicate was accepted.

Through this law, the Catholicos could have authority only in spiritual matters, this authority would be checked by a Synod Assembly, representative of the Government would be present in this Assembly, and no decision could be taken without the approval of this representative. The Catholicos could correspond with churches in other countries only through the intermediary of the Russian Ministry of Foreign Affairs. The election of the Catholicos would be made in Etchmiadzin by choosing between two candidates selected by representatives coming from other countries too. This choice would be made by the Tsar himself.

There was no question of the Catholicos or the other bishops having any kind of authority or privilege in secular matters.

It is possible that Etchmiadzin, facing an increasing Russification policy, and very severe measures against the Armenian nationalistic movement, was convinced, as we have stated above, that one day it would be altogether abolished, and thus attempted to persuade the Istanbul Patriarchate to establish an autonomous Armenia in the Ottoman Empire.

Such a thought was not in opposition to the interests of Russia.

We have thus brought the subject to the policies of the great powers.

2. The policies of the great powers

The policies of the great powers have not been established on a day-to-day basis, and they have not followed a fixed and uniform direction. Because it is impossible to set down in writing these policies one by one within the chronological development of historical events, we will attempt to summarize them as a whole, by looking at the period until the establishment of the Republic in Turkey.

We stated previously that the decline and fall of the Ottoman Empire coincided with the Karlowitz Pact of 1699. This pact opened the way for dispossessing the Ottoman Empire, for the first time, of large areas of land. Moreover, it was during this period that Russia began to make its presence felt in Europe.

At the beginning of the 18th century, the main power in Europe was, of course, the Austrian Empire. After the second siege of Vienna, Austria, who had not been able to achieve much with regard to the Ottomans for over two centuries, and had been dispossessed of many lands, now followed the policy of regaining the countries she had lost, which either belonged to her or were subject to her. Hungary, Bosnia, Herzegovina, and Serbia were among these countries. Whenever it was possible, Austria allied herself with Russia, in order to reach this goal. Russia took part in the war which ended with Karlowitz in 1699. Austria expanded her Empire following the 1716-18 war. As the Ottoman State declared war on Russia in 1736, Austria entered the conflict in 1737 to gain more lands through this war. However, Russia and Austria having lost the war, she had to return the lands she had gained by the Pasarovcha Pact of 1718.

Austria did not take part in the Russian War of 1768-74. But as Russia started descending towards the Balkans, she became concerned and felt need to intervene to bring the war to an end.

Because Russia, too, felt that she would not be left alone in the Balkans, she decided to ally with Austria, and Austria then entered the Ottoman-Russian war of 1787. Austria was not successful in this war, either, gained nothing when peace was declared in 1792 with the Zishtovi Treaty. This was the last war between the two countries, until both empires came to an end after the First World War. From this date on, Austria was concerned by Russia's expansion in the Balkans, and engaged in alliances with France, Britain, and Prussia.

When the German Empire was founded in 1870, Austria followed a policy parallel to Germany's, and Germany was the spokesman of this group.

At the beginning of the 18th century, Britain was busy attempting to destroy the French and Spanish hegemonies, and to establish its independent empire at the expense of these states. For Britain, struggling with France, Russia was a state which could put pressure on France and its ally, Prussia. For this reason, Britain made various pacts with Russia. The most significant was signed in 1755. 'With this pact, Russia would give 55,000 soldiers to Britain. When the troops were to go outside the Russian borders, Britain would pay £500,000 sterling per year to Russia, and when they stayed in Russia, she would pay £100,000 sterling per year. . . . The two states signed a non-aggression pact in 1776; when Catherine the Great was sending the Baltic Fleet to Turkish waters during the 1768-74 war, she was renting boats from Britain, and the British Admiral Samuel Greigh was the commandant of the fleet which destroyed the Ottoman Fleet in the Tcheshme harbour.'[18]

Britain became interested in the Ottoman Empire after the Kuchuk Kaynarja Treaty of 1774.

When the Ottoman-Russian War started in 1787, William Pitt, who headed the British Government, realized for the first time that the continuous advance of Russia towards the south would enable Russia become a strong power in the Black Sea, and constitute a danger to Britain. He thus felt the need to support the Ottoman Empire against Russia. The policy, started by Pitt in 1783, continued without change for a century, until Gladstone became Prime Minister. Pitt succeeded in persuading Austria to leave the alliance with Russia during the Ottoman-Russian War of 1787-92 and began to put pressure on Russia, with the help of Prussia after the French Revolution, and went so far as to decide to enter the war in order to end it and to ensure the return of Odessa. In the event, Britain did not enter the war, owing to disagreements within the government, and Russia was forced to end the war.

From this time until 1814 there was almost continuous war between Britain and France. Because of this, Britain supported Russia in the Russian-Ottoman war of 1806, and even sent its fleet into the Marmara Sea, despite its policy, in order not to remain alone against France. But when Russia and France made an agreement at Tilsit in 1807, the Ottoman-British friendship was restored. When the Congress of Vienna met in 1814, Britain attempted to have the Ottoman borders guaranteed by the Congress, but despite the support of the Austrian Chancellor Metternich, who was beginning to be concerned by the Russian danger, Tsar Alexander did not accede.

During the Greek rebellion, Britain supported Greece. Nevertheless, it would be an error to see this attitude of the British Prime Minister Canning as an alliance with Russia. Canning was convinced that Greece would sooner or later win her independence, and it would be preferable that Greece owe this to Britain, instead of to Russia, for Britain would then acquire a friendly country in the Mediterranean.

Britain remained a spectator of the 1828-30 Ottoman-Russian war which started during this rebellion. However, Britain and Austria were seriously worried when Moldavia-Wallachia became

subject to Russian rule. Britain became even more concerned when
Russia began to settle in Caucasia, for this might mean a
preparation to advance towards India.

It is for this reason that Britain did not accept the suggestion
made by Nicholas I, Tsar of Russia, to the British Ambassador in
1853: 'Well, we have here a sick man, a very sick man; it would be,
I tell you frankly, a great misfortune if, one of these days, we were
to lose him, especially before the necessary arrangements had been
made.'[19] Britain was on the side of the Ottoman Empire during the
Crimean War. It is known that Russia offered Crete and Egypt to
Britain, and wanted for herself Moldavia-Wallachia, Serbia, and
Bulgaria.

Russia, who came defeated out of the Crimean War, felt the
necessity to turn now to the east, to Asia, and after having
completed the conquest of Siberia by taking Vladivostock, began to
conquer Turkistan. These conquests in Asia, especially the
occupation of Turkistan, naturally constituted a danger for
Britain's Empire of India.

The 1860s were the years of unification of Italy and Germany
in Europe, and the years when Russia increased its policy of
Pan-Slavism, which was begun after Russia invaded Poland in 1863.

The Ottoman Empire was alone in the 1877-8 war, and signed
the Ayastefanos (San Stefano) Pact, whose stipulations were hard
on the Ottomans. However, both Austria and Britain objected to
this pact. As Bismarck joined them. the Berlin Congress was held
and the Berlin Treaty was signed. As a result of this agreement,
most of Russia's gains were taken away.

After the Berlin Congress, there was a major change in British
policy. Gladstone, who became Prime Minister for the second time
in 1880 changed the policy which had been followed for a century,
which Pitt initiated, and put an end to protecting the
administrative integrity of Ottoman Empire. We have mentioned
that the religious factors Gladstone's conformist point of view as
well as his hostility towards Muslims played an important role in
this change of policy.

Russia, who turned once more towards the Far East after the
Berlin Congress, started again to compete with Britain in Asia, and
returned to a friendly policy concerning the Ottoman Empire. But
this did not last very long either. When Russia was defeated in the
Russo-Japanese war of 1905, Britain and Russia made an
agreement in 1907, about their spheres of influence in Asia.
Subsequently Britain began scheming to divide the Ottoman
Empire with France and Russia, and this aim was achieved during
the the First World War.

The close relations of the Ottoman Empire with France began,
except for the time of Suleiman the Magnificent, under the reign of
Napoleon. After Napoleon's unsuccessful Egyptian campaign,
France had helped Ottomans against Russia; however, after the

Vienna Congress, France some time was no longer in a position to play a significant role in European politics.

France began her policy of expanding in Africa by invading Algeria 1830. After this date, she began to attribute more importance to the subject of protecting Catholics within the Ottoman Empire, and played the main role in the incident of the `Holy Places' which eventually led to the Crimean War.

Napoleon III, who acted with the Ottoman Empire during the Crimean War, had been unable after 1856 to concentrate on other matters, because he had been struggling unsuccessfully with Germany and Italy, who were attempting to achieve unification after 1856, and he suffered a blow following his defeat by Germany in 1870. While France participated in Berlin Congress, she did not play a significant role.

France, who was the cradle of philosophies of freedom and independence after the Revolution, had been closed to such thoughts in the period starting with Napoleon until 1870. She assumed this role once again after the Third Republic was proclaimed, and became a refuge for various classes in various countries, and those struggling against the State in the Ottoman Empire.

France, who did not forget the defeat by Germany, began to get close to Russia, who had left the 1878 Berlin Congress offended at Germany. She also resolved her conflicts with Britain. After the `Entente Cordiale' had been established, and the relations between Russia and Britain were also improved, these three powers shared the same opinion concerning Ottoman Empire, and France played an active role in the projects about dividing the Empire.

Germany entered the European scene with the Versailles Treaty in 1870. Although Prussia had played an active role until then in various matters, it had never possessed the weight of a unified Germany, and had often remained in Austria's shadow. After 1870, Germany became the strongest and most feared country of Europe. After the alliance with Austria and Italy, when Europe was divided into two groups, the Triple Alliance and the Triple Entente, there was no subject left in which Germany did not have a say.

Germany, who started her colonization drive after this date, saw the Ottoman Empire as a country which she could easily influence. The reason why she supported the Ottoman State during the Berlin Congress, and offended her ally Russia, was because she did not want the Empire to disintegrate before she could obtain some rights. As a matter of fact, Ottoman-German relations became closer. Nevertheless, Germany was to take part in the projects carried out by Russia, France and England to divide the Ottoman Empire into spheres of influence, and to claim her share. It is certain that the Ottoman Empire, which entered the First

World War as Germany's ally, would have come under the absolute authority of Germany, if Germany had come victorious out of the war.

We come finally to Russia. We stated previously that Russia made her presence felt, starting with Peter the Great (1682-1725). It is recognized that Peter the Great fixed three goals for Russia: to expand to the Baltic shores and to the Black Sea, and to take Poland. When Peter died, only one of these goals had been attained: the Baltic shores had been taken from Sweden through the Nishtad treaty. Although Russia took possession of the Azak castle in 1699, she had to return it to the Ottomans in 1714. The culmination of this policy established by Peter, fell to the lot of Catherine the Great (1762-96). Under her rule, Poland was divided between Austria and Prussia, and was wiped out from the European map; after the Kuchuk Kaynarca Treaty of 1774, the Ottoman-Russian border was pushed up to the Dniester river, the khanate of Crimea came under Russian jurisdiction to be annexed shortly after, and Russia settled on the northern shores of the Black Sea, ready to descend towards the south, from Caucasia on one side, from the Balkans on the other.

The goal of Russia to descend to the warm seas is a subject recognized by all, but it is less well known that two directions were chosen to achieve this goal. The first was to reach the Mediterranean through the Straits, the other was to reach India by taking advantage of water routes. Projects and plans of this second direction were accepted during the reign of Tsarina Anna (1730-40) in 1734, and Krillov was entrusted with the realization of the plan. After this plan was put into effect, Russia decided to advance in the two directions, and chose as a principle to focus on one direction temporarily, if there proved to be difficulties in the other direction. This plan, which was made in 1734, projected taking the regions of Bukhara, Samarkand and Badakhshan. Badakhshan is an area within the borders of Afghanistan and Russia had to wait until the 1980s to obtain this region.

It is possible to summarize the policy of Russia, since the reign of Peter the Great, concerning the Ottoman Empire: to expand Russia, at the expense of the Ottoman Empire, to restore Byzantium by taking Istanbul, and to make the Tsar the undisputed leader of the Orthodox world. After Peter the Great, the Tsars never forgot this policy; the more successful included Catherine II (1762-96), Nicholas I (1825-55) and Alexander II (1855-81).

Russia, until the reign of Catherine the Great, was far from having the power to struggle alone with the Ottoman Empire. However, the Kuchuk Kaynarca Treaty of 1774 demonstrated that Russia was now able to cause the collapse of the Ottoman Empire without the help of another country. But, from this date on, the other European countries made it apparent that they would not allow the Ottoman Empire to be absorbed by Russia, thus enabling

Russia to become an uncontrollable power. It is for this reason that Russia began to make preliminary projects for distribution with the other powers, as she was getting ready for another attack. The offer made Austria in the 1787 war, and to Britain in the 1853 war, are examples of this.

The main opportunity Russia had to attack the Ottoman Empire was to provoke and support the various Orthodox communities within the Empire to rebel, and then to declare war on the pretext of protecting them. The Serbian rebellion of 1806 was the source of the Russian war which started that year. The Greek rebellion gave rise to the 1828 war. The 'Holy Places' issue started the 1853 Crimean War. The 1877 war started with Herzegovina revolt.

From 1774 on, Russia considered herself as the sole representative of the Orthodox and Slav subjects of the Ottoman Empire, and in the case of an insurrection or rebellion, considered immediate intervention as natural. However, Austria, who had lost some areas to Italy as the unification of Italy was being realized, wanted, from 1870 on, to invade Bosnia-Herzegovina and became interested in Slavs because of the existence of a substantial Slav element within her Empire. Russia, keeping this in mind, succeeded, as the three emperors (Alexander II, Kaiser Wilhelm and Franz-Josef) met in 1875, in having the non-intervention principle accepted in the event of a possible rebellion of Christian elements of the Ottoman Empire. The aim of `non-intervention' is to avoid helping the Ottoman Empire to crush the rebellion. However, when the rebellion which started in Herzegovina in 1875 and spread to Bulgaria and Serbia in 1876 was crushed by Ottomans, Russia intervened on the side of the rebels, and the 1877 war started.

Russia obtained from the Ottoman Empire, through the Berlin Treaty the maximum of what the other powers would accept. Rumania, Bulgaria, and Serbia obtained autonomy and later independence. It was obvious that after this Russia would have no opportunity to obtain more land.

We have thus summarized the policies followed by the Powers concerning the Ottoman Empire. It is now necessary to examine the place of the Armenians within this framework.

In the 1870's the Armenians were not yet included in the policies of either Russia or the other powers. Even the Armenian authors of that time do not mention the existence of any dispute between the Armenian community and the Ottoman government.

The interest of Russia, which was closely following the rebellion of the non-Muslim subjects in the Ottoman Empire, and of Austria, which adopted the same policy after 1870, lay mainly in the Slavic elements. No one was interested in the Armenians, who were living in their country without any complaint. These years coincide in Russia with the period when Pan-Slavism was at its strongest, when liberation movements were brutally crushed, and when the rights of the Armenians in Russian Armenia were taken away from them. The clearest proof of this is that when the Patriarch asked to be allowed to take part in the Conference of Ambassadors gathered in Tophane to discuss the subject of the 1876 Balkan rebellions, he was told that the meeting had nothing to do with the Armenians. We shall return to this subject later.

Until this date, the interest of Russia in the Armenians had been limited to taking advantage of them on the eastern front during the wars with the Ottomans. This cooperation started during the Iran war which ended with the Turkmenchai truce, and continued in the 1828 Ottoman war, and to some extent in the 1853-6 war.

From the 1870's on, the Armenians began to seek the aid of the European powers, for the reasons we have stated above. These attempts were made by the Patriarchate (and Etchmiadzin) and the clergy.

It must be accepted that they were successful, and the 'Armenian question' appeared at the Berlin Congress, However, the factor which played a role in the emergence of this question, rather than the Armenians' attempts, was the fact that the political conjuncture necessitated taking advantage of them.

As a matter of fact, after the Berlin Congress, almost the entire Balkans (except for Rumelia, which would be lost in the Balkan war), were separated from the Ottoman Empire, and these regions could no longer be used as an excuse to declare war on the Ottoman Empire. Besides, Russia realized that the Balkans would not constitute a passage for her advance to the Mediterranean, and later saw that these countries, whom she actively helped to gain their independence, did not remain grateful to her.

Then she recognized that in the East only the Erzurum-Iskenderun axis remained to permit her descent to the south, and thought of taking advantage of the Armenians to obtain this axis. For this reason, she was to turn to the Armenian question especially after the Berlin Congress.

With this intention, Russia, just as she did in the Balkans, attempted to create incidents in Armenia, so that she could then interfere. She not only took advantage of the Armenian Church, but supported the revolutionary committees which were formed.

The Liberal Party and its leader Gladstone, who came to power in Britain after the Berlin Congress, were the main supporters of Russia in this matter, and appeared as the sole custodian of the Armenian question and almost as the tool of Russia's foreign policy.

However, as Russia realized that Britain had the aim of actually granting independence to Armenia, and she engaged once again in a power struggle with Britain in Asia, she ceased being interested in the Armenians, even started to oppose their ideas of independence, and followed the same policy with the Ottomans.

As was the case with Greek independence, the British were hoping that if an independent Armenia was established, they would have first of all a country grateful to them, and thus create a buffer state which would prevent the descent of Russia to the south. While Russia abandoned its support of the revolutionary committees, this time, France and Britain continued this support.

Russia, after being defeated by Japan in 1905, and having made an agreement with Britain concerning Asia, completely put aside the question of Armenian independence, and started its policy of dividing the Ottoman Empire into spheres of influence, which would later result in the dismemberment of the Empire. During the First World War which started in this climate, she went to the distribution agreement with the Sykes-Picot treaty.

Within these political developments, the Armenians would be nothing more than a tool, a means, and independence and autonomy would remain only as their wishes and dreams. The only ones who did not see this truth were the Armenians and especially the Armenian Church.

3. From the reform edict to the Berlin Congress

Now we can examine events in the Ottoman Empire until 1878. The struggle, from the 1856 Reform Edict on, among the Armenians and with which the Patriarchate too was involved, continued after the Armenian nation's regulation was accepted in 1863. However, this internal strife was confined to Istanbul, and there was no apparent discontent in Anatolia. Moreover, there were no known complaints to foreign countries in these matters.

Actually there was a revolt in Zeitun in 1862. But this, as we shall explain later, had entirely different causes, involving non-Armenian elements and being due to the feudal system which prevailed in various regions in the east of the country.

This situation started to change after Migirdich Hrimyan was elected Patriarch in 1869.

Pasdermadjian states that 'On the eve of the 1877-78 Russian-Ottoman War, the situation of Armenians in Turkish Armenia was as difficult and even worse than that of Serbians in Bosnia, or that of Bulgarians in Roumelia and Macedonia.' Later he writes: 'Until 1876, the Turkish policy, although it favored the Kurds in Armenia, did not have a real anti-Armenian character. The often tragic situation of Armenians came from their position as subject people, and the general conditions of the Empire, rather than from a concerted action of the government. In fact, the interventions of Constantinople in Armenian matters during the last decades were chiefly characterized by the concern to protect the independence of the Armenian Church over against the attempts of assimilation coming from the Catholic or the Orthodox side.'[20]

Pasdermadjian, just as he does not deem it necessary to state the extent of the influence of the Ottoman Empire in the 1870's in Bosnia-Herzegovina and even in Bulgaria, does not mention whether the condition of the Muslims, either in Europe or in Anatolia, was better than the condition of the Armenians.

During this period, the fall of the Empire was almost declared by the government with the Reform Edict, and the necessity of implementing definite measures as soon as possible was created. The sufferings were the same for every subject, and were even worse for the Muslims who could not benefit from the protection of a foreign country, and who did not have anyone to whom they could voice their complaints. It was a fact that banditry was prevalent in the east. But were the victims of the brigands only non--Muslim and especially Armenians? It must be remembered that Armenians and Greeks, too, had their own bands of brigands, and these would only attack Muslims. Consequently, Muslims were being attacked from two sides, by Muslim and non-Muslim brigands. Moreover, one must not forget that the Armenians, who were complaining so much of these conditions, were the richest sector of the population, having the largest opportunities.

According to the well-known book of Marcel Léart [21] if the numbers are correct, 141 of 166 exporters in Anatolia were Armenian, 12 were of other origin, and only 13 were Turks; 6,800 of 9,800 shop-owners and craftsmen were Armenians, 2,550 were Turks; out of 150 exporters, 127 were Armenians and 23 were Turks; of 153 industrialists, 130 were Armenians and 20 were Turks; of 37 bankers, 32 were Armenians. In the region which they call Turkish Armenia, they had in total 803 schools, 2,088 teachers, and 81,226 students.

The Armenian Church began to portray the Armenians, after Hrimyan became Patriarch, as a society moaning under continuous cruelty and torture, when the Armenians should be having at most as much right to complain as the Muslim majority, about the general administration of the country and the lack of order.

At this point it may be useful to examine Hrimyan's personality.

After the Gulhane reforms of 1839, and especially the Reform Edict, the main concern of the Patriarchate was the decline in its rights and privileges. Patriarch Matheos Chuhajiyan had resigned in 1848 for this reason. In 1858 he was elected the Etchmiadzin Catholicos. In the same year, Gevorg Kerestejiyan was brought to the Istanbul Patriarchate. Kerestejiyan resigned in 1860 because of the disagreements which appeared when the Armenian nation's regulation was being prepared. Armenian newspapers of the period reported that his resignation was due to his opposition to the regulation. [22] In 1866, Kerestejiyan succeeded Chuhajiyan and became Catholicos of Etchmiadzin.

In 1869, Hrimyan became the Istanbul Patriarch. In 1885, he was to become the Catholicos of Etchmiadzin. As Hrimyan resigned, and left the Patriarchate, Nerses Varjabetyan replaced him. To a large extent, this Patriarch was under the influence of Hrimyan; it is even claimed that some of his actions were due to Hrimyan's pressure. Nerses Varjabetyan was candidate in the election of the Catholicos in Etchmiadzin in 1884, but the Tsar did not approve his election and consequently he did not become Catholicos.

In contrast, the candidacies of Chuhajiyan, Kerestejiyan, and Hrimyan were approved by the Tsar, who also approved the candidacy of Matheos Izmirliyan to the Catholicate. Izmirliyan had been the Istanbul Patriarch between 1894 and 1896, and was brought once again to the Patriarchate in 1908. Consequently, he left the Patriarchate in the same year and went to Etchmiadzin where he became the Catholicos after Hrimyan.

It is obvious that the Tsar acted only in the direction which was most beneficial to Russian interests in his approval of the Catholicos. It therefore necessary to assume that those who could transfer to Etchmiadzin from Istanbul were serving the interests of the Tsar and Russian nation interests.

Although the interests of the Armenian Church did not always coincide with those of Russia, at times they did coincide.

While Russia maintained the influence of Etchmiadzin within Russia at minimum, she saw the continuation of this influence outside Russia as advantageous. At this point there was understanding with the Church. The Istanbul Patriarchate, especially, was far from satisfied at the decline of its authority.

The Armenian Church was aware that Russia did not want an independent Armenia. The Russians were also aware that the Armenian Church knew this, and that they wanted autonomy within the Ottoman Empire. Russia had realized that the other powers would not allow the invasion of the area called Armenia, and for this reason saw advantage in giving autonomy to this region, which inevitably would come under her jurisdiction.

The Armenian Church and Russia were concious that if conditions were to improve in the Empire after the attempted reforms, the complaints which the Armenians made in the 1870s about administrative malfunctions could not be made any longer. After the declaration of the Constitutional Government, when the Armenians were included in the Constitutional Assembly, there would be even less excuse for complaint. Under these circumstances there was a sense of urgency; something had to be done as soon as possible. (The abolition of the Constitutional Government was a source of joy for the Armenian Church.)

The authority of the Patriarchate had to be strengthened, the interest of the great powers had to be secured in order to gain independence, and their intervention had to be obtained. And this necessitated above all a continuous voicing of complaints. In all these matters, the interest of the Armenian Church coincided with that of Russia. Hrimyan was the individual who made the most significant contribution.

Hrimyan was born in 1820 in Van, and visited Etchmiadzin and Ararat in 1841 . Later he came to Istanbul and became a teacher. The years in which he started teaching coincided with the period when Chuhajiyan was the Patriarch. In 1854 Hrimyan joined the Church. During the time he was in Istanbul, he undoubtedly observed the problems of the Patriarchate. After he joined the Church he was appointed to Van. Later, he was sent to Mush. It is useful to remember that during this time, first Chuhajiyan, then Kerestejiyan was Catholicos in Etchmiadzin, and both of them resigned because the authority of the Patriarchate was declining. Hrimyan started printing two newspapers in Van and Mush, entitled *The Eagle of Van* and *The Eagle of Mush*, and began to focus on the theme of the Armenians' plight in eastern Anatolia. In 1869 he was elected Patriarch when he was only forty-nine years old, and had joined the Church only fifteen years earlier. It is not difficult to accept that he was elected because he knew of the problems of the Church, and tried to solve them. The Catholicos Kerestejiyan might also have used his influence in this election.

As soon as he became Patriarch, Hrimyan brought the condition of the eastern provinces to the agenda of the National Patriarchate Assembly. He demanded in circulars he sent to all the bishops that they inform him of matters which could constitute a complaint. A memorandum based on these reports was submitted to the Grand Vizier in February 1872. The government formed a Commission, which had an equal number of Muslim and Christian members, to investigate these complaints.

Hrimyan had also brought the subject of changing the Armenian National Regulation to the National Assembly; his aim was to expand the jurisdiction of the Patriarchy, to reduce the number of representatives in the National Assembly from 140 to 50 and to have the members who were not of the clergy elected in equal numbers from Istanbul and the provinces.[23] But all his efforts met the opposition of the political assembly. The representatives from Istanbul and the provinces in the National Assembly began to quarrel. Hrimyan resigned in 1873, as he realized that the Assemblies did not follow him, and that he could not impose on them what he wanted. He was replaced Nerses Varjabedyan.

Although the new Patriarch was not of the same opinion as Hrimyan, Hrimyan and his supporters continued their activities.

When the 1875 rebellion in Herzegovina spread, and the great powers intervened, demanding the implementation of reforms in this area, the Armenian Church became convinced that, by taking advantage of the situation, it could obtain autonomy for the eastern provinces. A group headed by Hrimyan, and including Izmirliyan who later was to become Patriarch, increased their pressure on Nerses. Finally, Nerses felt the obligation to act with them.

When it became known that a conference was to be held in Istanbul to discuss the events in Herzegovina and Bulgaria, a memorandum prepared by Izmirliyan, requesting that the problems of Armenians, too, be included in this conference, was sent to all the great powers in September 1876 Etchmiadzin supported these complaints by doing its share at the level of the Tsar. Actually the complaints were about isolated incidents, and the requests consisted of matters which the Babiali was already attempting to put into effect, such as the implementation of the decisions taken by the Babiali and the specially formed commission concerning the land administration, exempting the properties of the Church from taxation, the establishment of a commission in the Babiali in which representatives of the Patriarchate would take part, and which would prosecute cases of injustice and investigate matters communicated by the Patriarchate.

The Patriarch Nerses was also contacting the Embassies in Istanbul and trying to attract their attention to the Armenian question. A meeting he had with the British Ambassador is of great significance. Henry Elliot, the British Ambassador, wrote as follows in the report he sent on 7 December 1876 to the Foreign Office:

Yesterday the Armenian Patriarch paid me a visit. He expressed the hope, in the name of the large Christian community of which he is the leader, that the Conference would put pressure on the Babiali, that the privileges that are to be granted to the provinces which have revolted against the Empire also be granted to the provinces which remained calm, but which deserve equal treatment.

I replied with caution. I told him that the object of the Conference was to ensure order in provinces which have rebelled, and which endanger the overall peace, and that I did not think that it would handle the topic of the overall administration of the Ottoman Empire.

The Patriarch replied that his nation was very upset, and that if a rebellion was necessary to attract the interest of the European powers, then there was no difficulty in starting such an action.[24]

The Tophane Conference met in such an atmosphere, on 23 December 1876, to discuss the Herzegovina and Bulgaria events. On the same day the First Constitutional Government was proclaimed in the Ottoman Empire.

Despite all these efforts the Tophane Conference did not deal with the Armenian question.

The proclamation of the constitutional government was very well received inside as well as outside the country. All the non-Muslims expressed their joy in an honest fashion. But, after a while, the Armenian Church came to the conclusion that the constitutional government would work to its disadvantage, that if the situation and the administration of the country were to improve, then it would have to abandon its hope for autonomy, it set its hopes on a Russo-Ottoman War.

Russia declared war on the Ottoman Empire on 24 April 1877, as no decision was taken either during the Tophane Conference or in the diplomatic contacts initiated after the Conference was over.

An interesting point which showed the attitude of the Armenian community and Church was that, as the proclamation of war was being read in the Constitutional Assembly, the Armenian delegates applauded it enthusiastically.[25]

Moreover, when the Sultan asked that the non-Muslim subjects, too, do their patriotic duty, on 7 December 1877, the Armenian National Assembly took the decision, as requested by the Patriarch, that the Armenian nation be enlisted and participate in the war.[26] However, after Plevne fell on 10 December, the National Assembly met again on 18 December, and, in spite of the Patriarch, annulled the previous decision.[27]

It thus becomes apparent that the Russian Tsar had a good reason for not approving of Nerses, and refusing his candidacy to the Catholicate.

Another point that becomes apparent is that the Armenians were not willing to become subject to Russian rule, and that they were willing to fight along with the Ottomans to prevent this. But, as Plevne fell, and it became clear that the Ottoman Empire was going to lose the war, and that some of the eastern provinces would then be relinquished to Russia, the Patriarch got closer to Russia, with the thought that the only way of gaining anything would be through Russia.

Thus, as the 1877-8 war was ending, the Armenian question was becoming a European question.

4. The 1877-78 Russian war and the Berlin Congress

This war that began on 24 April was the shortest war between Ottomans and Russians, and the one with the hardest consequences. It is for this reason that it was recorded in Ottoman history as the 93 disaster, using the Muslim calendar.

With the declaration of war, Russian armies attacked under the command of Loris Melikof, of Armenian origin, on the eastern front. Before the commander of the eastern front, Ghazi Ahmet Mukhtar Pasha, had made the necessary military arrangements, Bayazit, which was defenceless, was invaded by the Russians on 30 April and Ardakhan fell on 17 May.

The Russian forces engaged in the first battle with the forces of Ahmet Mukhtar Pasha on 21 June, and retreated. The battle in Zivin, too, was won by Ahmet Mukhtar Pasha. After a short waiting period, on 24 August Ahmet Mukhtar Pasha attacked the Russian forces, who were attempting to block the road between Kars and Erzurum, won the battle of Gedikler, and forced the Russians to retreat. The battle of Yahniler, which started with a counter-attack by the Russians on 2 October, ended with the victory of the Turks after three days. However, Russian forces who attacked again on 15 November from Alajadagh could not be stopped this time. Ahmet Mukhtar Pasha was forced to retreat to Erzurum, and Kars fell on 18th November.

The Russians advanced up to Erzurum, but Erzurum resisted until the end of the war, and the Russian soldiers entered the city only eight days after the truce. Likewise, Batum was opened to the Russians only after the truce, according to the stipulation of the truce.

On the western front, the war ended on 31 January 1878 with the truce made in Edirne, as the Ottomans requested peace after Plevne fell and the road to Istanbul was opened to the Russians. The terms of peace were established in Ayastefanos (Yeshilkeuy). There was no clause in the truce concerning Armenians.

Whatever happened, happened between 31 January, when the Edirne Truce was signed, and 3 March, when the Ayastefanos (San Stefano) Treaty was signed.

It is known that Armenians engaged in extensive activities after the 18 December meeting where they annulled the decision to take part in the war. We can summarize the activities they engaged in as follows.[28]

It is understood that the Istanbul Patriarchate sent a letter of complaint to the Foreign Minister of each of the great powers before the end of the war, and that the Russian Armenians asked the Russian government to help the Armenians in Turkey.

When the war ended with the Edirne Truce, it was decided in a secret meeting held by the Armenian National Assembly that a memorandum should be sent to the Etchmiadzin Catholicate, to be submitted to the Tsar. According to Esat Uras, who cites an Armenian author named Saruhan, a request based on three possibilities was made to the Tsar: (1) that the regions up to the Euphrates he united with Ararat, and that they be part of Russia; (2) if no land annexation is to take place, then the privileges to be given to the Bulgarian nation he given also to the Armenian nation; (3) that the occupied lands he not vacated until the reform to be made is completed. (We have not found such information in the sources we have obtained. Because the annexation of the eastern provinces to Russia was not in the interest of the Armenians, we can assume that it was aimed at strengthening the second and third requests which were essential.)

It was also decided in the Armenian Assembly that a delegation should be sent to the Edirne Pact talks, and that a petition should be given to the Tsar and the Russian Prime Minister. It was requested in this petition, dated 1/13 February 1878, which is said to be included in Leo's book entitled *Documents of the Armenian question* (Tiflis, 1916), that the rights granted to the Christians in Roumelia be also given to them. It is apparent that the Catholicos did not approve of the subject of annexing the eastern provinces to Russia, and even of the request made to the Russians; this is reasonable because of the general conduct of the Armenian Church.

Despite all these efforts, an article about the Armenians could not be obtained in the Edirne Truce agreement.

When the peace talks started in Ayastefanos, thc Patriarch, again not to be left out, went to the Russian headquarters and personally requested from Archduke Nicholas that a paragraph concerning Armenians be included in the pact. (Although it is recorded in all Armenian sources that it was requested that the headquarters of Archduke Nicholas intervene, it is not mentioned that the Patriarch himself went to the headquarters to make the request.)

This time the Armenian Church was successful in its efforts, since the 16th paragraph provided that improvements and reforms required by local need should be implemented in areas inhabited by the Armenians, that their security should be guaranteed, and that the evacuation by the Russian army of the territories which it occupied in Armenia, and which were to be returned to Turkey, should not begin until these measures had been put into effect.[29]

The Armenians did not obtain autonomy through this article. If the article that stipulated that the evacuation of the provinces was dependent upon reforms had not been changed in the Berlin Congress, then maybe it would not have been possible to take back, besides Batum, Kars, and Ardakhan the areas up to Erzurum which were under Russian occupation, and then the Armenians living in those provinces might have fallen under Russian rule. Whether they would have been pleased with such a situation is another matter.

Even Russia did not think that the Ayastefanos Treaty would remain as it was signed. Actually, the signed document was called 'Mukaddemat-i Sulhiyye', a preliminary peace agreement.

As soon as the terms of this agreement were made public, Austria and Britain objected to it, with France naturally joining them. Finally, it was decided on bismarck's initiative that a new congress should meet in Berlin. The Congress met on 13 June, and the Berlin Treaty was signed on 13 July.

The Armenians did not remain idle between 3 March, when the Ayastefanos Treaty was signed, and 13 June, when the Berlin Congress met.

On 17 March, the Patriarch paid a visit to the British Consul in Istanbul. We summarize below the telegram sent by the British Consul Layard, which reports the statements made by the Patriarch during this visit, and his request that the Ottoman authorities should not hear of it. [30]

The Patriarch stated that last year they had had nothing to complain of in the Turkish administration, that they had preferred to remain under Ottoman rule instead of becoming part of Russia, and that they had even decided to go to war. However, after the Russian victory became certain, and moreover, it became known that some of the eastern provinces would be given to Russia, the situation changed. He stated that now the Armenians were very angry towards him, because he had previously adopted an anti-Russian stand, and that they might even stone him. (This report of Layard is sufficient to destroy all the Armenian claims, and the statements of the Patriarch must constitute a sufficient confession.)

The Patriarch, continuing his remarks, stated that the Armenians were determined to pursue their rights, that they demanded the same laws as the other Christian communities, that if they could not obtain these demands through the intervention of Europe, then they would turn to Russia, and that they would continue their agitation until their annexation by Russia, and he requested patronage for the establishment of an autonomous Armenia.

During this meeting, Layard asked the Patriarch what he meant by 'Armenia'. According to the Patriarch, 'Armenia' would include the pashaliks of Van and Sivas, most of Diyarbekir, and the old kingdom of Cilicia. As Layard stated that the overwhelming majority of the population of the region was Muslim, the Patriarch agreed, but stated that the Muslims, too, were not pleased with the present administration, and for this reason they would prefer a Christian government. As Layard expressed his doubt about the feasibility of such a project, the Patriarch asserted that if the rightful demands of Armenians went unheeded, then the whole area in question would rebel against the Turkish administration, and would be annexed by Russia.

This very important document clearly reveals Armenian intentions. Obviously, in view of these declarations made by Patriarch Nerses, it is unnecessary to look for other explanations for the Armenian rebellions that started later.

In his report, which we have summarized, Layard also mentioned the existence of serious intrigues which drove the Armenians to adopt such a stance, that an autonomous Armenia would sooner or later fall into the hands of Russia, and that if Russia were to have borders with Syria, this would not be in England's interest.

In his second report, [31] Layard stated that an Armenian who had held an important position in the Babiali had told him confidentially that the prominent leaders of the Armenian community were preparing a constitution for an autonomous Armenian province which they would present at Berlin, and that if their demands were not accepted, then they were determined to continue their agitation until they were accepted.

As a matter of fact, the Armenians did bring such a document to the Congress. Consequently, there is no reason to doubt that the second part of the warning, that is the rebellions, which cost many lives, were already being planned at that time.

The Patriarchate did not undertake these initiatives only in Istanbul. It also made efforts at the level of the great powers which were to participate in the Berlin Congress. The former Patriarch Hrimyan and Archbishop Horen Narbey were sent with the same intention to Paris and London, and Horen Narbey went to Russia and was received by the Tsar.

The former representative of the khedivate of Egypt, Noubar Pasha (the father of Noubar Pasha who presided over the Armenian delegations during the Sèvres and Lausanne talks), was also a member of this delegation at least during the meetings in France, for he paid a visit to the British Consul in Paris, Lord Lyons, with the delegation. [32]

When the Berlin Congress met, the Patriarch, too, wanted to go to Berlin When he was not allowed to go, Hrimyan and Narbey, who were still in Europe, went to Berlin on 13 June. This delegation submitted to the Congress the proposals which they had prepared for the establishment in Turkey of an Armenia. The text of these proposals has been included in various sources. [33] We present here the text as translated into Turkish by Esat Uras:

The organization proposals for the Armenia of Turkey submitted to the Berlin Congress by the delegation of Armenian representatives.

I

According to the enclosed map, Ottoman Armenia includes the provinces of Erzerum and Van, the northern part of Diyarbekir, that is the northern part of the *sanjak* of Harput, and in the west by taking the

Euphrates as the border, the *sanjak* of Ergani, the northern parts of Siirt - which form the Turkish part of Great Armenia - and the harbour of Rize which lies between Trabzon and Batum, and which is necessary for commerce and export.

Armenia shall be administered by an Armenian Vali [governor of a province] appointed by the Babiali, on condition that this appointment be approved by the guarantor countries, and the Vali shall reside in Erzurum.

The governor shall possess all the authority of the executive powers, shall be responsible for keeping order within the entire province, shall ensure the collection of taxes, and shall appoint the administration officers under his responsibility. He shall select and appoint the judges, shall convene the general assembly and preside over it, and shall look after the administrative branches of the province.

The governor-general, who shall be appointed for a period of five years, may be removed from his position during these five years only by agreement with the guarantor countries.

The province shall have a central administrative assembly which shall he presided over by the governor-general. Its members shall include: 1) Director of Finances, 2) Director of Public Works, 3) a judicial consultant, 4) Commander of Public Security, 5) Inspector of Christian schools, 6) Muslim Inspector. This latter shall be appointed by the governor-general with the approval of the Cadi.

The province shall be divided into *sanjaks*, which shall be further divided into *kazas*. The governors of the *sanjaks* and the *kaymakams* [the head officials of the *kazas*] shall be appointed by the governor-general. They shall represent the governor-general in the administrative divisions of the province. Advisors who shall be appointed by the governor-general shall help them in administrative matters.

II

Because the maintenance of order and public security shall be the responsibility of the province, only 20 per cent of the general revenues of the province shall be given every year to the State Treasury.

After the necessary allowance has been reserved from the remaining income of the province, for the civil service, the judicial organization, the gendarmerie, and the militia, the remaining sum shall be allocated in the following way: 80 per cent for the building and maintenance of roads and public utility works; 20 per cent for the construction, repair, and maintenance of schools; after the allowance has been reserved for institutions of higher education, the remaining portion shall be distributed to Christian and Muslim schools, in proportion to the number of members of every sect in every city.

III

A religious court leader shall he appointed by the Sultan, to inspect all the religious courts within the province. Canonical law courts shall only deal with cases among Muslims.

All legal, commerce, and murder cases shall be dealt with in regular courts, whether they have occurred among Christians, or between Muslims and Christians. These courts shall be formed of three judges one of which shall be president.

The governor-general shall appoint the judges and the president of these courts. Petty offences shall be handled by the head officials of the counties and the advisors. The organization of regular and religious courts, their jurisprudence and authority, shall he established by special statutes and regulations. Legal codes and criminal law shall be established according to the most recent legal principles in Europe.

IV

Absolute freedom shall be granted for religions and sects.

The administration of religious institutions and the employment of priests shall be the responsibility of every subdistrict.

V

The provincial public security force shall be formed by: 1) the gendarmerie, 2) the volunteer body. The volunteer soldiers shall be Armenians and individuals who have lived in the province for at least five years. Kurds, Circasians, and other nomadic tribes shall be excluded from this organization.

The gendarmerie shall be responsible for keeping order and maintaining it within the entire province.

The gendarmerie shall be headed by a commander appointed by the governor-general with the approval of the commander of the provincial military forces and the gendarmerie shall immediately be brought under his orders.

The volunteer soldiers shall be under the command of the commander of the provincial military forces and shall have the duty of helping the gendarmerie. The police force shall be composed of four thousand armed soldiers, and the Ottoman government shall not have the authority to send them, as in the case of other soldiers, to fortified areas of the province.

VI

The general assembly shall be formed in the following way:

Each county shall have two representatives, from each community, chosen by the Christian and Muslim inhabitants. These representatives shall meet in the centre of the *sanjak* and shall elect two representatives from each community, one representing the Muslim, and the other representing the Armenian community. They shall elect and be elected in an equal manner:

1. Those who are at least 25 years old, and have an income, or those inhabitants of the province who pay any amount of direct taxes.

2. Spiritual leaders and priests belonging to various creeds.

3. Teachers and lecturers.

Each leader of congregations belonging to recognized religions (one from each sect) shall be members of the assembly.

The assembly shall meet once a year in the provincial capital and shall examine the budget of the province, and establish the setting and distribution of taxes. The governor-general shall submit each year a report about the fiscal matters of the province to the assembly. The procedure for the setting and distribution of taxes shall be altered with the aim of increasing the wealth of the inhabitants of the province.

Every five years, the governor-general and the assembly shall fix together the amount of money to be given to the Babiali, in accordance with the above articles.

VII

Within three months of signing the Protocol, an international commission shall be formed by the guarantor countries to supervise the paragraphs of this regulation which will be put into effect.

[A schedule was added, showing the population:]

The provinces of Erzurum and Van are excluded from the areas which were decided to be given to Russia in the Ayastefanos Pact. The densely populated centres of these provinces are: Baybourt, Erzinjan, Malazgirt, Mush, Bitlis, and Van. The population has been reported as 2,066,000. When we subtract from this figure the population of areas which have been relinquished to Russia, which is 366,000, we obtain the figure of 1,700,000.

The distribution of this population in various communities is:

Armenian	1,150,000
Turk	400,000
Nomadic Kurd	80,000
Zazas or Dimbiliks having their own dialects	35,000
The Yazidis who workship the sun, who have their own dialects, and who are for the most part nomads	13,000
Nomadic Gypsies	3,000
Greeks and Jews	5,000
Assyrians	14,000
	1,7000,000

There are 109 churches in these two provinces.

The densely populated centres of the northern part of Diyarbekir, that is the eastern part of the *sanjak* of Harput (the beginning of the border is the west bank of the Euphrates), the *sanjak* of Ergani, and the northern part of the sanjak of Siirt, are: Harput, Eghin, Chimishkezek, Palu, and Siirt. The population of this region is:

According to the official yearbook	664,300
Less the number to remain in the province	302,000
	362,300

Its distribution according to the various communities:

Armenian	180,000
Turk	130,000
Nomadic Kurds	40,000
Zazas	2,300
Yazidis	2,000
Assyrians, Chaldonians	8,000
	362,300

There are 48 churches in this province.

General List

Provinces	Armenian	Turk	Kurd	Greek	Assyrian	Zaza	Yazidi
Erzurum, Van	1,150,000	400,000	80,000	5,000	14,00	35,000	13,000
The northern part of Diyarbekir							
	180,000	130,000	40,000		8,000	2,000	2,000
	1,130,000	530,000	120,000	5,000	22,000	37,000	15,000

There was 3,000 Gypsies in Erzurum and Van.

	Total
Armenian	1,330,000
Turk	530,000
Kurd	120,000
Other	82,000
	2,062,000

The Patriarch visited the British Consul in Istanbul again on 30 July. After having stated that they had submitted their proposals to the Congress, he asked for British support.[34]

The fact that the request of the Armenians was not handled at the Berlin Congress in the way and to the extent that they had wished was due to the attitude of the British. On 4 June 1878, an agreement of two paragraphs had been made between the British Consul Mr. Layard and the Ottoman Foreign Minister Saffet Pasha. According to the first article of this agreement, in the event of a Russian attempt to invade some areas of Anatolia other than the sanjaks of Batum, Kars, and Ardakhan, Britain would provide the Turks with military aid, and the Turks would engage in reforms in the eastern provinces. Meanwhile, Cyprus was left to be occupied by the British, to facilitate the military aid which Britain would be providing. According to the second article, the ratifications of the agreement would be exchanged in a month.

Through this agreement, Britain took on the responsibility of guarantee-ing the implementation of reforms that would benefit the Armenians. Because of this agreement, Russia followed a policy of not advocating reforms, and even of hindering them, with the aim that the Armenians would be disappointed in the British, and would then turn towards Russia.

The request of the Armenians was examined at the Berlin Congress for the first time on 4 July 1878. (The Conference lasted for thirty-one days, and during this time twenty sessions were held.) However, the discussion did not start with the Armenian request, but with a proposal by the British delegate Lord Salisbury asking that the 16th article of Ayastefanos be modified, and that the stipulation that the evacuation be dependent upon the reforms be annulled.

More discussions took place on 6 July, and on 8 July a new text replacing the 16th article of Ayastefanos was accepted.

This new text, which was the 61st article of the Berlin Congress, stated: 'The Babiali engages itself to put into effect, without delay, the reforms and reorganization needed by the Armenians, due to the local conditions of the provinces which they inhabit, and to protect their security and peace against the Kurds and the Circassians. It shall report the preventive measures it will be taking on this subject to the powers, as the need arises, and the powers shall supervise the application of these measures.'

According to the Berlin Treaty, Russia would keep, in the east, the *sanjaks* of Batum, Kars, and Ardakhan, but would return the *sanjak* of Bayazit; moreover, it was decreed that the fortifications of Batum, which was to become a free harbour, would be demolished. In addition the area of Kotur was relinquished to Iran.

The 62nd paragraph of the Berlin Treaty is worth remembering. This paragraph decreed that freedom to worship and to belong to a sect would continue absolutely, that changing one's religion or sect would not entail a change in other rights, that anyone, regardless of his religion or sect, could be a witness in court, and that the Consuls in the Ottoman Empire would have the right to officially protect religious institutions and charities.

It is clear that the Armenians would also take advantage of this decree.

The Patriarch paid another visit to the British Consul on 10 July. We do not think he was aware of the situation in Berlin, considering the limited means of communication of that time. During his visit, the Patriarch stated that the Armenians had been unable to persuade the Congress to accept their proposals, and requested that, at least, an article should be included in the agreement, that they would benefit from the protection of foreign powers when the need arose.[35]

In spite of all their efforts, the Armenians left the Berlin Congress without having obtained the autonomy of Armenia. According to a rumour, as the delegation left Berlin it made a protest, and stated that its request had gone unheeded because the Armenians were a peaceful nation, that this was a good lesson for them, and that they would return having learned their lesson.

Armenian autonomy was not obtained at Berlin. However, the Armenian question was established in international politics as the last question concerning non-Muslims in the Ottoman Empire and while the Congress was still continuing, a Russian wing was formed among the Istanbul Armenians.

Now it is time to study the Armenian question which became a European question. However, before studying the further developments, it is necessary to deal with the subject of the Armenian population in the Ottoman Empire.

5. The population question

The Armenian population is not really part of our subject during the periods that we are studying, the Armenian population in the entire world was only 3 million. Naturally, the numbers living in the Ottoman Empire were fewer-especially if, as Armenian sources indicate, there was a massive and continuous emigration of Armenians from the eastern region to Russia after the 1829 Edirne Truce.

However, the Armenians who came to the Berlin Congress with the hope of establishing an autonomous Armenia in the eastern provinces felt the necessity to prove that the Armenian population of the region was more than the Muslim population so that their request could be considered justifiable. Thus they gave figures, knowing no limit to exaggeration just as they have done in every matter. Their version of the Armenian population which did not coincide with the records of the Ottoman Empire, or those of other states, was not taken seriously at the Berlin Congress or later powers were in a position to be informed of the actual Armenian population through their own means.

It is obvious that the figures sent by the Patriarchate to Berlin were not taken seriously even by the Armenians themselves.

However, later, when it was a question of engaging in propaganda against the Ottoman Empire, the great powers, and especially Britain, saw no inconvenience in accepting these figures which they knew to be erroneous and stating that the difference from the actual figures corresponded to the population massacred by the Turks.

It is necessary, for this reason, to examine the subject of the Armenian population. Let us look at Armenian, Western, and Ottoman records in turn. We shall draw conclusions later.

(a) Armenian sources

Generally, Armenian sources give the figures provided by the Patriarchate. Contemporary Armenian authors prefer to give the figures reported by others, instead of submitting a figure themselves.

Hovannisian reports that the Armenian population in Turkey before 1914 was less than 2 million but more than 1.5 million.[36]

Pasdermadjian states that, in 1914, there were 4,100,000 Armenians in the world, 2,100,000 in the Ottoman Empire, 1,700,000 in Russia.[37]

Jacques de Morgan (we include him among the Armenian authors as he obtained his figures from Chobandjian) reports that in 1914 there were 2,380,000 Armenians in Turkey, that in the world there were 4,160,000, and that even if the population had declined as a result of recent events, it would still be around 3 million.[38]

Marcel Léart's book was published in 1913.[39] One would assume that he is French, but he was in fact an Armenian. We learn this from the letter sent by M. N. Moditchian to Toynbee on 17 February 1916. This correspondence coincides with the period when Toynbee was looking for documents for the Blue Book.[40] The real name of Léart was Krikor Zohrap. On pp. 59-60 of his book, Léart gives the Armenian population of Turkey for the years 1882 and 1912, and states that these figures were provided by the Patriarchate. The figures for 1882 are as follows:

Van	400,000	
Bitlis	250,000	
Diyarbekir	150,000	
Erzurum	280,000	
Elaziz	270,000	
Sivas	280,000	
		1,630,000
Adana	280,000	
Aleppo		
(Antep, Urfa, Kilis, Marash)	100,000	
		380,000
Trabzon	120,000	
Bursa	60,000	
Aydin	50,000	
Ankara, Kastamonu, Konya	120,000	
Syria, Beirut, Musul,		
Baghdad and Basra	40,000	
District of Izmir	65,000	
		455,000
Istanbul and its surroundings	135,000	
Edirne	50,000	
The rest of European Turkey	10,000	
		195,000
Total for Turkey		
		2,660,000

The population figures for six provinces in 1912, given by Léart and again attributed to the Patriarchate, are as follows:

	Total	Turks	Armenians
Erzurum	630,000	240,000	215,000
Van	350,000	47,000	185,000
Bitlis	382,000	40,000	180,000
Harput	450,000	102,000	168,000
Diyarbekir	296,000	45,000	105,000
Sivas	507,000	192,000	165,000
	2,615,000	666,000	1,018,000

We have been unable to find the documents in which the Patriarchate gave these statistics, but we have found the statistics it gave to the British Ambassador in 1880 and 1881 . In these statistics, the Patriarch gave the total Armenian population in 1880 in the eastern provinces as 658,000. Later, the Patriarch rectified the figure he gave for Sivas, and this total increased to 805,745. If one is to pay attention to Léart's list, this figure increases for the same date to 1,630,000; it is hard to imagine that the Patriarch could have thought of increasing these figures more than two-fold two years later, when even the 1880 figures were doubted by the British. Moreover, we have the figures submitted by the Patriarch in 1881. We shall give them below. For this reason, it is possible that the above list was a statistic prepared by Leart in 1913, at the suggestion of the Patriarch, in order to spread confusion.

Léart, or rather, Zohrap, tried to prove that the Patriarchate reports were even less, and with this intention translated the chapter on 'The tax levied non-Muslim subjects in lieu of military service on pp. 413 and 414 of the yearbook of the Ottoman Empire for the year 1298 (1882). His translation (p. 64) is as follows:

When we reexamine the net returns of this tax for the years 1292, 1293, 1294, we obtain the following figures:

Year 1292 (1876) 416,720 T.L.
Year 1293 (1877) 542,200 T.L.
Year 1294 (1878) 542.390 T.L.

By taking into account the fact that in the past three years, the return of this tax had been more than the average of the other years, due to the circulation of paper-money, we had to accept, as the eventual return for this year, the sum 462,870 T.L. [Turkish liras.]

If we evaluate the male non-Muslim population of the Ottoman Empire at a minimum of 4,000,000, the return of this tax should be at least double what it produces today.

When we look at the original text, we see that, first of all, it mentions, not the circulation of paper-money, but the rumour that it will be removed from the market, and it is stated that the taxes which were not paid because of these rumours had been paid. While this passage was erroneously translated, the statement 'if the non-Muslim male population was at least 4,000,000, the military conscription tax to be collected from them, would the amount shown above', was translated in a way to give it a totally different meaning. As Marcel Léart came from Istanbul, it is difficult to accept that he had a limited knowledge of Turkish.

A similar point can be found on p. 10 of his book. It is stated in a footnote that Lynch gives the Armenian population of Aleppo, Adana, Trabzon, Erzerum, Van, Bitlis, Diyarbekir, Elaziz and Sivas as 1,058,000.

However, the figures given by Lynch are as follows:

The six provinces	387,746
The rest of Asian Turkey	751,500
European Turkey	186,000
	1,325,246

Lynch gives the figure for the whole of Asian Turkey as 1,139,246. Among the non-Armenian foreign authors, Cuinet gives the highest figure for Asian Turkey. The figure he gives for Aleppo, Adana and Trabzon is 193,999. When we add this to the figures Lynch gave for the six provinces, we come up with 581,745.

Because we were unable to determine whether the statistics in this book attributed to the Patriarchate were in fact provided by the Patriarchate, we do not include them in our analysis below.

As for the figures that were given by the Patriarchate, we have determined them in the following way.

The figure given by the Patriarchate at the Berlin Congress for the Armenian population in the Ottoman Empire was 3,000,000;[41] the figure given for the Armenian population in the provinces of Erzerum, Van, Bitlis, Sivas and Diyarbekir was 2,000,000, and for the Turkish population it was 1,000.000.[42]

An Armenian clerical writer (Vahan Vardapet in an Armenian newspaper published in Constantinople, the *Djeridei Sharkieh*, dated 3/15 December 1886), who appears not to err on the side of exaggeration, has placed the entire Gregorian population, that is the great bulk of his countrymen in Turkey, at 1,263,900 souls. It is reasonable to suppose that the Armenian subjects of the Sultan number upwards of one and a half millions. [43]

The Patriarch sent some statistics to the British Ambassador about the population in the eastern provinces, for the first time, on 24 June 1880.[44] Later, he rectified the Sivas figures, and sent

another letter on 10 September 1880.[45] Meanwhile, Odian Efendi
from the Patriarchate gave a note containing some statistics to Sir
Charles Dilke from the Foreign Office in London, in the month of
July of the same year.[46] On 20 October 1881, the Patriarch sent new
statistics to the British Ambassador.[47]

We shall now show these statistics in tabulated form. But let
us first report some observations made by the British Embassy
concerning these statistics. Major Trotter wrote as follows in a
memorandum he prepared for the British Ambassador on 7
September 1880:

I would, however, beg to call your Excellency's special attention to
the discordant results of (3), (4), and (5), all of which have been supplied
at various times, directly or indirectly, from the Armenian Patriarchate.
When such large discrepancies are apparent in these three Armenian
estimates of the Armenian population, it is perfectly evident that still less
reliance can be placed on the corresponding estimates of the Mahommedan
population (vide (15) and (18) Tables C and D).[48]

The numbers in parentheses refer to the columns in the
statistics lists. We shall give them as we examine the provinces.

More significant than this is the memorandum presented by
Major Trotter to his Ambassador on 15 February 1882:

At a meeting last Autumn of the Armenian Assemble Nationale, M.
Sdépan Papazian, the reputed author of the statistical Tables presented to
the Berlin Conference, made a violent attack on the Patriarch for having
communicated statistical Tables to the Embassies without having
previously consulted the Nationale Assembly, in consequence of which the
enormous divergence between the Berlin and the more recent Patriarchal
figures had attracted attention, and called forth remarks tending to show
the untrustworthiness of both sets of figures

The Berlin compilation, by a glaringly unfair manipulation of official
figures tried to prove that, according to the said figures, the Armenian
population Erzerum and Van (including Bitlis and Hekkari) amounted to
1,150,000 soule. I have subsequently shown that, in all probability, the
real number does not exceed 450,000: while the Patriarchal figures
supplied to the Embassy in 1880 gave 373,500 Armenians, plus 85,000
Nestorians.[49]

It is my belief that the discrepancy between the figures given
at various times, as well as the two observations made by Major
Trotter, the expert on population in the British Embassy, show to
what extent the figures submitted by the Patriarchate should be
taken seriously.

Now we shall present the figures submitted by the
Patriarchate, adding to these the figures given by Marcel Léart, in
one table. During that period, the object was to prove that the
Armenians were in a majority in relation to the Turks, and for this
reason the statistics included figures for the Turkish population. In
the list below we shall give only the figures for the Armenian

population; the Turkish figures will be given later, under the provinces

The Armenian population in six provinces (including Catholics and Protestants), according to the Patriarchate, was:

	1878 (a)	1880 (b	1880 (c)	1881 (d)	1882 (e)	1912 (f)
Erzurum		215,177	111,000	128,478	280,000	215,000
Van	1,150,000	184,000	252,500	133.,859	400,000	185,000
Bitlis		164,508		130,460	250,000	180,000
Diyarbekir			88,000		150,000	105,000
Elaziz			155,000	107,059	270,000	168,000
Sivas			199,245	243,515	280,000	165,000

(a) in the statistics submitted to the Berlin Congress.
(b) The figures given to Sir Charles Dilke (FO. 424/106/200)
(c) The Patriarch's list 424/106/273, with the Sivas correction (424/107/135).
(d) The Patriarch's list (FO. 424/132/46).
(e) and (f) Marcel Leart's lists.

It is apparent that there is no possibility of taking these lists seriously.

(b) Foreign sources

Ludovic de Constenson gives the 1913 Armenian population in the world as 3,100,000, in Turkey as 1,400,000, in Russia as 1,550,000.[50]

Viconte de Coursons states in his book that he has used Cuinet's figures, which we give below.[31]

Christopher Walker states that before the First World War there were 1,500,000-2,000,000 Armenians in Turkey. [52]

H. F. Tozer, quoting Ravenstein, writes that in 1877 there were 700,000 Armenians in Asian Turkey.[53]

Clair Price reports the Armenian population in Turkey prior to the war as 1,000,000. [54]

Alexander Powell asserts that the Armenian population in the world does not exceed 3,000,000, that in Turkey there were 1,500,000 Armenians, and in Russia 1.000,000. [55]

Lynch examined the question of the Armenian population in a detailed manner. We shall see the figures he gives for the provinces when we come to study the provinces. He gives the general Armenian population in the following table: [56]

The Armenian plateau (Russian and Turkish Provinces)	906,984
Caucasia and the rest of Transcaucasia	450,000
Astrakhan, Bessarabia	75,600
The rest of Turkish Asia	751,500
European Turkey	186,000
Iranian Azerbaidjan	28,890
Colony of Julfa and the rest of Iran	14,110
Bulgaria, Eastern Roumelia	5,010
Roumania	8,070
Austria	1,230
	2,427,394

Lynch states on p. II/409 of his book that the population of the Armenian plateau in Turkey is 387,746 and the Armenian population of the Empire 1,325,246.

Among foreign sources, the one who has researched the population of the Ottoman Empire most thoroughly is, without any doubt, Vital Cuinet. In the foreword to his book he writes: 'The work which we present today, to the public in general, is a compilation of statistic notes gathered on the spot during various trips of exploration we have undertaken in the last twelve years.[57] It is known that Cuinet undertook these travels in the name and on behalf of the Debt Commission.

Leaving the detailed figures Cuinet gives for the provinces to be examined later, we shall now look at the figures he gives for the population Anatolian Turkey:

Muslim	14,856,118
Armenian	1,475,011
Other Christians	1,285,853
Jewish	123,947
Other foreigners	170,822
	17,911,751

The Gregorian, Protestant, and Catholic Armenians are included in the Armenian population.

Cuinet's figures appear in the French Yellow Book, and this shows the extent to which the French recognize these figures as official.[58]

In the 1910 edition of the *Encyclopaedia Britannica*, the world Armenian population is given as 2,900,000, and the Armenian population in Turkey as 1,500,000. (In the 1953 edition of the same work, the population of Armenians in Turkey is given as 2,500,550 for the same year. The article in the 1910 edition was written by a Briton, and the article in the 1953 edition was written by an Armenian.)

(c) Ottoman sources

It was repeatedly claimed that no census, in the modern sense, had been taken in the Ottoman Empire, and therefore the figures given by the Babiali were erroneous and imaginary.

Actually, this was not the case. When Sultan Abdulhamid received the new American Ambassador in 1886, the Ambassador mentioned the last census taken in America, and its advantages. The Sultan expressed his interest in the subject, and asked the Ambassador whether he would help to establish such an organization in Turkey. As the Ambassador gave a positive answer, the preparations for a census were undertaken with the Ambassador's help. Details of this subject will be found in Kemal Karpat's article.[59] The results of this census were published in 1893. It is recognized that the results of the census are reliable, because everybody was given identity papers during the census, and from that date on it was impossible to engage in any occupation without these papers. However, the census was not taken as it is taken today, by requiring everybody to stay at home and going from one house to the next, but by asking the head of every household and by filling in a card for every member of the household. When these cards were being filled in, the muhtars (headmen of the quarter or a village) were present.

The first president of the Statistics Bureau, founded in 1892, and which published the census results, was a Jew named Fethi Franko, and he was replaced by an Armenian named Migirdich Shinabyan. Shinabyan held this position between 1897 and 1903, and he was replaced by an American named Robert, who held the post until 1908.

After the census was taken, the new births and deaths were recorded through the census offices established in every district, and thus the recording of population changes became possible.

We give below the figures given by the Ottoman authorities concerning the distribution of the population, as recorded by Prof. Kemal Karpat:

	1893	1905	1914
Muslim	12,587, 137	15,508,753	15,044,846
Greek	2,332,191	2,823,063	1.729,738
Gregorian Armenian	1,001,465	1,031,708	1,161,169
Catholic Armenian	-	89,040	67,838
Protestant	36,268	52,485	65.844
Greek Catholic	-	29,749	62,468
Jewish	184,106	253,435	187,023
Latin	18,240	20,496	24,845
Syriac	-	36,985	54.750
Ancient Syriac	-	-	4,133
Chaldean	-	2,371	13,211
Jacobite	-	1,024	6,932
Maronite	-	28,738	47,406

Samaritan	-	262	164
Nestorian	-	-	8,091
Yazidi	-	2,927	6,957
Gypsy	3,153	16,470	11,169
Druse	-	-	7,385
Cossack	-	1,792	1,006
Bulgarian	817,835	761,530	14,908
Serbian	-	-	1
Wallachian	-	26,042	82
Foreigner	235,983	197,760	-
Roman Catholic	149,786	-	-
Monophysite	32,598	-	-
	17,388,562	20,884,630	18,520,016

It is apparent that the Greek, as well as the Catholic Armenians are included in the 1893 Catholic population figures. It can be accepted that all the Protestants were Armenian. Consequently, the Armenian community in the Ottoman Empire is:

in 1893   1,157,519   (30,000 Catholics have been considered Greek.)

in 1905   1,173,233
in 1914   1,294,851

If we are to summarize the figures we have given above from three different groups of sources, the Armenian population in Turkey is according to:

Patriarchate	1,780,000-3,000,000
Jacques de Morgan	2,380,000
Pasdermadjian	2,100,000
Hovannisian	1,500,000-2,000,000
Vahan Vardapet	1,263,000
Constenson	1,400,000
Walker	1,500,000-2,000,000
Ravenstein	760,000 (Asian Turkey)
Clair Price	1,500,000
A. Powell	1 ,500,000
Lynch	1,325,000
Cuinet	1,475,000 (Asian Turkey)
Encyclopaedia Brittannica)	1,500,000
Ottoman Empire	1,160,000-1,300,000

The fact that the Patriarchate did not repeat the 3,000,000 figure it gave to the Berlin Congress, but reduced it to 1,780,000, is significant.It is understood that the Patriarch spoke without reflection, thinking that autonomy was going to be obtained anyway, but that he did not repeat this figure, and even gave a figure under 2,000,000, when he saw that autonomy was not going to materialize, and he thought of the subject of taxes. Nevertheless, we shall see below that the figures given by the Patriarch for the six provinces too are quite exaggerated. It is also useful to remember that the Patriarch, who said he was basing his figures on the records of the Patriarchate, never revealed these records. Moreover, it is obvious that Catholic and Protestant Armenians would not be included in the Patriarchate records.

The Patriarchate figures being what they are, we can leave aside the Armenian sources who follow the Patriarchate, and Walker, who is obviously the standard-bearer of the Armenians. Besides, the figures given by Vahan Vardapet, member of the Patriarchate, clearly contradict them.

Western sources give figures between 1,300,000 and 1,500,000. However, among them Lynch, to some extent, and Cuinet have done serious research. Cuinet's figure, when Istanbul is included, can be accepted as 1,500,000.

The Ottoman statistics give, for the same date of 1896, the figure of 1,160,000. As the census was not taken by requiring individuals to stay at home, and by going from one house to the next, if we are to accept the number of Armenians who were not included in the census, for tax evasion reasons, as around 150,000, the Ottoman figure for 1896 is approximately 1,300,000.

If we are to take into account the fact that Cuinet's research was based on information obtained from local Churches, that these Churches continually tended to exaggerate, and if we remember that Vahan Vardapet gave the figure 1,300,000, then we can assume that this exaggeration was also reflected in Cuinet's computations. Moreover, Cuinet's statistics were before the 1894-6 revolts. Armenian authors are agreed that, following these revolts, hundreds of thousands of Armenians emigrated from the Ottoman Empire.

Under these circumstances, we can accept that the Armenian population in the Ottoman Empire in 1896 was approximately 1,300,000.

What is important for the Armenian question is, not so much the total population, but rather, the Armenian population in the eastern provinces where the Armenians wanted to establish an autonomous Armenia.

At the Berlin Congress, the Armenians had shown the borders of the country which would be administered by them as bounded by the Russia-Iran border in the east; in the west, by a line extending from Tirebolou on Black Sea coast to the point where the Kizil Chubuk stream joins the Euphrates; and in the south by a line extending from the Euphrates to the bitlis stream from the south of lake Van to the Iran border.[60]

According to the administrative division of the period, Tirebolou was a district centre. The six provinces, again according to the administrative division of the period, are Erzurum, Van, Bitlis, Diyarbekir, Elaziz, and Sivas. These provinces, according to the present-day administrative division, correspond to the provinces of Erzurum, Erzincan, Agri, Van, Hakkari, Bingol, Sivas, Amasya, and Tokat, and to the region of Shebin Karahisar to the south of Giresoun.

The Patriarchate, in the statistics it prepared for the purpose of proving Armenians were in a majority in the Provinces, counted all the Christians as Armenians, but when it came to counting the Muslims, it counted only the Turks. Moreover, it did not adhere to the provincial borders, and in some cases drew a border in the districts. Although it attempted in this way to confuse the foreign powers, it did not obtain any result, not because of the inaccuracy of the statistics, but because of the policies of the great powers that we have mentioned previously.

However, because these figures which were asserted then are also used today, it is necessary to examine them in detail.

Let us take a look at the letter sent by the Patriarch Nerses, on 24 June 1880, to the British Ambassador:

At a time when the question of reforms concerning Armenia, subject of the third collective note submitted to the Sublime Porte, is being discussed, I thought that your Excellency would be pleased to have at your disposal serious statisticaly documents. The previous censuses of the population have been done on the basis of number of houses; this method is absolutely erroneous, as the number inhabitants of every household are by no means identical, and depend on whether the houses are occupied by Christians or Muslims. According to Muslim traditions, different families cannot live in the same house; in Armenian customs, however, children and brothers, after as well as before their marriage, continue live together. As a result, while one must count at most three to eight inhabitants in a Muslim house, we can count twelve to sixty in an Armenian house.

Only a census based on the number of individuals can produce a reliable result. The enclosed table, which includes only the censuses of the six Armenian: provinces, properly so called, (there are besides, one million Armenians in the rest of Asian Turkey), has been prepared in such a way as to put the Christian population not above the actual figures, but below them. This will enable your Excellency to get a clear idea of the actual situation and of the proportion of the various elements which it is necessary to protect.

If we admit that we can, which is in fact erroneous, consider all the nomads as Muslims, the Christian population is still by far the largest; as for the Muslim population, properly so called, it does not even constitute one third of the total.

I consider it unnecessary to call the attention of your Excellency to the reflections which the study of these statistics calls forth; I realize how much your Excellency is already inclined in favour of the Armenian cause, which is the one of humanity and justice.

I beg your Excellency to accept my thanks for the past, and for the future, my respect, etc.[61]

This letter, which explains Turkish and Armenian customs and practices and which claims that an Armenian household may contain as many as sixty people, is a document which must be viewed from beginning to end with extreme caution.

But the following reply given by the Patriarch on 10 September 1880 to the Ambassador, as he pointed out the discrepancies in the figures, especially concerning the Sivas province, is even more significant:

I hasten to reply to the legitimate observations in your letter dated the sixth of this month, concerning the Table of the mixed population of the Sivas province which I had the honour of presenting to your Excellency.

While drawing up this Table, your Excellency, I only considered the Armenian part of this province, such as Sivas, Divrik, and the vicinity; I omitted, in consequence, all the south-eastern districts (sanjaks), which are not part of Armenia, such as for example, Tokat (Armenian Gomana), Derende, Gurun, Tonous, Azizie; the latter has recently been included in the Sivas province. , ,[62]

The Ambassador had this answer examined in the registry office of the Embassy, and a memorandum prepared by Lieutenant-Colonel C. W. Wilson for the Ambassador is enclosed in the same document in the British archives. Wilson wrote:

The letter of the Armenian Patriarch shows a great lack of knowledge concerning the local realities of the population of the province of Sivas and the Christian population. For example, Darende, Gurun, Tonous, and Azizie are stated to be *sanjaks* (sub-divisions of a province). Whereas, three of them are *kazas* (sub-divisions of a *sanjak*) and one of them is only a *nahiye* (subdivision of a *kaza*). Moreover, it is also stated that Azizie has recently been included with Sivas, which is totally inaccurate.

After these documents, quoted here to show the manner in which the Patriarchate worked and its intentions, let us now turn to the population distribution in the six provinces, by looking at the information in our sources.

(d) The province of Erzurum

Lynch writes that the population of Erzurum in 1827 was 130,000, and that 24,000 were Armenian; that after the 1829 Russian occupation, Armenians, too, left as the Russians were withdrawing; that the 1835 population of Erzurum fell to 15,000, that there were 120 Armenian families left among them, and that at the time of his visit to Erzurum (after 1896), the population was 40,000, of which 10,500 were Armenian.[63]

It is obvious that the subject is the central kaza of Erzurum. He gives the population of the province as 544,502 on p. II/412 of his book, the Armenian population as (106,765).

The Armenian Patriarch, in his letter dated 24 June 1880, gives the population of the province as 270,000, and the Armenians as 111,000. In 1881, he increases this figure to 128,478. The figure given in Britain is 215,177.

Cuinet records the Armenian population as 134,967 in a total population of 645,702.

It was shown in an estimate of the Ottomans in 1890 that the total population was 555, 159, the non-Muslim population being 113,488, and that the British Consul C. Lloyd agreed with this estimate.[64] As it is known that according to the Ottomans there were 3,356, according to Cuinet 3,725 according to the Patriarch 5,000 insignificant non-Muslim elements excluding the Armenians, then if we count their average total as 4,000,the Armenian population was 109,488.

The Ottomans made another estimate in 1895, through a control commission sent to the region as part of the reform programme. We also find this estimate in the same British document. It gives the population of the provinces as 669,717 and the non-Muslim population as 123,935.When we exclude, as in the above, 4,000 from these figures, we obtain 119,935 as the Armenian population.

Among the British documents, there are other estimates made by Major Trotter.[65] However, these were given cumulatively for the provinces of Erzurum, Van and Bitlis (excluding Siirt). Consequently, we shall examine these estimates cumulatively, after having recorded the separate estimates for the Van and Bitlis provinces.

We can now tabulate the various estimates made for Erzerum between 1880 and 1893: (Other elements are also included in the totals besides the Turkish and Armenian figures.)

Estimate made by	Muslim	Armenian	Total	Year of estimate
The Patriarch	351,990	215,177	582,879	1880 Britain
The Patriarch	120,000	111,000	270,000	1880
The Patriarch	196,269	128,478	337,767	1881
Ottomans	441,671	109,488	555,159	1890
1893 census	444,548	109,838	559,055	1890s
Cuinet	500,782	134,967	645,702	1892
Ottomans	545,782	121,935	669,717	1895
Lynch	428,495	106,768	544,502	c. 1896

(e) The province of Van

Lynch gives the general population as 197,873, and the Armenian population as 75,644 at the time of his travels, in 1896.[66]

The figure given by the Patriarch for 1880 is cumulative with the province of Bitlis. In 1881 he gave the 133,859 figure. The figure given in Britain was 184,000.

Among a total population of 430,000, Cuinet gives the Muslim population as 241,000 and the Armenian population as 79,998. The 1890 Ottoman estimate is 282,582 Muslims and 135,912 non-Muslims. As there were approximately 80,000 Nestorians in this province, the Armenian population was, then, 55,912. The estimate of Consul Lloyd was 115,000 Muslims and 155,988 non-Muslims. If we subtract from this figure the 80,000 Nestorians, then the Armenian population was 75,000.

According to the 1893 Ottoman census, the population of the province was 119,860. There were 59,412 Muslims and 60,448 Armenians. The Nestorians seem to have been excluded from this census.

The Ottomans' 1895 estimate was 207,028 Muslims, and 101,204 non--Muslims. When we subtract the Nestorian population, there were then 11,204 Armenians. It is apparent that in this estimate there was a confusion between Nestorians and Muslims. For this reason, it will be better not to include this last estimate in our list.

The summary of the Van province is then

Estimate made by	Muslim	Armenian	Total	Year of estimate	
The Patriarch	120,000	184,000	384,363	1880	Britain
The Patriarch	113,586	133,859	337,611	1881	
Ottomans	282.582	55,912	418,494	1890	
Consul Lloyd	115,000	75,988	270,988	1890	
Cuinet	241,000	79,998	430,000	1892	
1893 census	119.860	60,448	180,308	1890s	
Lynch	52,229	75,644	127,873	c.1896	

(f) The province of Bitlis

Lynch writes that the population of the province in 1814 was 12,000, half of which was Armenian; that in 1838 it was between 15 and 18,000, one third of which was Armenian; that in 1868 there were 4,000 families, 1,500 of which were Christian; and during his travels there were 27,673 Muslims, 16,089 Armenians, and 342 Assyrians.[67]

The Patriarch gives a cumulative figure for Van and Bitlis in 1880. The figure he gives in 1881 for Bitlis only is 130,460 Armenians. The figure given in Britain is 164,508. According to the Patriarch, there are no non-Muslims, other than Armenians. However, there were in Bitlis approximately 10,000 non-Muslims other than Armenians. We have subtracted 10,000 from the Ottomans' 1890 and 1895 estimates and Consul Lloyd's 1890 estimate in preparing the figures below:

Estimate made by	Muslim	Armenian	Total	Year of estimate	
The Patriarch	88,388	164,508	253,226	1880	Britain
The Patriarch	21,121	130,460	151,581	1881	
Ottomans	167,054	99,944	276,998	1890	
Lloyd	166,794	111,082	287.876	1890	
Cuinet	254,000	131,390	398.625	1892	
1893 census	167,054	102,856	276,998	1890s	
Ottomans	352,713	116,874	479,587	1895	
Lynch	145,454	97,184	242,980	c.1896	

Although the *sanjak* of Siirt was previously within Diyarbekir, in 1880 it became part of Bitlis. Siirt is not included in the Bitlis figures Patriarch's estimate.

Major Trotter has included Siirt in Diyarbekir in the cumulative comparisons.

The figures accepted by Major Trotter for Siirt are:

Muslim	47,098
Christian	23,678
(Armenian)	(22,450)
Total	70.776

If we subtract these figures from the Bitlis totals, and add them to the Diyarbekir figures, the general totals will not change, but the comparison will be easier.

We obtain the following table for Bitlis after the subtraction. We can include the figures given by the Patriarch and Lynch, as they give their figures excluding Siirt.

Estimate made by	Muslim	Armenian	Total	Year of estimate	
The Patriarch	88,388	164,508	253,226	1880	Britain
The Patriarch	21,121	130,460	151,581	1881	
Ottomans	167,054	99,944	276,998	1890	
Lloyd	166,794	111,082	287.876	1890	
Cuine	254,000	131,390	398.625	1892	
1893 census	167,054	102,856	276,998	1890s	
Ottomans	352,713	116,874	479,587	1895	
Lynch	145,454	97,184	242,980	c.1896	

We mentioned above that the Patriarch gave a cumulative figure for Van and Bitlis in 1880. Now, as we have established the other figures for Van and Bitlis, we can add these, and make a cumulative table including the 1880 figures of the Patriarch.
Cumulative population for the Van and Bitlis provinces:

Estimate made by	Muslim	Armenian	Total	Year of estimate
The Patriarch	208,388	348,508	537,589	1880 Britain
The Patriarch	151,500	252,500	489,000	1880
The Patriarch	134,407	264,319	489,192	1881
Ottomans	402,538	133,406	624,716	1890
Lloyd	234,969	164,620	488,088	1890
Cuinet	447,902	168,938	757,849	1892
1893 census	239,816	140,854	386,530	1890s
Ottomans	-	-	-	1895
Lynch	197,683	172,828	370,853	c.1896

We mentioned above that Major Trotter had given some other figures, but that these were cumulative for the provinces of Erzurum, Van and Bitlis (excluding Siirt). Now, by counting cumulatively also the figures which we have given for these three provinces, and including Major Trotter's cumulative figures, we can arrive at the table below.
Cumulative population for Erzurum, Van and Bitlis (excluding Siirt) provinces:

Estimate made by	Muslim	Armenian	Total	Year of estimate
Consul Taylor	724,700	290,500	1,130.400	1869 (a)
Berlin project	528,000	1,150,000	1,700,000	1878 (b)
Patriarchate	560,378	563,685	1,120,468	1880 (c)
Patriarchate	280,000	363,500	758,000	1881 (d)
Patriarchate	330,676	392,797	862,959	1881 (d)
Vahan Vardabet	-	440,500	-	1879 (e)
Ottomans	844,209	242,894	1,179,875	1890
Consul Lloyd	676,367	274,108	1,043,247	1890
Cuinet	948,684	323,905	1,403,551	1892
1893 census	734,364	250,692	945,585	1890s
Ottomans	-	-	-	1895
Lynch	628,178	279,596	915,355	c. 1896

It is necessary to give some information about the other figures provided by the British. (a) Taylor was Consul in Erzurum and Diyarbekir, and the figures he obtained were taken from the Blue Book Turkey 15 (1877). (b) Distributed by the Patriarchate at the Berlin Congress. (c) Given to Sir Charles Dilke in July 1880.

(d) Given by the Patriarch to the British Consul in 1880 and 1881, and included above. Major Trotter excluded the Alawis and the Poschas from the Erzurum figures. (e) Given by Vahan Vardabet, an agent in the services of the Patriarchate, to Major Trotter.

The differences in the four sets of figures which are given sequentially by the Patriarchate, together with the differences between these figures and the other estimates, speak for themselves. Above, the numbers (3,4,5) which Major Trotter refers to in his letter to the British Ambassador are the three separate estimates of the Patriarchate.

(g) The province of Diyarbekir

We have compiled the list below by adding the figures we have subtracted from Bitlis (to be able to compare them with the figures of the Patriarch and Major Trotter) to the figures for Diyarbekir. The additions have been made to the figures given by Cuinet and Consul Lloyd, to the Ottomans' 1890 and 1895 estimates, and to the 1893 census. The others were already given with the additions. Lynch did not give the population of Diyarbekir as a province.

Diyarbekir is not included in the list given by the Patriarchate in England and in its 1881 list.

Estimate made by	Muslim	Armenian	Total	Year of estimate
Patriarch	145,000	88,800	293,800	1880
Ottoman	328,000	76,958	416,082	1880
Ottoman	287,672	79,320	383,220	1890
Lloyd	351,682	90,034	541,580	1890
Cuinet	384,742	101,579	542,238	1892
1893 census	336,689	83,047	438,740	1890s
Ottoman	425,351	86,202	532,781	1895

(h) The province of Elaziz

We present below the corresponding figures:

Estimate made by	Muslim	Armenian	Total	Year of estimate
Patriarch	125,000	158,000	300,000	1880
Patriarch	172,584	107,059	280,163	1881
Ottoman	300,194	74, 158	374,352	1890
Lloyd	205,353	81,155	286,508	1890
Cuinet	505,446	69,718	575,31.4	1892
1893 census	300,188	79,974	381,346	1890s
Ottoman	494,881	84,422	579,303	1895
Lynch	182,000	93,000	276,756	c.1896

(i) The province of Sivas

The figures we have are as follows:

Estimate made by	Muslim	Armenian	Total	Year of estimate
Patriarch	388,218	199,245	605,063	1880
Patriarch	694,425	243,515	945,081	1881
Ottoman	735,489	116,712	892,201	1890
Cuinet	859,514	170,433	1,086,015	1892
1893 census	766,5S8	118,191	926,671	1890s
Ottoman	801,630	131,361	971,981	1895

(j) Total Armenian population

These are the six provinces. However, the Patriarch also included Halep, for some reason. Therefore we give the figures for the province of Halep:

Estimate made by	Muslim	Armenian	Total	Year of estimate
Patriarch	135,000	90,000	342,500	1880
Cuinet	792,449	37,999	995,758	1892
1893 census	684,599	61,489	787,714	1890s

Now, if we summarize the Armenian population of the six provinces, we obtain the following table. (We have taken the highest of the estimates made by the Patriarch and the Ottomans. In the other estimates, we have shown both the highest and the lowest figures.)

	Patriarch	Ottoman	Other Highest	Lowest
Erzurum	215,177	121,935	134,967 (Cuinet)	106,768 (Lynch)
Van,Bitlis	348,500	140,854	168,938(Cuinet)	164,620 (Lloyd)
Diyarbekir	88,800	86,202	101,579 (Cuinet)	90,034 (Lloyd)
Elaziz	158,000	84,422	93,000 (Lynch)	69,718 (Cuinet)
Sivas	243,515	131,361	170,433 (Cuinet)	170,433 (Cuinet)
Total	1,053,992	564,774	668,917	601,573

The mean of the highest and the lowest figures from the other sources is 635,245.

In view of the explanation given above about the figures of the Patriarchate, we can conclude that the Armenian population of the six provinces for the years 1895-6 was between 565,000 and 635,000.

As we can compute the general Armenian population of Turkey as 1,300,000, we can accept the Armenian population outside the six provinces as between 665,000 and 735,000.

If this population we have given for the years 1895-6 had been able to increase at a normal rate, it would naturally have attained a higher figure. However, owing to the emigration which occurred after the 1895-6 revolts, upon which all Armenian writers agree, the fact that this emigration increased after the Balkan wars, and the population living in the areas which Turkey lost between 1896 and 1914, the population in 1914 remained around 1,300,000.

We present below the provinces and independent sanjaks which, according to the official Ottoman statistics, had an Armenian population of at least 1,000 in 1914:

Province of Istanbul	84,093
Province of Edirne	19,888
Province of Adana	57,686
Province of Aydin	20,766
Province of Halep	49,486
Province of Ankara	53,957
Province of Beirut	5,288
Province of Bitlis	119,132
Province of Bursa	61,191
Province of Kastamonu	8,959
Province of Diyarbekir	73,226
Province of Erzurum	136,618
Province of Konya	13,225
Province of Elaziz	87,864
Province of Sivas	151,674
Province of Syria	2,533
Province of Trabzon	40,237
Province of Van	67,792
Sanjak of Bolou	2,972
Sanjak of Janik	28,576
Sanjak of Eskishehir	8,807
Sanjak of Izmit	57,789
Sanjak of Jerusalem	3,043
Sanjak of Kayseri	52,192
Sanjak of Kalei Sultaniye (Chanakkale)	2,541
Sanjak of Kara Hisari Sahip	7,448
Sanjak of Karasi (Balikesir)	8,704
Sanjak of Kutahya	4,548
Sanjak of Marash	38,433
Sanjak of Nigde	5,705
Sanjak of Urfa	18,370

Places having a population less than 1,000 are the ,Sanjaks of Antalya (630). Ichili (341), Menteshe (12), Chatalja (842), and Zor (283). When these are added to the above figures, we obtain a total Armenian population of 1,294,851, which is 6.9 per cent of the total population of the State of 18,520,016.

CHAPTER FOUR

The Armenian question

1. First attempts at reform

The British Foreign Secretary, Lord Salisbury, in the dispatch he sent to the British Ambassador in Istanbul, Sir Henry Layard, on 8 August 1878, instructed him to press the Ottoman government to implement the reforms to which it had agreed in the 4th of June Agreement (Cyprus) and the Berlin Treaty. Layard submitted a diplomatic note to the Babiali on 19 August.

The Ottoman government was not against the reforms. As a matter of fact, the intentions of the government were clear in the reply given to Layard's note on 24 October 1878. [1]

The Ottoman government stated that it was considering the establishment of a special gendarme force in the eastern provinces, that the Gendarmerie would be a central administrative body, in which European officers would be employed, that changes would be made in the legal system, and that in some central courts European judges would be charged as inspectors.

Although the Babiali was ready in principle to make these reforms, the Treasury was empty. We learn from the British documents that this financial situation was explained to Layard during his meetings with Abdulhamid and Prime Minister Mehmet Esat Saffet Pasha, and that the Sultan even requested the British government to provide a loan of £6 million sterling.[2] However, it is apparent that the British government was not able to give this loan. For this reason, soon after the Berlin Congress, the Ottoman government was unable to implement the measures which it had considered in good faith.

Immediately after the Berlin Congress, Russia began to provoke the Armenians of the Ottoman Empire with propaganda to the effect that the reforms would not be implemented, so that they would be driven to emigrate to Russia. The Russians were even spreading rumours that they would rebuild the city of Ani, which had come into their possession with the most recent land gains, and that they would make it the capital of Armenia. (Nothing was done in Ani, until it was returned to Turkey after the First World War.)

Layard reported these developments to the Sultan and called his attention to the need for security and order in the eastern provinces. Layard informed the Foreign Office that Ismail Hakki Pasha, commander of the eastern army, had been instructed, as a result, to take every possible measure for the Armenians' security and protection, and added that various intrigues originating abroad were inciting the Armenians to rebel against the Babiali. [3]

It was mentioned in the reports of British Consuls in Trabzon and Erzurum that the Russians' activities bore fruit, and that Armenians inhabiting the regions which would be evacuated by the Russians started to emigrate in large numbers.

However, although the Russians spread rumours, which encouraged emigration, they were also opposing emigration. The reason for this was clear. They could take advantage of the Armenian community, which was thus troubled, within the Ottoman Empire, instead of within Russia. If the Armenians could be maintained ready to explode in the eastern provinces of Turkey, when the time was ripe and the ground was prepared, this explosion could be ignited.

Faced with these developments, the Patriarchate did not follow a policy of reconciliation. As a matter of fact, the Patriarchate had almost adopted, especially after the Berlin Congress, the general policy of provoking the Armenians, instead of pacifying them, and had provoked incidents. We mentioned earlier that the Patriarch, during his conversations with the British Ambassador in 1877, had stated that if rebellions were necessary to gain the attention of Europe, they could be arranged.

Esat Uras reported by translating from the minutes of the Armenian Assembly the statements made by the Patriarch to justify himself, when he was required to give explanations to the Armenian National Assembly after his lack of success at the Berlin Congress. Some parts of this speech especially shed light on future events.

The Patriarch made the following statements in his written declaration read on 21 July 1878 at the Armenian National Assembly.

. . . . . When neither the question of Bosnia-Herzegovina nor the political situation of Bulgaria were existent, the Armenian question had been around for ten years. This question stemmed from the hostilities which the Armenians were subjected to in Armenia. . . . Then the problems of Bosnia-Herzegovina and Bulgaria came about. Related to these two problems, injustices and national independence arose. . . .

. . . . The Ottoman nation shed great quantities of blood on the battlefield, and after so much sacrifice when they were defeated, and due to the fact that it was ringing in their ears that the suffering was the fault of Christians, they became extremely excited.

Prudence and farsightedness are required more than ever, and at the same time we must act effectively. . . .

The Ottomans had not yet sent their qualified representative to Edirne, when my respectable friends and I started working.

As we obtained the 16th article of the Ayastefanos Treaty, which provided us with new spirit and strength, we began working with greater aspiration and zeal. . . . The 16th article was certainly going to be changed.

. . . 'The political situation of the region of Euphrates, too, had a close relationship with Britain's interests. . . . Britain would see that this article prepared the ground for the establishment of a new province in the region of Euphrates in the interest of one state especially among those who signed. Britain would certainly not accept this. . . .

Any impartial analysis will show that, if the Turkish-British Agreement had not made certain that the reform project for the Christian Asian community would be decided with agreement between the British and Turkish governments, the powers would decide on this project from the standpoint of their own interests. The 61st article of the Berlin Agreement is this [see above, p. 104]

The sad part of this article is that, it temporarily delayed the solving of our problem, did not fulfil the hopes of the nation, and did not provide a reward for the future. Which country has immediately obtained its desires. . . .

For this reason, I have considered it necessary to complain here to the Ambassadors, and in Berlin to the delegates. Let us continue the work we have started.

Such problems can neither be solved in one day, nor by a single man. Let us be prepared for the future. Let us not stay here and there. Let us go to Armenia. Let us send to Armenia the competent, reputable, patriotic ones of our nation, our educators, our Churchmen. Let our educators, our teachers, our fervent youth go to Armenia. . . ,[4]

The Patriarch had summarized in this manner what was and what would be accomplished. We do not think it is necessary to describe what had been accomplished and to speculate what would be accomplished, for the Patriarch's statements are clear enough.

Because of this attitude, when the British Ambassador pointed out the unfortunate consequences of provocation in the eastern provinces and of the discontent stirred among the people, and suggested to the Patriarch that he do something about it, the Patriarch stated that the Armenians accused him of having deceived them. He added that discontent would continue as long as Armenia was not granted autonomy, that the Babiali was no longer trusted, and that only when an Armenian governor was appointed to Armenia, would trust perhaps be re-established.[5]

Again, we are informed by the British documents that the British did not accept the idea of an Armenian governor. The British Consul in Trabzon, Alfred Bliotti, affirmed that the administration of the eastern provinces was indeed oppressive; this, however, was not directed specifically at Armenians, but, rather, was a general maladministration. He further stated that Muslims were more oppressed by this administration, for the non-Muslims could voice their complaints through the Consuls, whereas there was nobody the Muslims could complain to. Moreover, the Consuls did not see the necessity of speaking up against the treatment of

Muslims. He added that appointing an Armenian governor to the East would have no effect, other than to facilitate Russian intrigues, and consequently to harm British interests.[6]

Towards the end of 1878, Britain sent military Consuls to the main eastern provinces, with the aim of closely following Russian activities on the one hand, and supervising the reforms on the other. Thus Major Trotter was sent to Diyarbekir, Captain Clayton to Van, and Captain Everett to Erzurum. This was not well received by the Ottoman government.

On Wednesday, 4 December, 1878, the Grand Vizier Saffet Pasha was dismissed from office, and Senator Hairettin Pasha of Tunisia was appointed in his place. It is said that the dismissal was due to the fact that an informer reported to Abdujhamid that Saffet Pasha, along with members of the Cabinet, was thinking of dethroning the Sultan.

The subject of reform was mentioned in the imperial decree following the announcement of the new government, and the new Grand Vizier was asked to implement it without delay.

The new Grand Vizier, Hairettin Pasha, decided in February 1879 to send commissions to the eastern provinces with the aim of studying the condition of the region and the Christians' complaints. These commissions, which consisted of three members, also included an Armenian member. A commission in which Yusuf Pasha and Nuryan Efendi participated was sent to Van; another, which included Abidin Pasha and Manas Efendi, was sent to Diyarbekir and its vicinity; another, which included Sait Pasha and Sarkis Efendi, was sent to the province of Aleppo.

It is known that a project prepared by the Patriarchate entitled the Reform Project of the Province of Erzurum was submitted to the commission which was sent to Erzurum, and that the same project was also sent to the British Embassy in Istanbul. We have not included the text of this project because we have been unable to discover what formal procedures were undertaken concerning it. However, there was no mention in this project of either autonomy or an Armenian governor.

The prerequisite of any reform was the establishment of a police and gendarme force; this, however, was impossible, because the Treasury was empty. As a consequence, the year 1879 saw nothing but continued discussions between the British Embassy, the Patriarchate and the Babiali concerning the subject of reforms.

Because it was only Britain that was interested in the subject of reforms, Russia having ceased to be involved, and because Britain was continually sending reports of complaint to the Babiali through the military Consuls whom it had sent to various provinces, the Babiali and especially the Sultan began to hesitate. Moreover, the Patriarchate was in a suspicious position because of its work on the idea of an autonomous Armenia, and the discontent created in the eastern provinces. The attitude of Britain during the rebellion which occurred in Zeitun in 1878 (we shall discuss this subject on page 150.) indicated that the Armenians were on the point of creating a question in Anatolia, similar to a new Serbian or Bulgarian problem. Indeed, the British documents have proved that this was exactly the intention of the Armenians.

The year 1880 started in such an atmosphere, and the elections which took place in March in England brought the Liberal Party to power. Gladstone became Prime Minister, and Lord Granville Foreign Secretary.

2. The internationalization of the subject of reform

We have mentioned Gladstone's opinion regarding the Ottoman Empire and the Turks. It was expected that he would use every opportunity to benefit the Armenians. Whereas Salisbury had preferred that Britain should handle the matter alone, without the involvement of other powers, Granville adopted a totally different policy and invited other powers to work with Britain.

With this intention, he sent circulars in May to the British Ambassadors in Paris, Berlin, Vienna, St Petorburg and Rome urging them to persuade the governments of the countries to which they were accredited to put pressure on the Babiali to implement the reforms put forward in the 61st article of the Berlin Treaty.

While he sent this instruction, Granville changed the Ambassador in Istanbul and appointed Goschen to replace Layard. From this time forward, it was Goschen who was to play a major role in Istanbul. However, before looking at his activities, it is useful to look, first, at the last report Layard sent to the Foreign Office before he received the order to return. Layard wrote:

The Armenians who expected that, after the announcement of the Cyprus Agreement, Britain would immediately have the reforms implemented, were disappointed when they saw that nothing was done, and Russia, taking advantage of the situation, began to encourage them to ask its help. Such a situation would prepare the ground for the occupation of these provinces by Russia. It was necessary to have the Ottoman Empire take action.

The Armenians, if absolute autonomy was not possible, expected partial autonomy. But under these circumstances, to provide them this possibility would eventually result in disaster for the Armenians, for it would lead to the oppression of the Armenians, who are everywhere in a minority, by the majority of the population, and this would open the way for Russian intervention. While it cannot be expected that Russia would grant autonomy or independence to the Armenians, it would be inevitable that the. Armenians would be lost in the Russian Empire.[7]

The accuracy of Layard's statements cannot be refuted. However, Granville was not of the same opinion, and considered granting independence to the Armenians. But, to do this, he had to obtain the consent of Russia. Russia. knowing that Britain coveted Arabia, did not see any benefit in the establishment of an independent Armenia. The Ottoman Empire, too, realized that Britain would cease to protect the integrity of its territory, but would rather try to obtain whatever it could get, and subsequently began to see the advantage of turning towards Russia.

It is impossible to affirm that the Sultan's opinion was erroneous, for the period of pillaging the Ottoman Empire had begun. In 1881 France would obtain Tunisia, and Thessaly be relinquished to Greece; in 1882, Britain would occupy Egypt; in 1885. Eastern Roumelia would become part of Bulgaria. Although the 'Turks were to win the 1897 Turco-Greek War, they would have to recognize the autonomy of Crete. It cannot be assumed that Abdulhamid had foreseen all this, but the fact that he was determined not to let the last Anatolian territory go, knowing that he had no chance in Europe and Asia, is an attitude that can easily be understood.

However, the Ottoman Empire was not in good condition. It was impossible to talk of a continuous and stable administration. The only continuity was in the Sultan, and he seemed determined not to let any government stay in power. Indeed, we can easily see this if we enumerate the Ottoman Grand Viziers from the Berlin Congress to the establishment of the Second Constitutional government:

Saffet Pasha	4. 6. 1878-4. 12. 1878
Hairettin Pasha of Tunisia	4. 12. 1878-29. 7. 1879
Ahmet Arifi Pasha	29. 7. 1879-18. 10. 1879
Mehmet Sait Pasha	18. 10. 1879-9. 6. 1880
Mehmet Kadri Pasha	9. 6. 1880-12. 9. 1880
Mehmet Sait Pasha	12. 9. 1880-2. 5. 1882
Abdurrahman Nurettin Pasha	2. 5. 1882-11. 7. 1882
Mehmet Sait Pasha	12. 7. 1882-1. 12. 1882
Ahmet Vefik Pasha	1. 12. 1882-3. 12. 1882
Mehmet Sait Pasha	3. 12. 1882-25. 9. 1885
Mehmet Kamil Pasha	25. 9. 1885-4. 9. 1891
Ahmed Cevad Pasha	4. 9. 1891-8. 6. 1895
Mehmet Sait Pasha	8. 6. 1895-1. 10. 1895
Mehmet Kamil Pasha	2. 10. 1895-7. 11. 1895
Halil Rifat Pasha	7. 11. 1895-9. 11. 1901
Mehmet Sait Pasha	18. 11. 1901-14. 1. 1903
Mehmet Ferid Pasha	14. 1. 1903-22. 7. 1908
Mehmet Sait Pasha	22. 7. 1908-4. 8. 1908

18 Grand Viziers in 30 years, and 14 Grand Viziers in 18 years between 1878 and 1896, which we can consider a critical period, was quite high for the execution of an important task.

When Goschen arrived in Istanbul in June 1880, an agreement had been made between the powers for common action. At that time, the Grand Vizier was Mehmet Kadri Pasha, and the Foreign Minister was Abidin Pasha, who had gone to Diyarbekir and its vicinity as the chairman of the investigation commission.

The joint note of the six powers was submitted to Abidin Pasha on 11 June 1880. This note mentioned the Armenian topic, among various reform matters, and requested information as to what had been accomplished regarding the 61st article of the Berlin Agreement. The attention of the Babiali was drawn to the responsibility that would arise from new delays in the application of those measures, which the great powers agreed were necessary in the interest of the Ottoman Empire and Europe.

When Goschen submitted this note, he did not have the time or the opportunity to learn the opinion of his staff in Istanbul. He did this later on. He gathered the opinion of the Embassy staff and the Consulates. Lieutenant-Colonel Wilson from the Embassy, too, had prepared a long memorandum. We summarize below the opinion of Lieutenant-Colonel Wilson in the memorandum sent by Goschen to Foreign Secretary Granville on 16th June:

The Armenians are divided into the Gregorian (Orthodox), Roman Catholic, and Protestant sects, which are usually at variance with each other, and rarely combine for any common object. Not only do the different sects intrigue against each other, but the Gregorians are rarely if ever united among themselves on any question of local politics. [There is a paragraph which extensively describes the weak and corrupt character of Armenians which we prefer not to include here.] The mixed population of Anatolia has not reached the maturity necessary for reforms in the Western sense. The masses of the people are generally uneducated and far from civilized. Possible reforms would be re-assembly of the Imperial Parliament, [the Sultan had closed the Assembly eleven months after its opening on 13 February 1878], the execution of existing laws, the implementation of the reform envisaged in the 1867 Vilayet Law, abolition of the system of ruling the people by religious communities, the improvement of civil service regulations, to enable Christians to become government officials, the reorganization of local administration budgets, reforming the tax laws, improving the courts, making a civil law for various cases, the modification of laws concerning bribery and embezzlement, reforming the jails, establishing a real gendarmerie, and appointing selected European full-pay officers for the gendarmerie, having Christians, too, become gendarmes, agrarian reform, improving the educational system, granting freedom for the press. encouraging various industries, and to give them to foreign capital.[8]

This is all very well, but there is no information in the report as to how the necessary funds would be found. The reports coming from the Consuls emphasized that the Armenians were preparing to secede from the Ottoman administration and that their goal was autonomy.

The Consul of Erzurum, Everett, in particular, wrote in his report dated 25 June that the Armenians did not believe Europeans would help them to obtain autonomy, and that they had prepared themselves for the necessary action: that teachers coming from Istanbul attempted to give direction to the people; that they imported arms; that he had heard weapons were hidden in all the Armenian houses; that they were not yet ready, but serious troubles would arise when the tie came.[9]

The Ottoman Empire gave a reply to the joint note of the six powers on 5 July 1880.

It was stated in this reply, signed by Abidin Pasha, that meticulous investigations were carried out in the eastern provinces, and that the work had begun; that commissions would be established in nahiyes, formed by a president belonging to the sect of the majority of the nahiye, a vice-president of the minority sect, and 4-6 members, which would be responsible for the administration; that the bujaks would have their own gendarmerie; that a gendarmerie force would also be established in the province; that itinerant courts would be formed for penal matters; that in principle the right to become government officials had been granted to non-Muslim, and that this right would be extended even more; that one-tenth of the sum remaining after having subtracted local expenses from provincial income would be left in the province for public works and educational services; and that a regulation was being drafted for all the Anatolian provinces. The note ended with the following statement: 'Before concluding my reply, I would like to inform you that it was established in the census arranged by the Babiali in the provinces of Van, Diyarbekir, Bitlis, Erzurum, and Sivas, where Armenians are present in large numbers, that only 17 per cent of the total population were Armenians, approximately 4 per cent were other non-Muslims, and 79 per cent were Muslims.'

It is clear that Goschen especially focused on the information given about the Armenian population.

The Armenian Patriarch, too, had provided him with some statistics on the population subject. (We noted them in Chapter 3.) Goschen began an investigation on this subject through his local organization. (Major Trotter's conclusions were based on this investigation.) Parallel to this, the Ambassadors in Istanbul of the six powers began to work together to submit another note concerning matters which were not satisfactory in the reply of Abidin Pasha. The Patriarch took part indirectly in this, by providing them with various information.

A new note was subsequently prepared and, after the concerned governments' approval had been obtained, was submitted to the Babiali on 7 September 1880. Abidin Pasha was still the Minister of Foreign Affairs when the note was submitted. However, three days later the Grand Vizier was dismissed, being replaced by Sait Pasha, and the new Minister of Foreign Affairs was Asim Pasha. Consequently, the responsibility for examining and answering the powers' note was left to the new cabinet.

This note, dated 7 September is quite long. We summarize its main points:

The six powers, after having stated that the explanation given by Abidin Pasha was in no way satisfactory, and that it did not comply with the obligation of article 61 of the Berlin Agreement, make the following observations.

There is no indication that reforms have been applied to the legal organization. Although the reform concerning all provinces is pleasing, priority must be given, above everything else, to the provinces mentioned in the 61st article. Not only the *bujak* leaders, but higher officials too, must be selected from among the sect of the majority. The gendarmerie organization must also include non-Muslims as officers and privates. The authority of governors must be extended. The population question must be established as soon as possible through a special commission, but this must not cause delay in other respects.[10]

The Babiali did not answer this note separately. However, in the note sent by Minister of Foreign Affairs Asim Pasha to the powers on 3 October 1880, concerning the reform to be implemented in Roumelia, this subject, too, was mentioned, and information was given about the decisions taken following the investigations made by delegations sent to the eastern provinces, most recently by Baker Pasha.

We summarize below the information given by the Babiali to the powers.

The courts of Diyarbekir, Bitlis, Van, and Erzurum would be reformed, the police and the gendarmerie would be reorganized in these provinces, the colonels of gendarmerie would be appointed from the Ministry of War, other officers would be selected by regiment assemblies and they would be appointed through the suggestion of the governors, by the Ministry of War. The *bujak* organization mentioned in the note dated 5 July 1880 would be completed shortly. 10 per cent of provincial income would be allotted to the province for educational and public services. Provincial administrative offices would be open to every subject.

Military courts would apply the civil code and the other statutes in force.

This constituted a sufficient answer to the powers' note. However, they, and especially Britain, were not willing to consider it as an answer, and from this date on, some sort of dispute began between Britain and the Babiali. Various endeavours we shall mention, before going into detail, will clarify this point.

Ambassador Goschen, in a telegram he sent to the Foreign Office on 16 November 1880,[11] mentioned that the Babiali had not replied to the joint note, and stated that the Armenians did not have the patience to wait endlessly, that they could attempt to revolt, and that it would be well to invite the powers which had signed the Berlin Agreement to a new joint undertaking.

The Gladstone cabinet wanted such an undertaking anyway. However, Russia did not want the Armenian question to be put forward, when the Karadagh and Greek topic was being discussed. Germany and Austria did not find it appropriate to put pressure on the Ottoman Empire. For this reason, Granville was unable to send Goschen the instructions he wanted concerning a joint undertaking.

In March 1881, Tsar Alexander II was shot by a nihilist. From this date on, Russia began to apply a policy of opposing any kind of liberation movement, and taking as priority the russification of the country. Subsequently it lost almost all interest in the subject of implementing reforms to the advantage of the Armenians in the Ottoman Empire. Britain was thus left totally alone.

Goschen made no new attempts until he finally left Istanbul in June 1881 . He was replaced by Lord Dufferin in that month.

Dufferin mentioned the Armenian question the first time he saw Sultan Abdulhamid, and suggested that a competent governor should be sent to the region.[12] The British Ambassador repeated his views when he was received in July by the Grand Vizier Sait Pasha.

Not only did the British Embassy make these attempts, but it was also in the process of preparing proposals concerning the reform to be made. We have mentioned these activities during the time of the former Ambassador Goschen. The new Ambassador also got involved in this subject, and had Lieutenant-Colonel Wilson, who was the Embassy expert on these matters, prepare new proposals.[13] We mention this, not to report these proposals, but to show the extent to which the British took this matter seriously.

A report by Dufferin dated 23 August informs us that during another visit he paid to the Grand Vizier Sait Pasha on 22 August he mentioned these proposals which he was having prepared.[14]

On Dufferin's instruction, Lieutenant-Colonel Wilson and Major Trotter prepared a new note on 23 August and submitted it to the Ambassador.

On 29 August Dufferin organized a meeting with the Ambassadors of the other five powers, and suggested that a joint note should again be submitted to the Babiali, and that an answer to their note dated 7 September 1880 should be requested.

On 9 September 1881, the Ambassadors met again at the British Embassy. Dufferin suggested that the six powers should write a new joint note and request from the Babiali first of all that a general-governor should be appointed to the East, that they should state that their opinion in their note dated 7 September 1880 had not changed, and that they should insist on the subject of reform. He also suggested that the Ambassadors should prepare reform proposals among themselves.

The Ambassadors accepted these suggestions, can condition that their respective governments approve of them; however, the Russian Ambassador suggested that, instead of submitting a joint note, they should separately make these requests orally, using the same terminology, and this, suggestion, too, was accepted.[15]

When Dufferin was received by the Sultan on 15 September, he mentioned the subject and elaborated on the idea of sending a governor-general, stating that it would be time to implement the reforms when the governor-general was in control of the situation and when he had dealt with complaints. We are informed by Dufferin's report dated 19 September 1881 that Sultan Abdulhamid replied that he would send a high-ranking official to the region in a month. [16]

On 1 October 1881, the Ambassadors met again, at Dufferin's invitation, to study the reform proposals prepared by Lieutenant-Colonel Wilson and Trotter. It was decided at this meeting that the Russian Ambassador Novikoff and Dufferin should work as a subcommittee, that they should prepare a memorandum, and that the Ambassadors should meet again.

In November, Dufferin made various requests to be informed about the progress of the decision to send a governor-general to the East; he was told that reform proposals were being prepared, and that he would soon be informed of them.[17] This was at the time when the Zeitun incidents, which we shall describe on page 150 occurred.

On 22 November, Dufferin paid a visit with the Russian Ambassador to Minister of Foreign Affairs Asim Pasha, and mentioned the subject of appointing a governor-general.

When Dufferin learned in December from the secretary-general of Foreign Affairs, Artin Efendi, that the Sultan would do nothing about the Armenians without the insistence of Germany, he asked his Ministry to approach Germany. [18] Germany did not want to exert pressure, nor was a British approach to Austria successful.

Dufferin was received by the Sultan on 14 January 1882. During the meeting, the Sultan told him that difficulties arising from the application of the decrees established by the Berlin Treaty concerning the eastern borders had been overcome; that the subject of reform in the eastern provinces had also been examined, and that it would be put into effect; that a qualified governor-general had not been appointed because one had not yet been found, and that he needed time. [19]

In 1882, Britain encouraged Germany to act with it. The German Minister of Foreign Affairs stated, in the instruction he sent to the Embassy in London, that they would lose the Sultan's trust if they interfered in Turkey's internal affairs, and that they wanted to maintain this trust from the perspective of European peace. [20]

No further attempts were made, because 1882 continued with unrest in Erzurum.

When the British Foreign Secretary realized that he was not going to succeed in obtaining the support of other powers, he decided to resort to threats. And he decided to dwell on the Cyprus Agreement.

On 10 May 1883, Dufferin, following the instructions of his government, paid another visit to the Sultan, and when they were discussing the Armenian question, told him that the 4 June 1878 Cyprus Agreement put forward obligations on both sides; that if the Ottomans would not fulfil theirs by implementing reforms, then the obligation on Britain to protect Turkey would be annulled. The Sultan then asked the British Ambassador why, in that case, they still remained in Cyprus. This approach, too, proved fruitless.

In 1883, the Foreign Secretary, Granville, made new approaches to Germany and Austria. However, these too were fruitless. The German Minister of Foreign Affairs stated the following points in his instruction No. 84 which he sent to his London Ambassador on 17 May 1883:

I do not understand what England will gain by putting the Sultan in an uneasy situation. The matters called Armenian reform are ideal and theoretical requests, and they have been included in Congressional discussions, with the thought that they could be useful in Parliaments. Their practical value and the result they will give are doubtful, and constitute a double-edged sword for the Armenians. In our opinion it should not he part of British policy, to weaken the Ottoman Empire, and to cut the ties connecting Armenians to Turkey. To interfere in such internal matters is the surest way to bring distressful results. I find Dufferin's attempt unfortunate for European peace and the tranquillity of the East. [21]

The Austrian Minister of Foreign Affairs was not so categorical. However, he did not conceal that he wanted to maintain the friendly attitude of the Sultan, and that consequently he could not act with Britain.

The stubborn insistence of the British, the fact that in the meantime they invaded Egypt, and the fact that they remained in Cyprus despite their declaration that they would not keep their obligations under the Cyprus Agreement (Britain did not annul the 4 June 1878 Agreement until Lausanne) clearly indicated the new policy of Britain and its intentions concerning the Empire.

This change in British policy was the main reason why the Ottoman Empire turned towards the Central powers. It was for the same reason that Von der Gotz Pasha came to Turkey (in the spring of 1883) and began the reform of the Ottoman Army.

In spite of the attitude of Germany and Austria, Granville insisted on his policy. But nothing was obtained in 1883, because of Britain's unnecessary insistence. After 1883, the attitude of Russia towards the Armenians became even harsher. Naturally this left Britain more isolated.

In 1885, the Liberals lost the election in Britain, and Lord Salisbury became Prime Minister. However, Salisbury's government did not last long, a new election became necessary and Gladstone again became Prime Minister in February 1886.

One of the first subjects that the new Foreign Secretary, Lord Rosebery, became occupied with was, as was to be expected, Armenian reform. He requested the Ambassador in Istanbul, Sir E. Thornton, in June 1886 to remind the Ottoman Empire of the obligations of the 61st article, since there was no other bone of contention left.

Instead of making this request orally, the Istanbul Ambassador preferred to submit a memorandum when he visited the Minister of Foreign Affairs, Sait Pasha, on 16 August 1886. This memorandum had no result other than angering the Ottoman government. The Grand Vizier Mehmet Kamil Pasha even demanded that the memorandum be taken back.

This last attempt of the British was not welcomed by Germany and Austria. In the meantime there was a new Foreign Secretary, Lord Iddesleigh replacing Lord Rosebery. Lord Iddesleigh was compelled to reply to the German and Austrian Ambassadors that the instructions had been sent by the former Foreign Secretary, and that their Ambassador had not felt the need to request a new instruction before making an approach to the Babiali.

3. Armenian preparations for revolt

We have mentioned that, at the beginning of the Berlin Congress, when talking to the British Ambassador, the Armenian Patriarch stated that if revolt was necessary to gain the attention of the European powers, it would not be difficult to achieve. We have also pointed out that the Patriarch, in the speech he made at the Armenian National Assembly after the Berlin Congress, encouraged teachers, radicals, and enthusiastic youth to go to the eastern provinces.

The information coming from the British Consuls in the eastern provinces from 1880 on showed that the Armenians were beginning to be restless. At that time only Russia and Britain had Consulates in the eastern provinces, Britain at Trabzon, Erzurum, Van and Diyarbekir, and Russia at Erzurum and Van.

Reports were coming from the provinces through the governors-general and the security offices to the Ministry of the Interior, but because these were more case reports, and did not include evaluations, and because the Consul's reports in some cases included information given by Armenians, we have preferred to analyse developments on the basis of the latter.

The Consul of Van, Captain Clayton, wrote in his report dated 12 October 1880[22] that he was informed that associations were being formed in Russian Armenia to send weapons to the Armenians of Turkey, and that agents had been engaged for the distribution of these weapons. In November, Clayton stated that the Armenians were preparing to rebel, and that an American missionary in Van had stated that weapons were continuously being sent from Russia. [23]

The Consul of Erzurum, Everett, gave similar information concerning his region, and wrote in his report dated November that it was a certainty that weapons were being gathered in Russia; because it was out of the question that these weapons would be used in Russia, it should be accepted that they were gathered to be used in Turkey. He then stated that the Russian Consul General in Erzurum, M. Obermüller, had confirmed this, but that he did not know what his government thought about it.[24]

On 23 December 1880, the Consul of Izmir, Colonel Wilson, wrote on the basis of the information he had gathered that he had heard that Armenians would want to use force, and that many young people had gone to Istanbul, Tiflis, and Van. He added to his report a memorandum by Lieutenant Herbert Chermside.[25] In this memorandum, the lieutenant wrote that a rebellion movement could be organized in Van; that he had obtained a letter written by a doctor named Rufrenian (who had previously been employed in Turkey, and who had gone to Ighdir in Russia) to his wife, in which he stated that he had become the leader of an organization formed in Russia against Turkey.

The Consul of Van, Clayton, reported in the last days of 1880 that the Russian Consul-General, Major Kamsaraghan, had informed him that the Armenians were preparing to revolt, but that he was trying to persuade them not to. [26]

The Consul of Trabzon, Alfred Bliotti, in his report dated 5 March 1881, gave an account of a discussion he had with the Russian Consul-General of Erzurum. He wrote that the Russian Consul-General had told him that 'the Russian Consul in Van, who is of Armenian origin, was attempting to create incidents in Armenia, that he had reported the situation to his government, but that he was dismissed instead of the Consul'. Bliotti went on to say that the former chief translator of the Istanbul Embassy, Belotsercovetz, had been appointed to the Trabzon Consulate, and that this individual had played a very active role in the Bulgarian rebellion. [27]

At the beginning of 1882, Everett wrote that evidence was increasing that the Armenians were preparing to revolt.[28] The Consul had been provided with two documents, in Armenian, which were used to register volunteers. The first document was used for the oath of loyalty of the volunteer, and the second was used for the employment of the taker of the oath. The Consul General reported that the quality of the paper indicated that they had been printed in Russia, and that the watermarks showed that they could have been printed between December 1880 and August 1881. (When this information was submitted to Dufferin, he instructed the Consul that there was no need to inform the local authorities.)

Everett, in his report of June 1882,[29] stated that he had received his information from totally reliable sources, that the attempts of the Armenians were preparations, that they were working to raise the people's consciousness, to strengthen nationalistic feelings, that the activities extended in the south to Mush and Van, that Van was one of the main centres, that the activities were supported by Russia, and that the main agent was the Russian Consul in Van, Kamsaraghan.

The new Consul of Erzurum, Eyres, in a report he sent to his Embassy on 9 December 1882,[30] wrote that the day before the government had discovered a rebellion attempt of Armenians, that there were about 40 arrests, and that the government knew the identity of approximately 700 participants. (We shall return to this subject on page 130.)

Portakalian was one of those who worked with Hrimyan in Van. When arrests started following the Erzurum incident, and he was forbidden to reside in Van, Portakalian decided to leave the country with some of his followers. He went to Marseilles and in 1885 began to publish there a newspaper, Armenia, which is still published. One of Portakalian's sup-porters, Avetisian, return to Van and organized a revolutionary party, 'Armenakan'.

Following Portakalian, an Armenian group in England began to publish a newspaper, Hayastan. Later, this group succeeded in founding the British-Armenian Committee in England in 1888. This committee, which included some prominent members of the Liberal Party, became one of the most important propaganda centres of the Armenian question.

In 1885, the Armenakan Party was founded in Van, in 1887 the Hunchak Party was founded in Switzerland, followed by the Tashnak Party, and the revolt activities became the responsibility of these parties and committees.

4. Associations and committees

The first association founded by Armenians within the Empire was the 'Benevolent Union' founded in Istanbul in 1860. The aim of this association was to restore Cilicia. The association included such well-known figures as H. Shishmanian, M. Beshiktashian, N. Sivajian, S. Tagvorian, and Dr H. Katibian. It is reported that the association did not secretly get involved in the subject of revolt, but that some of its members took part in the 1862 Zeitun events, and the names of Hasip Shishmanian and Migirdich Beshiktashian are given. [31]

Between 1870 and 1880, the societies of Araratian' in Van, `The Friends of the Schools' and 'The East' in Mush, and `Nationalistic Women' in Erzurum appeared. Later, the 'Araratian', `Friends of the Schools', and 'East' united and formed 'The United Association of Armenians'. In outlook, all of these associations were committed to social affairs. [32]

Revolutionary associations were also founded alongside these societies. In 1878 the association of 'Black Cross' was founded in Van. This association was similar to the Ku Klux Klan in the United States. In 1881 , the association of `The Defenders of the Motherland' (Pashtpan Haireniats) was founded in Erzurum. Its aim was to arm Armenians to protect them from attacks. It was this organization whose activities had been discovered in 1882, and whose members had been arrested. (We shall return to this subject.) This association only lasted for one and a half years, from May 1881 to November 1882.

The first revolutionary political party was the Armenian Party. Although he had nothing to do with the founding of the party, Migirdich Portakalian's name is associated with Armenakan. Portakalian, who was born in Istanbul in 1848, was a teacher who spent many years in Van teaching in the school he had founded, and trained a generation of revolutionaries. [33]

When, in 1885, he was forbidden to reside in Van, as we have mentioned, he went to France and began to publish the *Armenia* newspaper there. Although in the beginning he presented himself as a loyal Turkish citizen, his views changed with time; he became a real revolutionary, and began working on the slogan that independence would not be gained without shedding blood.

In the autumn of 1885, nine individuals who were Portakalian's students founded the Armenakan Party. These nine individuals were Migirdich Terlemezian (Avetisian), Grigor Terlemezian, Ruben Shatavarian, Grigor Adian, Grigor Ajemian, M. Barutjian, Gevord Hanjian, Grigor Beozikian, and Gareghin Manukian. It is believed that Avetisian was the leader of this organization and that he made the contact with Portakalian. Although the newspaper *Armenia* was connected with this party, it never became the official newspaper of the party. Despite the fact that in August 1885 *Armenia* was not allowed to enter Turkey, it continued to be secretly introduced. (In 1886, it was forbidden that the newspaper enter Russia.)

The Party Programme was written by hand in seven or eight copies, and was published for the first time after the Second World War.[34] We summarize it below.

The Party was founded in order to obtain the right of Armenians to rule themselves. Only Armenians can be Party members. To attain its goal, the Party shall unite all patriotic Armenians who share the same cause, shall spread revolutionary ideas, shall teach members to use weapons, shall teach them military discipline, shall provide weapons and money, shall organize guerrilla forces, and shall prepare the people to a general movement. The Party shall be formed of active and auxiliary members; the latter shall only provide financial support. A central organization shall be formed, and regional committees shall be established. The Central Organization shall be formed by representatives of Regional Committees. An additional committee shall be formed to ensure cooperation with other revolutionary groups.

It is also reported that the Russian Consul Major Kamsaraghan gave instruction about using weapons and military strategy in the Armenian School in Van.

It is reported in Nalbandian's book that the known activities of the party were the shoot-out between three revolutionaries disguised as Kurds (Hovannes Agripassian, Vardan Goloshian and Karabet Kulaksizian) and Turkish gendarmes, Avetisian's attack with three accomplices on a Kurdish group, and various murders, including that of police officer Nuri Efendi in Van on 16 October 1892.

There is also a rumour that the Armenakan Party became in time the Ramgavar Party. The two organizations which we must focus on are, without any doubt, the Committees of Hunchak and Tashnak.

(a) The Revolutionary Hunchak Party

In Armenian, Hunchak (Hinchak or Henchak) means Bell. The founders of this party were the children of well-to-do families, who had never set foot in the Ottoman Empire, who were sent to Paris to study, and who had adopted Marxist theory. It is accepted that it was Portakalian and the newspaper *Armenia* which he published that united them. As a matter of fact, Avetis Nazarbekian, who wrote fervent revolutionary articles in the newspaper *Armenia*, was a student in Paris. In the summer of 1886 he went from Paris to Geneva with his fiancée Marian Sardinian. At that time they were both only in their twenties. In Geneva they met four Russian Armenian students, Gabriel Kafian, Ruben

Hanazad, Nicoli Martinian, and Migirdich Manu-charian. All were readers of *Armenia*. Because *Armenia* dwelled on the situation of Armenians in the Ottoman Empire, the main topic of conversation between these six students was how to save the Armenians of Turkey, which they had never seen. Later, Manucharian left the group, but another student, Gevorg Harajian from Montpellier, joined.

This six-member group decided to organize a society, and asked Portakalian to lead them, but did not receive a positive answer. The group then decided to publish another newspaper in response to *Armenia*, and began a campaign to raise money. They applied to the Mekhitarist Monastery in Vienna, and requested Armenian type for a newspaper to be published in Armenian. While waiting for the type they formed a three-member committee (Nazarbekian, Vardanian, and Harajian) towards the end of 1886 and began preparing the programme of the future organization. We give below the main points of the project which was later announced as the programme of the Revolutionary Hunchak Party. [35]

1. The present order must be removed by a revolution and must be replaced by a new society based on economic realities and social justice.

2. The first goal of the Party is to obtain the political and national independence of Turkish Armenia. After having attained this goal, an attempt will be made to reach various political and economic aims. The political aims are:

- the establishment of a Legislative Popular Assembly to be elected with free elections by general and direct vote;
- the election of national representatives from all classes of society;
- extensive provincial autonomy;
- extensive city autonomy;
- the right for every individual to be employed in any office;
- absolute freedom of press, speech, conscience, assembly, organization, and vote;
- general military service.

3. The economic aims shall be established after a careful study of the people's needs and wishes. Probably a progressive tax above a certain income level will be applied.

4. The method to be used to attain goals which will be realized in Turkey through revolution is propaganda, provocation, terror, organization and the peasant and worker movements.

The propaganda will consist of explaining to the people the basic reasons and the appropriate time of the revolt against the Government. Provocation and terror are necessary to increase the people's courage. The main methods of provocation are demonstrations against the Government, not paying taxes, not wanting reform, creating hatred against the aristocratic class. Terror is the method for protecting the people and obtaining their trust in the Hunchak programme. The Party's aim is to use terror against the Ottoman Government, but the Government will not be the only target. Terror will also be used against dangerous Turks and Armenians working for the Government, spies and informers.

5. A special branch will be formed to organize these terrorist activities.

6. The Party shall include a central committee. Two large revolutionary groups shall he formed by workers and peasants. In addition to these groups, bands of guerrillas shall be formed.

7. The most appropriate time to realize the revolution will be when Turkey is at war.

8. Syriacs and Kurds must be won over in the struggle against Turks.

9. After the independence of the Armenia of Turkey, the revolution will be extended to the Armenia of Russia and Iran, and a Federative Armenia will be established.

It appeared that the Hunchak programme was both nationalist and communist. First it based the revolution on class struggle against economic exploitation, and then it aimed at establishing a nationalist state.

It was clear that the students who had drafted the programme had adopted the views of revolutionary Russians; they were in contact with Plekhanov and Zasulich, Russian revolutionaries who were in Geneva.

This project was unanimously accepted by the students, and the Hunchak Party was founded de facto in Geneva in August 1887. However, it was later called, in 1890, the Revolutionary Hunchak Party, referring to the newspaper it published.

The Armenian type arrived in 1887, and the Hunchak newspaper began to be published in Armenian. The Party Programme was published in the October-November 1888 issue.

The economic and social views of the Hunchaks did not find an audience among the middle- and upper-class Armenians in Russia, or in Turkey. The Hunchaks chose Istanbul as their centre of operation, and sent organizers to other regions (Bafra, Merzifon, Amasya, Tokat, Yozgat, Arapkir, Trabzon). The Hunchaks were supported by young people, and began to gather supporters among them in Turkey, Russia, and Iran.

According to Esat Uras, those who came to Istanbul to open the Centre were Shimavon from Tiflis, Megoveryan from Batum, Danielian from Iran, and Rupen Hanazad from Russia.[36] This last was one of the founding members of the Party in Geneva.

The Hunchak Party took responsibility for the demonstrations of Kumkapi and the Babiali, and the rebellions of Sassun and Zeitun. We shall later examine each of these in turn.

When it became apparent that the activities undertaken in Turkey did not produce the desired result, the Hunchak Party was split into two factions. One group claimed that the European powers did not support them because of the socialist ideas of the Party programme. They wanted to exclude all socialist principles from the programme. This difference of opinion resulted in a split into two factions in 1896, the Nazarbekian faction, and the anti-Nazarbekian faction which wanted to abandon socialist ideas. This second faction held a meeting in 1896 in Alexandria and founded the 'New Hunchak Party'. The Revolutionary Hunchak Party held its second general congress in London in 1896 and continued to exist.

(b) The Revolutionary Armenian Federation (Dashnaksutyun)

In Armenian the word Dashnaksutyun means Federation. Because this party was born through the unity of various Armenian groups, especially those in Russia, it was called the Federation. The word was shortened into 'Tashnak' when using it in Turkish.

The factions which gave rise to the federation can be divided into three main groups.

The first, called non-socialist revolutionary nationalists, was formed by individuals who were interested in the independence of the Armenians of Turkey, and who leaned towards the Armenakan Party. Most of them were students studying in St Petersburg, and their spokesman was Konstantin Hatisian, a wealthy Russian Armenian. This group was called the Northerners, based on the name of the boarding house where they gathered (Severnye Nomera = Northern Boarding House).

One group of the socialist revolutionaries wanted to cooperate with Russian and Georgian revolutionaries and abolish the Tsarist regime. A second group focussed only on the Armenians of Turkey. Both socialist groups were generally supported by students in Moscow. They were called the Southerners from the name of the hoarding house where they gathered in Tiflis (Iuzhnye Nomera = Southern Boarding House), Within the group which focused on theArmenians of Turkey there were some who were members of the Hunchak Party.[37]

It is not known how and when these various groups came together. However, it is known that Christopher Mikealian, Stepan Zartan, and Simon Zavarian made unification possible in the summer of 1890, and that Ruben Hanazad took part in the meetings in the name of the Hunchak Party.

It is said that, at the beginning, a secret bureau established in Geneva organized and administered the activities, and that this bureau managed the other members with very strict discipline.[38] Even so, the area where the main activity took place and where the most important leaders were was Tiflis. According to another report, Trabzon was chosen as the centre. Nalbandian, who gives this information, states that `The Central Committee was formed of five members, and most of them continued to live in Tiflis.

These five individuals who were elected to the executive board were C. Mikaelian, S. Zavarian, Abraham Dastakian, H. Loris Malikian, and Levon Sarkisian.[39]

When the federation was formed in 1890, it appeared that the Hunchak Party was included in it. This unity, however, did not last long. The Hunchaks severed their ties with the federation on 5 June 1891, claiming that the Tashnaks were very slow in organizing their activities. Obviously it was hardly practical for the Hunchaks, who had communist tendencies, to remain in the federation.

The Hunchaks were followed by non-socialist leaders such as Konstantin Hatisian. Discontent arose from the fact that the Tashnaks had first announced a Manifesto, before drafting a programme. They decided to hold a General Congress in the summer of 1892, and began to publish the newspaper *Droshak*, one of the Party's official journals.

The programme of the Tashnaks was drafted during this 1892 meeting. The programme stated that the Party would form revolutionary groups to reach its goal by means of revolts, and indicated that the methods of the Russian nihilists would be adopted.[40]

The methods to be used by revolutionary bands organized by the Party were as follows: [41]

1. To propagandize for the principles of the Dasnaksutyun and its objectives, based upon an understanding of, and sympathy with, the revolutionary work.

2. To organize fighting bands, to work with them with regard to the above-mentioned problems, and to prepare them for activity.

3. To use every means, by word and deed, to arouse the revolutionary activity and spirit of the people.

4. To use every means to arm the people.

5. To organize revolutionary committees and establish strong links between them.

6. To stimulate fighting and to terrorize government officials, informers, traitors, usurers, and every kind of exploiter.

7. To organize financial districts.

8. To protect the peaceful people and the inhabitants against attacks by brigands.

9. To establish communications for the transportation of men and arms.

10. To expose government establishments to looting and destruction.

The Party also drafted an organizational regulation and founded the Eastern and Western bureaus. The Eastern bureau included the area east of the Giresun-Harput-Diyarbekir axis, Caucasia, Russia, and Iran. The Western bureau included the area west of Giresun-Harput-Diyarbekir, the Balkans, America, Egypt, and other foreign countries. The Western bureau also organized the activities of these bureaus. [42]

From the moment it was founded, the Tashnak Party was a terrorist organization. While the Hunchak Party wanted to form a politically independent Armenia by uniting the Armenians of Turkey, Russia, and Iran, the Tashnak Party did not even mention the word independence in its 1892 programme. It also did not claim a separation from the Ottoman Empire. Nalbandian states that `the fact that the political goals of the Tashnaks were almost identical to the reform project submitted by the Patriarch Nerses to the Berlin Congress, was expressed in the first editorial of Droshak'. In 1919, during their 9th General Congress, the Tashnaks expanded their programme, and adopted the goal of founding an autonomous and independent Republic by uniting the Armenians of Turkey and Russia.

The Tashnaks, who started their activities as a terrorist organization, assumed responsibility for the attack on the Ottoman Bank, the 1904 revolt in Sassun, and the assassination in Yildiz. In addition there were various other incidents. We shall examine these later.

Let us first make the following observation. Before the Tashnaks appeared as an organized party, they had started their terrorist acts. The Tashnaks had assassinated Gerekjian, the former president of the 'Defenders of the Motherland' Society, in 1891 in Erzurum, acting on the decision taken by the local central committee. Gerekjian's error had been to oppose immediate revolutionary activity and to suggest prudence and preparations. The local central committee had him killed, following the motto that he who is not with us is against us. In 1892, the Tashnak Central Committee disapproved of this assassination, but did not punish Aram Aramian who was responsible for it. [43]

The ideas of rebellion which developed after the Church and the religious factor on one side, and the policies of the powers on the other, had prepared the ground, were easily utilized by the terrorist organizations, and the epoch of rebellions came. In this period, propaganda became a very effective weapon.

5. Terrorist activities, rebellions

Before describing Armenian terrorist activities and rebellions, it will be useful to record various reflections and observations that have been made regarding this topic.

We cited one, from Sydney Whitman, in Chapter 2.[44] During his discussion with the British Consul in Erzurum, Whitman asked whether, in his opinion, any killings would have taken place, if Armenian revolutionaries had not arrived in the country to encourage the people to revolt, and the Consul had replied, 'No, without any doubt, not one Armenian would have been killed'.

We can read the following lines in Price:

> . . . the Capitulations were more than merely a legal process. They constituted a mental attitude toward the Ottoman Government. 'They made it the Western habit to disregard the Ottoman Government and to establish contacts with its subjects quite independently of the existing relations with that country. Under the Capitulations, the West long ago established contact with the Ottoman Government's Christian subjects and a code of governmental conduct was unwittingly built up which the West applied to that Government alone. Under this code, any Ottoman Christian was given the right to rebel against the Government but the Government, although it was the only body charged with the maintenance of peace in the country, was denied the right to put down Christian rebellion. This code the West has applied to no other Government. [45]

Let's take a quatation from Langer, too:

> One of the revolutionaries told Dr. Hamlin, the founder of Robert College, that the Hentchak bands would 'watch their opportunity to kill Turks and Kurds, set fire to their villages, and then make their escape into the mountains. The enraged Moslems will then rise, and fall upon the defenceless Armenians and slaughter them with such barbarity that Russia will intervene in the name of humanity and Christian civilization.' When the horrified missionary denounced the scheme as atrocious and infernal beyond anything ever known, he received this reply: 'It appears so to you, no doubt; but we Armenians have determined to be free. Europe listened to the Bulgarian horrors and made Bulgaria free. She will listen to our cry when it goes up in the shrieks and blood of millions of women and children. . . . We are desperate. We shall do it'. [46]

Hogarth's words are much more impressive:

> The Armenian, for all his ineffaceable nationalism, his passion for plotting and his fanatical intolerance, would be a negligible thorn in the Ottoman side did he stand alone. The Porte knows very well that while Armenian Christians are Gregorian, Catholic, and Protestant, each sect bitterly intolerant of the others, and moreover while commerce and usury are all in Armenian hands, it can divide and rule secure; but behind the Armenian secret societies (and there are few Armenians who have not committed technical treason by becoming members of such societies at some period of their lives) it sees the Kurd, and behind the Kurd the Russian; or, looking west, it espies through the ceaseless sporadic propaganda of the agitators Exeter Hall and the Armenian committees. The Turk begins to repress because we sympathize, and we sympathize the more because he represses, and so the vicious circle revolves. Does he habitually, however, do more than repress? Does he, as administrator, oppress? So far we have heard one version only, one party to this suit, with its stories of outrage, and echoing through them a long cry for national independence. The mouth of the accused has been shut hitherto by fatalism, by custom, by that gulf of misunderstanding which is fixed between the Christian and the Moslem.

In my own experience of western Armenia, extending more or less over four years up to 1894, I have seen no signs of a Reign of Terror. . . . Life in Christian villages has not shown itself outwardly to me as being very different from life in the villages of Islam, nor the trade and property of Armenians in towns to be less secure than those of Moslems.... There was tension, there was friction, there was a condition of mutual suspicion as to which Armenians have said to me again and again, 'If only the patriots would leave us to trade and to till!'. . . . The Turk rules by right of five hundred years' possession, and before his day the Byzantine, the Persian, the Parthian, the Roman preceded each other as over-lords of Greater Armenia hack to the misty days of the first Tigranes. The Turk claims certain rights in this matter-the right to safeguard his own existence, the right to smoke out such hornets' nests as Zeitun, which has annihilated for centuries past the trade of the Eastern Taurus, the right to remain dominant by all means not outrageous. [47]

Sir Mark Sykes wrote the following:

As for the tactics of the revolutionaries, anything more fiendish one could not imagine - the assassination of Moslems in order to bring about the punishment of innocent men, the midnight extortion of money from villages which have just paid their taxes by day, the murder of persons who refuse to contribute to their collection-boxes, are only some of the crimes of which Moslems, Catholics, and Gregorians accuse them with no uncertain voice . . . the Armenian revolutionaries prefer to plunder their co-religionists to giving battle to their enemies; the anarchists of Constantinople throw bombs with the intention of provoking a massacre of their fellow-countrymen.

If the object of English philanthropists and the roving brigands (who are the active agents of revolution) is to subject the bulk of the Eastern provinces to the tender mercies of an Armenian oligarchy, then I cannot entirely condemn the fanatic outbreaks of the Moslems or the repressive measures of the Turkish government. On the other hand, if the object of the Armenians is to secure equality before the law, and the maintenance of security and peace in the countries partly inhabited by Armenians, then I can only say that their methods are not those calculated to achieve success. [48]

We are taking a quatation from Pears:

Under such circumstances the revolt of a handful of Armenians had not a chance of success and was therefore unjustifiable. As a friend to the Armenians, revolt seemed to me purely mischievous. Some of the extremists declared that while they recognised that hundreds of innocent persons suffered from each of these attempts, they could provoke a big massacre which would bring in foreign intervention. Such intervention was useless so long as Russia was hostile. Lord Salisbury had publicly declared that as he could not get a fleet over the Taurus mountains he did not see how England could help the Armenians, much as she sympathised with them. [49]

Dixon-Johnson, a year later, wrote:

The advent of these revolutionary agents into Kurdistan had the inevitable result of embittering the former good relations of the Turkish Government and the resident Moslem population with the Christian, and especially the Orthodox Armenian section of the inhabitants.

This was natural for the reason that in Turkey the people have a horror of secret societies and plots, founded on the experience of their own suffering at the hands of the Greek Hetairia and the Bulgarian Komitadjis. The fears of the Turks and the Kurds were genuine. They believed that the members of the once loyal 'millet-i sadika' (the loyal nation) no longer merited that title, and that they were arming and preparing to massacre the Moslems. The whole country became like a powder magazine. . . . [50]

These passages that we have quoted were taken from books written after the rebellions, and during the First World War, and whose authors were mostly Armenian sympathizers. These books, and others, include many degrading passages about the Armenian character. However, we have preferred to exclude   such passages degrading the Armenian nation as a whole.

We shall cite one more author before examing the events themoolves. the reply of the Armenian representative, Avetis Aharonian, to Lord Curzon on 8 April 1920, when Curzon asked for the Armenians' attacks on the Azerbaijani Turks in Caucasia to be stopped: ' "Your Lordship of course knows that the hone of contention here is our land," I replied. "Zangezour is Armenian; Karabagh is Armenian; Nakhitchevan has been an inseparable part of our land for a thousand years. It is natural that when our enemies are trying to seize our lands we are forced to defend them, no matter what." [51]

(a) The arrest of the 'Defenders of the Motherland'

We have mentioned that the British Consul, Eyres, reported to Istanbul that approximately forty arrests had taken place in Erzurum on 8 December 1882. Those who were arrested were members of the `Defenders of the Motherland' society. The documents obtained by Everett at the beginning of 1882, which pointed to the founding of a revolutionary society, concerned this society.[52] 'The founders of the "Defenders of the Motherland" were Hachatur Kerekchian, Karabet Nishkian, Agop Isgalatsian, Aleksan Yetelikian, Hovannes Asturian, and Yeghishe Tursunian. The society began its activities in May 1881. and within three months had obtained the oath of more than a hundred people. The Erzurum Bishop Ormanian was aware of this, and had informed the Patriarch in Istanbul, who had approved the establishment of the organization.'[53] As soon as the Government officials obtained the oath documents published by the organization, the arrests began. Bishop Ormanian was summoned to Istanbul.

While investigations concerning this matter were still in progress, the British Ambassador Dufferin visited the Sultan, and stated that if reforms were not implemented, Britain would not abide by the Cyprus Agreement.

The case of 76 individuals who were arrested began in 1883 in Erzurum; 40 of them were convicted. Kerekchian was sentenced to 15 years, and the others received sentences of 5-13 years. However, through the continuous mediations and favours of Patriarch Nerses and Bishop Ormanian, most of the convicts were pardoned by the Sultan in July 1884, and founding members such as Kerekchian, Ishgalatsian and Asturian were pardoned in September 1886.

After this date, the Armenakan Society established in Van engaged in a continuous propaganda campaign, through the efforts of Portakalian on the one hand, and of Agopian, who was at the head of the organization in England, on the other. Agopian was immediately informed of every arrest, and presented many petitions to the British Government on this subject.

Here is a very interesting point. In a letter he sent to Salisbury on 29 March 1888, Agopian stated that five innocent individuals had been arrested, and gave their names.[54] One of the five was Migirdich Terlemezian. We have mentioned above that Terlemezian was the founder of the Armenakan Party. It is impossible for us to state whether the British were indeed uninformed of the establishment and aims of this party, or claimed to be unaware. We know, however, that Salisbury, who received this letter from Agopian, sent instructions to the Ambassador in Istanbul, Sir William White, and requested that he investigate the matter. It is impossible not to accept that the Ottoman Government was right to arrest Terlemezian, whose deeds were proclaimed as national heroism after everything was over, and many years had passed. Although the Empire was badly administered in those years, there is no doubt that the authorities had easily obtained information about the events, at a time when informants were prevalent. Possibly the Ottoman administration could have prevented the Armenian rebellion, had the constant intervention, mixed with threats, of the powers not occurred.

(b) The incident of Musa Bey

To report the incident of Musa Bey is useful in that it shows the extent of British interference. It was claimed that Musa Bey, the leader of the Mutki tribe, and one of the feudal princes of the Mush area, had abducted an Armenian girl, had raped her, then had wanted her to marry his brother on condition that she convert to Islam; that, when the girl refused to convert, he had beaten her, and injured one of her eyes. The Patriarchate had reported this incident to the Sultan as an example of the cruelty and torture inflicted on Armenians. Abdulhamid ordered that Musa Bey be tried, and he was summoned to Istanbul.

Because the Armenian Press exaggerated the incident, especially outside the country, the trial which took place in August 1889 was followed by many foreign journalists and the representatives of Embassies in Istanbul. Everything seemed to be normal up to this point. However, the British Ambassador acted almost as a special official to demonstrate his role as the defender of the Armenian people, and engaged in constant attempts to ensure the conviction of Musa Bey. The reader may find the correspondence between the British Embassy and the Foreign Office in the British Archives, in dossier F.O. 424/162. Musa Bey was acquitted at the end of the public trial, but the British Ambassador had made this into a matter of honour. He continued his attempts at the Babiali level and finally the Sultan was forced to send Musa Bey into exile to a distant region. This decision, which was taken about an individual who had been acquitted in court, was unfortunate, not only for the Ottoman Empire, but for the British Government as well.

(c) The shoot-out with the Armenakan band members

A major event in the party's history was the sanguinary encounter between three revolutionaries and some Turkish officials in May 1889. The comrades Karapet Koulaksizian, Hovhannes Agripasian, and Vardan Goloshian, armed with rifles and disguised in Kurdish costume, left the village of Hatvan, in the Salmast district in Persia, for Van, on the night of May 16, 1889. After nine or ten days of travel by foot, they passed the Persian frontier into Turkey. As they proceeded on their journey to Van, they were stopped on the Bashkaleh road near Van by four zaptiehs ('Turkish police) who were accompanying a caravan. The zaptiehs demanded that the three men disarm. When they refused, the zaptiehs fired on them. [55]

The important point to emphasize here is that these three Armenians were disguised as Kurds, and that the zaptiehs fired on them when they refused to disarm. This incident is enough to refute the claim that Ottoman soldiers connived at brigands' attacks on Armenians.

As a result of the firing, Goloshian was killed, Agripasian was seriously injured and Kulaksizian managed to escape unharmed.

These two individuals would have been buried without even their identity being known, had it not been for letters found on them, letters which had come from Portakalian from France and Patighian from England, and which mentioned that a secret society had been founded and that it needed funds and members. However, the documents which were found, and especially the fact that Portakalian, in the letter he sent to Kulaksizian, stated that he had published the information Kulaksizian had given him in his newspaper, and that he asked him to continue sending him such information about the region, made the situation much clearer.

As a consequence, this was a case for the police and at the same time provided the Government authorities with new information about the secret society. It may be assumed that the British Consul did not need to be interested in this case, and if he did, he did not need to go further than to report it. However, the British Consul in Van, Derey, had sent pages of reports with the intention of proving that these individuals were not revolutionaries. [56]

As we examine these events after some 100 years, and see how the British Consuls in the area presented these events which Armenian writers still report with pride, it is easy to understand how propaganda against Turkey was fed and developed. Nevertheless, we must add that not all the British Consuls acted in this manner, although the points which they reported with honesty were not brought into the open in England, owing to the increasing activities of the British-Armenian Society and the Armenian newspapers published in London.

(d) The Erzurum incident

While these secret parties were organized within the Empire, the Hunchak and Tashnak parties were founded outside the country, the Armenian societies were established in France and England, and the fact that they engaged in systematic propaganda against Turkey drove the Babiali and the local authorities to follow the Armenians and their activities closely, the identity of the old `millet-i sadika' began to disappear and the Armenians began to be considered a dangerous element.

On 20 June 1890, a revolt occurred in Erzurum. Let us first note how the incident was described in an article written by Han-Azad (one of the founders of the Hunchak Party), for the anniversary of the incident, in the *Hayrenik* newspaper published in America in 1927.

The founder of the Sanasarian School had died in 1890. The government had been informed that there was a workshop in this school which produced weapons. It was thought that the informers were the Armenian Catholic priests. Two hours before the search, an individual named `Bogos the dog', belonging to the `Defenders of the Motherland' Society, spread the news that the school would be searched. Immediately, national history books, notebooks, objects which would draw suspicion and curiosity were concealed. Nothing was found during the search. Armenians cried out that the entering of the Turks into the Church was filth and indecency. The men of Gerekchian, who was one of the founders of the `Defenders of the Motherland' Society, and who was later killed by the decision of the Erzurum centre of the Dashnaksutyun Committee, began to engage in provocations among the people. Shops were closed, worship in Church was forbidden, bells were not rung. As soon as they were in control of the situation, they seized this opportunity to yell that

Armenians have been free for three days, and that they shall defend their freedom with arms. They demanded that the government reduce taxes and abolish the military conscription tax, that the Church which was desecrated be demolished and built a new, that the 61st article of the Berlin Treaty be implemented. Armenians stayed for 3-4 days in the cemetery, in the Church and in the School yard. Some prominent Armenians, who were trying to disperse the Armenians, were beaten. The order of the government, which demanded that everybody go back to their business, went unheeded. The committee members went around encouraging the people. Meanwhile, Gerekchian's brother shot two soldiers and fighting began in the city, and continued till evening. It was believed that there were many casualties. The following day the Consuls visited the city. There were more than 100 dead on both sides, and 200-300 wounded. . . . [57]

This is the version coming from a Hunchak leader, who was in a position to know the causes of the incident better than anybody else, and is the same, with its incomplete details, as the Ottoman version. The differences in detail were as follows. The denunciation made to the Government was that weapons were produced not only in the school, but also in the church. The church and the school were searched in the presence of the church priest and the school president. (This is the reason for the charges that the church was desecrated.) The revolt did not occur on the day of the search, but the following day (it is obvious from the Armenian version, how the people were provoked). Shots were fired on the soldiers who were sent to establish order, one soldier was killed, and four were wounded. Following this the Muslims and the Armenians who had rebelled began fighting, 8 Armenians and 2 Moslems were killed, 60 Armenians and 45 Moslems were wounded. [58]

The report sent by the British Consul, Clifford Lloyd, to the Embassy clarifies certain points:

The order to search the Armenian institutions in Erzurum had come from Istanbul. This search had created some discontent among the Armenians. They decided to close the shops and schools, and send a letter of protest to the Sultan. The Consul tried to pacify them, and to persuade them to open the shops. The Muslims and the local authorities saw the closing of the shops as an antagonistic act. The governor-general discussed for this reason with the Armenian bishop, and the Bishop who returned to the Church advised the people, but the people began demonstrations against the Bishop. Upon this, the Bishop had asked the help of the soldiers, a battalion of soldiers had arrived, and the Armenians had shut themselves in the Church. It was then that some Armenians had opened fire on the soldiers, had killed two soldiers, and had wounded three. (In the Ottoman version it was stated that there were one dead and four wounded; it is possible that one of the wounded died later.) Upon this the Muslims attacked the Armenians with sticks and daggers, and chased them as far as the neighbourhoods of the Consulates. The British Consul had informed the governor-general and had asked for help. The unit arrived shortly and was in control of the situation. Meanwhile 12 Armenians were killed and 250 individuals were wounded. [59]

The Consul's report does not mention any Muslims who were killed or wounded.

These accounts of the Erzurum incident, from three different sources, are in near agreement. However, the incident was reported in Europe as a massacre of Armenians. Europe accepted that this was a massacre, and the incident entered the literature as the first accusation of massacre concerning Armenian revolts, which would be continued.

The matter did not stop here. The Armenians who were caught and sent for trial, accused of having opened fire on the soldiers, were freed on 28 September as a result of undertakings by the representatives of the great powers in Istanbul (there were 28 accused), and the Attorney-general who had arrested them was dismissed from office.[60] Thus, Gerekchian's brother, whom we know today, through Hanazad's article, had opened fire and killed a soldier, was freed without punishment.

We can assume that this will have encouraged the rebels in the future.

(e) The demonstration of Kumkapi (Kumkapu)

The Hunchakian Revolutionary Party revealed its power for the first time in Constantinople on Sunday, July 15, 1890, when it organized the Demonstration of Kumkapi. The purpose of the demonstration was '. . . to awaken the maltreated Armenians and to make the Sublime Porte fully aware of the miseries of the Armenians.' The demonstration started in the Armenian Cathedral in the Armenian Quarter of Kumkapi. Here Patriarch Khoren Ashikian was addressing a large congregation gathered for the Vartavar (Transfiguration of our Lord) services. In the cathedral, Haruthiun Jangulian, a party member, read a Hunchak protest directed to the Sultan which advocated Armenian reforms. Afterward, he went to the Patriarchate and smashed the 'Turkish coat of arms. Although the Armenian Patriarch protested, he was forced by the Hunchaks to join them in presenting the protest to the Sultan. Hardly had the procession toward Yildiz Palace started when it was blocked by Turkish soldiers, and a riot ensued in which a number of people were killed and wounded. Jangulian, who was considered the Hunchak hero of the demonstration, was arrested and sentenced to life imprisonment. [61]

This account by Nalbandian is accurate, but it is necessary to examine the preparations for the incident in more detail.

First of all, it must be recorded that the Hunchak Party wanted to organize a movement in Istanbul, because the Erzurum revolt, and the incident of Musa Bey, did not produce interest in Europe to the extent that had been expected. This demonstration would be partly against the Babiali and partly against the Patriarch himself, because the Hunchak Party was convinced that the Patriarch Ashikian was not protecting the interest of the Armenian nation. The decision to hold a demonstration was taken by the Istanbul Committee of the Hunchak Party. Among them were prominent individuals such as Hanazad Negovarian and Simeon, but it was decided that these individuals would not take part in the demonstration because they were Russian citizens. The demonstration would be led by Jangulian, Murad and Damadian. Later, Mihran Damadian organized an anti-Turkish demonstration in Athens in July 1891 , and participated in the Sassun rebellion in August 1891. Hamparsoun Boyajian, who was using the nickname of Murad, had also taken part in the Sassun rebellion, and entered the Assembly as the Kozan representative during the Second Constitutional Government. We shall return to him later.

In the Kumkapi Church, the Patriarch, seeing that the situation was out of control, fled to the Patriarchate, but the Armenians also raided the Patriarchate, and tried to put him in a carriage and take him to the palace by threatening him (some say that he was shot at). The soldiers who arrived in response to the request for help of the Patriarchate, brought the situation under control. Jangulian reported the intervention of the soldiers: 'Our men were savagely firing shots one after another at the soldiers, and the soldiers were trying to arrest those who were shooting. 6-7 soldiers fell to the ground, seriously wounded, approximately 10 of them were also wounded. Two of us died.[62] However, two soldiers were killed during the incident.

The Ottoman Minister of Foreign Affairs, in the circular telegram No. 97842/19 that he sent on 30 July 1890 to the Embassies to inform them of the incident, reported that only the Gendarmerie Commander Server Bey had died in the fight; it is therefore apparent that one of the wounded died later. [63]

Jangulian and the other leaders were arrested and tried. On 20 August, Jangulian was sentenced to death, and the others had various sentences. Abdulhamid changed the death sentence to a life sentence. Thus, this demonstration, too, ended without having produced the intervention desired by the Armenians. However, as the German Ambassador in Istanbul stated, 'the Patriarch who was for peace, was sacrificed, and it became apparent that even in the capital of the Empire an Armenian revolt was possible. The propaganda of Armenians living in foreign countries, which encouraged revolt, here too, attained their goal, and endangered the tranquillity of the Armenian community living in Istanbul and its vicinity, who were outside such movements, and who constituted the majority.' [64]

In spite of everything, the Armenians believed that the demonstration of Kumkapi had drawn the attention of Europe to the Armenian question. The Hunchak newspaper, in its issue of 7 September 1890, wrote: `Armenians shall refuse European proposals that are contrary to their supreme objective, and are ready to fight for this cause until their last drop of blood.'

Nalbandian observes: 'These party declarations were bold statements, which, when analyzed, bring up the following questions. How much blood was to be sacrificed for the revolution and who were to die for the cause, only a few Hunchak revolutionaries or numerous Armenian inhabitants of the interior provinces? What would be the value of an independent country whose people had been nearly wiped out in the revolutionary process? The opponents of the Hunchaks were not willing to see a large part of their nation destroyed in order that the Hunchaks might attain a dubious political goal.' [65]

Although the activities of the Armenian Committees were arousing reactions in Europe, they had no effect on the powers at governmental level.

The German chargé d'affaires in St Petersburg stated in his report dated 15 September 1890:

In the most recent meeting I had with Giers [the Russian Minister of Foreign Affairs], he told me that Russia's interest in the Armenian topic was only moral rather than political, and consequently, although they were not uninterested, they were passive. . . . Despite the fact that the articles concerning Armenians of the Berlin Treaty had not yet been implemented, Russia was not interested in them, and was doing nothing to speed their implementation. The British attempts to force Russian involvement in Asia Minor failed. . . . Giers stated that England was the only state which had a political interest in the Armenian question, that the British wanted to establish an independent Armenian principality on the Russian harder, which would prevent Russia from reaching the Mediterranean. He added that Russia had no desire to create a second Bulgaria, and that an autonomous Armenian Principality would constitute a danger, while it would be a temptation for the Armenians in Russia. [66]

The German Ambassador in Istanbul reported the following statements the British Ambassador made in a meeting, in his report to his Ministry dated 28 September 1890:

Sir William White said that an autonomous Armenia was the request of Committees only in foreign countries, and especially in England. that it had been supported only by Mr. Gladstone, and that the present government paid no attention of it. A little while ago, Mr. William Summer, from the Liberal Party, had come here. He was one of the followers of the Armenian question. He had told the British Ambassador that the only reason why Gladstone and himself were interested in the Armenian question, was to create difficulties for the Salisbury cabinet. [67]

But it was impossible for them to stop the Hunchaks. In 1591, the Hunchaks joined the Eastern Federation formed by the revolutionaries of Macedonia, Albania, Crete and Greece, in order to synchronize their activities. As we have mentioned above,

Mihran Damadian organized a large demonstration against Turkey in Athens in July 1891. In 1892, various incidents occurred in some of the provinces of Turkey.

(f) Other incidents before the Sassun rebellion

At the beginning of 1891 , Abdulhamid declared an amnesty for Armenians. As a result, Armenians when had been arrested were freed. 76 Armenians who were thus freed in Istanbul went to the Patriarchate and gave an oath that they would never take part in such movements again. [68]

However, the agents of the Hunchak Party continued their activities. The hostile and false propaganda outside the country became increasingly harsh. A claim was made that Armenians were being forced to convert to Islam.

The following statements of the Armenian Bishop of Izmir, Melchizedech, against the claim that Armenians were being forced to convert, are worth recording:

Our devotion to truth makes a duty for us to say that the Ottoman Government has given clear instructions to have those who wish to convert to the religion of Islam, sent to their own religious leaders, for a last suggestion to keep their old faith, let alone torture us, or restrict our religious freedom. As the Bishop of Izmir, I have personally witnessed many similar cases. [69]

These statements, however, fell on deaf ears.

Now, the revolutionaries had begun to collect funds for their 'national cause', by sending anonymous letters to wealthy Armenians, threatening them. This activity was especially practised in Van. Naturally, this led to more arrests. Similar cases occurred in Harput, and in Arapkir.

In March 1892, 250 Armenians who had petitioned the Russian Government to be under its protection were arrested. Those who were arrested usually received short prison sentences. Invariably, these incidents were used by the Committee in London and by Garabet Agopian as examples of Turkish oppression.

In the summer of 1892, Gladstone was returned to power. This gave even more hope to the revolutionaries.

In December 1892 they attempted to assassinate the governor-general of Van. [70]

In the summer of 1892, an organization was established which would ensure the systematic distribution of various pamphlets and other publications published outside the country and which encouraged Armenians to rebel. For this reason, Merzifon was chosen as the centre because of its proximity to the Samsun harbour, and branches were established in Kaiser, Yozgat, Chorum, and other areas. From 1893 on, posters began to be posted on the walls.

In January 1893, placards were posted in Amasya, Merzifon, Chorum, Tokat, Yozgat, Ankara and Diyarbekir, directly accusing the Sultan, declaring that he was incompetent and that a great state which ruled millions of Muslims would soon come to help.

Upon this, various suspect Armenians were arrested in these cities. Armenians claimed that these placards had been posted by Muslim fanatics. ('The announcements had been signed by the Patriotic Muslims Committee.) Nalbandian records that these announcements had been posted by Armenians, referring to Max Balian, who was one of them. [71]

The same placards had been posted on the walls of the Anatolian College belonging to the American missionaries in Merzifon. (Years later, Max Balian stated that he himself had posted these placards.) Tumanian and Kayayan, who were among the school teachers, were arrested. Bliss states that these two professors had been arrested without any evidence. [72] He also states that 'The Armenians said that the placards were posted by the Turks; the Turks returned the charge upon the Armenians. Just where. the truth is, it will probably be some years before it is possible to state with accuracy. [73]

The fact that they were posted by the Armenians has been proved today through their own confessions. We find the following statement in Nalbandian's book: 'We are informed by Aderbed (Sarkis Mubehadjian) of the Hunchak Committee, that Tumanian was carefully followed by the Government, and that since the beginning of 1891, he and the other Hunchaks were consulting with one another and planning a revolution against the State.'[74]

This shows that the Ottoman authorities, in spite of maladministration, were not totally unaware of the situation, and that the arrests, as stated by Bliss, had not arisen out of a hatred against a missionary school. Despite this, these two professors, who had been arrested, were pardoned by Abdulhamid.

Again, at the beginning of April 1893, Abdulhamid declared a general amnesty for the Armenians who had been arrested in various provinces for posting placards, and they were subsequently freed. Naturally, those who had been arrested for murder and other common crimes did not benefit from this amnesty. Their trial took place in Ankara. Five individuals were sentenced to death, and others received various prison sentences. The sentences were carried out.

The revolutionaries continued their activities in Merzifon. Finally, in September 1593, the authorities found the house in which this group was operating, and the house was raided. The Armenians who were in the house opened fire and threw a bomb at the soldiers. Twenty-five soldiers died or were wounded; 4 of the Armenians were caught dead, and the other 4 alive.

In December 1893, an Armenian revolt occurred in Yozgat. In this city too, shots were fired at the soldiers, but the incident was crushed before it got out of control.

On 27 April 1894, there was an attempt to assassinate the Patriarch Ashikian in Istanbul. The Armenian aggressor was arrested. The Patriarch resigned after this incident.

On 4 August 1894, an Armenian band attacked the mail coach, killed the courier, and stole the mail. They were caught after they fought with the detachment which had been sent after them, after having killed a gendarmerie sergeant.

Finally, in August 1894, the Sassun rebellion began.

(g) The first Sassun rebellion

It is said that the Sassun rebellion began with simple confrontations between various tribes of the area (Bekhranlu, Hayanlu, Yapanlu, Vilikan) and Armenians, but the truth is more complicated.

Mihran Damadian, who was one of the organizers of the Kumkapi demonstration in Istanbul, had escaped from Istanbul to Athens, had returned to Turkey after the Athens demonstration of July 1891 , had arrived at Sassun, where he organized a band, and had begun to encourage the people to rebel. This Damadian band had raided the village of Avzim in Mush in December 1892, killed a Turk named Sergeant Ishak in the street, and fled. Subsequently, the Gendarmerie had pursued the band. In 1893 army commanders informed Istanbul that the bands were increasing.

In June 1893, Armenian bands killed a member of the Hayanlu tribe; upon this, the tribes of Bekhranlu and Hayanlu attacked Taluri to take revenge. A few people died on both sides. The tribes retreated because the Armenians were better organized. As soon as the incident was known, soldiers were sent to the region and brought the situation under control.

During the activities of the bands in 1893, Damadian was caught wounded, and sent to Istanbul. He was later freed there.

When Damadian was still in the region, Hamparsum Boyajian, with the nickname Murad, came to the area, and cooperated with him. After Damadian was arrested, he continued the preparations for rebellion. Boyajian's aim was to incite the Armenians to attack the local tribes, provoke intervention by the army, and thus stir up Europe by claiming that Armenians were being massacred.

Naturally, Boyajian did not express this aim. He told the Armenians of Taluri that he had come from Europe; that if they rebelled, the European powers would intervene and found an Armenian state. It is known that Boyajian's activities were successful, especially in Shirik, Semal, Gulguzar, Herenk, and Taluri. Those who participated in the revolt were from these areas.

The Armenian villages of the Sadak township remained outside the events. It is a fact that Murad succeeded in inciting 3,000 Armenians to rebel, including those who came from Mush, Koulp, and Silvan.

It was even stated in the report compiled by the foreign Consuls who were included in the investigative delegation sent to the region after the incidents that Damadian and Boyajian had arrived in the region with a concealed political aim, and had attempted to create confrontations between Armenians and the other inhabitants of the region. [75]

The Boyajian band organized many attacks on various tribes of the area in 1894. They pillaged the properties of the Bekhran and Zadian tribes. They killed more than ten individuals during separate attacks, including the son of a prominent member of the Bekhran tribe. These incidents gave rise to an armed confrontation between the Bekhran tribe and the Armenians. The Armenians, who had expected such a confrontation, retreated and gathered on the Antok mountain, where they had previously sent their women and children. (The fact that all the children, women, and cattle had been sent before, was even included in the Consuls' report: Document No. 31, p. 136.)

When the Government heard of the events, it sent soldiers to the region. The Armenians who had retreated to the Antok mountain resisted the soldiers with arms. After a quick operation, the rebellion was crushed. [76] It is known that the insurrection began in mid-August and ended on 23 August with Murad's arrest.

This rebellion gave rise to much anti-Turkish propaganda in Europe. For example, A. W. Williams cites the following statement made by an Armenian native of Sassun: 'There is hardly a man left alive in Sassun, and pleading women and little children, all together, old and young, have been sacrificed by the swords of the Turkish soldiers. They besieged the village from the last of April until the first of August, and during all these weeks we fed on vegetables and the roots of grasses.' Again according to Williams, 6,000 Armenians were killed in Sassun. [77] The soldiers arrived in Sassun on 14 August. (Williams notes this on p. 327 of his book, but sees no inconsistency in quoting the above account four pages later.)

Bliss does not fall short of Williams. Then followed a general attack upon the different villages. The Armenians had the better situation, and defended themselves with considerable success. . . . The result was that for nearly three weeks from the latter part of August there was a general campaign of butchery. So bitter was the contest, that the Governor of Mush, fearing that he had not sufficient force at hand, sent word to the general commander of the Turkish forces in Eastern Turkey.' [78] According to Bliss, more than 6,000 Armenians were killed.

Pastermadjian writes that the Ottoman soldiers used the confrontation between the tribes and the Armenians as an excuse and engaged in massacring the Armenians of the area, butchering 3,500 of 12,000 Armenians. [79] But he does not mention the fact that the Armenians put up armed resistance to the soldiers, and does not explain why the 12,000 Armenians had not all been killed if the aim was to get rid of Armenians.

With regard to the number of Armenians killed, we find the best reply to this exaggeration, which was to constitute an example to the future rebellions, in the Consuls' report and in the British documents.

In my opinion, before making an observation, we should first examine the region. The Taluri valley, which was the area of the rebellion, is a mountaineous area to the south of the plain of Mush. The region has many villages which are in close proximity to one another. Some of the villages are inhabited by Armenians, and some by Muslims. Very few of the villages are mixed. According to Cuinet's statistics. there were 8,369 Armenians in the entire Sassun region.

It is stated in the Consuls' report that the number of those who were reported dead, and whose names were established, was 114 individuals in the village of Shenik, 65 in Semal, 40 in Guliguzar, 22 in Ahgpi, 10 in Ispagank, and 14 in Taluri, the total being 265 individuals. [80] The British representative who took part in the delegation of Consuls states in his memorandum dated 12 October that, taking as a basis the number of houses, it would be established that there were at most 10,000 Armenians in the region, and that taking into consideration those who were alive, the number of those who had died could not exceed 900. [81]

The interesting point is that nobody mentioned the number of Muslims who were killed.

The Sassun rebellion ended, as we have mentioned above, on 23 August, 1894.

However, the repercussions of this rebellion in Europe once again brought Britain to the fore. Britain suggested that the powers which had Consuls in Erzurum should each send a representative along with the Commission of Enquiry. While theBritish Ambassadors in Paris and St Petersburg were suggesting this, the British Ambassador in Istanbul forced the Babiali to accept it. As France and Russia accepted the British suggestion, the Consuls or representatives in Erzurum of the three powers went to the area. Even the report dated 20 July 1895, which they prepared in common, could not prove that the Armenians had been innocent and that they had been massacred. (The report of the Turkish delegation is included in the Yildiz Palace Archives; Documents of the year 1312 on Armenian affairs No. 666: 302-180595-1.)

In order to find the original report today, one must apply to the official archives. In the references made in Armenian books to this report, generally Damadian and Boyajian are not mentioned.

The subject of the Sassun rebellion was thus closed.
This rebellion gave Britain the chance to involve France and Russia, and to make a new joint attempt in the matter of reform. We shall return to this attempt, which began the second period of pressure on the Babiali, and the developments which followed it, after the discussion of the rebellions.

(h) The Babiali demonstration .

In the years 1895-6, there were Armenian rebellions or attempts at rebellion in many provinces of Anatolia. Most of them lasted for one or two days; only the rebellion of Zeitun and the second rebellion at Sassun kept the Babiali busy for long. We shall leave these two rebellions to last, and first quickly examine the others. Although departing from chronological order, it is useful to examine first the Babiali demonstration, which can be considered the most important, owing to its repercussions. Nalbrandian writes:

In the Turkish capital there were two separate Hunchak committees. One was the Board of Directors; the other was the Executive Committee. The Board gave instructions for nearly all of the revolutionary activity in Turkey, with the knowledge and approval of the General Headquarters at Geneva. The Executive Committee of Constantinople directed the organizational work according to the instructions of the Board of Directors. The members of the Board of Directors and the Executive Committee did not know one another, but there was complete cooperation between them. This cooperation was achieved by having one man, called the Representative of the Two Committees, who acted as the intermediary between the two groups.

The Executive Committee, after receiving the order from the Board of Directors to organize the Demonstration of Bab Ali, chose three men to supervise the project. The leader was Karo Sahakian (Hevehili Karon). Patriarch Mattheos Ismirlian, hearing rumors of a demonstration, called Karo and asked if the rumors were true. If there was to be a demonstration, the Patriarch insisted that it should be a peaceful one. Karo also wished a peaceful demonstration, but some members of the Committee did not agree; the matter was left to the Board of Directors, who decided that it should be peaceful.

Months of secret preparations ended on September 16/28, 1895. On that day the Hunchaks presented a letter, written in French, to the foreign embassies and to the Turkish government. [82]

As can be seen, the Patriarch was aware of the matter from the beginning, as he knew the individual named Karo (and probably his position in the Hunchak Committee.)

This letter dated 28 September. signed by the Revolutionary Committee, stated that 'The Armenians of Constantinople have decided to make shortly a demonstration, of a strictly peaceful character, in order to give expression to their wishes with regard to the reforms to be implemented in the Armenian provinces. As this shall not be an aggressive one, an intervention by the police or the Armed Forces to prevent it could create remarkably unfortunate results, and the responsibility will not fall on us.'

In this letter, two points call for attention. First, despite the fact that such demonstrations were forbidden in Istanbul, the Hunchaks submitted their decision, without even asking permission. Second, they declared before-hand that in the event of intervention, unfortunate results could occur.

The French Ambassador in Istanbul, Paul Cambon, summarized the development of the incident, in report No. 174 which he sent to his Ministry, dated 3 October:

. . . the origin of the September 30 bloody demonstration is now evident. In the beginning, the date of the demonstration had been established as September 22nd, but for various reasons, this was postponed to the later date.

On Saturday, September 28th, (received the letter which I have enclosed [the letter quoted above] from the secret Istanbul Hunchak Committee. The Committee stated that they had decided to hold a peaceful demonstration, and declared beforehand that they would not be responsible for the results in the event of intervention. This letter was also sent to the other Embassies, the Ministry of Gendarmerie, and the office of the Attorney General.

The Ottoman Authorities did not rely upon this assurance and took dispositions to prevent the demonstration, in case of necessity with force. [The Ambassador's logic is interesting. He seems to think that it was necessary for the government to remain inactive, when it received the communication of this secret revolutionary committee.] On the morning of Monday, September 30th, I received a petition. The said demonstration had begun as I received the petition.

At nine a.m. a crowd including men, women, and children, went to the Armenian Patriarchate. It was the Epiphany day, and the Church was full of people, where, the day before, 5,000 people had been baptized, possibly in the desire to be killed in battle. The Patriarch, who was at his summer residence in Buyukdere, had returned the night before to Kumkapi when the event was announced. [We are informed by Nalbandian that the Patriarch had been told of the event much earlier.] The people demanded to see him. They told him the miserable condition of the Armenian nation . . . and announced their decision to give a petition to the Grand Vizier, as the reforms had not been implemented. The Patriarch tried to dissuade them, told them that he could give the petition himself, and asked that the crowd disperse. [We know that he wanted the demonstration to be peaceful.] The Armenians did not accept this. . . . They wanted the Patriarch to accompany them. Izmirlian tried to explain to them that this was not possible.

Meanwhile another group gathered in Sultanahmet at the beginning of a street going to the Babiali, and the crowd increased with Armenians coming from every direction.

In my telegrams Nos 128 and 131 , I reported a march of 2,000 people. [The Ambassador's telegram No. 131 is interesting. In that telegram he reports the march in the following manner: 'The Kum Kapu group gathered behind the Patriarchate Church. The Sultanahmet group, which was approximately 2,000 people, marched to the Babiali between 10 and 11 p.m., led by a priest.' Is it possible to claim that the Patriarch could not control the priests?] In front of the iron door of the Babiali, an officer who was at the head of the gendarmes tried to stop them. The Armenians stated that they wanted to give a petition to the Grand Vizier, that they would give the petition and disperse if they were let alone. The officer told them that he would not permit their passage, and told them to disperse. As the Armenians refused, he ordered the gendarmes to disperse the crowd. However, after many demonstrators had been beaten with rifle-butts, an Armenian fired a shot and killed the officer. Your Excellency knows very well how demonstrations turn into armed confrontations. Soon, the dead and the wounded were piled around.[83]

Let us turn now to the observations of the British Ambassador:

As I telegraphed to your Lordship on the 30th ultimo, a communication bearing the seal of the 'Hindchag', the Armenian Revolutionary Committee, was addressed to the Embassies on the 28th ultimo, stating that a strictly peaceful demonstration was about to be made by the Armenians in order to express their desire for reforms. . . . The demonstration took place on the 30th ultimo, but unhappily it had not the peaceful character attributed to it. The demonstrators were armed with pistols and knives of a uniform pattern which had no doubt been issued to them by the organizers of the movement.

There is good reason to suppose that the object of the 'Hindchag' was to cause disorder and bloodshed with a view to inducing the Powers of Europe to intervene on behalf of the Armenians.

It is stated that 3,000 persons took the Sacrament in the various Armenian churches on the preceding Sunday in order to be prepared for death.

On the morning of the 30th ultimo, crowds of Armenians assembled in various quarters of the town, the largest assemblage being in the Armenian quarter of Koum Kapou. They proceeded towards the Porte in numbers, estimated by eye-witnesses at about 2,000, though this is probably an exaggeration.

The authorities appear to have taken some steps to organize a counter-demonstration, and it was observed that an unusual number of Softahs and other Turks armed with sticks were collected in the streets.

The police appear to have made some effort to induce the crowd to retire peaceably.

According to the statement made by the Minister of Police to one of the Dragomans of the Embassy, he deputed Server Bey, a Major in whom he had special confidence, to urge the crowd to disperse.

On their refusing to do so, and stating their intention of proceeding to the Porte, he ordered his men to drive back the crowd with the flat of their swords and the butt-end of their muskets. At the same time, two mounted gendarmes seized upon the leader of the procession, who carried the Memorial which it was intended to present to the Porte. Shots were then exchanged. [84]

In another telegram, the British Ambassador stated: '. . . Shots were exchanged, and the officer of the gendarmerie was killed. About fifteen gendarmes and sixty Armenians fell. The police then dispersed the Armenians, pursuing them and arresting large numbers. [85]

In another telegram he stated: 'It appears that the police charged the Armenians and struck them with the butt of their muskets and flat of their swords, and seized upon their leaders; but there seems no doubt that it was the Armenians who fired the first shot. [86]

We can read the government version in the report of Nazim Pasha, the Minister of Gendarmerie:

The Armenian organizations held a meeting on September 30th in the church of the Patriarchate. . . . It was investigated that they wanted to create an insurrection by attacking the Babiali, and obtain the intervention of Europe. The superintendent of the police, Husnu Bey, was sent to the Patriarchate and the situation was explained to the Patriarch.

The Patriarch said that there was not enough time, that the people were also desperate, that he could not be much help, and thus showed that although he was capable of preventing an attempt at revolution, he did not wish to prevent it.

Under these circumstances . . . we had recourse to preventive measures. . . . The Police and the Gendarmerie were given the order to refrain from force and shooting . . . that the crowd he dispersed without shedding blood . . . by the mounted gendarmes.

. . . . A group of individuals from the crowd of more than 1,000 who had gathered in the church went to the Patriarchate and spoke there, then they began walking armed with pistols and daggers. The crowd increased in number as they were joined in Divanyolou by companions coming from various quarters. . . . In spite of warnings made until the last moment, they did not hesitate to reply by firing shots. . . . They brutally killed Major Servet Bey, a member of the Istanbul Gendarme regiment in front of the people. Then they fired shots on the Muslim and Christian people they encountered, and on the gendarmes on duty, and wounded many individuals.[87]

As can be seen, these three versions are in agreement, the only exception being that the report of the Embassies does not mention the fact that the superintendent of police had gone to the Patriarch. There is no reason to doubt that he had.

As the Armenians fired shots and killed a few privates along with Server Bey, the police and the gendarmes opened fire. The Armenians then began to the in various directions, and continued to fire shots indiscriminately on the people as they made their escape.

Incidents continued after 30 September. Armenians opened fire on the people collectively from the quarters they resided in. Incidents occurred in Chukur Cheshme, Kasimpasha, Karagumruk, Eyub, and Vanikeuy, and there were armed confrontations between Muslims and Armenians.

The Embassies' telegrams and the report of the Minister do not include the number of dead and wounded. If it is possible to believe Lepsius, 172 Armenians died in this incident.[88] Bliss gave the same figure. We have not found another figure anywhere else.

It can be assumed that the majority of the persons who died were killed, not during the incident, but during the confrontations between Muslims and Armenians which occurred after the incident. The incidents were suppressed by the army troops, as they took control of every quarter of the city.

The following statement was made by the German Ambassador, Saurma, in the report he sent to his Ministry, dated 6 October:

All the Armenian rebellion attempts here and there, are organized by the revolutionary committees. This is, in anycase, recorded in their programme. However, the Turkish Government had to be prepared, and had to have prevented, by using the army troops, which have now occupied Istanbul, armed confrontations between the antagonistic demonstrators, as they occurred the last time.

Most of the Armenians here have not taken part in this.

Only a group of them, those who were scared by the revolutionary committees who took arms and money, participated in the demonstration.

For this reason, a very unfortunate panic occurred, and it can be assumed that the Committees will take advantage of it, and new excesses may be expected. [89]

It may well be that the German Ambassador was right to some extent, that the Government had to give orders to the troops beforehand. However, as the French Ambassador stated, mass psychology must be kept in mind. The Ambassador stated that the Government did not trust the assurance that this would he a strictly peaceful demonstration, and took measures to prevent it. However, it is apparent that the Government did not take adequate measures thinking that the Armenians would not attack with arms, that the demonstration would, after all, be held peacefully, and that it could easily be dispersed by mounted gendarmes. When events occurred contrary to these expectations, and the Muslims were agitated, it naturally took time to control every quarter of the city. Moreover, it is also apparent that Armenians again opened fire

on the police from their hideouts. It is of course usual to attempt
to arrest those who participate with arms in a demonstration by
a revolutionary organization. The incidents caused by those
who resisted the investigations led to the continuation of the
confrontations.

The Babiali demonstration, having prepared the ground for
concluding the joint attempt made by Britain, France, and Russia
concerning the reforms after the Sassun rebellion, was hailed by
the Hunchak Party as their own victory.

(i) Incidents in other cities during 1895-6

After the three powers made a joint attempt at reform,
following the Sassun rebellion, the Hunchak Committee decided to
bring its activities to the final stage. It was assumed that the reform
which was considered and whose preparations had begun could
thus lead on to independence.

It was stated in a report sent by the British Embassy in
Istanbul to the Foreign Office, dated 18 July 1895, that 'The
Armenian Committees are determined to provoke another
massacre and it is rumoured that they are preparing rebellions in
various areas.'[90]

This information of the British Embassy was not inaccurate.
As a matter of fact, many incidents created by Armenian
revolutionaries in every part of the country occurred in 1895.

Let us examine these incidents chronologically.

On 1 July 1895, Karabet Kuyumjuian, who did not want to
take in the Hunchak Committee, was killed in Merzifon.

On 12 July, the Turkish School in Merzifon was set afire; 30
houses, 20 shops and 3 inns were also burnt in the fire that spread.

In August a fire was started in Amasia; 58 houses, 16 shops,
2 inns, 1 mosque, 1 Muslim theological school, 1 dervish lodge and
1 Turkish school were burnt.

All the British Consuls in Anatolia stated that in the months
of July and August 1895 the activities of the Committee had
reached such a point that incidents could occur at any time. We do
not see the necessity of citing each of these reports. Those who wish
may find them in the British Blue Books Turkey No. 1 (1896) and
No. 2 (1896).

These preparations made by the Committee gave results
which were in their interest. Almost in every province insurrections
of a similar nature occurred approximately at the same time.

We give below the dates and localities of these insurrections or
disorders in chronological order. In most cases, these incidents also
spread to the neighbouring townships and villages.

In parenthesis are given the names of the provinces, according to the administrative division of that time.

29 September 1895 - Divrighi (Sivas)
2 October 1895 - Trabzon
6 October 1895 - Eghin (Elaziz)
7 October 1895 - Develi (Kayseri)
9 October 1895 - Akhisar (the gubernatorate of Izmit)
21 October 1895 - Erzinjan (Erzurum)
25 October 1895 - Gumushane (Trabzon)
25 October 1895 - Bitlis
26 October 1895 - Baybourt (Erzurum)
27 October 1895 - Marash (Aleppo)
30 October 1895 - Erzurum
2 November 1895 - Diyarbekir
2 November 1895 - Siverek (Diyarbekir)
4 November 1895 - Malatia (Elaziz)
7 November 1895 - Harput (Elaziz)
9 November 1895 - Arapkir (Elaziz)
15 November 1895 - Sivas
15 November 1895 - Merzifon (Sivas)
16 November 1895 - Antep (Aleppo)
18 November 1895 - Marash (Aleppo)
22 November 1895 - Mush (Bitlis)
3 December 1895 - Kayseri (Ankara)
3 December 1895 - Yozgat (Ankara)

Let us now examine quickly the reasons and the manner in which the most significant of these incidents started.

The Trabzon incidents began when the former governor-general of Van, Bahri Pasha, and the Trabzon commander, Hamdi Pasha, were attacked on Wednesday, 2 October 1895 (20 September 1311) by two Armenians, and were wounded. The aggressors, who escaped, had been pursued, and measures had been taken to prevent an incident occurring in the city. The actual incident began when an Armenian named Shinark opened fire on the people from the balcony of an inn on 8 October, upon hearing that a relative of his had died during the Istanbul incident. The Muslims and the Armenians began to fight and the incident was stopped by the intervention of the army. [91]

The incident in Erzinjan began when a few Armenian volunteers shot a few Muslims on 21 October in the local weekly market place. The army brought the situation under control. [92]

The incident which occurred in Bitlis on 25 October 1895 began when Armenians attacked a mosque as the Muslims were praying in the Friday noon service. An investigation showed that the Protestant missionary George had provoked the incident. [93]

The incident which occurred in Marash on 27 October began when Armenians opened fire on Muslims. [94]

The Erzurum incident of 30 October began when a group of armed Armenians entered the Government Office with the aim of assassinating the governor and the staff, and killed the gendarmes who encountered them.[95] The incident spread when fire was opened on the soldiers who arrived there, and was crushed with difficulty.

The incident in Diyarbekir began on 2 November, when shots were fired on the Muslims who were praying in the mosque for the Friday noon service. In the fire that was later started, mosques and Muslim theological schools, as well as shops, 90 per cent of which belonged to Muslims, were destroyed. [96]

The Malatya incident began on 4 November, when a Muslim named Hemo went to the barbershop to be shaved, and the Armenian barber, Ehlijanoghlu Serkis, cut his throat with a razor and killed him.

The Harput incident began on 7 November, when an Armenian named Baghjian Kirkor fired shots from his house and wounded three Muslims named Hoca Mustafa Efendi, Vartafilli Ali Efendi, and Bekir Efendi.

The year 1895 ended with such confrontations between Turks and Armenians. Armenian sources give unbelievable figures for the number of dead as a result of these confrontations, which lasted for a day or a few days. Naturally the figures are not supported by any document, and nowhere is it mentioned how many Muslims lost their lives. Moreover, the fact that almost all these figures are in the hundreds or thousands, without any variance, indicates how these figures were computed.

The Ottoman Government established the number of Muslims and non-Muslims who were killed or wounded as a result of the confrontations in 1895. [97]

	Men		Women		Children		Total	
	Dead	Wounded	Dead	Wounded	Dead	Wounded	Dead	Wounded
Muslim	1,683	1,409	134	23	11	1	1,828	1,433
Non-Muslim	8,247	2,049	401	184	59	5	8,717	2,238
Total	9,930	3,458	535	207	70	6	10,545	3,671

The overall table, which will be published among the Ottoman documents, gives an account of the townships within the provinces one by one, as well as the number of dead and wounded for men, women, and children within each community.

According to this list, the total of those who were killed during the confrontations in 1895, having added the figure 72 given by Lepsius for those who died in the Babiali demonstration to the list of the Armenians who were killed, is 10,617, 1,828 of which were Muslims, and 8,789 were non-Muslims.

In 1895, apart from the incidents we have enumerated, a rebellion occurred in Zeitun. However, we shall include those why died in this rebellion in the 1896 total, because this rebellion lasted until that year.

In our opinion, the fact that the number of wounded is relatively low is because it included only those who were brought to the hospital to be treated. Otherwise, in these confrontations where 10,545 people died, the number of wounded must have exceeded 3,671.

(j) The Zeitun rebellion

Zeitun was a township centre, under the jurisdiction of the province of Marash, by a stream which was the confluent of the Ceyhan river at the foot of the Berit mountain; it was located in a very mountainous and unfruitful area. (Its name today is Suleimanli.)

The inhabitants of Zeitun claimed that they had received a decree from Sultan Murad IV exempting them from taxes, since they had asserted that they lived in a very poor region, and had no means. According to their claim, through this firman which they said had been destroyed in a fire in 1884, the Sultan had fixed the annual tax for the town of Zeitun at 15,000 kurush, and had ordered that no other Sultan might modify this firman, and that Ottoman officials were not to reside in the town. [98]

The very idea that a Sultan such as Murad IV, who struggled the most with the rebellious tribes of Anatolia, could have decreed such a firman is absurd. However, the inhabitants of Zeitun who rebelled, giving as an excuse this fictitious firman, were a rebellious community unequalled in Anatolia. Esat Uras has enumerated the rebellions which occurred in Zeitun to 1852 on pp. 488-9 of his book:

The Governor of Marash, Omer Pasha, ordered that the taxes be directly paid to Marash during the 1774 Russo-Ottoman war: as a result a rebellion occurred in 1780, during which Ömer Pasha was killed, and Zeitun was besieged for 7 months. After Omer Pasha, Ali Pasha started action against Zeitun in 1782, and was defeated in the area of Göredin.

In 1808, Kalender Pasha, a sanjak governor of Marash, came to Zeitun and besieged the town for 9 months, and forced the inhabitants to accept a tax of 6 purses of gold.

In 1819, as Chapanoghlu Jelal Mahmut Pasha was returning after having punished the son of Hulbul in Aleppo, he marched on Zeitun at the request of the inhabitants of Marash, but did not obtain any result.

In 1829, the Governor of Kayseri, Köse Mehmet Pasha, was sent, but was unable to obtain anything substantial.

In 1832, Beyazitoghlu Suleiman Pasha marched on Zeitun, and tried to disseminate discord among them.

After Suleiman Pasha, Tosun Pasha imprisoned some inhabitants of Zeitun in 1835 for the accumulated 7-year tax debt; the Zeitunites retorted by abducting various prominent members of Marash. The two sides compromised by releasing the prisoners.

In 1836, the incident of Deli Keshish occurred when Topalian was killed in Marash.

In 1840, the Akchadagh operation was organized.

In 1842 an armed confrontation occurred with the inhabitants of Tejer.

In 1852, Mustafa Pasha of Scutari, the sanjak governor, marched on Zeitun for their tax debt of 150,000 kurush.

In 1853 the first 'ideological preacher', Melikian Ardzruni Hovagim, came to Zeitun from Constantinople and acquired a very important administrative position. Hovagim, among other things, took steps to strengthen the defenses of the town. To secure additional funds for this purpose, he planned a journey to Russia in 1854. The Ishkhans (local notables) tried to discourage him from making the trip because of the dangers he might encounter as a result of the Crimean War then in progress. Disregarding these warnings, Hovagim started on his unsuccessful mission. In Erzurum he was arrested and hanged by the Turkish authorities.

Hovagim's presence in Zeitun, together with his contemplated journey to Russia, indicates the national character of his activity. It implies that as early as the 1850's Armenians in Constantinople had direct interests in Zeitun and that the Armenians in Russia were concerned with the political situation in Turkish Armenia. [99]

Another rebellion broke out in Zeitun in 1862. This time, the Bahiali sent a bigger force to crush the rebellion. The inhabitants of Zeitun, through their connections in Istanbul, requested the mediation of the French. Their connections were members of the Benevolent Union. As a result of the French mediation, the forces which had been sent were called back.

During the 1877-8 Russo-Ottoman War, there was another rebellion in Zeitun. This time the British mediated.

In 1895, it became known that some Hunchak revolutionaries had arrived in Zeitun with the aim of causing an insurrection.

I was born in the Taurus mountains. In 1888 I left my village and went to Istanbul to study, in 1891 I went to France, and in 1893 I went to Cilicia at the request of my fellow countrymen. I felt that after the Sassun massacre, a similar incident would also threaten our region, and I began to take precautions to defend the people against possible attacks by the Muslims. The patriotic youth of the country did not remain uninterested in my calls, and began defence preparations, in spite of their limited means. . . .

I took upon myself the responsibility of fulfilling this mission in Zeitun. I was accompanied by my friends Abah, Mleh, and Hratchia. Towards the end of July, we arrived in Zeitun. [100]

These statements are taken from the diary of Aghasi, who began the 1895 Zeitun rebellion. Aghasi goes on to say:

> This brave population, who for a while had been forced to show restraint, voluntarily came to our call. A great number of Zeitunites came to join us in the mountains where we had been hiding. . . . They had all come with arms; there were even children who carried a knife or a gun. [p. 189]
>
> On August 7th, the first encounter between Armenians and the gendarmes occurred. The Armenian named ,Jellad, who had gone with a friend to the village of Dashaluk, to visit his mother, had been surrounded by 40 gendarmes. Both of them defended themelves for half an hour and succeeded in putting the 40 gendarmes to flight. . . . On September 30th, a big demonstration was organized in Istanbul by Armenians. . . . On October 10th the government of Zeitun had sent for the last time two gendarmes to Alabash, to examine, in secret, the situation of the Armenians, in view of a detinitive attack. The inhabitants of Alabash, in an outburst of anger, tied these two gendarmes to a tree, and burnt them alive. [p. 193]
>
> On October 24th, we hung a red flag in the valley of Karanlik Dere. From that morning forward, the prominent leaders of all the Armenian villages started arriving with some fighters. Among them were Vartabed Bartholomeos, the priest Der Mardiros, Prince Nazareth Yeni Dünya. . . . At noon, we began negotiating. The discussions lasted for two hours; we established the plan of our struggle. [p.197]

The Zeitun rebellion was thus begun. According to the West, the crushing of this rebellion was a massacre. We do not intend to summarize Aghasi's book; however, we want to cite a few more passages, because they may constitute an example for all the rebellions, and because they cannot be refuted, as they were written by an Armenian.

> Then we saw Vartabed Sahag, a 90-year-old lame man; he seemed happy and was crying out to thank God: 'Praise the Lord! I was afraid of dying before smelling for the last time gunpowder; the perfume of incense was beginning to disgust me, and sometimes I would put gunpowder in the incenser'. [p. 214]
>
> The women, armed with axes, guns, daggers, and sticks, chased the Turkish prisoners who were escaping, and killed most of them, only 56 of them were able to escape. [p. 289]

Finally, we quote the following to reply to the massacre claims:

> From the beginning until the end of the insurrection, the Turks lost 20,000 men, 13,000 of whom were soldiers, and the rest were bashi-bozuks [irregulars]. We had lost only 125 men, 60 of whom had died in battle, and 65 of whom were dastardly killed during the cease-fire. [p. 306]

This is what Aghasi states. However, according to Lepsius, 6,000 Armenians were killed in Zeitun. [101]

The Zeitun rebellion, which began on 24 October 1895, ended on 28 January 1896. The 50 officers and 600 soldiers who were in the barracks in the town were taken prisoner in a surprise attack. Aghasi informs us of their fate.

On 3 November 1895, the rebels of Zeitun informed the British Consul in Aleppo that their ammunition was running low, and requested the intervention of the British Government. The British Ambassador requested the Babiali to treat the Zeitunites with mercy if they surrendered. [102]

On 24 December, the armed forces besieged Zeitun. Approximately 5,000 rebels fled the town and the barracks in the direction of Kills. Some of them were captured, and to capture the rest was no longer a difficult task. This time the six powers proposed an agreement which was accepted. [103]

On 31 January, the Russian, Italian (representing Germany and Austria), French, and British Consuls in Aleppo came to Zeitun.

As a result, the rebels surrendered under the agreement that they return their arms, with a general amnesty, allowing five revolutionaries to leave the country, the annulment of past taxes, and a reduction in public taxes. Thus the rebellion ended.

When the rebels no longer had the power to resist, the fact that Britain, followed by the other powers, saved the rebels without even granting the right to the Government to try the guilty ones, as if she were ending a war, is interesting. The actual cases of death occurred among the Armenians of Zeitun after this, due to epidemics of typhus, dysentery, and variola. Naturally the Muslim villages were not preserved from these epidemics. The Armenian villages which had been demolished during the rebellion were rebuilt with the help of American missionaries. Nobody was interested in Muslim villages.

The Hunchak revolutionaries who started the rebellion left Zeitun on 13 February under the protection of the British Consulate, and on 12 March they departed from Mersin to Marseilles.

The Zeitun rebellion was thus concluded.

With the Zeitun rebellion, the activities of the Hunchak Party in Turkey ended. The Party had acted in order to gain the attention of Europe and obtain independence for the Armenians, but had failed. Actually, the subject of reform was reopened after the Sassun rebellion, and Abdulhamid, as we shall see later, announced reform principles. But their implementation was not possible.

The Hunchak Party, as we have stated above, split into two factions in 1896, and began to deal with its internal problems. Although some of its members took part in some incidents in Turkey, such as the Van rebellion, this participation was no longer a result of instructions coming from abroad.

After 1896, the Tashnak Party was slowly becoming the main actor in Turkey.

(k) The Van rebellion

Although the Van rebellion occurred on the night of 14 June, preparations for it had begun much earlier. General Mayewski, Russian Consul for six years in Van, and later in Erzurum, wrote:

In 1895, the revolutionaries of Van were working to draw the attention of Europe once again to the Armenian question. Letters were sent to wealthy Armenians asking for money, threatening them with death. During this time, some political crimes were committed by order of the revolutionary committee of Van. The most important of these crimes was perpetrated on January 6th, that is on the day of the biggest Armenian holiday, on the person of the priest Bogos, as he was on his way to church to celebrate the holy service. The poor old man had been condemned to death, as he had strongly opposed the ignominious deeds of certain revolutionaries.

During the winter of 1895-96, young Armenians gathered in the spacious rooms of the houses near the Russian consulate [in Van], where they engaged in patrol and even detachment drills, and sometimes, transported by their zeal, they practised shooting.

As happens everywhere, with spring, the preparations of the revolutionary movement began to gain importance. One even heard of certain attempts, such as the murder of some Kurds in the proximity of the city, whose bodies had been cut to pieces. The revolutionaries, seeing that no investigation was carried out in regard to these murders, increasingly plucked up courage. However, the patience of Muslims was being exhausted in proportion to the Armenians' audacity. [104]

The British Consul Williams, too, foresaw the future. The Tashnaks have in Van about 400 members. With the Hunchaks, who in my opinion do not exceed 50 members, they terrorize their coreligionists, and provoke the Muslim community with their excesses and frenzy, and are an obstacle to the implementation of reforms. If they can be silenced, I am certain that the main obstacle to the region's security will disappear.'[105]

Saadettin Pasha, the Military Commander in Van, seemed to be of the same opinion. In fact, from October 1895 onward, isolated incidents continued to occur in Van, and he was constantly vigilant. It appears from the provincial reports that until the date of the rebellion, twenty-three incidents were recorded. Saadettin Pasha, in his report subsequent to the rebellion, stated these points and summarized developments before the rebellion.[106] We shall summarize the passages of this report regarding the beginning and the development of the rebellion.

On the night of the third Monday of June, Armenian bands opened fire on the detachment patrolling behind the Armenian quarter of the Van orchards, and seriously wounded the commander Recep Efendi and a soldier. In the morning, the prosecutor, the coroner, the commander of the gendarmes, and the superintendent of police went to the site of the incident, made investigations, but were not successful. The only road from the orchards to the city had houses on both sides inhabited by Armenians.

At 4 p.m. shots were fired from these houses on the Muslims who were walking on their way home. The soldiers intervened to prevent an incident, and attempted to advise the Armenians, who retorted by firing shots and did not let anyone approach them. On the contrary, the houses were almost fortified and prepared for a skirmish. On June 6th, the British, French, Iranian, and Russian Consuls were sent to the Armenians to ask them to lay down their arms, but the Armenians refused the offer. On the night of June 8th, shots were exchanged between thc rebels and the soldiers. On June 9th and 10th when shots were no longer fired from the fortified houses, it was understood that the rebels had fled, and the neighbouring localities were informed.

When it was known that a group of 780 of the rebels who had fled, had passed through the *kaza* of Hamidi, and had attacked the Muzerki tribe in the village of Elbak, soldiers were immediately dispatched to the area, and the rebels who fled again took refuge in the Isbestan village. When they were asked to surrender, they refused, and attempted to escape next morning to Iran, but were caught.

It became known that the 286 men from Troshak and Hunchak group which had escaped from Van had attacked the Shemiski tribe in the village of Salhane of the Jermeliye *kaza*; soldiers had been sent to the area, and as a result of an armed confrontation with the soldiers, all of them had been killed except for one who succeeded in fleeing to Kotur.

Among the local brigands, those who were from the *kaza* of Shitak escaped from Van to Shitak, but surrendered there.

In this rebellion, the number of casualties in Van was 879. Among them 340 Muslims were dead, and 260 were wounded. Of the Armenians there were 219 dead and 59 wounded.

[Until this point, the report is in agreement with the report dated 28 June 1896 by Major Williams, the British Consul: the Consul gives the number of casualties as 500 Armenians and 300 Muslims. (Turkey No. 8 (1896), No. 337, enclosure 1.)]

When these incidents were occurring in Van, incidents occurred in neighbouring *kazas* as a result of Armenian attacks on Muslims. In the confrontation which began on June 5th, when Armenians murdered Suleiman Agha and Mahmut Agha in the village of Olgullu, and ended on June 7th, 12 Muslims had died, and 16 had been wounded, whereas 205 Armenians had died.

In the confrontation which began after the attack of an Armenian band in the *kaza* of Kuvash, 4 Muslims and 100 Armenians had died, and 8 Muslims had been wounded.

During the pursuit of the two Armenian groups who had escaped from Van, it was recorded that 39 Muslims had died and 38 had been wounded. [We noted above that only one person had escaped of the two groups, one group being 780 people, and the other 286 people.]

During the confrontation with the brigands who had escaped to Shitak, 15 Muslims had died, and 30 had been wounded, 30 Armenians had died, and 8 had been wounded.

6 Muslims, and 27 Armenians had died, 8 Muslims and 4 Armenians had been seriously wounded in the confrontation which began when Mehmet Agha of the Haydaranli tribe was killed on June 5th in the village of Berdek of the kaza of Erjis.

Moreover, 30 Armenians had died in the villages of Gurzot and Anguzk, 8 in the village of Nekes, and 31 in the *kaza* of Adiljevaz. Among the Muslims, 2 had died and 3 had been wounded.

Thus, the Van rebellion continued between 15 and 24 June, and in total, in the separate incidents we have indicated above, 418 Muslims and 1,715 Armenians had died, and 363 Muslims and 71 Armenians had been wounded.

After this date separate incidents occurred in Van, with bands coming from Iran, but these did not constitute a rebellion.

(1) The raid on the Ottoman Bank

The last incident in 1896 was the raid on the Ottoman Bank on 26 August. This incident was entirely organized by the Tashnak committees. After those attempts in which the Hunchaks had not been successful, the Tashnaks wanted to try their luck.

The organizers of the raid were three Armenians named Varto, Mar, and Boris, who had come from Caucasia. Karekin Pasdermadjian, who used the nickname Armen Garo, who later was elected deputy to the National Assembly from Erzurum during the 1908 Constitutional Government and fought against Turkey in Caucasia with his band during the First World War, came from Athens to join them.

Before the Armenian revolutionaries had surrendered and had been sent to Marseilles, they had stayed on the yacht of Sir Edgar Vincent, the president of the Ottoman bank. The president's secretary, too, had stayed with them. The revolutionaries had told secretary F. A. Baker of the plans they had prepared. Below, we summarized the secretary's report on the subject.

The events of the 20th were schemed and planned out some three months ago by the Foreign Committees, and the chiefs of the various bands, only came to Constantinople some three weeks back. The attack on the bank was one part of their programme, as they told me that the following points and places had been singled out for their demonstrations: the Sublime Porte, the Armenian Patriarchate, that part of Stamboul sloping down towards Makri-keui [today Bakir-keuy], the Ottoman Bank (occupation), the Credit Lyonnais Bank (occupation), the Vaivoda police-station (bomb attacks), the Galata Serai police station (bomb attack), the Aia Triada Greek Church (bomb attack).

The bombs were made by them here, they had obtained their dynamite here. The Bank was attacked at 01:00 hours and at the same time a raid was made on the Vaivoda police-station in order to prevent assistance being sent to the Bank by the latter.

They gave me the following reasons for having singled out the Imperial Ottoman Bank and Credit Lyonnais for occupation. As these establishments contain people of so many nationalities, all the Powers would be ready to assist in obtaining their demands from the Turks, in order to save the lives of their subjects; that the Bank was the easiest building to resist a siege and to defend; that being the most prominent building in the town, more attention would be attracted to their attempts to bring the Armenian cause before the lower classes and thus instil more ardour in their weaker brethren.

They used bombs because, they said, they were more destructive, and caused more consternation, owing to the novelty of the thing.
The assailants were all Turkish subjects, and, with the exception of the three chiefs, of the 'hamal' porter class.
One of the chiefs was killed. Two of the chiefs were not Armenians from Constantinople, but from Van, and of superior education, knowing Russian, French, Turkish, and Greek.

The third had evidently lived a long time here and knew the place well. They were all most determined men, and repeatedly told me that they would not give themselves up, but were most anxious as to how far their ultimatum to the Turks would be successful. For free pardon they did not care, except in as much as if not obtaining the reforms they asked for they would be alive for a new attempt, which they declared would be more terrible than anything known yet.

Their hatred of the Turks was beyond all description. They declared that they would return here, through Macedonia, and were confident of success in their next demonstration. They were anxious to know whether their fellow men had done much damage with their bombs, whether many soldiers had been killed, and whether the soldiers had been firing on the Armenians. They also told me that it had been their intention to kill all the Turks in the employ of the Bank before blowing the latter up, but that they had not time to do so, as things finished sooner than they expected.[107]

This was the revolutionaries' plan and intention. Esat Uras has quoted from pp. 160-3 of Vartanian's book, *History of Dashnaksutyun*, written in Armenian, where Hayik Tiryakian, who took part in the movement, gives an account of the occupation which took place on 26 August.[108] We summarize this passage below.

August 26th, 6:30 in the morning. 6 people were sufficient to begin the occupation. We set out early, with sacks full of bombs on our shoulders and guns in our hands. As we approached the Bank, we heard the sound of guns, and bombs thrown by our vanguard friends. We rushed into the Bank. They thought we were robbers. I told them not to be afraid. The bombs were giving incredible results, they did not kill instantly, but tore their flesh apart, and made them writhe with pain, and agony. We went with Garo to the President's office, and wrote down our conditions. We demanded that the Powers fulfil our requests, that those who took part in this confrontation be freed; if not, we would blow up the Bank with ourselves. There were 17 left who could fight. 3 had died, 6 of our friends had been wounded. Our enemies' casualties were also heavy.

The demands of the revolutionaries were:[109]

- the appointment of a European as Chief Superintendent of police, chosen by the
six powers;
- the appointment of the governors of provinces, and *sanjaks*, and the head officials of districts, by the Chief Superintendent of police, with the Sultan's approval;

- the militia, the gendarmerie and the police to be recruited from the local people, and to be under the command of a European officer;

- a judiciary reform consistent with the European system to be instituted;

- absolute freedom of religion, education, and the press;

- the allocation of three-quarters of the country's income to local needs;

- the annulment of tax debts;

- a tax exemption for five years, and the next five-year tax to be assigned for the damage done in the recent disorders;

- the immediate return of embezzled properties;

- the emigrants to be allowed to return freely;

- an amnesty for Armenians sentenced for political reasons;

- a temporary commission to be formed with representatives of the European countries, which would supervise the implementation of the above demands.

In the end, the General Director of the Bank, Sir Edgar Vincent, went to the Palace with Maximoff, the head dragoman of the Russian Embassy, and obtained authority to solve the problem. It was guaranteed that they would leave the country freely. 17 people left the Bank with Maximoff, and went to Sir Edgar's yacht. From there, they set out for Marseilles on the French ship *Gironde*.

The occupation of the Bank was thus concluded. However, the bombs thrown and the bullets fired on that day by Armenians on the police and the people aroused the Muslim community of Istanbul. The disorders in Istanbul lasted for a few days. This was not only an attack by Muslims on Armenians. The Armenians, too, continued their attacks.

The British Embassy in its telegram dated 30 August, wrote that 'In Istanbul and Bosphorus, tranquillity was totally established as of last night and today. However, this evening, around 6 p.m. some Armenians threw a bomb in Galata near the Ottoman Bank and the soldiers replied to this by opening fire . . . It cannot be denied that this constant bomb throwing by Armenians has seriously provoked the Turks.' Likewise, the British Embassy informed its Ministry that the Armenians had thrown yet another bomb on 3 September.[110]

According to Western sources, the number of Armenians killed as a result of this incident was between 4,000 and 6,000. A document concerning this subject has not yet been found in the Ottoman archives. However, in our opinion, the figure 6,000 is exaggerated. In the case of the Babiali demonstration, too, the disorders continued for a few days, but the number of dead did not exceed 172. To be able to reach the figure 4,000-6,000, the incident had to last for weeks. Moreover, it is written in all the sources that the Muslims fought with sticks and knives, and it is hardly possible to kill so many people with these means. We have nowhere encountered the number of Muslims killed. But according to the British document, 120 soldiers of the Grand Vizier were killed, and there were approximately 25 wounded.[111] Again in the same document it is stated that about 300 Muslims were arrested because of the incidents, and that the preventive measures taken by the Government were satisfactory.

A special court was established for this incident, and the Muslims and the Armenians who were arrested were tried in this court.

(m) The second Sassun rebellion

The first attempt of the Tashnaks did not produce any result. They attempted their second blow in July 1897. The Tashnak bands generally entered Turkey from Iran by way of Van. However, the Mazrik tribe which was on their way used to annoy them. In order the eliminate the tribe, they attacked the tribe's tents in Honasor in July 1897 (with a hand of 250) as the sun was rising. However, they did not succeed and were forced to retreat and flee, having faced the danger of being surrounded.[112]

After this date, the Tashnaks extended their activities to the region of Sassun and Mush. Antranik now had responsibility for organizing the activities of the bands. Antranik was born in 1866 in Sharki Karahisar, had entered the committee at an early age, had been imprisoned for the murder of a Turk, and had gone to Batum after the Committee helped him escape from prison. He later made a reputation through his band fights during the First World War, and he became Regimental Commander. His name first appeared during the period we are examining.

The Ottoman Government decided in 1901 to build barracks on the hills of Talouri and Shenik to put the administration of Sassun in order. The Armenians opposed this project. The struggle with the bands led by Antranik began at this date, but the actual rebellion began to spread from 1903 onward, in the entire region. On 13 April 1904, soldiers were dispatched against the rebels. The rebels were unable to resist for long, but the struggle with Antranik's band continued until August. In the end, Antranik was forced to flee to Caucasia. Esat Uras quotes from *The Antranik Battles*, a book written in Armenian by K. Kukulyan and published in 1929 in Beirut:

In April 1904, the Armenian rebellions spread from the hills of Sassoun and the plain of Mush to Van. The Consuls mediated and offered an agreement with Antranik. Among the band leaders were the renowned Tashnak Committee members of Mush and Sassoun, Murad of Sivas, Sebuk, Kevork, Mko, and the new revolutionary Sempad. . . . The Dashnaksutyun bureau met with the representatives of the Mush Central Committee, and chose Antranik to be the commander. Sebuk was seriously wounded. Keork of Akcha died. The renowned Hirayr, who did not want to leave Sebuk to the enemies, and tried to take him along, was also shot. [113]

The passage reported the confrontations as well as the number of Turks and Armenians killed during each confrontation. During the confrontations which occurred on 14, 16, and 22 April, on 2 May and 17 July, 932-1, 132 Turks were killed, as opposed to only 19 Armenians. These are figures provided by Armenians. But this rebellion, too, was included in the literature as a massacre. However, earlier interest was not renewed, for in this period the powers were concerned with other subjects.

(n) The Yildiz Palace assassination attempt

The final effort by the Tashnaks was the assassination attempt on Abdul-hamid. Papazian states that "The attempt on the life of Sultan Abdul-Hamid in 1905 constitutes the last episode of the revolutionary attempts of the A.R. Federation on behalf of Turkish Armenia. This was another of the spectacular but futile acts of the Dashnagtzoutune. Its success would not have helped the Armenian cause; its failure probably saved our people from greater misfortunes."[114]

The assassination attempt occurred on Friday, 21 July 1905. The bombs, which were planted in the carriage the Sultan would take, exploded before he got in, while he was talking with the Sheikhulislam. The Sultan pardoned the assailants.

(o) Overall picture of the rebellions

The assassination attempt at the Yildiz Palace was the last assault organized by the revolutionary committees. In 1908 another insurrection took place in Adana, but the nature of this revolt was different.

The period starting with the 1890 Erzurum incident and ending with the 1896 Van rebellion is known in the West as the period of massacres.

Nalbandian states that in this period 50,000-300,000 Armenians were killed.

David Marshall Lang writes that between 1894 and 1896, 200,000 Armenians were killed. [115]

According to Pastermadjian, 100,000-110,000 died.[116] Misseskian states that at least 300,000 were killed.[117]

The figure given by Lepsius is 88,243. However, there is no indication as to the source of this figure. For example, he states that in 1896, 20,000 persons died in Van. However, most of the bands in Van had come from Iran, and there is no reason to doubt the figures given by Saadettin Pasha. Likewise, he states that 6,000 died in Zeitun. Aghasi writes that they had 125 casualties. It is stated in the British documents that approximately 3,000 died of the epidemics after the rebellion, and these deaths have no direct relationship with the rebellion.

The figure for 1895 given by Bliss is 35,032. When we add to this figure the number of those who died during the 1896 incidents (Zeitun, Van, Ottoman Bank), which according to the West is 6,000-7,000, we obtain a figure of 42,000, approximately.

The figure the Ottomans give for 1895 is 8,717. When we add to this the figure 3,715, the number for Van being 1,715 and for the Ottoman Bank being 2,000, and having raised to 1,000 the figure 125 for Zeitun given by Aghasi, we obtain 13,432.

One thing is certain, and that is, even if we are to include the Armenians killed by the bullets of the Armenian rebels as having been killed by Turks, the number of Armenians who died during the rebellions in the 1890's will hardly reach 20,000.

There is a great difference between 20,000 and 300,000. At the very least it would be fair for those who give these figures to remember how many people lost their lives in rebellions or disorders in their own or other countries, and think how much right they have to use the term massacre.

In the meantime it is also necessary to compute the number of Muslims who died in the same period. If we are to take seriously Aghasi's statement that they killed 20,000 Turks in Zeitun, then the Muslim casualties would approach 25,000, and would be twice the Armenian casualties. We leave aside this exaggeration. The number of Muslims who died during these rebellions in a two-year period is not less than 5,000. Most of these Muslims were killed without provocation, by shots fired on them or with bombs, so that the rest would be aroused and attack the Armenians. This is the real murder, the real massacre.

6. Further attempts at reform

We left the subject of reform with the memorandum submitted by the British Ambassador to the Babiali on 16 August 1886, mentioning the Cyprus Agreement.

We have mentioned that Patriarch Ashikian resigned after the assassination attempt on his person in April 1894, that the Sassun rebellion started in August 1894, and that an investigative delegation was sent to the region on the insistence of Britain after the rebellion had been crushed.

The year 1895 began with the election of Mateos Izmirlian, who looked to be another Hrimyan, to the Patriarchate, and in the same year the British Ambassador, Sir Philip Currie, re-opened the subject of reform. The Ambassador asked permission to show the Russian and French Ambassadors the proposals he had asked the Military Attaché, Colonel Chermside, to prepare, and to submit them to the Babiali, if they agreed. The Earl of Kimberley granted permission.[118]

On 17 April the British Ambassador met the Russian and French Ambassadors; and they agreed to prepare a final draft of the reform proposals which they would submit to the Babiali, and to submit them first to their Governments for approval. The proposals were approved by the French and Russian Governments, and were submitted to the Babiali, along with a memorandum, on 11 May.[119] We shall not dwell on the details, as it will be sufficient to report the text accepted by the Babiali.

On the same day, the proposals were also submitted to the German, Austrian, and Italian Ambassadors.

As Abdulhamid delayed his reply, the British Foreign Secretary suggested that the powers should press for a reply jointly. However, the Russian Minister of Foreign Affairs stated that they would not take part in such an approach.[120]

On 3 June, the Babiali gave its answer to the Ambassadors and stated that it would not accept some paragraphs of the proposals.

On 4 June, the Russian Minister of Foreign Affairs explained to the British Ambassador in St Petersburg that they did not consider the reform proposals as an ultimatum, that they would not approve the use of threatening language in view of the Babiali's counter-offers, that Russia would not accept the creation of an Armenian state in Asia Minor, which would constitute the nucleus of an independent Armenia and was clearly the aim of the Armenian Committees.[121]

On 14 June, the Russian Minister of Foreign Affairs, Lobenoff, was even more explicit, and told the British Ambassador:

...Russia would be pleased by the development of the Turkish administration, by the Christian community having greater security for their lives and property, but oppose the creation of a country in Asia where Armenians would benefit from exceptional privileges. According to the Ambassadors' proposals, this country would be quite large, and would comprise almost half of Asia Minor. Russian Armenians have become very excited, and the authorities have been forced to take measures to prevent them from sending arms and money to the other side of the border. I understand that the Government of Her Majesty is somewhat unconcerned with the subject, due to the great distance between England, or more specifically, between the lands under British rule, and the said region, but Russia cannot allow the creation of a second Bulgaria on its borders.[122]

On 27 June, the Babiali appointed Mushir Shakir Pasha as the inspector of the eastern provinces. This appointment almost complied with the suggestion of the three powers that a High Commissioner should be appointed. At the same time, the Liberal government of Rosebery resigned and Lord Salisbury formed a new government.

'Lord Rosebery, in a speech he gave on July 5th, as the opposition leader, stated that the Liberal Government had reached an agreement in Istanbul with Russia and France concerning the subject of exerting strong pressure to save the Armenians from this unbearable oppression, torture and barbarity, that he hoped that the new government would continue this policy, otherwise the United Kingdom would be forced to take into account all the Christian population of the Ottoman Empire.' The German Ambassador in London, Hatzfeld, informed his Ministry of these statements, and added that Rosebery probably gave this speech to put his opponent in a difficult position. [123]

As there was no agreement to exert pressure on the Babiali, it is obvious that the speech was delivered to create problems for the new government, but in fact the speech did not have this effect, for Salisbury now had a different view of the subject. To preserve the integrity of the Ottoman Empire was no longer in accordance with British interests. An independent Armenia in eastern Turkey could very well be useful to Britain. However, as she would not be able to achieve this because of Russia, and as the Ottoman Empire would disintegrate anyway, an alternative might be to come to an agreement with Russia, to obtain Syria and Iraq, and to relinquish the eastern provinces to Russia.

The ultimate partition of the Ottoman Empire finally became part of British policy. What was once considered by Tsar Alexander was now the view of Salisbury,

Under these circumstances, Germany would certainly not be excluded.

As we shall see, this policy of Britain's became increasingly clear.

The conversation Salisbury had with the German Ambassador Hatzfeld on 9 July may be considered as the first indication of this new policy. The British Prime Minister, after having stated that he would not be able to abandon the former Cabinet's policy concerning the Armenian question and that the Sultan had at least to suggest an acceptable governor for the eastern provinces, added that one day Britain and Russia might once again share the same viewpoint, and that this would mean the end of Turkish sovereignty.

As the German Ambassador pointed out that Russia would never permit the creation of an independent Armenia, Salisbury stated, `That is true. However, the changes that will occur may also be in Russia's interest.'

The German Ambassador who reported this discussion added the following remarks to his telegram: `Although our conversation was strictly confidential, I did not want to follow up this point, but I am absolutely certain that the Minister, with the changes he mentioned, was thinking of dividing Turkey, and relinquishing the Turkish provinces on the Russian border to Russia, rather than granting them autonomy.' [124]

We shall not follow developments in this subject step by step, as it is not our object to examine British foreign policy. However, we shall note some turning points as they occur.

The Babiali presented a new paper on 2 August, on the subject of the reform proposals, indicating which articles would be accepted and which would not. This paper was entitled `Observations concerning the proposals submitted by the Ambassadors of the three powers about the reform to be implemented in various provinces in Anatolia',[125] and had been prepared by a Commission charged with examining the proposals.

Correspondence regarding this subject continued for a while between the Babiali and the Embassies, between the Embassies and their Ministries, and on 30 September the Babiali demonstration occurred. These incidents encouraged the three powers to press the subject of reform.

Finally, on 22 October 1895, agreement having been reached on a text on reforms, it was sent with a diplomatic note to the three Embassies, to six provinces as instructions, and to Mushir Shakir Pasha.[126]

We summarize below the text of the reform measures that were now agreed. The original text written in French and English is in the document Turkey No. 1 (1896) no. 204 and enclosures. The text in Turkish is given on pp. 345ff of Esat Uras' book.

It appears from the title of the decree that the reform was to be implemented in the provinces of Erzurum, Bitlis, Van, Diyarbekir, Elaziz, and Sivas. Its main points are:

Art 1. A Christian assistant shall be appointed for each Governor.

Art 2. In *sanjaks* and *kazas* with a high proportion of Christians, a Christian Assistant shall be appointed to the Muslim Governor of the *sanjak* and to the Muslim *kaymakam* [head official of a kaza].

Art 3. The *kaymakams* shall be chosen from among the graduates of the School for Civil Servants, regardless of sect or religion, and shall be appointed by order of the Sultan.

Art 5. In the six provinces local officials shall be appointed in accordance with the proportion of the population.

Art 9. If the inhabitants of a *bujak* [sub-district] belong to one single community, the members of the Assembly shall be selected only from that community.

Art. 20. Police officers shall include Muslims and Christians in proportion to the population of the province.

Art. 22. Officers of gendarmerie, low-ranking officers, and privates shall be selected in proportion to the population.

Art. 28. It is forbidden for the members of the Hamidiye regiments to bear arms and uniforms outside training.

Art. 31. The tithe [*ashar*] shall be collected by the tax contractors.

Art. 32. A permanent Supervisory Commission, comprising a Muslim President, and Muslim and non-Muslim members in equal numbers, shall be formed. The Commission shall operate in the Babiali and supervise the reforms.

These are the main articles of the regulation, which has 32 articles in all.

This decision was accepted, but the subject was not concluded. Rebellions had made headway in almost every city of the country. The fact that the Sultan established and announced the Supervisory Commission did not change much.

The powers insisted that the text of this decree should be officially announced but Abdulhamid demurred. He asserted that it was sufficient for the decision to be published in the code of laws [*Düstur*] and that an announcement might create discontent among the Muslim community. In view of disorders which broke out with the Van rebellion in June 1896, and the raid on the Ottoman Bank on 26 August, the powers focussed once again on the subject of reform, joined this time by Germany and Austria, and began to insist that it would be announced with a decree (*irade*).

The Russian Ambassador, too, made great efforts to have the reform measures made public. The Russian Ambassador, Nelidov, informed the British Ambassador that on 4 October a decree had been prepared and that it would soon be published, and also sent the text to be published.[127] When publication was once again delayed, Salisbury took the initiative himself, suggesting on 20 October 1896 to the Governments of the other five powers that they should secure publication of the decree, if necessary by exerting pressure, and that they should give authority to the Ambassadors in Istanbul for this purpose.[128]

The Sultan informed the powers on 25 October that preparations for reform were concluded.[129]

It appears that the decisive factor for the Sultan was the fact that on 3 November 1896 the Armenian question was brought to the agenda of the French Assembly. After the French Minister of Foreign Affairs, M. Hanotaux, announced that the six powers were acting jointly to improve the administrative system without endangering the integrity of the Ottoman Empire, and without interfering with its internal affairs, the Sultan told the French Ambassador in Istanbul that the reforms would be extended to all provinces, that this would be accomplished in the quickest manner, and that political prisoners would be pardoned.

The *Iradei Seniye* (official decree) was published in the newspapers on 11 November 1896. The decree extended the application of the text drafted a year earlier to all the provinces, instead of only six provinces, but excluded some articles of the previous text, such as those concerning regiments and the judiciary inspectors. The British Ambassador was quick to inform London that he found the decree insufficient.[130]

The Sultan kept the promise he gave to the French, and pardoned political prisoners, except those who were sentenced to death, on 23 December 1896. Those who were sentenced to death were sent to a fortress to be freed at a later date.

In the meantime, Maghanian Ormanian was elected to the Patriarchate, which was vacant, on 18 November 1896.

Britain continued its attempts to complete the parts of the reform which had been excluded. The powers agreed that their Ambassadors in Istanbul should work to this end. Meetings were held in Istanbul. However, except for Britain, motivation was lacking. A meeting held on 23 December 1896 was probably the last meeting. The year 1897 was bringing new problems. When the Turco-Greek War began on 18 April 1897, the subject of reform was put aside until the end of the Balkan War.

7. The Adana incident and the end of attempts at reform

(a) The Adana incident

The years 1897-1914 constitute the most disastrous period of the Ottoman Empire. Within and outside the country, incidents were occurring every day, and the Empire was clearly disintegrating.

The regime within the country was now unbearable. The administration could no longer control the insurrections and rebellions, and followed such a policy that it seemed to vent its anger, arising out of its inability to control, on a silent community. As a result of this, secret organizations were founded inside and outside the country, working to put an end to this absolutist regime.

Although the Turco-Greek War ended in victory, the Ottoman Empire came out of the war empty-handed, owing to the intervention of the great powers, and had to recognize the autonomy of Crete. Moreover, France landed soldiers on Lesbos in 1901, the Macedonian rebellion occurred in 1902, and the Arabian peninsula was in turmoil.

The struggle which was begun by the Committee of Union and Progress (Ittihad ve Terakki Cemiyeti), in the hope of putting an end to this process, ended on 24 July 1908 with the declaration of the Second Constitutional Government. However, this Government was unable to find any way of improving the condition of the Empire. On 5 October 1908, Austria occupied Bosnia-Herzegovina, on the same day Bulgaria declared its independence, and on 6 October Greece annexed Crete.

The first Assembly of the Second Constitutional Government was opened on 17 December 1908 in this situation.

On 13 April 1909, the reactionary coup known as 'the event of 31 March', aimed at abolishing the Constitutional Government, took place in Istanbul.

The next day a confrontation between Muslims and Armenians occurred in Adana, and the last bloody stage of the Armenian question began.

At this time, Adana was like a barrel of gunpowder ready to explode at any moment. The British documents clearly attest to this. We read as follows in the report of the British Embassy:

[After the proclamation of the constitution] nearly no one in Adana was really satisfied. The Turks hated the idea that they were no longer masters. The Armenian wanted to rush into Home Rule. The Greek mistrusted the constitution because he had not made it himself and because under it he seemed likely to lose certain facilities he had enjoyed under the old venal system. . . .

Under the constitution all men might bear arms. From the delightful novelty of the thing, many thousands of revolvers were purchased. Even schoolboys had them and, boy-like, flourished them about. But worse followed. The swagger of the arm-bearing Armenian and his ready tongue irritated the ignorant Turks. Threats and insults passed on both sides. Certain Armenian leaders, delegates from Constantinople, and priests (an Armenian priest is in his way an autocrat) urged their congregations to buy arms. It was done openly, indiscreetly, and, in some cases, it might be said wickedly. What can be thought of a preacher, a Russian Armenian, who in a church in this city where there had never been a massacre, preached revenge for the martyrs of 1895? Constitution or none, it was all the same to him. 'Revenge,' he said, 'murder for murder. Buy arms. A Turk for every Armenian of 1895.' An American missionary who was present got up and left the church. Bishop Mushech, of Adana, toured his province preaching that he who had a coat should sell it and buy a gun.[131]

It appears that the Governor and the Commander in Adana at the time were not capable of resisting an incident of any kind. In his memories, Jemal Pasha wrote:

A young priest who passionately sought authority, named Mushech, was at the time a member of the Adana Armenian Delegation, and was also one of the leaders of the Hinchaks.

Monsignor Mushech had begun to have rifles and revolvers brought from Europe to arm his men. He was publicly announcing that [Armenians were now armed, that they would no longer fear incidents such as the 1894 massacres, and that should so much as a single hair on an Armenian's head be disturbed, ten Turks would be destroyed.]

It is here that the biggest responsibility of the Adana government begins. . . . To arrest and imprison His Excellency Mushech and his accomplices, to undertake legal investigation with regard to them, and even to declare a state of siege in the province was the best short cut.

Unfortunately in Turkey . . . such a government did not exist in 1908.

At that time, the province of Adana was administered by Governor Jevat Bey, who was a perfect example of a cultured gentleman. However, his lack of administrative talent could not be replaced by his culture. In short, he was not the man to serve as Governor of Adana at such a time.

As for the Division Commander, he was an old soldier named Ferit Mustafa Remzi Pasha.

The Governor of the Jebelibereket *sanjak* was Asaf Bey. I cannot understand how this faint-hearted man who was afraid of his own shadow could become a governor.

In the beginning of 1909 there were rumours circulating in Adana, that soon the Armenians would rebel and annihilate the Turks, that the European fleet would invade the province on this pretext, and that they would ensure the establishment of Armenia.

The Turks paid so much attention to these rumours that some of the notables attempted to send their families to safer areas.

In the month of April 1909, there was so much tension between the two sides, that nobody had any doubt that a confrontation would occur at any moment.

Finally, on April 14th, the [Adana incident] occurred, first of all with the Armenians' attacks on the orders of Monsignor Mushech.

Such horrible massacres had begun in Adana, Hamidiye, Tarsus, Misis, Erzin, Dortyol, Azizli, in short in every area where the Armenians were in a majority, that reading their details would afflict one with great hatred.

The Government, which was quite helpless in the provincial centre, demonstarted its stupidity to the extent of ordering a general insurrection to prevent attacks against the Muslim folk under its jurisdiction. When he was informed that the Armenians of Dortyol were advancing with an armed convoy to the town of Erzin, the centre of the *sanjak* of Jebelibereket, the *sanjak* governor Asaf Bey, without even leaving his office, sent telegrams to all the places under his jurisdiction, as well as to the neighbouring *sanjak* of Kozan, stating that it would be necessary (for every patriotic Turk to take his arms and rush to the aid of the *sanjak* of Jebelibereket, as the Muslims here were in danger of being massacred].

These are the reasons and causes of the first Adana incident. The second Adana incident occurred eleven days after the first, and was restricted to the city of Adana. It began when some Armenian youths opened fire on the soldiers' camp at night, and this in turn triggered worse massacres in the city of Adana.

In my opinion, the sole responsibility for the Adana massacres lies in the person of the renowned author of *Les Vêpres Ciliciennes*, Monsignor Mushech. The Adana government of the time, which realized the harm this individual was capable of, and did not take any preventive measures, is also responsible.[132]

We have exactly quoted into our pages, what Cemal Pasha had written concerning the Adana incident. In these memoirs, Asaf Bey, the Governor of Cebelibereket Province was seriously accused. However, in the book written by Mehmet Asaf Bey where the writer had also published his memories, denied all the allegations that had been brought against him, what Mehmet Asaf Bey has written concerning Cemal Pasha is as follows:[133]

"The appointment of the famous Unionist Cemal Bey as the governor was celebrated by the Armenians whereas this was a reason for the Muslims to mourn. This was because he sacrificied all the Muslims but adulated the Armenians as a means to hinder the involvement of foreign factors in the issue"

Despite the fact that Asaf Bey, had been interrogated by an investigation committee consisting of representatives, he was declared to be innocent by two martial courts and was not reassigned to his former post. Following his aquittal Asaf Bey returned to Istanbul and he met with Grand Vizier Hüseyin Hilmi Pasha. The details concerning the content of the conversation Asaf Bey had with Hüseyin Hilmi Pasha can be found in the 63-64 pages of his memoirs. We understand that during this conversation Hüseyin Hilmi Pasha reiterated all the allegations brought against Asaf Bey whereas the latter responded by stating that the government had remained completely passive during the incidents and refused to send any directions, leaving aside conveying the requested assistance.

The details concerning the occurance of the Adana incident are broadly expressed in Asaf Bey's memoirs.

The British also shared Jemal Pasha's view of Bishop Mushech. The above-mentioned document also includes the following footnote:

Since writing the above on Bishop Mushech I got another view of him and his conduct, which may be of some interest. I was urging on one of the Delegates of the Patriarch the necessity of finding some modus vivendi between the two races. In the forefront of his conditions for peace he placed the pardon of this Bishop.

'He has done nothing,' he said, 'nothing at all. It is true that he took bribes from Bahri Pasha. It is true that he was in the arms trade, and sold the people bad arms for good money. It is true that he preached to them to buy arms, and thereby made much money. It is true that he made foolish speeches. It is true that he used to go to the vineyards with a rifle and bandolier on his shoulder. It is true that he had himself photographed in the costume of the old chiefs of Armenia, But what of all that? It is nothing.'

At the time of the incidents, Mushech was in Egypt. Without doubt he would have taken an active part in the incidents, if he had been in Adana. The British Ambassador, in another report dated 4 May 1909, states that the Armenian Patriarch was responsible to a great extent for the incidents.[134]

The incidents spread when Armenians killed two young Muslims and refused to hand over the assailant, and Muslims and Armenians fought in the streets for three days.

The government immediately dispatched soldiers from Dedeaghach to Adana. Their arrival rekindled the incidents, but this time they were easily crushed. Jemal Pasha writes that in the Adana incident 17,000 Armenians and 1,850 Muslims were killed, and that, had the population ratios been in favour of the Armenians, the statistics would have been reversed. The inclinations shown by both sides during the fighting did not differ from one another.

The Patriarchate gives the number of dead as 21,300 based on the investigation it carried out. The Edirne representative, Babikian Efendi, had prepared a report to be submitted to the Assembly. He gave the number of dead as 21,001 in his report which was not discussed in the Assembly, as he died shortly after.[135] Because the figure given by Jemal Pasha pertains to the time after the trials, it can be accepted that the number of Armenians who died is closer to 17,000 rather than 20,000, as it is possible that some had returned after having fled during the incidents.

The Adana incident appears as a case in which Armenians were responsible in so far as they engaged in provocation until it erupted, and the local government was responsible in that it was unable to control it once it happened. However, this was not in any way a case of one side massacring the other, as the Armenians and the Muslims both fought fiercely. As Jemal Pasha pointed out, if the Armenian population had been in the majority, instead of being one-tenth of the Muslim population, the numbers of dead might well have been reversed.

The British Ambassador, in the reports mentioned above, stated that it was not possible to make the two sides declare a cease-fire, and that the cease-fire which was obtained with the soldiers' intervention was disregarded as soon as the soldiers left the area.

After the incident, martial law was declared in Adana. The Armenian and Muslim culprits were sent to the military court martial. Jemal Pasha, who was appointed to Adana after the incident, wrote as follows:

Four months after I arrived at Adana, I had 30 Muslims, among the martial court convicts, hanged, only in the city of Adana, and 2 months later I had 17 Muslims hanged in the town of Erzin. Only one Armenian was hanged. Among the Muslims who were hanged, there were young members of the most established and wealthy families of Adana, as well as the mufti of the *kaza* of Bahche. This mufti had great influence on the local Turks. I regret deeply that I was unable to capture Monsignor Mushech as he escaped in a foreign ship to Alexandria, on the second day of the Adana incident. If I had captured this person, who was rightly sentenced to death in default, I would have hanged him opposite the mufti of Bahche.

While reading this statement we should also bear in mind what Asaf Bey has written.

The last incident of Adana was thus concluded.

(b) Final attempt at reform

The incident of Adana, which, if it had occurred at a time of tranquility, would have aroused a storm in Europe, had in fact occurred at the same time as the 31 March rebellion. Attention was chiefly directed to Istanbul, on the attempt to de-throne the Sultan. Moreover, conflicts were brewing in the Balkans, incidents were continuously occurring. In 1910, a rebellion began in Albania, in

1911 the Benghazi war with Italy broke out and finally, on 8
October 1912, the Balkan War began.

Report No. 1129 sent by the British Ambassador to the
Foreign Office on the last day of 1912 indicates how this last
period of the reform attempts began.

[The Armenians] would seem to feel that now that article 23 of the
Treaty of Berlin has eventuated in the freeing of the Macedonians, the time
has come to deal with the provinces affected by article 61 of the same
treaty. Recent despatches from his Majesty's consular officers at Erzurum,
Van, Bitlis, etc., would point to an increase in these expectations of the
Armenians; while their communities in Geneva, Paris, Marseilles,
America, Egypt, and notably in the Caucasus, would seem to cherish the
hope that the present chapter of Balkan history will not be closed by
Europe without the commencement of a better era for the Asiatic provinces
inhabited by the Armenians.

Here in the capital-though for obvious reasons the movement is not
so overt as, e.g., in the Caucasus- the Armenian community, numbering
over 150,000 souls, is also preoccupied with the immediate future of their
`millet' [nation]. On an intimation from the Armenian Catholicos, George
v, or supreme spiritual head of the Armenian Church, who resides at
Etchmiazin, in the Caucasus, it has been decided to appoint as bishop of
the Armenian communities in Europe Mgr. Ormanian, who was Patriarch
during the last twelve years of Abdul Hamid's reign, and who was
unceremoniously deposed by the violent agitation of the Tashnag
Armenians, allied to the Committee of Union and Progress, shortly after
the inauguration of the Young Turkey regime in 1908. False charges of
simony and corruption were trumped up against him and now that the
majority of the Tashnags have broken off their alliance with the
Committee of Union and Progress, owing to its failure to carry out any of
its promises and undertakings to the Armenians, the Armenian
Patriarchate and the National Assembly are taking steps to exonerate and
rehabilitate Mgr. Ormanian before he proceeds to Europe, where part of
his mission will be to make known and plead the cause of the Armenians
in European centres.

The son of Boghos Nubar Pasha is reported to have endeavoured to
gain the sympathies of M. Poincaré in the Armenian cause and to have also
spoken on the subject with Rifaat Pasha, the Ottoman Ambassador in
Paris, urging that the reforms of 1895 should be put into execution by the
Porte on its own initiative. On receipt of Rifaat Pasha's reports on the
subject, Reshid Bey, the Minister of the Interior, with the sanction of his
government drew up a fresh scheme for the improvement of conditions in
four of the six Eastern Anatolian vilayets, and a Ministerial commission,
composed of the Grand Vizier; Gabriel Effendi; the Minister of the
Interior; and Damad Sherif Pasha, Minister of Public Instruction, has
discussed the matter with four prominent Armenians, viz., Mgr.
Ormanian; Diran Kelekian, formerly Secretary-General of the Patriarchate,
and now chief editor of the `Sabah' newspaper; Gulbenkian, an Armenian
established in England; and Dr Djavarian, deputy for Sivas. These
Armenians urged that the scheme should apply not to four, but to the six
vilayets to which the 1895 reforms were applicable, viz., Erzurum, Van,
Bitlis, Kharput, Diyarbekir, and Sivas; and this was agreed to in principle,

it being also decided to divide the six provinces into two groups, the first comprising Bitlis, Van, and Erzurum, with head-quarters at the latter town, and the second Sivas, Diyarbekir, and Harput (also called Mamouret-ul-Aziz), with head-quarters at Kharput. The valis (governors) of the six provinces would be abolished, and each province reduced to a sanjak with a Mutessarif as governor, while each of the two groups would be administered by a commission sitting at the head-quarters and composed of seven members, to wit: two Armenians, two Moslems, and two foreigners, with a third foreigner as president, the latter preferably English. The gendarmerie and police would be officered by Europeans, while there would also be European judicial inspectors. The military forces in each group of provinces would be under the command of a marshal, who would also be inspector-general. The Armenians consulted by the commission further advocated that the local revenues should be assigned to the provinces. .

While these matters were under discussion at the commission, the Armenian Patriarch and community informed the Government that the four Armenians consulted by the commission were not representative, as they had not been chosen by the National Assembly of the Armenian 'millet'. It would appear that while the Patriarch and his council are both at the present stage to appeal to foreign Governments, the four Armenians in question and a section of the community would prefer that a Government scheme should be drawn up and that an endeavour should be made to induce Europe to have the matter discussed and sanctioned by the meeting of Ambassadors in London or a European Congress, should it be decided to convene one to give the imprimatur of Europe to the changes to the Treaty of Berlin resulting from the Balkan War. There is, however, in Armenian circles a growing conviction, based on the bitter experiences of the last thirty-odd years, that the Turkish Government is incapable of executing real reforms in non-Turkish Ottoman provinces, that a general European guarantee, even on a Lebanon basis, as suggested in the enclosure in your despatch No. 560 of the 11th instant, cannot, owing to international divergences of interest and rivalries, be effective, that the time is gone by for palliatives based on status quo theories and that nothing short of autonomy or the cessation of direct Turkish administrative rule in such provinces will meet the necessities of the present time. The holders of these views would prefer to see Europe give a mandate to Russia, as was given to Austria in 1878, to take in the case of Bosnia and Herzegovina, to introduce reforms in the six vilayets under the suzerainty of the Sultan. The Turco-Russian railway agreement as to the basin of the Black Sea and the corresponding self-denying arrangements as to the north-eastern provinces of Asia Minor accepted by Germany at Potsdam, seem to them to have simplified such a solution from the international stand-point. . . .[136]

This telegram is significant for two reasons. First, it shows to a great extent the future of the Armenian question; second, it clearly demonstrates that the Ottoman Empire was in the process of being divided into spheres of influence.

Let us briefly examine, without going into detail, the division of the Ottoman Empire into spheres of influence, as it concerns, even if indirectly, the Armenian question, or rather the Armenians within the Ottoman Empire.

The aim of dividing the Empire into spheres of influence was to give the privileges of public works and industry in specific regions to certain powers.

The Ottoman Empire, through the dual treaties and agreements, had given the privileges of the Baghdad Railway construction to the Germans. The text of the general agreement to be made in this subject could not be signed until the First World War, and was later abandoned. On 19 March 1913, the Ottoman Petroleum Company, in which the Ottomans had very few shares, was founded, and the privileges of Iraqi Petroleum were given to this company. Approximately three-quarters of the capital was British. On 29 July 1913, the Shattularab (the area of the united Tigris and Euphrates from their junction to the sea) Agreement was made with the British, the privilege of operating ships on the Euphrates and the Tigris was given to the British, and it was decided that a mixed commission should administer Shattularab. Moreover, the irrigation of Iraq was left to the British. On 29 October 1913, an agreement was reached to the effect that the privileges of the railways to be constructed to the east of Trabzon-Pekerich-Harput- Diyarbekir should be given to Russia. On 9 April 1914, an agreement was made, which gave the French extensive privileges in Western Anatolia.

When we say an agreement was made, it is only in a manner of speaking. Actually these agreements were almost forced onto the Ottomans.

Although an agreement was reached with the Italians giving them privileges to construct a railway in the region of Antalya, it did not produce any result, owing to the objections of the British.

Making an agreement with the Ottoman Empire was not sufficient. This agreement had to be sanctioned by the other powers. On 15 June 1914 Britain and Germany made an agreement, to the effect that each would recognize the privileges given to the other. A similar agreement was made on 15 February 1914 between France and Germany. In February 1914 Britain and Russia, too, made such an agreement. France and Britain had previously reached agreement, and on 5 December 1912, Sir Edward Grey, the British Foreign Secretary, had even told Paul Cambon, the French Ambassador, that Britain did not covet Syria, and had offered Syria to France.

When the First World War began, as a result of these agreements every inch of Ottoman Anatolia had been divided into spheres of influence controlled by various powers (see Map 1).

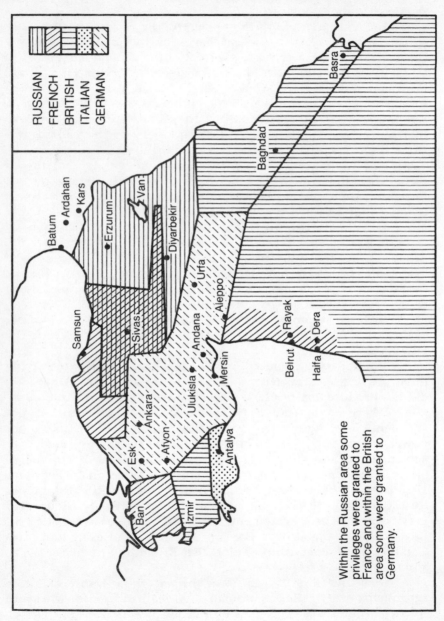

RUSSIAN
FRENCH
BRITISH
ITALIAN
GERMAN

Basra

Baghdad

Batum
Ardahan
Kars
Erzurum
Van
Diyarbekir

Urfa
Aleppo
Rayak
Dera
Beirut
Haifa

Samsun

Sivas
Andana
Mersin

Ankara
Ulukisla
Esk.
Afyon
Antalya
Ban
Izmir

Within the Russian area some
privileges were granted to
France and within the British
area some were granted to
Germany.

Map 1. Spheres of influence according to the 1913–1914 Agreement

It is useful to take a look at some German documents to understand how this distribution was arrived at. Because these documents were translated by Yusuf Hikmet Bayur, we quote them from his book. The statements in parentheses in the German documents are the observations written by Kaiser Wilhelm as he read the telegrams.

The German Ambassador to Moscow sent the following report dated 23 January 1913 to his Prime Minister, Bethmann-Hollweg:

During my most recent discussions with Mr. Sazanov, my attention was drawn to the fact that, when we were discussing the dangers which would arise, should the Balkan War continue, he brought the conversation a few times to Armenia (This is now an old story) and stated his fears that a massacre of Christians might occur there. (These would be organized so that this would constitute a pretext for intervention and annexation. The fleet show will be useful for the same reason.) Minister (Sazanov) made the following remark: 'Disorders which would occur on our borders will not leave us unconcerned and should something like this occur, we cannot not intervene'.

According to reliable sources here, the local authorities are split into two groups. One group advocates action in Armenia, so that Russia is not left empty-handed when the problems in the Near East are solved, and the other group opposes such a policy.

In many instances it is claimed that the Ministry of Foreign Affairs supports the first group. I do not agree with this claim, taking into account the fact that Mr. Sazanov until now has been moderate and prudent in the Balkan crisis. Nevertheless, some newspapers which have obvious relations with the Ministry of Foreign Affairs are openly attempting to arouse interest to the advantage of Armenia, and to point to the necessity of Russian intervention, with the aim of protecting the Christians who live there, should this be necessary. (Good bait catches fine fish.)

According to my investigation, among the opponents of an active Russian policy in Armenia is the Governor-General of Caucasia. According to a well-informed diplomat here, when Voronzov-Dashkov was asked his opinion, he pointed out the dangers that Russian action in Armenia would create for the Caucasus. The governor-general defended the following viewpoint.

The goal of such an action should be, first of all, reform and autonomy. However, it can be expected that the Armenians, who live in the Caucasus in great numbers, would demand the same rights as soon as they heard of the privileges granted to their fellowmen in Turkey, and that disorders would arise in the Caucasus.

Apparently, Mr. Sazanov yesterday told the councillor of the Austro-Hungarian Embassy (Count Chernin), 'I insistently suggested to the Turkish Ambassador here, that he offer his Government to implement reforms in Armenia, to prevent disorders there.' (Like in Macedonia? This is exactly what Voronzov is afraid of.) Turhan Pasha did not mention this Russian suggestion to me; however, he talked about the Russian intentions in Armenia in the most suspicious manner. (He was right.) Until a few weeks ago, the Ambassador fully defended the moderate and honest character of Russian policy. Now he tells me that the Minister's attitude towards him has completely changed, and that this makes him suspicious.

(Of course, because everything in Istanbul is in a mess.) He is afraid that Russia is preparing a plan which she does not want to make public. (For weeks this was obvious to the non-diplomats.) Turhan Pasha stated that the claim that the Christians in Armenia were in danger was totally unfounded, but on the other hand, there was no doubt that creating disorders in Armenia by way of the Caucasus was entirely within the Russians' powers, if they could benefit from these disorders. (He's right. That's how it will be.)

A point which drew my attention is that the Italian chargé d'affaires (Tommasi della Torretta) who openly supports Russia (he has assured me until now that Russian policy is not based on interests) (The fool.) has mentioned his fears about the Russian aims in Asia Minor. When I made the observation that Russia has to take England into account when she wants to expand into Asia Minor (The opposite is true, they have no need, London does whatever Benkendorff wants.), Marquis Toretta's reply was: 'What if the states of the Triple Entente have agreed on this subject?' (Right.) The charge d'affairs then pointed to the attention France paid to Syria (A blow to the Bagdad railway.) and stated that it was not impossible that England was coveting the Arab shores of the Red Sea. (Right.)

Marquis Toretta stated that he had no clear indication that the members of the Triple Entente have reached such agreements. I am not in a position to report events which point to the existence of such agreements. However, I did not think it was right not to include in my report the distrust which began to be felt here among diplomatic circles against the Russian plans. (Quite late, I've had this fear for very long, but they never believe me, finally Petersburg has begun to spoil the game, which has aroused this general distrust.)[137]

The German Ambassador in Istanbul, Vangenheim, sent the following report dated 21 January 1913:

. . . However, with another observation having no relation to the Balkan alliance, one reaches the conclusion that Germany will be under the necessity of defending the perpetuation of Asiatic Turkey after peace is made. If Turkey is left alone, it is possible that the process of disintegration which caused the breaking up of European Turkey will spread soon to Asia Minor. The conviction that Asiatic Turkey in a few years will fall victim to being divided, as long as the central system is not changed, and the army continues to interfere constantly in the inner politics of the country, is prevalent not only among the Turks of Istanbul, but among the inhabitants of Asia Minor as well. Russia and France keep in mind the possibility that the situation in Asia Minor will evolve in a way to justify intervention in Europe to protect Russian and French interests that are in danger. Today, Asia Minor resembles the state Morocco was in before the conference of Algeciras. The subject of dividing Asia Minor can be brought up, sooner than expected. We have few interests in Morocco, but we are engaged in Asia Minor through hundreds of millions and our prestige which is linked to the Baghdad railway. The possibility that the areas which were opened to world transport, thanks to German achievements, might fall into the hands of foreigners, is an unbearable thought for the German national consciousness. If we do not want to be excluded from this division, we must from now on come to an agreement with the interested powers, and especially with England. Our relations with Great Britain are now improving thanks to Your Majesty's dominating and prudent policy. This is also being felt here. However, it is yet quite doubtful that this policy of approaching England is popular in England, to the extent that the British Government will consent, without pondering much, to Germany obtaining an area in Asia Minor, and especially to occupy a harbour on the shores of Asia Minor. A German Mersin, or a German Iskenderun will probably be a more unpleasant thought to the British today, than a German Aghadir. Every rational German politician would hope that something comes out of this modest beginning of the German-British entente. But this delicate plant needs many years to flourish, and at this point, it must be handled with care. However, if the Turkey of Asia Minor is not supported in an energetic and substantial manner by friendly powers, this country will not be able to survive for long. The future of Asiatic Turkey has been discussed recently by my Austrian and Italian colleagues in detail. As soon as peace is made, Marquis Pallavicini as well as Marquis Garroni will suggest to their Governments that they defend the thesis that the Triple Alliance must give its support to Turkey.[138]

The German Ambassador in London sent the following report on 24 January:

Sir Edward Grey has just discussed with me the incidents which occurred in Istanbul [He refers to the toppling of the Kamil Pasha Cabinet by the Young Turks and Enver Bey Pasha], and stated that 'A coup d'état does not necessarily mean that the war will rekindle'. First of all the intention of the Young Turks is only to take power into their hands. In fact, it will be difficult for them to give up Edirne from now on, but everything is possible with the Turks. We should first wait for the reply note. Grey has said this to their plenipotentiaries in the Balkans, and suggested to them that they should not take action and should return to their country.

Taking advantage of this opportunity I mentioned the issue of Asia Minor, and told him, 'We are ready to guarantee the countries under Turkish rule, along with the other powers. Because we have no intention of obtaining any country, we do not want other countries to have such an intention.' He gave me this reply: 'First of all peace must be obtained. It is impossible to focus on other issues before it is obtained, because we cannot know beforehand whether the war will spread to Asia Minor or not.' Then he asked what we would do, should anarchy arise and our interests and the Baghdad railway be in danger, and stated that we might engage in military intervention, that our situation in Mesopotamia corresponded to the situation of the French in Syria. I replied that 'We should never, and we shall not cross the boundary of protecting our economic interests; on the other hand, we expect the same from France and other powers.'

I had the impression that he (Grey) was preoccupied with the question of the disintegration of Asia Minor, and that although he does not want to take part yet in the division into spheres of interest, he is thinking of Russia and France, and for this reason he will not be able easily to approach the agreement which is being considered.[139]

The opinion of the German Government is clear in the telegram sent by the Chancellor Bethmann-Hollweg to their Ambassador in London on 27 January 1913.

I entirely agree with the phraseology used by Your Highness during the conversation which took place on the 24th of the current month with Sir E. Grey on the subject of Asia. As long as we only have economic interests in Asia Minor, and should inner conflicts arise, it is true that there is no reason for us to cross the boundaries of these economic interests on condition that France and other powers do likewise, because we are pleased with the present administrative system of Asia Minor, and we are far from wanting the abolition of Turkish rule or that it be threatened. On the other hand, if there is an attempt to change the present situation of governing, and to begin the division of Asiatic Turkey, then it is natural that our interests which are only economic will immediately become first class political interests. (Yes.) Then we will be forced to interfere and obtain our share from the inheritance, because Germany is engaged in Asia Minor, not only through hundreds of millions, but through her prestige. German national consciousness will not allow areas which have been opened to , culture and international transport through German achievements to fall into entirely foreign hands.
Germany would not desire that Asiatic Turkey be eliminated today. Our relations with Great Britain are, in fact, being improved. But it is doubtful whether this development is popular in England to the extent that the British government will quietly accept that Germany settle in Asia Minor, and even on the coasts of Asia Minor. For this reason, our intervention today in Asia Minor would encounter the opposition of England. (?) Moreover, it should be added that the provinces Germany would demand in the event of a partition constitute the core and backbone of the Turkish state and are inhabited by a Muslim community which has remained extremely loyal to the Sultan and his chalifs. Disintegration in Turkey has not reached such a point that we should not take into consideration these elements which are the best in the population. Should we attempt to settle in Anatolia, we must also count on the fierce resistance of the people. However, England in Arabia, Russia in Armenia, France in Syria will be more successful because of the liberation movements which have been present in these areas for a long time. For this reason, not only will it be necessary to use substantial military forces for the realization of our action, but it also seems doubtful whether it is justified to leave the motherland in such an unguarded state, when one bears in mind the relationships between the great powers today.
The above observations, presented with the only aim that Your Highness has an idea of the situation, show how much vital interest we have in the continuation, as long as possible, of Turkish rule in Asia Minor. For this reason, within the framework of the instructions submitted to you, we request that, at all costs, you prevent the Asia question from being brought up.[140]

While this attitude of Germany made the other powers forget the subject of partitioning the Ottoman Empire, it showed the need to strengthen spheres of influence, and as a result of this, the agreements we have mentioned above were reached.

For the same reason, the Armenian question was not brought up during the London talks which concluded the Balkan Wars, but the Armenians, of course, had no idea then that this would happen.

Without doubt, the Babiali was informed of the activities the Armenians engaged in, and especially of Bogos Nubar Pasha's contacts. Bogos Nubar Pasha had even met Javit Bey, who at the time was meeting the French in Paris, and had not concealed his opinions.

The Babiali felt that European pressure was likely, and began to consider ways of preventing it. It is necessary to study the conversations reported by the British Ambassador in his telegram against this background.

Accordingly, the Babiali enacted the law of General Provincial Administration dated 13 March 1329 (26 March 1913) which gave authority to make decisions in local matters in the provinces to the provincial assembly, and which accepted special budgets for the provinces; the law of the Justices of the Peace (*Sulh Hakimleri Kanunu*) dated 11 April 1329 (24 April 1913) which would permit the establishment of new courts in various areas; and other laws. At the same time, in 1913, the Babiali made an approach which it thought would please the European powers, requesting experts and officers for gendarmerie from Britain to work in eastern Anatolia and in the Ottoman Ministry of the Interior.

This request made the Armenian question reappear. Russia very strongly opposed this. However, still on 23 January, Russia declared that it did not find it convenient to bring up the Armenian question at that time.[141]

We shall not dwell on the details. Russia claimed that sending foreign experts, who would work on the topic of the Armenians, to Turkey, could only be done within the framework of general reform, and that this subject should be discussed between Russia, France and Britain at the level of the Ambassadors in Istanbul.

Germany asserted that the subject concerned all the great powers. As a result, Russia invited France, Britain, Germany, Austria and Italy to handle this subject through their Ambassadors in Istanbul, with a circular note it sent on 6 June 1913.

This time, Germany suggested that the Turks should also participate in the discussions. Russia strongly opposed this.

Finally, Russia's suggestion was acted on. The Ambassadors were headed by the Austrian Ambassador who had seniority in service, and met in his waterside residence in Yenikeuy. During this meeting on 30 June 1913, the Russians submitted proposals. (These had been prepared by the Russian, British, and French experts.)

The text of the proposals was:

1. The provinces of Erzeroum, Van, Bitlis, Biyarbekir, Kharpout, and Sivas shall be united as a single province. Some of the bordering areas of these provinces shall be excluded from this new province. (The region of Hakkari, the region of Birejik in Siirt, south of Malatya, the north-west of Sivas [that is, approximately today's province of Tokat].)

Attention shall be paid to ensuring that the population is homogeneous as far as possible within each subdivision, as the new vilayet is divided into *sanjaks, kazas, and nahiyes.*

2. The governor-general of this `Armenian province' shall be appointed for a period of five years by the Sultan, with the consent of the great powers. He will be an Ottoman Christian, or preferably a, European foreigner.

3. This governor-general will be the executive officer of the province and may, without exception, appoint and dismiss all the officials. Likewise he will appoint the judges. The police and the gendarmerie are directly under his command. When he requires it, the army too will be placed under his command to establish order.

The officials, the judges, the police, and the gendarmerie will be formed of Muslims and Christians in equal numbers. When the governors of the *sanjaks* and the head officials of the districts are being selected, the number of various elements and their economic importance must be taken into consideration. The organization of the police and the gendarmerie shall be given to foreign officers, who will be in the service of Turkey, and who will also have the high command of the police and the gendarmerie.

4. The governor-general shall have an administrative assembly in an advisory role. Its members will be: (a) Presidents of various departments, (b) Spiritual leaders of various congregations and (c) six advisors, three of whom will be Muslims and the other three Christians, selected from among the members of the provincial assembly.

An administrative assembly of the same nature and formation shall be established in each *sanjak* and *kaza.*

5. The provincial assembly shall be formed of Muslim and Christian members in equal numbers.

The Assembly memberships which shall be given to various Muslim and Christian peoples shall be established separately for every *kaza.* These numbers will be proportionate to the numbers of various elements in each kaza, on condition that the above-mentioned equality in numbers of Muslims and Christians as a total is maintained.

This assembly will possess great powers to enact the budget and the laws. The decree of the Sultan approving or rejecting these laws must arrive within two months. If there is no reply within two months, this means that the law is accepted.

6. The boundaries of the *nahiyes* will be established in such a way that they include, as far as possible, villages having a homogeneous population. The *nahiye* will have an assembly selected by the inhabitants. This assembly will elect from among its members the governor of the *nahiye* and his assistant. The governor will belong to the community in the majority and his assistant will be from the community in the minority.

7. The centre of each *nahiye* and *kaza* will have a justice of the peace appointed by the governor-general. The justice of the peace of the *nahiye* will belong to the creed of the majority.

Even in the courts the principle of having Muslim and Christian judges in equal numbers will be respected.

8. In peace time, the population of the province will do military service within the province. The light cavalry regiments of Kurds (the former Hamidiye regiments) will be abolished.

9. The right to vote in various elections, and the right to be elected is restricted to the sedentary inhabitants. [That is, the tribes and nomads are excluded.]

10. All laws, regulations etc., shall be published in three languages (Turkish, Kurdish, Armenian). Likewise, in the courts, in the official requests, these three languages may be used.

11. Every community living in the province may found a private school of any level, and may collect taxes from its members for this reason. Turkish will be compulsory in these schools, and their inspection will be the responsibility of the governor-general.

12. The governor-general shall appoint a commission to examine the subject of returning the lands taken from the Armenians.

13. The various privileges of the Armenian community and the rights it obtained through the 1863 organization will not be infringed.

14. Nomads will not be allowed to settle in the province.

15. Measures will be implemented in accordance with the principles above, to improve the condition of the Armenians outside the new province and especially in Cilicia.

16. A commission formed of the delegates of the Ottoman Government and of the great powers will establish the constitution of the new province.

17. The great powers will pay attention to the implementation of these principles, and will ensure their implementation.[142]

It is useful to look at the telegram dated 30 June, sent by the German Ambassador to his government concerning this meeting.

Mr. Giers made the following observations today during the meeting of the Ambassadors:

1. This conference is organized through Russia's encouragement.

2. Russia is more interested than the other powers in the question of eastern Anatolia and the Armenians.

3. The discussions must be concluded as soon as possible. Following this, Von Giers submitted Mandelstam's proposal. According to this proposal, the six provinces must be united into one province under the supervision of a governor- general to be appointed by the Sultan, or better, of a European governor-general. From an administrative and military point of view, this province will be entirely separated from the Ottoman states. The officials and judges without exception will be nominated and appointed by the governor-general. Military troops will include only Armenians and during peace time will be used only in that area. This proposal goes beyond the 1895 programme and even beyond the status of Lebanon. Acceptance of this proposal will create an Armenia, more than half of Anatolia, which is flimsily bound to Turkey only with the sovereignty of the Sultan.

Because the other half of the Armenians live in Russia, Russia claims a first class right in this subject. This subject means the beginning of the division [the division of Ottoman Asia]. France will implement this action in Syria, likewise. If we do not want to abandon Anatolia, we will request a similar regime for the region we are interested in. The Russian proposal also protects the province of Diyarbekir, which is partly our region, in the name of Armenia. Upon the suggestion of the most senior Ambassador [Austria], the proposal was referred to a commission formed by Embassies' delegates to be examined. I plan to be represented through Schönberg, the Turkish translator of the Embassy. Marquis Pallavicini and I are giving instructions to our representatives not to engage in any argument about the main points, but to insist that a comprehensive discussion take place concerning the separate points of the Russian programme and study of the Turkish offers. Above all, the important point is to gain time so that the detachments which are about to return may re-enter Armenia, and in this way, time is gained for the British position. If England consents to Russia's offer, this would prove that England is not willing to delay the division.[143]

As for the Ottoman Government, it informed the Ambassadors of the reform which would be implemented through the changes made on the subject of the general administration of the provinces on 1 July. Thus two sets of proposals had appeared. These were discussed during eight meetings held between 3 and 24 July at the subcommission formed by the Ambassadors, and no result was obtained. Germany, Austria, and Italy supported the Turkish thesis during these meetings, and the British seemed to lean towards them.

Russia realized that in order to have the proposal approved, it had to obtain the consent of Germany. We shall not dwell on the details. The German Ambassador Vangenheim and the Russian Ambassador Giers began discussions and reached an agreement on a new proposal. The text, which the other powers did not object to, was submitted to the Babiali by the Russians. Between September 1913 and February 1914 offers and counter- offers were made between the Russian Ambassador and the Grand Vizier. Now Russia was taking the initiative on the subject, with the consent of the other Ambassadors, and was informing them of developments. Each time the Grand Vizier requested support from the other powers, they replied that he should conclude the matter as soon as possible.

Thus, the final text was signed on 8 February 1914. We quote the text from Hikmet Bayur:

An agreement has been reached between His Highness Prince Said Halim Pasha, the Grand Vizier and the Minister of Foreign Affairs of the Ottoman Empire, and Excellency Constantin Gulkevitch, the chargé d'affaires of Russia, that after the designation of two inspector-generals who will be brought to the head of the two sectors of Eastern Anatolia, the Babiali shall send the following note to the Great Powers:

Two foreign inspector-generals will be brought to the head of the two Eastern Anatolian sectors: Mr. A— will be at the head of the sectors including the provinces of Erzurum, Trabzon, and Sivas, and

Mr. B—will be appointed to the provinces of Van, Bitlis, Kharput, and Diyarbekir.

The inspector-generals will have control of the administration, the judiciary, the police, and the gendarmerie in their sectors.

Should the general security forces there not be on hand in time, upon the request of the inspector-general, the armed forces will be given under his command for the implementation of the measures he has taken, within the boundaries of his jurisdiction.

The inspector-generals will dismiss officials, as need may be, should they detect any incompetence or poor conduct on their part, and will send for trial those who have engaged in activities punishable by the courts. They will replace the lower officials whom they have dismissed by officials who are qualified according to the rules and regulations. They possess the right to submit the names of officials who will replace the higher officials to the Government of His Majesty the Sultan. The inspector-general will immediately inform the interested Ministry with a telegram, and a short memorandum, and within eight days they will send the dossiers of these officials, along with the detailed memorandums, to the same place.

In serious cases, which necessitate quick implementation of measures, the inspector-generals have the right to suspend officials of the judiciary who cannot be dismissed (such as judges), on condition that they immediately inform the Ministry of Justice.

Should it be detected that the governors are engaged in acts requiring that urgent indispensable measures are taken against them, the inspector-generals will inform the Ministry of the Interior of this with a telegram, and the Minister will make a decision at most within four days of receipt of the inspector-general's telegram.

The agrarian conflicts [the lands claimed by the Armenians to have been taken away from them] will be resolved under the direct supervision of the inspector- generals.

More detailed regulations will be drafted, concerning the duties and jurisdictions of the inspector-generals, after these have been appointed, and with their cooperation.

Should there be a vacancy during the next ten years in the office of the inspector generals, the Babiali will rely on the benevolent assistance of the great powers for their election.

Laws, regulations, and official communications will be announced in every area in the local languages. If the inspector-general regards it as feasible, everyone will have the right to use his own language in the courts and in government offices. Court sentences will be given in Turkish, and when possible they will be translated into the language of the interested parties.

The portion allotted to each community for the public instruction budget in each province will be proportional to its portion of the tax levied for public instruction. The Imperial Government will not oppose in any way that within a congregation, those who are of that faith, help in the administration of their schools.

During time of peace and tranquility, each Ottoman will do his military service within the military inspectorship of his residence. Nevertheless, the Imperial Government, till further orders, will send land army units, formed by recruits from all parts of the Empire, in accordance with the population ratio of those areas, to the remote areas of Yemen, Asir and Nejd in Arabia; likewise it will draft soldiers from all parts of the Empire for the navy.

The Hamidiye regiments will be organized as reserve cavalry. Their arms will be kept in military depots, and will be given to them only during mobilization and manoeuvres. These regiments will be under the orders of the commander of the army corps of their region. During peace time the commanders of the regiments, companies, and squads will be chosen from among the Regular Army officers of the Imperial Army. The privates of these regiments will do their military service for one year, and to enter the regiment, they will themselves provide their horses with all their equipment. Everybody of that area who accepts these conditions will be taken into the regiment regardless of religion and origin. When they are gathered for mobilization or manoeuvres, these units will be subjected to the same disciplinary measures as the regular army units.

The authority of the provincial general assemblies has been established according to the principles of the law dated March 13, 1329 [26 March 1913, i.e. the law of the general administration of the provinces].

A definitive census will be made as soon as possible within a year, under the supervision of the inspector-generals, and will establish the proportion of the various religions, communities, and languages in the two sectors. Until then, half of the members elected in the general assemblies and committees of the provinces of Van and Bitlis will be non-Muslims. If the definitive census is not made within one year, then the members of the general assembly of the province of Erzurum, too, will be elected in the same proportion as the two provinces mentioned above. The members of the general assemblies of the provinces of Sivas, Kharpout, and Diyarbekir will be elected according to the present principle of proportionality. (This refers to the proportion of various religions.] To achieve this, until the definitive census is made, the number of Muslim voters will be established based on the tables used during the last census, and the number of non-Muslim voters will be established according to the tables provided by the congregations. However, if some financial difficulties make the implementation of this temporary census system impossible, the inspector-generals have the right to suggest a system better suited to the present needs and conditions of the provinces of Sivas, Kharpout, and Diyarbekir, for the distribution of the memberships in the general assemblies of these provinces among various communities.

In all the provinces based on the principle of proportionality in the elections of the general assemblies, the minorities will have members on the committees.

The elected members of the administrative assemblies will be Muslim and non- Muslim in equal numbers.

If the inspector-generals have no objection, as there are vacancies in the police force and the gendarmerie of the two sectors, the principles of equality among Muslims and non-Muslims will be the basis in the employment of new officers. This principle of equality will also be the basis as far as possible for the distribution of all the other officials in the two sectors.

In confirmation of these articles, the above mentioned individuals have initialled and sealed this document.[144]

Because this agreement was made with Russia, Russia was its supervisor. That is, the other five powers left Russia to act freely in the matter of the
eastern provinces.

The Ottoman Government did not have the courage to announce this agreement to the people. The following news item was published in the newspaper *Tanin* on 11 February 1914:

As we have written previously, the discussions which have been occurring for some time concerning the reforms to be implemented in the eastern provinces have reached a good result, and a total agreement has been made in all the reform principles. As the Government has decided to communicate soon through the press, the text of this communication is being finalized and presented by the Babiali.

Although some of our associates have written that a protocol would be organized and signed, this is an erroneous statement. However, the Babiali will restrict itself to submit the reform principles to the Embassies. [145]

The only thing that remained was the election of the inspector-generals. This was not easily achieved, as the powers had difficulty in reaching agreement. Finally, Major Hoff of the Norwegian army was chosen for the region of Van, Bitlis, Harput and Diyarbekir; Westenek of Belgium was chosen for the region of Trabzon, Erzurum and Sivas; and the Babiali signed a contract with them on 25 May 1914.

On 28 June 1914 the heir to the Austrian throne, Archduke Francis Ferdinand, was assassinated in Bosnia, and the developments leading to the First World War began. When the Ottoman Empire entered the war on 1 November, the inspector-generals had not begun their work.

On 31 December 1914, the Babiali announced with an official decree that it had dismissed them.

The subject of reform for the benefit of the Armenians was thus concluded.

CHAPTER FIVE

The First World War

1. The Armenians during the war

Nearly three-quarters of a century has passed since 1914, and the question whether the Ottoman Empire could have avoided entering the war is still being discussed today. As no one at that time knew with certainty why the Empire entered the war, and no discussion took place when the decision was made, it is not clear why it is being discussed today.

The subject is outside our topic of discussion, and we shall not dwell on it. We only wish to mention a point which most people are still unaware of, owing to the erroneous explanations made intentionally by those who were largely responsible for entering the war, to defend themselves.

In 1914, the Ottoman Empire was pursuing an agreement with any one of the Triple Entente or the Triple Alliance. There were very few prominent members of the government who supported Germany's groups, that is the Triple Alliance. In fact, Enver Pasha was probably the only one.

Jemal Pasha, Talat Pasha and Javit Bey were supporters of the Triple Entente. They made many unsuccessful attempts to reach agreement with France or England. Then they turned to Germany. Contrary to what is generally known, Turkey made the request to Germany, rather than Germany to Turkey. At that time, Germany was convinced that Turkey would only be an impediment to its allies.

On 23 July, Enver Pasha courteously asked the German Ambassador whether an agreement could be reached with Germany. The First World War was about to begin.

We do not find it necessary to include it here, but the telegram sent by Wangenheim to Berlin concerning this meeting is worth reading (telegram dated 22 July 1914).[1] Upon instructions given by the Kaiser himself, in the belief that even one more rifle would be useful in the coming war, it was decided to make an alliance with Turkey, and this agreement was signed on 2 August. The First World War had already begun on the 1st.

This agreement was not the decisive reason why the Ottoman Empire entered the war, for the agreement was drafted as a defensive alliance against Russia. The war began with Germany declaring war on Russia, so Turkey was not under any obligation to enter the war.

In spite of this, the Ottoman Empire entered the war on 31 October.

In order to explain the attitude of the Armenians during this period, we must refer to an incident which occurred in 1909.

After the event of 31 March and the Adana rebellion, an agreement was made between the Party of Union and Progress and the Istanbul delegation of the Tashnak Committee. We quote this agreement, which was published on 3 September 1909 in the *Tanin* newspaper, from Esat Uras' book.

In order to ensure the independence of the country, to protect till the end its integrity and policy, to eradicate the evil thoughts appearing in various individuals, and to establish good relations between Ottoman subjects, total agreement has been reached between the Committee of Union and Progress and the Armenian Tashnaksutyun Committee on the following points.

1. The two said committees shall work without sparing any sacrifices, and to the utmost of their ability, to strengthen the constitutional government and to maintain the cultural education of the people on solid principles.

2. They shall act in a determined and specific direction within the limits of legal conditions, against the possibility of any reactionary movements.

3. Because the only aim of the activities of the two committees is to spare the sacred Ottoman country from any partition and separation, attempts will be made to eradicate the rumours that Armenians are leaning towards independence, rumours present in public opinion and which have remained from the period of despotism.

4. Both committees agree on [extending the authority of the provinces] necessary for the country's progress and development.

5. The Committee of Union and Progress and the Tashnaksutyun Committee consider the incident of 31 March and the Adana disaster as a warning, and have decided to work hand in hand for the implementation of the above principles.[2]

We have been unable to find a document to the effect that the Tashnak Central Committee approved this agreement made by the delegation responsible for Istanbul.

It is known that the Tashnak Committee held a congress at Erzurum in June 1914. Because, at that time, an agreement had been reached with Russia concerning the eastern provinces, and the inspector-generals had even been designated, Erzurum had become a place where the Tashnaks could speak freely on any topic.

Esat Uras reports the decision which was taken during this Congress: 'The Tashnaksutyun Congress, bearing in mind the contradictory economic, social, and administrative policy implemented for a long time by the Government of Union and Progress in regard to the Christian communities, and especially to the Armenians, has decided to remain in opposition to the Government of Union and Progress, to criticize its political programme, and to engage in a fierce struggle against it and its organization.'[3]

Y. H. Bayur has included this decision in his book, quoting from Esat Uras. However, Esat Uras gives no reference for this decision, and we have not found it in any other source.

On the other hand, it is reported in all the sources that representatives of the Committee of Union and Progress took part in this congress. Esat Uras denies this, asserting that there is no document to support it, and that this was a claim made by the Tashnaks in a book published in 1920 in Istanbul. We do not think that it was entirely impossible for the representatives of the Party of Union and Progress to have taken part in this Congress. Nevertheless, it seems impossible to establish what they suggested, if they did take part.

Clair Price wrote as follows on this subject:

The Armenian bloc in the Parliament at Constantinople was holding its 1914 congress at Erzurum in the eastern provinces when the Enver Government entered the war. Government emissaries visited them there and laid before them the Pan-Turanian project whose immediate object was to throw Russia back. A partition of Russian Trans-Caucasia was proposed, the conquered territory to be divided between Armenians, Georgians and Tartars, each to be accorded autonomy under Ottoman suzerainty. The Armenian bloc replied that if war proved necessary they would do their duty as Ottoman subjects but they advised the Government to remain neutral.[4]

Toynbee's memorandum, which we referred to earlier, says: '. . . In the fall of 1914, Turks came to the Armenians' national congress in Erzurum , and offered them an autonomous Armenia (on Turkey's and Russia's lands) if they would actively help Turkey during the war. The Armenians refused this offer.'[5]

Papazian states:

When the world war broke out in Europe, the Turks began feverish preparations for joining hands with the Germans. In August 1914 the young Turks asked the Dashnag Convention, then in session in Erzurum, to carry out their old agreement of 1907, and start an uprising among the Armenians of the Caucasus against the Russian government. The Dashnagtzoutune refused to do this, and gave assurance that in the event of war between Russia and Turkey, they would support Turkey as loyal citizens. On the other hand, they could not be held responsible for the Russian Armenians. . . . The fact remains, however, that the leaders of the Turkish-Armenian section of the Dashnagtzoutune did not carry out their promise of loyalty to the Turkish cause when the Turks entered the war. The Dashnagtzoutune in the Caucasus had the upper hand. They were swayed in their actions by the interests of the Russian government, and disregarded, entirely, the political dangers that the war had created for the Armenians in Turkey. Prudence was thrown to the winds; even the decision of their own convention of Erzerum was forgotten, and a call was sent for Armenian volunteers to fight the Turks on the Caucasian front.[6]

Kachaznuni wrote:

In the beginning of fall 1914, when Turkey had not yet entered the war, but was preparing to, Armenian volunteer groups began to be organized with great zeal and pomp in Trans-Caucasia. In spite of the decision taken a few weeks before at the General Committee in Erzurum, the Dashnagtzoutune actively helped the organization of the aforementioned groups, and especially arming them, against Turkey. . . . There is no point in asking today whether our volunteers should have been in the foreground. Historical events have a logic of their own. In the fall of 1914 Armenian volunteer groups were formed and fought against the Turks. The opposite could not have happened, because for approximately twenty years the Armenian community was fed a certain and inevitable psychology. This state of mind had to manifest itself, and it happened.[7]

Kachaznuni was one of the prominent leaders of the Tashnak Party, and had been Prime Minister of the independent Armenian Republic. Consequently the information he gives is not based on hearsay, but carried his personal responsibility. His book, in fact, is his speech which was read in 1923 at the Party Council, and was not approved because it criticized the Party. He later published this speech, together with a letter written to a friend of his, named N.N. Towards the conclusion of the letter we read the following sentences: `You say "As we were unable to prevent the communication being read, I hope that it is forgotten as soon as possible". I find it dangerous and useless that this subject too, causes arguments. . . . For me the publication of this communication was a moral obligation on behalf of the Armenian cause. If I had not written, I would have committed a great sin. Because the General Council was unable to meet, I submitted my communication to the Advisory Council and I was told to "shut up". (This may be the reason why it is not possible to find this book in the world libraries.)

These sources we have quoted, indicate the possibility that representatives of the Committee of Union and Progress went to the Erzurum congress. However, the Armenians may also have discussed among themselves the kind of action to be taken during the war. Various dates are given as to when the congress was held. It seems logical that the date should be August or later. It also appears that it was decided during the congress that in the event of a Russo-Ottoman War, the Armenians in Turkey would not oppose the Government. But we are also informed by authorized Armenians that this decision was not followed.

It is apparent that the volunteers mentioned in all these sources were Armenians of Turkey. It is natural that the Armenians of the Caucasus were recruited and took part in the war, as they were Russian subjects.

When the Ottoman Government decreed mobilization, the Catholicos of Etchmiadzin sent a letter to Vorontsov-Dachkov, the Governor-General of the Caucasus, on 5 August 1914, and received a reply on 2 September. We quote a passage from the Catholicos' letter:

Based on the information I have received from the Istanbul Patriachate and the Armenian Assembly, I am convinced that any reform to be implemented by the Government which today rules Turkey, for the improvement of the condition of the Armenians, will not survive long, as long as it is not based on particular and solid engagements. . . . I request from Your Highness that you present to His Majesty the Emperor, the devotion of his faithful subjects on my behalf and on behalf of my congregation in Russia, the sincere loyalty and attachment of the Armenians of Turkey, and at the same time that you defend to the Czar the hopes of the Armenians of Turkey. . . .[8]

This passage clearly indicates cooperation between the Istanbul Patriarchate and Etchmiadzin, and that the Catholicos could speak on behalf of the Armenians of Turkey. We shall now quote a few statements from Vorontsov-Dachkov's reply:

I wish that the actions of the Armenians here, as well as those on the other side of the border, be now in accordance with my instructions. I request that you use your authority over your congregation, and ensure that our Armenians and those who reside in the border regions implement the duties and services which I will ask them to carry out in the future, in the event of a Russo-Turkish war, as in the situation of Turkey today.

The text of these letters was included in Gr. Tchalkouchian's work entitled *The Red Book* which was published in Armenian in Paris in 1919. The second letter, in particular, indicates clearly the kind of instructions the Armenians of Turkey would be given in the event of a war. The quotation we have given from various sources show that they did indeed receive these instructions when the day arrived.

There is another document which few people remember today.

When the Ottoman Empire had not yet entered the war, but as soon as it declared mobilization, Turkish Armenians living in Marseilles held a large meeting on 5 August 1914, and drew up a declaration which was published in various newspapers. We quote below a few passages from this declaration which was published over Aram Turabian's signature.

The Russian Armenians, in the ranks of the Muscovite army, will do their duty, to revenge the insult made on our brothers' corpses; as for us, the Armenians under the domination of Turkey, no Armenian rifle must be turned towards the friends and allies of France, our second land.

Turkey is mobilizing, she calls us on active service, without telling us against whom.

Against Russia? Surely not! We shall not go and fight against our own brothers of Caucasus, against the Balkan States, for which we have nothing but sympathy. Never! Gentlemen, you came to the wrong address; let us not forget the past, without being certain of the future yet.

Armenians, Turkey calls you to fight without telling you against whom: join as volunteers the ranks of the French Army and of her allies, to help destroy the army of Wilhelm II, whose railway is built on the corpses of our 300,000 brothers. . . .[9]

In this book, an alphabetical list of 400 individuals who enlisted as volunteers, complying with this summons, is included.

In fact, we find in almost every source that the Armenians cooperated with the Russians when war broke out. Let us give a few examples.

Rafael de Nogales writes:

After hostilities had actually commenced, the Deputy to the Assembly for Erzurum, Garo Pasdermichan, passed over with almost all the Armenian troops and officers of the Third Army to the Russians; to return with them soon after, burning hamlets and mercilessly putting to the knife all of the peaceful Mussulman villagers that fell into their hands. These bloody excesses had as their necessary corollary the immediate disarmament by the Ottoman authorities of the gendarmes and other Armenian soldiers who still remained in the army (probably because they had been unable to escape) and the utilization of their labour in the construction of highways and in carrying provisions back and forth across the mountains. The altogether unjustifiable desertion of the Armenian troops, united to the outrages they committed afterwards, on their return, in the sectors of Bash- Kaleh, Serail, and Bayacet, did not fail to alarm the Turks and rouse their fear lest the rest of the Armenian population in the frontier provinces of Van and Erzurum revolt likewise, and attack them with the sword. This indeed is precisely what happened a few weeks after my coming, when the Armenians of the vilayet of Van rose en masse against our expeditionary army in Persia; thus giving rise to bloody and terrible occurrences which, under the circumstances, might have been foreseen.[10]

Let us now turn to Philips Price: 'When war broke out the Armenians of these regions [the Eastern provinces] made secret contact with the Russian authorities in the Caucasus, and an underground network was created which enabled recruits to be gotten from these Turkish provinces for the Russian Army.'[11]

Philippe de Zara, who is not well known, writes:

After having accomplished the minimum of their duty as Ottoman citizens, the Armenians began to encourage the activities of the enemy. Their ambiguous attitude had certainly little to do with loyalty. But which Westerner would have the right to accuse them, when a tradition taught by Europe made the insubordination of the Sultan's Christian subjects the most sacred of obligations? An insubordination which was often sanctioned by granting autonomy, if not sovereignty. Nevertheless, how can anyone deny that, in the opinion of the Turks, according to the law of all the states, the conduct of the Armenians, facilitating during the war the task of the adversary, can be recognized as anything but a crime of high treason? . . . The committees, divided among themselves for internal issues, were often in agreement to facilitate the advance of Russian armies: they were attempting to obstruct the retreat of Turkish troops, to stop the convoys of provisions, to form bands of francs-tireurs. Mass desertions took place in the Eastern provinces: Armenians thus formed many troops officered by Russian officers. Here and there local revolts occurred. The leaders were setting the examples: two Armenian deputies fled to Russia. A literature of hatred was recalled: `Let the Turkish mothers cry. . . . Let's make the Turk taste a little grief.' The culpability of Armenians leaves no doubt.[12]

Clair Price, too, has focussed on the subject of cooperation with Russia:

Under the 1908 Constitution, the Enver Government had a right to mobilize Armenians of military age as well as Turks, but armed opposition broke out at once, notably at Zeitun. . . Along the eastern frontier, Armenians began deserting to the Russian Armies and the Enver Government, distrusting the loyalty of those who remained, removed them from the combatant force and formed them into labour gangs. . . .

In April, Lord Bryce and the `Friends of Armenia' in London appealed for funds to equip these volunteers, and Russia also was presumably not uninterested in them. . . . These volunteer bands finally captured Van, one of the eastern provincial capitals, late in April and, having massacred the Turkish population, they surrendered what remained of the city to the Russian Armies in June. The news from Van affected the Turks precisely as the news from Smyrna affected them when the Greeks landed there in May, 1919. The rumour immediately ran through Asia Minor that the Armenians had risen.

By this time, the military situation had turned sharply against the Enver Government. The Russian victory at Sarykamish was developing and streams of Turkish refugees were pouring westward into central Asia Minor. The British had launched their Dardanelles campaign at the very gates of Constantinople, and Bulgaria had not yet come in. It does not seem reasonable to assume that this moment, of all moments, would have been chosen by the Enver Government to take widespread measures against its Armenians unless it was believed that such measures were immediately necessary. Measures were taken.[13]

Felix Valyi has written:

In April the Armenian revolutionaries seized the town of Van, established an Armenian 'General Staff' there under the command of Aram and Vardan, which delivered up the town to the Russian troops on the 6th of May, after having 'freed' the district of Van from Mohammedans. . .

Amongst the most notorious of the Armenian chiefs was Karakin Pastermadjian, a former member of the Turkish Parliament, known by the name of 'Garo', who put himself at the head of the Armenian volunteers at the time of the opening of hostilities between Turkey and Russia, and the Turks accuse him of having set fire to all the Mussulman villages he found on his way and of massacring their inhabitants. It is known that the attempts made by Turkey to win the support of the 'Dachnakzoutioun' party against Russia at the beginning of the War were repulsed in the month of September, 1914, by the Armenian Congress at Erzurum, which declared itself `neutral'. Nevertheless the thousands of Russian bombs and muskets which were found in the hands of its members prove what this neutrality meant. And indeed the Turks attribute the Russian invasion of the north of Asia Minor to the behaviour of the Armenian bands whose attitude made the defence of the country exceedingly difficult.[14]

It must not be assumed that these authors we have quoted are friendly to the Turks and hostile to the Armenians. Rather, most of them are Armenian sympathizers. The passages we have quoted from them indicate the grounds for the relocation decision. Actually, if we had continued quoting, we would have arrived at passages referring to this decision. However, it was necessary, in our opinion, to examine first the developments within the borders of the Ottoman Empire through concrete incidents rather than by making general statements. We shall do this now, based on the Ottoman documents.

The Ottoman Government decreed mobilization on 3 August. The Armenians of Zeitun did not want to be under the Ottoman flag, and wished to protect their region by forming a volunteer regiment of Zeitun led by their own officers. As their request was naturally denied, they rebelled on 30 August.[15] As a result of the pursuit, approximately sixty rebels were caught with their weapons, and although tranquillity was established for a while, in December the Zeitunites began to attack civil servants and gendarmes.

In February 1915, it was necessary to send soldiers and ammunition to Zeitun from Marash. (It must not be forgotten that the country was at war.) The Armenians who attacked the troops guarding the ammunition killed six gendarmes, wounded two, and then escaped, and in the meantime cut communication links with Marash by breaking the telegraph lines. Almost all of those who had been enlisted from the area deserted. The rebellion of the Zeitunites continued until the implementation of the relocation decision. The brigands who had not been caught left the region when there was no place left to hide, and order was restored. In the pursuits which took place during the rebellion, 713 rifles, 21 shotguns, and 12 mausers were found, and 61 brigands, including their priests who had led them, were arrested.

We want to mention here a report sent by the American Consulate in Aleppo to its Ministry concerning these incidents which occurred in Zeitun during the war.[16] The Consul included in his report a letter written by a Protestant priest, John E. Merill, an American missionary of the region. We quote a few passages from this letter:

> Before a confrontation occurred in Zeitun, a Committee formed by Herr Blank, a Protestant missionary, and two Gregorians, went to Zeitun with the approval of the Government to obtain, if possible, a friendly agreement. As they met the inhabitants of Zeitun, they were told by the Zeitunites that they had attempted everything in order to persuade the outlaws to surrender, but that they were unable to persuade them. Naturally the Committee was not successful. The outlaws number around thirty, and hide in the hills between Zeitun and Marash. They have water, food, and ammunition, and the only road that leads to their hide-out is a path large enough for one person. . . . later the Zeitunites were persuaded to hand over these outlaws, and in return they have stipulated that their villages be not harmed. . . . But later some of the villagers were transferred to Marash. . . . The inhabitants of Zeitun have been duped by the Government. . . . To force the educated and competent Christian community of the Marash region to migrate is a direct blow to the interests of the American missionaries. The results of more than 50 years of work and thousands of dollars is being threatened. . . .

This report is quite amazing. Missionaries are attempting to reach an agreement with outlaws in a country at war (these are deserters), and they consider the deportation to Marash of certain families who feed and hide them a blow to the missionaries' interests. If these outlaws are killed in an armed confrontation, this is considered a massacre.

One of the main reasons for the misfortunes of the Armenians is this missionary mentality, and the uproar made by those who believe their claims.

A report sent on 30 August 1914 by the Eleshkirt Border Battalion Command to the 3rd Army Command stated that the Russians searching houses in the villages near the border gave the arms they found to the Armenians, and that the Armenians of the region were engaged in propaganda to escape to Russia.[17]

A message sent by the Supreme Military Command to the 3rd Army Command on 6 September[18] stated that information had been received to the effect that the Armenians of Van were in contact with the Russians.

On 13 September 1914, the Governor of Erzurum sent a memorandum to the 3rd Army Command, stating that he had been informed that the Russians were attempting to bring the Armenians to their side and were preparing to engineer a rebellion in the eastern Anatolian provinces whenever they wanted; that an individual named Aramayis, who had been exiled to Siberia after having been sentenced to one hundred and one years, had been freed by the Russians, and that he was now organizing bands in

Kars; that a band had arrived at the village of Pasinler and was engaged in propaganda, telling the villagers to rebel when the Ottomans entered the war, and to desert if they were enlisted.

On 18 September 1914, the Governor of Bitlis, Mustafa Bey, sent a similar message to the 3rd Army Commander, and stated: `According to the recent decisions and suggestions of prominent Armenians, if there is a war, the Armenian soldiers in the Army will desert with their arms to the enemy. If the Ottoman Army advances, they will remain calm, if it retreats, bands will be formed to prevent passage to and from the front.'[19]

A message dated 2S September sent by the Supreme Military Command to the 3rd Army Command, stated that 'The Armenian Tashnakzutun and the Hinchakian Committees in the Caucasus have agreed with Russia to incite the Armenians of Turkey to revolt in the event of a war.'[20]

The Governor of Trabzon, Jemal Azmi Bey, in a message he sent to the Ministry of the Interior on 8 October 1914, stated that 'A band of 800 people comprising the Ottoman and Russian Armenians in Russia, has been armed by the Russians, and sent to the vicinity of Artvin. We have been informed that they will spread out between Artvin and Ardanuch, that their number will be increased to 7,000, and that they will be used to disturb security within the Ottoman country.'[21]

On 11 October 1914, the 3rd Army Commander sent the following message to the Supreme Military Command: `It has been established that the Russians are forming bands in the Caucasus by arming Russian and Ottoman Armenians and Greeks, that they will send them here and enlarge the bands in our territory. The Armenian desertions from our detachment are increasing.'[22]

On 13 October 1914, the Commander of the 2nd Cavalry Division informed the 3rd Army Commander that the Russians were distributing arms to the Armenians of Narman.[23]

On 14 October 1914, the Governor of the *sanjak* of Beyazit sent the following message to the Ministry of the Interior: 'We have been informed that on September 26th, Sehpat of the Armenian revolutionaries in Russia came to Hoy with 600 Armenian volunteers, and that they went to Selmas. Most of these Armenians are Ottoman citizens and are inhabitants of Van, Mush, Bitlis, Kars, and Gumru. It has been established that they are waiting for the arrival of their commander Antranik. We have been informed that pharmacist Rupen Migirdichian living in Erjish in the region of Van, along with Toros Karakashian and Portakalian, and Surin, who is doing business in Beyazit, are thinking of going to Selmas with the force they have gathered in the regions of Ighdir and Revan, that the individuals named Melkon and Ohannes have gone from Hoy to Van to make propaganda.'[24]

On 22 October 1914, the Commander of the 2nd Cavalry division informed the Army Commander that Armenian volunteers were gathered in the regions of Mush, Van, and Bitlis, that Armenian brigands were present near the borders, and that 30-40 brigands were present in the village of Pertos.[25]

A report sent by the 3rd Army Command to the Supreme Military Command on 25 October 1914 stated: 'Approximately 800 people, most of them Armenian deserters with Ottoman citizenship, have gathered in Kaghizman. They are armed by the Russian Government. The Armenians named Surien of Beyazit and Hachik Sirup, who have gone to Russia, have each gathered 2,000 people. We have been informed that one group will attempt to go to Mosson by way of lake Abbas, and that the other group will go to Beyazit or Iran.'[26]

On 24 October, the Governor of Erzurum stated in a report that he sent to the 3rd Army Commander: `According to the statement made by Sitrak who is one of the brigands who a few days ago attacked the mail coach on the border of Gumushhane, and who was caught, his companions are in Bayburt and Surmene, and the head official of Bayburt has gone to arrest these individuals.'[27]

On 28 October, the Governor notified the authorities that these individuals had been arrested.

In November, the Ottoman Empire was at war. The first reports concerning the planned Van rebellion came, on 29 November, from Kazim Bey (Ozalp), the Gendarmerie Division Commander. Kazim Bey stated that, according to the statements of two spies who had been caught, a rebellion would occur in Van soon, and that the enemy was gathering the weapons of the Muslims in the areas it invaded, and giving them to the Armenians, thus forming detachments. All the Armenians in the division whose weapons had been taken, had deserted.'[28]

The following day, 30 November, the Governor of Van, Jevdet Bey, stated in his telegram: `I am working to prevent the Armenians from creating an incident. The Russian Forces are advancing from Kotur. I do not think that the Gendarmerie Division will be able to resist these forces for long. I will start sending families to Bitlis.'[29]

It may be appropriate here to depart from the chronological order of events, and to describe the Van rebellion.

A telegram sent on 2 December from the province of Van to the Ministry of the Interior stated: 'At this point, Armenians are calm in the capital and in other areas; however, all the Armenians of the region of Selmas are working with the Russians. The person who leads the bands along the border is the notorious Antranik and his companions, who had once engineered the Taluri rebellion [the second rebellion of Sassun). After the Hanik battle, some Armenian privates deserted and joined the ranks of the enemy. I was informed that an Armenian bishop was in contact with the Russian Commander in Gari. I had him placed under police supervision.'[30]

A telegram sent on 15 December from the Ministry of the Interior to the Governor of Van stated that some of the telegraph lines of Reshadiye and Karjigan had been destroyed by the Armenians, and that the superintendent of the post had reported an armed confrontation with these Armenians. Additional information was requested.[31]

The Governor of Erzurum, Tahsin Bey, sent the following report to the Supreme Military Commander on 20 December: 'The Armenians of the *kazas* of Kerchikan and Gevash in Van are preparing to rebel. They have cut the telegraph lines of the area and have killed a corporal. Gendarmerie and militia have been sent to the area from Bitlis, and armed confrontations have begun. Because our forces are few, and the Militias have insufficient arms, more forces are needed.'[32]

The Governor of Bitlis sent the following telegram to the Ministry of the Interior on 21 February 1915: 'The Armenians of the *nahiye* of Haksef have rebelled. In the village of Siranun under the jurisdiction of the central kaza of Mush, shots were fired on our detachment, and the confrontation continued for two hours. In the village of Kumes, under the jurisdiction of the *bujak* of Akan, shots were fired at the house where the *bujak* superintendent and the gendarmes were staying, and the confrontation lasted for eight hours.'[33]

The same day, the governor of Bitlis, in a second telegram, stated: 'Armenians have revolted in many villages. I became suspicious when I saw that among the Armenians who opened fire in Kumes, a village in the *bujak* of Akan, were Rupen, the Tashnak delegate of Van, Zovin, and Eshroone of the Tashnak leaders in Mush. As a precaution, I had the delegate of Van, Papazian, be a guest of the *sanjak* governor, to hold him as a hostage.'[34]

On 27 February, about 300 volunteer soldiers from Siirt, who were on their way from Adiljevaz to Van, wanted to spend the night in the Armenian village of Arin. The Armenians, who attempted to prevent this, opened fire and killed eight privates. Upon this a detachment was sent from Erchish to Van, but the Armenian bands escaped to Lake Van.

On 4 March 1915, the head official of the district of Mahmudi in the province of Van sent the following telegram to the Ministry of the Interior: 'As a result of the investigation carried out after our *kaza* was taken back from the enemy, the following profile with regard to the torture and massacre which took place emerges:

Those who were killed in the village of Merkehu	41 men, 14 women
Those who were killed after having been raped	4 women
Those who were killed in the village of Ishtuju	7 men, 4 women
Those who are alive among those who have been raped	5 women
The wounded	3 men, 2 women[35]

A telegram dated 16 March sent by the Van Gendarmerie Division Command stated that in the *kaza* of Shatak of the province of Van, Armenians had attacked the gendarmerie station and the soldiers and had destroyed the telegraph lines, and that armed confrontations had occurred between the forces sent to the area and the Armenians. The incident began when a revolutionary teacher named Osep was caught with his weapon.[36]

On 20 March, the Governor of Van stated: `In all parts of the province, armed confrontations continued until the evening and have now increased. It is thought that the rebels number more than 2,000. We are trying to crush the rebellion.'[37]

The Governor, in a telegram he sent on 23 March, stated that 'the inhabitants of the villages of Bayrik, Alakoy, Iblankanis, and Buganis, which are at a distance of four hours from Van, are holding the strategic points above the village of Bayrik, and have besieged the village of Kusha. The number of rebels has increased to 1,000. Forces must be sent.'[38] Following this, the rebellion spread to the entire province.

Ali Ihsan Pasha wrote about this rebellion:

Jevdet Bey, the governor of Van, had informed the First Army Commander and the Supreme Military Command, as early as March 1915, that the Van rebellion was about to begin, and finally the rebellion occurred on April 17, 1915 in all parts of the province. The same day, the First Army was only able to arrive at Rumiyo. [This is the force of which Rafael de Nogales was a member.] After the rebellion began, it proved necessary to use the main part of the Van Mobile Gendarmerie Division to crush the rebellion.

If the First Army had not spent weeks in Mussul and Revandiz, we might have repelled the Russians in the vicinity of Dilman, before the Armenian rebellion occurred in Van, by using all the forces of the Van Mobile Gendarmerie Division. As time passed, the Armenian rebellion made it necessary to use an important part of our forces, and in mid-April, to make use of most of the Van Mobile Gendarmerie Division in fighting against the rebels in the rear. On the other hand, the Russians took advantage of the situation to increase the number of their forces in the vicinity of Dilman.

In April 1915, the First Army encountered the Russians, engaged in an offensive (together with part of the Van Mobile Gendarmerie Division on the eastern border of the province of Van) against the Russians on 1 May 1915 near Dilman, and retreated having suffered a great number of casualties. Because of the Armenian rebellion in Van, and the Russian forces advancing towards Van, the army was unable to free Van and was forced to retreat in the direction of Bitlis, through the mountains to the south of lake Van.[39]

On 20 April 1915, the Governor of Van sent the following telegram to the 3rd Army Command: 'The rebels have begun to open fire on our police stations near the Armenian quarters of Van, and on the Muslim houses. We are resisting and defending. In the confrontation which occurred near the village of Atalan until yesterday evening, most of the rebels have been crushed. The telegraph lines of Gevash have been repaired and opened to communication. Today the telegraph lines of Bashkale, Havasor, Memortki, Shersat have been cut. We have begun their repair. In the city, the confrontations are continuing with all their might. The insurrection is widespread. We request help and artillery.'[40]

On 24 April, the governor sent the following telegram to the Ministry of the Interior: 'Until now approximately 4,000 insurgent Armenians have been brought to the region from the vicinity. The rebels are engaged in highway robbery, attack the neighbouring villages and burn them. It is impossible to prevent this. Now many women and children are left homeless. It is not possible nor suitable to relocate them in tribal villages in the vicinity. Would it be convenient to begin sending them to the western provinces?'[41]

On 8 May, the Armenians began their offensive and started burning down the Muslim quarters. Upon this, the Governor, Jevdet Bey, ordered the evacuation of Van. On 17 May, the Turkish soldiers left Van, then the Armenians began to set fire to the Turkish quarters which had been evacuated. The Russians then entered Van. (The booklet entitled Zeve about the Van rebellion is worth reading.)

The Turkish forces engaged in an offensive on 22 July 1915, and repossessed Van. In August they lost it again to the Russians.

The rebellion in Van had spread to Mush. The Van Mobile Gendarmerie Division was charged with crushing this rebellion, and the operation continued until 11 July 1915.

On 2 May, before the fall of Van, the Deputy Commander-in-Chief, Enver Pasha, sent the following message to the Minister of the Interior, Talat Bey:

Around lake Van, and in specific areas known by the Governor of Van, Armenians are constantly gathered and prepared to continue their insurrection. I am convinced that these Armenians who have gathered must be removed from these areas, and that the rebellion's nest must be destroyed. According to the information provided by the 3rd Army Command, the Russians brought the Muslims within their borders into our country under wretched and miserable conditions, on 20 April 1915. In order to respond to this, as well as to reach the goal I have stated above, it is necessary to either send these Armenians and their families to Russia, or to disperse them within Anatolia. I request that the most suitable of these two alternatives be chosen and carried out. If there is no inconvenience I would prefer that the families of the rebels and the population of the region in rebellion are sent outside our borders, and that the Muslim community brought into our borders from abroad are relocated to their place.[42]

This message is the first indication of the relocation decision.

Let us continue now with the chronological account of events, which we interrupted to report the Van rebellion.

On 17 December 1914, the Commander of the 12th Army Corps in Antakya stated that it was feared the Armenians of Antakya would engage in an offensive.[43]

The Commander of the 11th Army Corps stated in a telegram he sent on 19 February 1915 from Elazigh to the Ministry of War, that Armenians, in various villages of the region, had opened fire on the gendarmes, and that the confrontation with the rebels had been continuing for the past three days.[44]

On 21 February, the same Army Corps sent the following telegram to the Ministry: 'Approximately 40-50 Armenian revolutionaries who were in the village of Siranun, two and a half hours away from Mush, have attacked villages, and have fought with the police and the cavalrymen who had been sent there.'[45]

On 25 February 1915, the Commander of the 11th Army Corps informed the Supreme Military Command that they had been notified that bombs were being produced in the *kaza* of Develi, and that during the search that was carried out, bombs, guns, gunpowder etc. had been found.[46]

The 10th Army Corps notified the 3rd Army Command in a report dated 27 March that the Armenians of the village of Purek in Sushehri had opened fire on unarmed volunteer soldiers who were passing by, that after the village was searched, 95 deserters and 25 guilty privates were arrested, and that guns and bullets had been found.[47]

On 30 March 1915, the Commander of the 11th Army Corps wrote to the Supreme Military Command that a gendarmerie detachment had fought for two hours with an Armenian band near the village of Murfe, which is at a distance of four hours from Bitlis.[48]

On 22 April 1915 the Governor of Sivas sent the following telegram to the Ministry of the Interior: 'Within the province the areas having a dense population of Armenians are Shebinkarahisar, Sushehri, Hafik; Divrik, Gurun, Gemerek, Amasya, Tokat, and Merzifon. Until now, during the searches carried out in the Armenian villages of Sushehri and its vicinity, in the villages of Tuzhisar and Horasan of Hafik, and in the *nahiye* of Olarash of the provincial capital, a great number of illegal weapons and dynamite have been found. According to the statement of the suspects who were caught, the Armenians have armed 30,000 people in this region, 15,000 of them have joined the Russian Army, and the other 15,000 will threaten our Army from the rear, if the Turkish Army is unsuccessful. Armed confrontations took place between the Armenians and the security forces who were sent to the village of Tuzhisar where Murat, of the Armenian Tashnak Committee, was hiding; those who escaped are being pursued.'[49]

The Governor of Diyarbekir wrote on 27 April 1915: 'In Diyarbekir searches have been carried out for deserters, weapons, and bullets. As a result a great quantity of arms, ammunition, military uniforms, and explosives was found. In the capital alone, among the Armenian revolutionaries, more than 1,000 deserters were found.'[50]

Such was the internal situation of the country in May 1915, when the Russians were advancing in eastern Anatolia, when the British and the French were threatening the Dardanelles, and the canal operation was in progress in the south.

Rebellions had occurred in Zeitun, Van, and Mush; the Van rebellion resulted in the Russian occupation of the city: the rebellions of Zeitun and Mush were still continuing. Every inch of the country was filled with deserters, every part was subject to the attacks of brigands. Because every Turk capable of bearing arms was recruited, the field was left to the Armenians. On the one hand, the state was fighting the war, and on the other, it was forced to deal with these insurrections.

The following information about the Zeitun rebellion is worthy of inclusion.

On 24 February, the Russian Ambassador in London went to the Foreign Office and stated: 'An Armenian of Zeitun has consulted Count Vorontzov-Dachkov, the King Regent of the Caucasus, and told him that they have gathered a force of 15,000 to attack the communication lines of the Turkish Armies, but that they lacked guns and ammunition, and that it would be very convenient to provide them with their needs. The French and the British might send the provisions by way of the Antakia harbour. How would England react to this possibility?'[51] The project was abandoned as the British refused.

Under these circumstances, the Ottoman Government was forced to take the decision for relocation.

We have quoted various authors as they summarized the events leading to the relocation decision. None of these authors considered the decision unjust.

Before dealing with the subject of relocation, we want to mention a few more points:

The term *tehjir* (relocation) is Arabic and derives from the root *hijret* (emigration). It is used in the sense of 'having one emigrate'. This word has no connotation of putting one in a concentration camp, but indicates 'changing one's location'. For this reason, the term 'deportation' used by the British and French is incorrect. Deportation has the connotation of forcing one to settle in a place under custody, that is, having one exiled. The individual who is exiled, who is deported, is not free in the place he is sent to. He lives in a specific place, in a prison, fortress, or camp, without any contact with the outside world.

The word *tehjir* has none of these meanings. If it was still used in Turkish today, we would be able to explain, for example, the transfer of those villagers whose villages were located on the site of the newly built Keban Dam, to other areas, using this term. Now, we use the term 'relocation' instead. In every language there are equivalents of this word *tehjir*. That they are not used, is another matter. In fact, even the term *tehjir* was not used in the decisions which were taken, as we shall see.

The second point we want to mention is that every country, during war, sends citizens of the enemy within its borders to concentration camps. This is an established practice implemented in every country. There have been cases when this practice was taken further, against individuals who had become citizens of a country. Now, naturally, it will be said that the Armenians were not foreign subjects. This is true, and for this reason they were not sent to concentration camps. However, remembering the attitude of the Armenians during the First World War, should they be considered Ottoman subjects or Russian subjects? This question cannot be easily answered. But one thing is certain, although the Armenians were legally Ottoman subjects, they acted in fact as Russian subjects. We shall return to this point later. We shall see that the Armenian leaders attempted to be known as belligerents.

A third point is that any country at war will consider as traitors those who work for the enemy, and even those who interrupt the war effort of the country. The punishment for traitors is invariably the most severe punishment in that country. For example, if the Ottoman Government had executed the insurgents of Zeitun who rebelled after the war started, along with those who helped the insurgents by hiding them, or by providing them with clothing, food, weapons and ammunition, this would have been a legal and justifiable attitude under the circumstances. To relocate them instead of executing the insurgents surely cannot be considered more inhumane. During war, the first obligation of the State is to protect the country, and this means to struggle with the enemies of the country according to the rules of war. We have seen the strangest and most far-fetched application of this rule, even in countries that were accusing Turkey most strongly. Oden Hedin has written:

At a time when the British were pleading for the Armenians in the entire world, when Lord Kitchener invaded Sudan, he established order in the country by exterminating the whole population capable of bearing arms. The French Archives are full of atrocious pictures of concentration camps in the Transvaal, where tens of thousands of Boer women and children starved to death. 'As the British', wrote the Irishman George Chatterton-Hill in the magazine 'Ord och Bild' (1916, p. 561), 'could not annihilate them [the Irish] through outright murder or through laws which would force the entire nation out of the country, they attempted another method, which they have also tried in India: organized hunger. And this method proved itself to be very efficacious. In a period of seventy years, from 1841 to 1911, the population of Ireland fell from 8,196,597 to 4,381,951! During the three years of the so-called great famine (1846-8) over one million people died of hunger in Ireland in the midst of rich fields of grain! During these three years, not less than 50 Million Pounds worth of foodstuff (grains and cattle) was taken out of Ireland under the charge of British bayonets, in order to pay taxes to the British State and rent to the absentee British landlords. During the next three years (1849-51) approximately 400,000 more people died due to privation.'

If the 'Protector of the small nations'; of 380 Million people, does not have enough elbow-room for her philanthropic activity, then she should knock on the door of her closest ally! In Russia, there is much more to be improved than in Turkey!'[52]

The author of these statements is a Swede. Certainly many more examples can be added to the above, starting with the rebellion of the Sipahies in India. We have already mentioned, in Chapter 2, the treatment of individuals of German origin in England during the First World War.

There are many versions as to the number of people killed by France, another protector of the Armenians, during its notorious 'pacification' policy in North Africa, during the struggle for independence of Algeria and Tunisia. But what is important is not the number of dead, but the attitude of the State. What is even more interesting in France is the condition of those who were killed by court sentences, or even without them, after the liberation at the end of the Second World War, because they collaborated with the Germans during the occupation. Again there are divergent numbers of dead. But we repeat, the important point is not the figures, but the attitude. After everything was over, and the country was liberated, old accounts were still being settled. It must not be forgotten that after 1923, no Armenian or Greek, let alone Turk, was persecuted. However, there were quite a few who collaborated with the Allied occupation forces in Istanbul.

As for the Russians, even if we do not dwell on how many people were killed during the rebellions under the Tsarist regime, what can be thought of the Crimean population which was collectively transferred to Siberia, on the grounds that they had collaborated with the Germans during the Second World War?

The same examples can be given for every state. The reason why we have mentioned only these three states is that they were the main defenders of the subject at that time. Thus, the attitude of every state during a rebellion, even when this rebellion does not occur within its borders but in occupied areas, is always the same. We have not encountered in the history of any state that the treatment was more merciful, when a rebellion occurred during wartime.

Moreover, the agreements made during the war by these three states we have mentioned, with regard to the dismemberment of Turkey, in which the Armenians were not mentioned, indicate to what extent these states were sincere in their interest in the Armenians. We shall return to this subject later.

As we shall see in the next section, before the Armenians were relocated their ringleaders were arrested on 24 April 1915 in Istanbul. The same day, the President of the USA received the following telegram from Catholicos Kevork of Etchmiadzin:

Honorable President, according to the most recent information we have received from Turkish Armenia, massacres have started there, and organized terror has endangered the existence of the Armenian community. At this delicate time, I address to the noble feelings of Your Excellency and of the great American nation, and request, in the name of humanity and the Christian faith, that your great Republic interfere immediately through its Diplomatic Representatives, to protect my people in Turkey left to the horrors of Turkish fanaticism.[53]

For the telegram to be received on 24 April, it is necessary for the Catholicos to have learned beforehand of the arrest, and to have sent the telegram before the 24th. As the American Ambassador sent his telegram about the arrest on the 27th,[54] the telegram of the Catholicos is enough to point to the guilt of those who were arrested.

On 27 April, the Russian Ambassador in Washington requested the intervention of the USA. The telegram sent by Bryan, the Minister of Foreign Affairs of the USA to the Embassy in Istanbul, informs us that the Russian Ambassador stated that quite a few Muslims were living in Russia, but that these people were not exposed to terror for religious reasons.[55]

It is interesting that these arrests were seen as stemming from religious intolerance. The real significance of these initiatives is clear in the light of the information we have given above.

In the next section we shall examine the relocation decision and its implementation, but let us first state that when the decision was made and its implementation was begun, the destructive activities of Armenians did not stop, and this situation made it necessary for the relocation to be implemented over a wider area.

As a matter of fact, rebellions occurred on 23 July 1915 in Boghazlian, on 1 August 1915 in Findikchik (Marash), on 9 August 1915 in the village of Germush of Urfa, on 14 September 1915 in Antakya (Musa Mountain), on 29 September 1915 in Urfa, on 7 February 1916 in Islahiye, on 4 April 1916 in Akdaghmadeni, and on 9 April 1916 in Tossia.

2. The relocation decision and its implementation

We have mentioned that Enver Pasha, in the message he sent to Talat Pasha on 2 May 1915, stated that the Armenians always start a rebellion where there are large Armenian communities, and that it was either necessary to force them into Russia, as the Russians had done with the Muslims, or to disperse them within Anatolia. It is clear that Enver Pasha's intention was to prevent the Armenians raising another rebellion. If the Armenians could be relocated in such a way that they would not form large communities, but would live in small groups far from each other, then the chance of organizing a rebellion would disappear.

It is again apparent from Enver Pasha's message that relocation was being considered for the instigators of rebellions and brigandage. As a matter of fact, the relocation was carried out in this manner.

We sincerely believe that the uproar created by the powers at that time was due to the fact that they realized that the Armenian rebellions, upon which they had set great hopes, were now impossible. The initiative made by the Russians in the USA on 27 April cannot be explained otherwise. We have also mentioned, in Chapter 2, the real intention lying behind the massacre rumours.

In order to believe that the politicians who appeared as perfect humanitarians, and who shed tears claiming that Armenians were being killed, were concerned and saddened by the fate of the Armenians in Turkey, one must be not only be rather naive but stupid.

Let us now examine in chronological order the measures which the Ottoman Empire was compelled to take regarding the Armenians, for the reasons stated earlier, and their implementation.

On 6 September 1914, the Ottoman Government sent a coded circular to provinces with a dense population of Armenians, and instructed them to keep the activities of the leaders of the Armenian political parties under constant supervision.[56]

On 25 February 1915, the Supreme Military Command gave the following instruction to all the units, with order No. 8682.

In Bitlis, Armenian brigands have appeared and some Armenian deserters are engaged in brigandage. In Aleppo, in Dortyol, Armenians have attacked soldiers and gendarmes, and in the *sanjak* of Kayseri a great number of bombs, codes in French, Russian, and Armenian were found in Armenian houses. Although these incidents are not serious at the moment, they indicate that preparations for rebellion are being made by our enemies within our country. Consequently, it has been deemed necessary to circulate and announce again the points below.

1. Armenians shall strictly not be employed in mobile armies, in mobile and stationary gendarmeries, or in any armed services. They shall not be employed even in the suites and offices of the Commandants and the Headquarters.

2. The Commanders of the Army and the Army Corps, the Assistant Commanders of the Army Corps and the Divisions, and the regional Commandants are authorized and compelled to have recourse to the Armed Forces immediately to eradicate aggression and opposition, should they be aware of any opposition, armed attack; or resistance to the Government from the people. Likewise, the Commanders have authority to declare martial law immediately whenever necessary.

3. Although vigilance will be maintained in all areas, in areas where there is no indication of aggression one must refrain from putting pressure on the people, which would terrify them. Thus, the conviction that those who have remained loyal and obedient will not be harmed must be strengthened, and the people must not be driven to rebellion by making them desperate.

4. Because all matters concerning defence and public order are the responsibility of the military authorities, owing to general mobilization, civil service officials will refer these matters to the Commanders. Only the officials of the province of Istanbul will refer to the General Headquarters for matters and measures related to public order.

5. For matters concerning public order, the highest authorities in the sectors of the Third and Fourth Army and Iraq are the Army Commanders. In the sectors of the First and Second Army, the highest authorities are the Commanders of the Army Corps. These Commanders of the Army Corps will provide information to the Army Commander and to their Assistant Commanders.

6. The Commanders of the Third and Fourth Army will immediately inform the Assistants of the Commander-in-Chief of the preventive measures they have conceived and adopted.[57]

On 24 April 1915, the Ministry of the Interior ordered with a circular that the Armenian Committee Centres be closed, that their documents be seized, and that the committee leader be arrested.[58] On 26 April, the Supreme Military Command sent a similar circular to the units, requesting that the leaders be sent to military courts and that the guilty ones be punished.[59]

Upon this instruction of the Ministry of the Interior, 235 people were arrested in Istanbul. This day, 24 April, on which the Armenians hold demonstrations each year claiming it is the date of the massacre, is the day when these 235 people were arrested.

On 26 May 1915, the Supreme Military Command sent the following message to the Ministry of the Interior:

It was orally decided that the Armenians be sent from the eastern Anatolian provinces, from Zeitun, and from such areas which are densely populated by Armenians, to the south of the province of Diyarbekir, to the valley of the Euphrates, to the vicinity of Urfa and Suleymaniye. The following points must be taken as a basis for settling the Armenians to ensure that pockets of rebellion do not reappear:

a) the Armenian population must not exceed 10 per cent of the tribal and Muslim population in the areas where Armenians will be settled;

b) each of the villages which the Armenians will found must not exceed 50 houses;

c) the migrant Armenian families must not be allowed to change residence even for reasons of travel or transport.[60]

On the same day, the office of the Prime Minister received the following memorandum from the Ministry of the Interior:

Some of the Armenians residing in quarters near military areas are hindering the activities of the Imperial Army which is engaged in protecting the Ottoman borders against the enemies of the State. They combine their efforts and actions with the enemy, they join the ranks of the enemy, they organize armed attacks within the country against the Armed Forces and innocent people, they engage in aggression, murder, terror, and pillage in Ottoman cities and towns, they provide the enemy with provisions, and manifest their audacity against fortified places. As it has proved necessary that such revolutionary elements be removed from the area of operations, and that the villages which serve as a base of operations and refuge for the rebels be evacuated, some measures are being taken. We have begun to transfer the Armenians residing in the provinces of Van, Bitlis and Erzurum and in the villages and towns of the *kazas* of Iskenderun, Beylan, Jisri-i Shuur, and Antakia, with the exception of the city of Adana proper, the city of Sis proper, and the city of Mersin proper, to the southern provinces. We have begun to transfer and settle them in the *sanjaks* of Zor and Mussul, with the exception of the southern area bordering with the province of Van, to the southern part of Urfa, with the exception of the city of Urfa proper, to the southern and southeastern part of the province of Aleppo, and to the eastern part of the province of Syria. The Armenians are being settled in quarters designated and assigned for this purpose. This course of events is considered favourable to the essential interests of the state.[61]

In short, Armenians residing in the provinces bordering the area of military operations and in proximity to the Mediterranean Sea would be relocated.

On 27 May (14 May 1331), 'the temporary law concerning the measures to be adopted by the military authorities for those whose activities are against the Government in wartime' was adopted, and was published on 1 June (19 May 1331) in the *Takvimi Vakayi* (the Ottoman official gazette). We quote from Y. H. Bayur, who has included this law in his book:

1. In wartime should the commanders of the Army, the Army Corps, or the divisions face any opposition, armed aggression, or resistance to operations and arrangements related to the decrees of the government, the defence of the country, and the maintenance of public order, they are authorized and compelled to immediately implement punishment through the Armed Forces, and to suppress the aggression and resistance.

2. The commanders of the Army, the Army Corps, and the divisions may transfer and settle in other quarters the inhabitants of villages and towns should they engage in spying or treason, or in view of military exigencies.[62]

The third article of the law states that the law will come into effect on the date of its publication.

Finally, on 30 May the Council of Ministers took the following decision:

It is absolutely necessary to annihilate and destroy by effective operations this possible harmful activity which has a bad effect on the war's operations which are designed for the benefit of protecting the state's security and existence.

The goal of the operation begun by this order of the Ministry is obvious. It is stated in the memorandum of the Ministry of the Interior that the Armenians who must be transferred, of those residing in the towns and villages, will be sent to their allotted local dwellings. Their transfer will be made in comfortable circumstances, their comfort will be provided on the way, and their lives and possessions will be protected. Until they are settled in their new dwellings, they will be fed through funds of the emigrants' appropriation. In proportion to their previous economic and financial condition, they will be given property and lands; the Government will construct dwellings for the needy ones, will distribute seeds for sowing, tools, and implements to the farmers and craftsmen who need them. Possessions and belongings left behind will be returned to them in an appropriate way. After the value of the possessions and immovable property belonging to the transferred emigrants has been calculated and registered, it will be distributed to the immigrants. Immovable properties such as warehouses, factories, shops, orange groves, vineyards, olive groves, orchards; which would remain outside the specialized sphere of the immigrants, will be sold at auction, or will be leased, and their value will be deposited in financial offices for safe-keeping to be paid to their owners. A regulation has been implemented by the said Ministry to the effect that the expenditures arising from these transactions and procedures be paid from the appropriation set aside for the emigrants. Through this decree, the administration and maintenance of the abandoned properties will be ensured. The general transactions concerning the emigrants will be accelerated, regulated and supervised. Commissions will be formed, which will employ salaried officials who will have the duty and authority, and who will be directly dependent on the Ministry of the Interior. These commissions will be composed of one president and two appointed members, one of whom will be selected from among the officials of the Ministry of the Interior, and the other from among the officials of the Ministry of Finance. These commissions will be sent to their regions, and the quarters where a commission will be present, the Governor will submit to the said Ministry a note stating that they have begun the application of the said regulation, and they will give information to the responsible departments.[63]

These are the texts concerning the relocation decision. As can be seen, the text does not even mention the word 'relocation'. The temporary law says 'transfer and settle in other quarters', the note of the Ministry of the Interior and the decision of the Council of Ministers refers to 'transferring' and 'settling' in the designated and appointed quarters.

First of all, we must point out that the relocation process was begun before the Council of Ministers decreed it. This becomes clear in the memorandum of the Ministry of the Interior, as well as in other instructions which we shall quote below:

It can be accepted that the process was initiated after the instructions dated 24 April.

Secondly, although the Council of Ministers could put the relocation process into effect on its own responsibility without the need of a separate law, a temporary law was enacted in order that the military authorities, too, could be given the same authority.

Thirdly, a temporary law had to be enacted because Parliament was not in session. The Assembly opened on 15 September, and this temporary law was accepted by the Assembly.

A regulation was prepared on the subject of relocation. Below we quote Articles 21 and 22 of this regulation whose original text is in the British Archives. (We shall return to this in section 5. For the original text, see Salahi Sonyel, *Shocking new documents*, London, 1975; F.O. 371/9158 E. 5523.)

Article 21. Should emigrants be attacked on their journey or in camps, the assailants will be immediately arrested, and sent to martial law court.

Article 22. Those who take bribes or gifts from the emigrants, or who rape the women by threats or promises, or those who engage in illicit relations with them, will immediately be removed from office, will be sent to the martial law court and will be punished severely.

A temporary law was passed on 26 September 1915 to conclude the process of liquidation. The text of this law follows.

Article 1. The properties, debts, credits left behind by each person who was transferred to other quarters with the temporary law dated May 4, 1331, will be liquidated by the courts according to the official report which the commissions formed for this matter will prepare for every person.

Article 2. The rented foundation properties [house properties and landed properties] which the individuals mentioned in the first article possessed at the time of their transfer will be transferred to the Ministry of Foundations, and the other immovable properties will be transferred to the Treasury, and their equivalent value will be included in the liquidation which will be made according to the first article. . . .

Article 3. The credits will be collected by the commissions through lawsuits, the deposits will be taken out of the banks, the movable properties will be sold by auction. The revenue will be deposited for safekeeping in the name of the owner to the financial office, and will be included in the liquidation. At the end of the liquidation the remaining sum will be paid to their owners . . . .[64]

The relocation process was begun on the basis of these principles. Now let us see how this operation was implemented by referring to documents that we found in the files of the Ministry of the Interior during our research, which began in 1981.

On 18 May (5 May 1331) a message was sent from the Ministry of the Interior to the gubernorate of Erzurum.65 It stated that it was necessary for the Armenians who were evacuated from Erzurum to be sent to the southern parts of Urfa and Mussul and to the *sanjak* of Zor.

On 23 May (10 May 1331), the following instructions were given to Erzurum with message No. 14, to Van with message No. 21 and to Bitlis with message No. 14:

The Armenians within the province will be transferred and settled in designated areas of the southern part of the province of Mussul with the exception of its northern part bordering with the province of Van, in the *sanjak* of Zor, and in the *sanjak* of Urfa with the exception of its central *kaza*. The Armenians arriving at their new settlements will be relocated in dwellings which will be constructed in the towns and villages, or in villages they will found in areas designated by the local government. The responsibility for transferring and relocating the Armenians who must be transferred belongs to the local administrators. The administrative officials along the way are responsible for protecting the lives and possessions of the Armenians sent to their new settlements, for feeding them, and for ensuring their rest. The Armenians who will be required to emigrate may take with them all their movable possessions. This transport will of course be made in areas free of war operations.[66]

On the same day a message was sent to the gubernorate of Mussul, and to the governors of the *sanjaks* of Urfa and Zor, which stated:

The Armenians who will be sent from Van, Bitlis, and Erzurum will be transferred and settled in parts of Urfa which Armenians do not inhabit, in the southern part of the province of Mussul, in areas designated by the local government.

The Armenians arriving at their new settlements will either be resettled in small groups in dwellings they will construct in existing towns and villages, or in the villages they will found in areas designated by the local government. It will be necessary for the towns and villages where the Armenians will settle, and the villages which they will found, to be at least 25 km away from the Baghdad railway and other railways. The officials on duty are responsible for protecting *en route* the lives and possessions of the Armenians being transferred, for feeding them, and for their rest. Armenians who are required to emigrate may take all their movable possessions. [67]

Message No. 17 sent on 27 May from the Ministry of the Interior to the province of Erzurum stated: `Because the province borders with Russia, no Armenian must be left there. It is of course in their discretion that the Armenians in some areas are hastily transferred, and that the transfer of others is delayed. It has not been deemed necessary that the Armenians of Elazigh, Diyarbekir, and Sivas be required to emigrate.[68]

On 1 June 1915 the Ministry of the Interior sent a circular notice to all provinces, drawing their attention to the following points: 'It has become apparent that in some areas the instruction concerning the arrest and relocation of dangerous Armenians and committee leaders has been misinterpreted. In many areas people who are not guilty have been arrested and transferred from one place to another, while no measures have been taken about the actual harmful individuals.[69]

On 5 June 1915, a message was sent from the Ministry of the Interior to the *sanjak* of Zor: 'There is no harm in Armenian muleteers going and coming to Aleppo. However, it is necessary for their movements and attitude to be watched constantly.'[70]

A message dated 9 June: 'Because the equivalent value of the immovable properties of the Armenians will be paid by the Government to their owners, it is necessary that the properties left behind are protected, and that they are sold by auction in the name of their owners. It is suitable that the transfer of those who work in the Army, and of the feeble women is delayed.'[71]

A significant message was sent on 14 June 1915 (1 June 1331):

The province of Erzurum has informed us that a convoy of 500 Armenians who were evacuated from Erzurum has been killed by tribes between Erzurum and Erzinjan. It is expected that efforts will be made to protect the lives of the Armenians being transferred, and those who try to escape *en route* and attack the officials responsible for protecting them will be punished. But under no circumstances will the people be allowed to interfere. Incidents resulting in such killings will not be allowed to occur. For this reason it is absolutely necessary that every possible measure is taken to protect the Armenians against attacks by tribes and villagers, and that those who attempt murder and violence are severely punished.[72]

On 21 June, message No. 83 sent by the Ministry of the Interior to Mussul stated: `The Armenians who will be sent into the province to be relocated and those who have already arrived must under no circumstances be brought near the northern and eastern part of the Baghdad railway, and must be settled only in areas to the west of the said railway.'[73]

A message was sent on 22 June 1915: 'Among the Armenian families, the girls up to age 20, and boys up to age 10 who are orphaned will not be sent to the south, but will be adopted by families.'[74]

On 23 June, message No. 21 was sent to the *sanjak* of Zor: 'During the settling of the Armenians it must be ensured that the inhabitants of the same county and locality are settled in different areas, that the Armenians are not allowed to open Armenian schools in their new places of residence, that their children are required to attend the public schools, that the villages which will be founded are at a distance of five hours from one another, and that they are not founded in high places which would facilitate defence.'[75]

On 26 June 1915 a message was sent from the Ministry of the Interior to the governor of Elaziz: 'The Armenian convoys sent under protection from Erzurum have been attacked and killed by the brigands of Dersim. It is required that measures are immediately taken to ensure the protection of the convoys. These consistent attacks by the brigands of Dersim must be stopped.'[76]

On 1 July 1915 (18 June 1331), the Ministry of the Interior sent a circular message: 'It has been understood that some Armenians are converting to Islam collectively or individually, to be able to stay in their areas of residence. They must be transferred despite their conversion.'[77]

On 4 July 1915 (21 June 1331), the Ministry of the Interior sent a message to the provinces of Trabzon, Sivas, Diyarbekir and Elaziz, and to the *sanjak* of Janik: 'It is ordered that the Armenians and their families whom the Government considers dangerous be removed, and that the merchants and artisans who are harmless be retained but that they be required to move out of their towns within the province.'[78]

The relocation areas were extended by a circular of the Ministry of the Interior dated 5 July 1915.[79]

This message was sent by the Ministry of the Interior to the province of Elaziz on 10 July 1915: 'It is ordered that children are to be adopted in accordance with Muslim traditions by prominent people residing in towns and villages where Armenians are not present. If there are a great many children, they may also be adopted by less wealthy, but honourable and honest families, who will be paid 30 kurush per month per child. It is required that a list be made of the families which have adopted these children and that a copy of this list be sent to the centre.'[80]

On 12 July 1915 (29 June 1331), the Ministry of the Interior sent a message to the province of Diyarbekir: 'We are informed that in recent times some Armenians within the province have been taken out of the city at night and had their throats cut like sheep. The number of those killed until now is estimated to be 2,000. It is ordered that this be absolutely prevented and that we are informed of the actual situation.'[81]

On 12 July 1915 the Ministry of the Interior sent a circular: 'It is ordered that no one else will be sent to the *sanjak* of Zor, whose population ratio has exceeded 10 per cent.'[82]

The Ministry of the Interior sent a circular message on 24 October 1916: 'The transferring of Armenians to other localities has been delayed. Information is requested as to the names and number of those harmful individuals who must be transferred.'[83]

These telegrams are sufficient to determine the reasons behind the relocation decision, its extent and implementation. As can be seen, the Government particularly emphasized the protection of life and property, and continually gave instructions for necessary measures to be taken.

Individuals who did not comply with these instructions, and those who were guilty, were arrested and sent for trial. A special investigative council was formed at the Ministry of War to examine such irregularities, and this council performed its duty until the beginning of 1918, when its duty was over.[84] Those who were found guilty were sent to the martial law courts. The number of these individuals was as follows.

From the province of Sivas	648
From the province of Elaziz	223
From the province of Diyarbekir	70
From the province of Bitlis	25
From the sanjak of Eskishehir	29
From the sanjak of Shebinkarahisar	6
From the sanjak of Nighde	8
From the sanjak of Izmit	33
From the province of Ankara	32
From the sanjak of Kaiseri	69
From the province of Syria	27
From the province of Hudavendigar	12
From the province of Konya	12
From the sanjak of Urfa	189
From the sanjak of Janik	14 [85]

The total is 1,397. They were given various sentences including execution.

Talat Pasha, in the speech he gave at the last Congress of the Party of Union and Progress on 1 November 1918, mentioned the subject of relocation. This speech, which was published in the 12 July 1921 issue of the *Vakit* newspaper, has been quoted by Bayur, from whom we quote:

The subject of relocating the Armenians is one of the most discussed subjects in the war cabinets in and especially outside the country.

First of all, it must be said, that the rumours of relocation and killings have been grossly exaggerated. The Armenian and Greek press, conscious that the rumours of oppression would have a great effect on public opinion in Europe and America where the Turks are unknown, or more exactly are known incorrectly, have created great uproar in the world through their exaggerations.

I do not wish to deny the incidents. I only wish to tell the truth, to destroy the exaggerations.

Notwithstanding these exaggerations, such relocation incidents probably occurred. However, the Babiali never acted in any of these incidents, based upon a previously made decision. The responsibility for the incidents lies above all, on the elements who committed unbearable acts which caused the relocation. Undoubtedly, all Armenians are not responsible for this. But is was of course necessary not to tolerate activities which obstructed the movements of the army during a great war which would determine the life or death of the state, and which endangered the security of the country and the army by creating rebellions.

The Armenian bands which obstructed the operations of our armies in the region of Erzurum were given support and refuge in the Armenian villages. When they were in difficulty, the villagers would answer their call, and rush to their aid by grabbing the weapons kept in the churches. We could not have tolerated the perpetuation of dangers which would continually obstruct our line of retreat and the services behind the front. Information received from the armies, communications constantly sent by the provinces, finally brought forth the necessity of adopting a definitive measure on this question.

Thus the relocation question arose above all from the measures adopted as a result of this military requirement.

What I mean to say is that the relocation was implemented everywhere in an orderly manner and to the necessary extent. The hostilities which had accumulated for a long time then exploded and brought forth abuses which we in no way desired. Many officials used force and violence more than was necessary. In many areas some innocent people unjustly fell victim. I admit this.[86]

Before we conclude the subject of relocation, a point we must mention is the number of individuals who were required to emigrate.

In a report submitted by the Ministry of the Interior to the Grand Vizier on 7 December 1916, it was stated that about 702,900 individuals had been relocated; in 1915 25 million kurush had been spent for this purpose; until the end of October 1916 86 million kurush had been spent; and until the end of the year 150 million kurush more would be spent.[87]

According to anti-Turkish propaganda, 2,000,000 Armenians were massacred during the relocation.

The figure given for those who died was 300,000, c. 1915. This figure increased with each passing year, and in the 1980s it reached 2,000,000. Although it is normal for the population of a society to increase with the year, the reproduction of individuals who died at a specific time is an occurrence peculiar to this subject.

We shall not dwell on who gave what figure on which date. Various deaths occurred for various reasons during the relocation. Some of the deaths were due to epidemics, some were due to climatic factors, some were due to the hardships suffered during the journey, some were due to attacks, because officials did not protect them or because some officials engaged in illegal acts. Moreover, many died during the rebellions or the band fights started in 1914 even before the war, and continued after the relocation decision was made until 1916. Many others died while fighting against the Turks in the Russian Army which they joined as volunteers.

Who are the one who can be pointed to as ' 　　　 murdered' in these deaths? Certainly not the ones who were killed while fighting, nor those who died of epidemics of typhus, typhoid fever, cholera, and variola, which were then widespread in Turkey, or of famine. It cannot be claimed that they would not have died if they had stayed in their homes, because the epidemics spread to the areas of their residence and took hundreds of thousands of lives. The number of those who died in Turkey at the fronts during the First World War is 550-600,000. The rest, more than 2,000,000 people, died of epidemics, malnutrition, and the attacks of Armenian and Greek bands although they were not soldiers. Therefore this group, too, must be excluded.

Should we include in this group those who died because of climatic factors and the hardships of the journey during their emigration? We do not think so. Again, it will be claimed that they would not have died if they had stayed in their homes. That is true, but there is a point which should be remembered. Among the nations Turkey fought during the First World War, the Armenians were included. And these were Armenians living in Turkey, Armenians who were Turkish citizens. Just as the Arabs after May 1916. Certainly it cannot be denied that Turkey was at war with the Armenians of Turkey.

The meaning of the telegram which reads: `I would like to thank the inhabitants of Van for their sacrifices' sent after the fall of Van by the Russian Tsar to the Russian Army Command of the region of Beyazit on 18 May 1915 is quite clear. The article published on 13 August 1915 in the newspaper Le Temps in Paris about Aram Manoukian is similar: `At the beginning of this war, once again Aram relinquished his comfort and business, resorted to arms, and took the leadership of those who rebelled in Van. Russia, who now controls this province, appointed Aram as governor to please the Armenians who did their part extremely well in this war against Turkey.'

An article published on 9 February 1916 in the Soleil du Midi stated:

. . . According to detailed information we are receiving, especially the declaration given by M. Sazanoff at the Duma, the Armenians, numbering 10,000, under the leadership of Aram Manoukian, have resisted the Turkish troops in Van for a month, and succeeded in putting them to flight before the Russian armies arrived.

In the mountains of Sassun, 30,000 Armenian revolutionaries have been fighting hopelessly for nine months, while waiting for the arrival of the Russian armies as well as of the troops of Armenian volunteers.

In Cilicia, in the mountains of Kessab, thousands of Armenians as well are awaiting the arrival of the French and the British. . . .[88]

The statement Sazanoff had made in the Duma was that 'In this war the Armenians are fighting with the Russians against the Ottoman Empire.'

The details we have given in this chapter leave no doubt that during the war the Armenians of Turkey were fighting against their country, with its enemy. As a matter of fact, they themselves stated as much during the Sèvres talks.

General Bronsart, who was Chief of Staff to the Ottoman Commander- in-Chief, wrote as follows in an article in the 24 July 1921 issue of the newspaper *Deutsche Allgemeine Zeitung*:

As demonstrated by the innumerable declarations, provocative pamphlets, weapons, ammunition, explosives, &c., found in areas inhabited by Armenians, the rebellion was prepared for a long time, organized, strengthened and financed by Russia. Information was received on time in Istanbul about an Armenian assassination attempt directed at high ranking state officials and officers.

Since all the Muslims capable of bearing arms were in the Turkish Army, it was easy to organize a terrible massacre by the Armenians against defenceless people, because the Armenians were not only attacking the sides and rear of the Eastern Army paralysed at the front by the Russians, but were attacking the Muslim folk in the region as well. The Armenian atrocities which I have witnessed were far worse than the so called Turkish brutality.[89]

Let us quote now a few statements from an anti-Turkish book. Hassan Arfa writes:

When the Russian armies invaded Turkey after the Sarikamish disaster of 1914, their columns were preceded by battalions of irregular Armenian volunteers, both from the Caucasus and from Turkey. One of these was commanded by a certain Andranik, a bloodthirsty adventurer. . . .

These Armenian volunteers, in order to avenge their compatriots who had been massacred by the Kurds, committed all kinds of excesses, more than six hundred thousand Kurds being killed between 1915 and 1916 in the eastern vilayets of Turkey.[90]

The Armenians were forced to emigrate because they had joined the ranks of the enemy. The fact that they were civilians does not change the situation. Those who were killed in Hiroshima and Nagasaki during the Second World War were also civilians. Those who were killed during the First World War in France, Belgium, and Holland were also civilians. Those who died in London during the Battle of Britain were also civilians. We gave above some examples as to how the civilians were killed. Turkey did not kill them, but relocated them. As it was impossible to adopt a better solution under the circumstances, it can not be accepted that those who died because they were unable to resist the hardships of the journey were killed by the Turks.

Let us give a similar example. During the struggle for independence, the French evacuated Marash; and 5,000 Armenians left Marash with the French. The date was 10 February 1920. The journey lasted until 14 February. `The result: 200 dead, among which 7 officers, and commander Marty; 300 wounded were brought back; 11 wounded were abandoned in Marash; 150 evacuated had their legs frozen; 2-3,000 Armenians died during the retreat.[191]

Did the French massacre these Armenians?

There remain only those who were killed *en route*, defenceless. The responsibility here lies with the Government because it was unable to protect these individuals, or because officials winked at the killings. The Government arrested those who were responsible for this, as far as it was able to determine the culprits, and sent them to the martial law court. Quite a few of them were executed.

How many individuals lost their lives as they were killed defencelessly? Even at that time it was not possible to determine this, and it is impossible to determine it today.

The statistics given as the death toll today are invariably the total of the individuals who died for all reasons we have stated above, from the declaration of war until the armistice. The figure which is increased today to 2,000,000 is this total. In his blue book, Toynbee wrote that the number of Armenians who died might be 600,000.[92] He computed this number by subtracting the number of Armenians who were alive after the emigration from the Armenian population before the war. Today we are able to do this computation more easily, by comparison with the existing documents.

Dr Fridtjof Nansen's report states that, according to the League of Nations Emigrants' Committee, the number of Armenians who emigrated during the First World War from Turkey to Russia was between 400,000 and 420,000. This figure is the number of Armenians who emigrated from Turkey, and who were living in Russia at the end of the war. It is apparent that these emigrants went to Russia before the Moscow Treaty with Russia, which was signed on 16 March 1921.

In 1921, the Istanbul Patriarch, in a statistic he gave to the British, showed the number of Armenians living within the Ottoman borders before the Sevres Agreement as 625,000, including those who returned after they had emigrated.[93]

Including those who emigrated to Russia, we reach the figure of 1,045,000.

As the Armenian population in Turkey in 1914 was approximately 1,300,000, the total number of Armenians who died during the war cannot be more than 300,000.

Another method of computation is possible. In Toynbee's computation in the document we have mentioned above (note No. 92), it is stated that on 5 April 1916, in the regions of Zor, Aleppo, and Damascus, the number of emigrants was 500,000. It is natural that this figure will have considerably increased up to the end of 1916, because the process of emigration continued until the end of 1916, and because all those who had been required to emigrate were not sent only to these three regions.

We stated that the number of those who were required to emigrate was 702,900. Even if the emigrants who were alive on 5 April 1916 were from these three regions, and even if all those who emigrated after this date died, the number of those who died during the emigration would be 200,000. Because it is impossible that the sum of those who emigrated other than to the regions of Zor, Damascus, and Aleppo on 5 April 1916 and the sum of those who emigrated after this date could have died, it is apparent that, based upon this computation, the number of those who died from all causes was well below 100,000. And this would indicate that most of the casualties occurred during armed confrontations outside the process of emigration.

A third computation method would be based on the population of the Republic of Turkey.

In the Turkish Republic the first census was held in 1927. At that time the Armenian population of the country was 123,602.

In the 1931 census in France it was established that there were 29,227 foreigners, who were born in various countries, 5,114 who were born in Turkey, but who were French citizens. There were approximately 35,000 Armenians. It is obvious that all of them had come from Turkey.

The Canadian records show that 1,244 Armenians had come from Turkey between 1912 and 1914 (Imre Ferenczi, *International Migration*, Vol. 1, New York, 1929, p. 891).

In the same period, 34,136 Armenians emigrated to the United States, all of them from Turkey (Robert Mirak, *Armenian Emigration to the U.S. to 1915*).

In 1928, the number of Armenians who emigrated to Greece was 42,200 (League of Nations A. 33-1927).

The Bulgarian statistics record that in 1920 there were 10,848, and in 1926, 25,402 Gregorian Armenians (*Annuaire statistique du Royaume de Bulgarie*, 1931, p. 35). It is apparent that the difference of 15,000 Armenians came from Turkey.

Again according to the statistics of the League of Nations, 2,500 Armenians went to Cyprus.

Hovannisian gives the number of Armenians who emigrated to the Arab countries and Iran in the following list ('The Ebb and Flow of the Armenian Minority in the Arab Middle East', *Middle East Journal*, Vol. 28, No. 1(Winter 1974), p. 20):

Syria	100,000
Lebanon	50,000
Jordan	10,000
Egypt	40,000
Iraq	25,000
Iran	50,000

When we add to these figures the 420,000 Armenians who emigrated to Russia, we reach 824,560, or 825,000 if we round it up. If we count those who went to other European countries, the missing and the forgotten as 50,000, we reach the figure of 875,000. With the population of 123,000 in Turkey, we obtain 998,000. When we subtract this number from the Armenian population in Turkey in 1914 of 1,300,000, we obtain 302,000.

Therefore, every computation indicates that the number of casualties (we use this term because this is a society at war) of the Armenians of Turkey, for all reasons, did not exceed 300,000. It is obvious that among these casualties the number of deaths which occurred for whatever reason during the emigration will be less than this figure, and the number of those who can be considered as having been killed will be even less.

A murderer is a murderer, no excuse can be given. Just as we do not condone the fact that the Armenians massacred the Turks, we do not condone the fact that the Turks massacred the Armenians. However, the Armenians who were massacred were not massacred on the orders of the Government. As we have stated above, the culprits who were arrested were sent to the courts, were given sentences, including the death sentence, and the sentences were carried out.

We would have wished that the Armenians who massacred the Turks had also been punished. But, in Armenian books, they are portrayed as national heroes.

There is one more point we must mention before we conclude this subject.

The British were the leaders among those who were spreading the rumours of Armenian massacres throughout the world, and who were attempting to shape public opinion in that direction during the First World War. The famous Masterman bureau, which we mentioned in Chapter 2, had created a massacre story by publishing the blue book, which we have referred to on various occasions, in order to win over American public opinion and to turn the Islamic world against Turkey. Later, Toynbee made great efforts to substantiate these items of information sent to him, but was not successful.

There is another person who dealt extensively with this subject, .Dr Johannes Lepsius. Today the Armenians attach even more importance to Lepsius' work, as they are aware that the blue book was published by the propaganda bureau.

We think it important to examine Lepsius' background and his aims. For this reason we shall refer to Frank G. Weber:

Lest other Armenians of the Ottoman Empire attempt to imitate the insurrectionaries of Van, Enver decided to suppress all Armenian schools and newspapers. Wangenheim regretted these orders as both morally and materially deleterious to Germany's cause . . . Nevertheless, the Ambassador instructed his consuls to collect any kind of information that would show that the Germans had tried to alleviate the lot of the Armenians. These notices were to be published in a white book in the hope of impressing Entente and German public opinion. (German Archives Band 37, No. A.20525.)

The last found a powerful voice in Dr. Johannes Lepsius. 'The son of a famous archaeologist and himself a noted traveller and writer on the Near East, Lepsius was delegated by various Protestant Evangelical societies to enter Armenia and verify the atrocity stories at first hand. Wangenheim did not want the professor to come. He was as certain that the Turks would charge the Germans some sort of retribution for causing them this embarrassment as that not a single Armenian life would be spared because of Lepsius' endeavours. But Lepsius convinced the Wilhelmstrasse that his intention was not to put pressure on the Turks but instead to argue the patriarchal entourage into greater loyalty toward the Ottoman regime. Alleging this as his reason, he got as far as Constantinople, where the Armenian Patriarch acclaimed him but Talat refused him permission to travel into the interior. He had badgered Wangenheim unmercifully with letters, and the Ambassador described his reaction to Lepsius' proposals as something between amusement and contempt. Yet Lepsius emphasized an argument to which the Ambassador was always open: the liquidation of the Armenians would seriously and perhaps irreparably diminish the prospects of Germany's ascendancy in Turkey after the war.

When Lepsius returned to Germany, he devoted himself to keeping the German public unsparingly informed about the Armenian massacres. Though the German newspapers were not as chary of this news as might have seemed desirable in the interests of the Turkish alliance, the professor still preferred to make his disclosures in the journals of Basel and Zurich. What he wrote was not always up to date or unbiased. Much of it came from Armenian informants in the Turkish capital, and a large source, reworked with many variations, was given him by Ambassador Morgenthau at the time of his visit to Constantinople in July 1915. Morgenthau showed him a collection of American consular reports detailing the atrocities and suggested that the Armenians be removed from the Ottoman Empire and resettled in the American West. Lepsius took up that idea enthusiastically. . . .

. . . Lepsius pointed out to the Chancellor that if Germany made herself popular in Turkish Armenia, the Russian Armenians would be more likely to put themselves under German protection after the war.[94]

Lepsius had not set foot in Anatolia, had not talked to one single Armenian there. All the information he gathered consisted of what he learned from the Patriarchate and to some extent the reports which the American Ambassador Morgenthau showed him. We shall see in section 5 that these reports were all based on hearsay.

It is necessary to put Dr Lepsius on the same level as the Protestant missionaries, and to give the same value to his writings.

There was another decision taken during the war with regard to the Armenians of Turkey. This decision concerned the Patriarchate. With a new regulation published in the 10 August 1916 issue of the *Takvimi Vekayi* (Ottoman official gazette), the Armenian Churches in Turkey were no longer connected to Etchmiadzin, the Catholicates of Sis and Akdamar were united, the centre of the Catholicate was transferred to Jerusalem, and the Istanbul Patriachate was brought under this Catholicate. It was ruled that the Istanbul Patriarch could only establish contact with the Ministry of Sects.

The regulation reorganized the election of the Patriarch and the Patriarchate Assemblies. (A detailed explanation of this regulation may be found in Bayur's work, Vol. II, Chapter 3, p. 57-9.)

3. The partition of the Ottoman Empire

Because they directly concern the Armenians, it is necessary to mention the agreements on the partition of the Ottoman Empire when we examine the First World War.

We have mentioned the division of the Ottoman Empire into spheres of influence before the outbreak of the war. When the war began, Russia, France and Britain naturally excluded Germany, and began bargaining among themselves with the aim of an actual division and partition of the Empire. These attempts did not begin by collective meetings of the three powers, but two by two.

In the beginning, when the Babiali had not yet begun to make the Armenians emigrate, Russia coveted all the lands inhabited by Armenians, including Cilicia. The Tsar stated that 'I cannot put them [the Armenians) again under the Turkish yoke. Should I include Armenia in my country? I will only do this by an explicit and definitive request by the Armenians, or I will establish an autonomous administration for them.'[95]

However, we know that on 15 March 1915 Russia was willing to relinquish Cilicia to the French. Without going into details, we shall briefly state the result. Nevertheless, we wish to report one point which is also mentioned by Armenian authors. After the Russian Army had taken Erzurum, it was stated in an order by the Supreme Military Command that the Armenians did not have the right to reside in Erzurum. It is a historical truth that towards the end of 1915 the Archduke Nicholas stated: `As there is no Yakut problem in Russia, there is no Armenian problem.' These statements surely indicate the real intentions of Russia.

During these negotiations to decide the partition of the Ottoman Empire neither the Armenians nor Armenia was mentioned. The lands called Armenia were divided between Russia and France. Even this indicates that the reaction shown by the three powers with regard to the issue of relocation was entirely hypocritical, and that they used the Armenians simply as a means of relieving the burden of their own war efforts.

During the partition negotiations France was represented by George Picot, the former consul-general in Beirut, and Britain by Sir Mark Sykes, who was considered an expert on eastern affairs. In Russia, Sazanoff, the Minister of Foreign Affairs, was personally involved. The agreements that were reached are known as the Sykes-Picot Agreements.

The first negotiation consisted of the discussions between Russia and Britain on 12 March 1915, concerning the relinquishing of Istanbul and the area of the Straits to Russia. Britain accepted this on condition that commercial ships could pass freely through the Straits, and that the region which had been recognized as neutral through the 1907 agreements should now be included in Britain's sphere of influence.[96]

On 3 January 1916 the French and the British reached an agreement. According to this, Britain would dominate the region that included Baghdad and Basra in the south of Iraq; Beirut and the shores of Syria would be given to France, where Arab states would be formed under the protection of France and Britain, under the sovereignty of Hussein, the Governor of Mecca; Palastine would be an international zone; the southern part of a triangle extending with a narrow strip from the Syrian shores to Cilicia and Sivas would be given to France.

On 26 April 1916 France and Russia reached an agreement. Russia officially recognized the agreement between France and Britain, and obtained the provinces of Erzurum, Trabzon, Van and Bitlis (with the borders of that date), and the area extending to a locality to be selected to the west of Trabzon on the Black Sea. Russia was also given Mush, Siirt, and the valley of the Tigris. In return, Russia recognized French domination of the area between Aladagh and Kayseri, between Yildizdagh and Zara, and between Eghin and Harput.

Finally, on 16 September an agreement was reached between Britain and Russia similar to the one between France and Russia.[97]

It is apparent that these agreements were reached over a map.

When it was decided that Italy would join the Triple Entente during the war, she too was included in the partition plan, being offered the region of Antalya. Italy also wanted to have the province of Aydin (Izmir is part of the province of Aydin) but Russia opposed this, stating that under these circumstances Turkey would not survive. Nevertheless in the St. Jean de Maurienne agreement (19-21 April 1917) made with Italy there was a clause giving Izmir to Italy, on condition that Russia gave her approval. This clause was not implemented as Revolution broke out in Russia before she had given her approval. Later on, the province of Aydin was offered to Greece, which resulted in a dispute between Italy and her allies after the truce:

The extent of these agreements can best be understood from Map 2.

None of these agreements mentioned the Armenians. It was only when the Revolution broke out in Russia, and she withdrew from the war, that the idea of founding an Armenia in the regions which fell to her share reappeared.

Another subject which was to create problems later was the 'Balfour Declaration' made by the British Government on 2 November 1917. With this declaration, Britain proclaimed that a 'national Jewish homeland' should be created in Palestine. It appears that this intention was officially announced to Hussein, the Governor of Mecca, in January 1918, and he replied that they did not see any inconvenience in this as long as the rights of Arabs in Palestine were respected.[98]

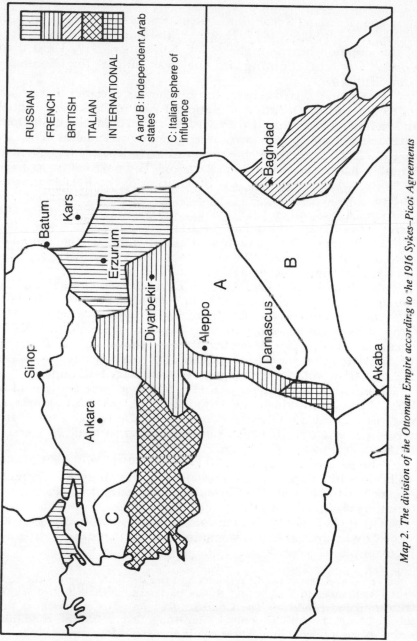

Map 2. The division of the Ottoman Empire according to the 1916 Sykes–Picot Agreements

RUSSIAN
FRENCH
BRITISH
ITALIAN
INTERNATIONAL

A and B: Independent Arab states

C: Italian sphere of influence

Baghdad

Kars
Batum
Erzurum
Diyarbekir
Sinop
Aleppo
Damascus
Akaba
Ankara
A
B
C

4. The elimination of the eastern front

The Russian Revolution began with the insurrection in Petrograd on 8 March 1917. However, the Bolsheviks took control of the situation on the night of 7-8 November 1917. Until then Russia was still fighting in the war under the Kerensky administration.

When they seized power, the Bolsheviks declared first of all, on 15 November 1917, that all nations living in Russia were equal and sovereign, and that if they wished they could break off from Russia and establish their own independent governments. The fact that the Armenians were able to found an independent Armenian Republic had its basis in this declaration. The next few years have shown to what extent this first declaration of the Bolsheviks was sincere.

On 24 November 1917 the Bolsheviks began to publish the secret agreements which had been made during the war. The agreement about the division and partitioning of the Ottoman Empire was among them. We do not know whether this agreement opened the Armenians' eyes.

On 28 November Estonia, on 6 December Finland, and on 24 December the Ukraine declared their independence.

On 26 November the Russians requested a truce. The Ottoman-Russian peace negotiations began on 4 December 1917 in Erzurum, and on 18 December the truce was signed. Its main articles stated that the two armies would remain where they were, and that they would not engage in new military build-ups.

Meanwhile the general peace negotiations were being held in Brest- Litovsk, in which the Ottomans took part. An agreement was reached on 15 December and on 17 December a cease-fire agreement was signed, which remained effective until 14 January 1918.

The peace talks began on 20 December 1917 in Brest-Litovsk. To begin with, Turkey was represented by the Minister of Foreign Affairs, Ahmet Nesimi Bey. From January 1918, Talat Pasha, the Grand Vizier took part in the talks.

On 13 January 1918 a declaration known as `Decree No. 13' signed by Lenin and Stalin was published in *Pravda* in Petrograd. Its main points were:

The Government of the Workers and the Peasants supports the right of the Armenians in Turkey and Russia to determine their destiny if they wish until independence. The Council of Commissars is convinced that this right can be fulfilled only by ensuring first of all the conditions necessary for a referendum. These conditions are as follows:

1. The retreat of armed forces from the borders of Turkish Armenia, and the formation of an Armenian militia, to protect life and property there.

2. The return of Armenian emigrants who have taken refuge in nearby areas.

3. The return of Armenians who have been exiled by the Turkish Government since the beginning of the war.

4. The establishment of a temporary National Armenian Government formed by deputies elected in accordance with democratic principles. The conditions of this government will be put forward during the peace talks with Turkey.

5. The Commissar for Caucasian Affairs, Shomian, will assist the Armenians in the realization of these goals.

6. A joint commission will be formed in order that Armenian lands can be evacuated by foreign troops.[99]

This decree indicated that the Russians would leave Turkey only after having armed the Armenians.

We shall not dwell on the details. The Brest-Litovsk negotiations ended on 3 March 1918 when the Peace Agreement was signed. Russia considered that this agreement had been virtually dictated, but signed it nevertheless because peace was necessary if the revolution was to continue.[100] The general agreement stated that Russia would do everything possible to evacuate the eastern Anatolian provinces and return them to Turkey, that the regions of Ardakhan, Kars, and Batum would also be evacuated, and that Turkey and the other states of the region would determine the new situation there.

The main articles of the Ottoman-Russian Agreement which was added to the general agreement were:

Article I:

1. Eastern Anatolia will be evacuated within 6-8 weeks.

3. Until the arrival of the Turkish Army, the Russians will establish order there, and will prevent incidents of revenge and brigandage.

4. The Russians will have a division every 150 km to guard the border.

5. The Armenian bands will be disarmed and dispersed.

7. Until the general peace, the Russians will not have units larger than a division in the Caucasus. If the situation requires otherwise, Russia will inform the four allies beforehand.

Because Turkey is fighting other enemies, it is necessary for her to have her army constantly mobilized.

Article III:

Three months after the approval of this agreement, the Turkish-Russian Commission will draw the border including the regions of Ardakhan, Kars, and Batum. The border will be the one before the 1877-8 war.

Article VI:

Because all existing agreements, pacts and treaties between the two states have been annulled, both states will sign consulate pact and other necessary agreements as required by the first appendix of the general agreement and within the period of time stated in that appendix.

Article VIII:

The agreements concerning the division of Iran have been annulled, and this country will be evacuated.

Article XI:

The Muslim elements in Russia have the right to emigrate to Turkey, either by disposing of their possessions, or taking them with them.[101]

When the Brest-Litovsk Agreement was being made the situation in the Caucasus was as follows:

When Kerensky was still in power in Russia, a National Assembly election was held. The Bolsheviks had dissolved this Assembly. The deputies elected in the Caucasus for this Assembly held a meeting on 10 February 1918 [This is the old Russian calendar; it would be 23 February according to the Gregorian calendar], and announced that the nations in the Caucasus [that is the Georgians, the Azerbaijanis, the Daghistanians and the Armenians] had founded the 'United Socialist Republic of Transcaucasia'. A provisional government was established under the leadership of Y. Ketetchgoni, a Georgian menshevik. Upon the request for peace made by Vehip Pasha, the first negotiations for peace began in Trabzon.[102]

As a matter of fact the Eastern Army Commander of the Ottomans had invited them to discussions. However, it was not a question of making a separate peace agreement, but rather of establishing friendly relations with the Caucasian states within the framework of the principles agreed with the Russians. Besides, when the Russian army left after the truce and was replaced by the Armenians, and when this situation became clear with the declaration of 13 January, the Ottoman Army had begun its operations and had freed Erzinjan on 13 February, and Trabzon on 24 February.

When the Caucasian delegation arrived at Trabzon on 8 March 1918, this operation was continuing. The Ottoman Army recovered Erzurum on 12 March, Sarikamish on 5 April, Van on 7 April, Batum on 14 April, and Kars on 25 April.

In his memoirs, Twerdo Khlebof, the Commander of the Russian Second Artillery regiment, narrates the cruelties and torture inflicted by the Armenians on unarmed Muslims during this period in regions they seemed to have inherited from the Russians, and especially in Erzurum, and the wicked deeds of prominent individuals such as Torkom, Andranik and Jamboladian. We shall not dwell on these subjects.[103]

As can be expected, the discussions in Trabzon did not have any result.

Let us now follow the attitude of the Armenians in this period from Kachaznuni's work:

The Armenians neither wanted to separate from Russia, nor expected anything from the Turks. The Armenians were still thinking of stopping the Turks by force of arms. In April a National Armenian Assembly met only to discuss this subject in Alexandropolis. In spite of the explanation I gave, this Assembly refused the Brest-Litovsk Agreement and decided to continue the war [paragraph 14] . . . Kars fell on April 25th. There was almost no resistance. . . . The Seym (the Assembly of the Republic of the Caucasus] immediately took the decision to continue the discussions interrupted in Trabzon, and to recognize the border of Brest-Litovsk. The discussions began at the beginning of May in Batum, where Turks had already settled. But the Turks had changed their minds. The Brest-Litovsk Agreement was no longer sufficient. They were saying 'we shed blood after Trabzon, it must be indemnified'. They wanted new concessions from Armenian lands [paragraph 15].

The Batum Conference had met on 11 May 1918. This time Halil Pasha was requesting the area including Ahiska, Ahilkelek, Gumru (Alexandropol), and the Kars-Gumru-Julfa railway.

As a matter of fact the war had not ended. The forces of Yakup Shevki Pasha had requested on 14 May that way be made via Gumru-Hulfa in order to send soldiers against the British in Iran. When he did not receive an answer he occupied Gumru and defeated the Armenians near Karakilis.

Meanwhile the Armenian and Bolshevik units in Baku had begun their advance to come to the help of the Armenian army in Gumru-Karakilis, and were demolishing Muslim villages on their way.

We continue to quote Kachaznuni:

Armed confrontations continued in Sardarabad until May 22-26, and in Haraklis until the 25th-28th. Maybe last efforts were being made for the Armenian nation to continue its existence. And doubtless this fight at the front and this brave resistance (it was not the army which was fighting but the people, because there was no army left) somewhat restored our esteem in the eyes of the Turks, and enabled a peace agreement to be made. [paragraph 17]

This time peace was achieved. A truce was signed on 4 June with Armenia, Azerbaijan and Georgia, on 8 June with Daghistan. Nahjivan was given to the Ottomans and thus contact was established with Azerbaijan.

However, peace was not established in the Caucasus because of the Baku conflict. The British had landed in Baku. The Turkish forces began their operations on 14 September, and took Baku on 15 September.

This is the incident about which the British Army published an official declaration stating that the Armenians had abandoned the war, and about which Toynbee wrote memoranda asserting that 'we must not inflict shame on the Armenians'. We have referred to these earlier, and in any case the events of the Caucasus are outside our topic.

As we conclude this discussion we want to mention one more point.

In Batum, the Turks had promised that they would intervene in order that the Caucasus states might make peace with the other allies (Germany, Austria, Bulgaria). For this reason the envoys of the Caucasus states had arrived in Istanbul. The delegates who came from Armenia were Aharonian and Hadissian. Vahdettin received them on 6 September 1918 in the 'Selâmlik'. The following telegram sent by Aharonian after this, on 9 September 1918, to Prime Minister Kachaznuni, is worth reading:

On September 6th, after we were in the `Selâmlik' we had an audience. We presented our congratulations on his accession to the throne. We submitted our best wishes for the development of the Empire and its well-being. We stated that the Armenian nation would never forget that it was the Ottoman Government which first conceived the idea of founding an independent Armenia, and recognized it, that the Armenian Government would do everything possible to protect friendly relations between the two countries and to strengthen them. His Majesty thanked us. He stated that he was very happy at seeing the envoys of independent and free Armenia, that he wished not only her development, but that she be strong in order to retain her independence. His Majesty is entirely convinced that friendly relations will always exist between the two neighbouring countries, Turkey and Armenia, in order that both of them may develop. He concluded his remarks by stating that he was very happy to see that Armenia had the strength to found an independent state which was able to send envoys to Istanbul, and repeated his best wishes for our country.

Talat Pasha went to Berlin to discuss the Caucasian matters. He is expected to return in two weeks. We hope that the issue of the Istanbul Conference will be resumed there.[104]

On 8 October 1918, the Talat Pasha cabinet resigned, having requested peace on the basis of the Wilson principles. The request for peace was made through the Spanish Embassy in America, which was protecting Turkish interests, by requesting America's mediation.[105] On 14 October, Ahmet Izzet Pasha formed a new Government. Britain gave Admiral Calthrope full powers for the peace discussions, which began on 27 October 1918 in Mondros, and the armistice was signed on 30 October.

Articles 11 and 24 of the armistice, concerning our subject, are:

Article 11. The order which was previously given, concerning the withdrawal of the Ottoman Army present in the north-eastern part of Iran, behind the border in effect before the war, will be carried out immediately. Because it was previously ordered that the Ottoman Army partially evacuate Transcaucasia, the remaining areas will be evacuated if such an action is requested after the allies have examined the local situation.

Article 24. The Entente Powers have the right to occupy any area of the six provinces should any insurrections occur in the said provinces.

Let us read about the situation in the East on the actual day the armistice was signed, from Kazim Karabekir Pasha's book:

I was the Commander of the First Caucasian Army Corps. My headquarters were in Tabriz. The 2nd Caucasian Division had occupied the Iranian Azerbaijan and the 9th Caucasus Division had occupied the region of Nahjivan (which was 6 kilometres south of Erivan) from the Turkish-Armenian border up to the Aras river. That is, it was covering an area of hundreds of square kilometres. Just as the Armenians were weakened through several blows, a British detachment which had approached Tabriz at a distance of three days had been expelled from Iranian Azerbaijan by successive offensives. Three aeroplanes had been shot down recently. On 15 September 1334 (1918) Baku was taken by our army, no enemy was left even in Azerbaijan. Georgia, too, was silent like Armenia, but had come under the protection of the Germans.[106]

After the armistice the situation naturally changed. The British entered Baku on 17 November 1918', demanding that the Turks retreat. By taking advantage of the fact that the Ottoman armies had retreated to the 1914 borders, the Georgians took Ahiska on 1 March 1919, the Armenians took Kars on 19 April, and on 20 April the Georgians entered Ardakhan.

We shall deal with later events on the eastern front in Chapter 6.

On 13 November, the fleet of the Entente Powers, consisting of sixty ships, arrived at Istanbul, and on 14 November soldiers were disembarked.

The victorious powers began to invade the areas which they had reserved for themselves through the secret agreements made during the war.

5. Armistice and hunting of the offenders

As soon as news of the relocation of the Armenians and the massacre claims were beginning to circulate in Europe as elements of war propaganda, the British and French Governments announced in May 1915 that they would hold responsible for these murders the members of the Ottoman Government, and those who had taken part or would take part in the massacres.

When the armistice was signed and Turkey was occupied, it was necessary for this engagement to be carried out.

However, before the occupation forces acted, the Ottoman Government acted. Upon this, the invading powers, or rather Britain, because the French seemed uninterested in this subject, preferred to wait for a while.

For this reason the pursuit of the offenders which began with the armistice occurred in two stages. We summarize below the first stage, which consisted of activities carried out by the Ottoman Government.

After Talat Pasha resigned, the duty of forming a new cabinet was given to Ahmet Izzet Pasha on 14 October 1918. On 19 October Izzet Pasha read his Government's programme in the Assembly. The following passage was included: `We decided that the citizens who were made to emigrate and resettle in other parts of the country due to necessities of wartime may return to their original places of residence, and we have begun to carry out this decision. A proposed law which was necessary for freeing those who were exiled by administrative and military decrees, and for declaring a general amnesty for political prisoners, will be prepared and submitted to the Assembly.[107]

Towards the end of 1918, upon the request of Vahdettin, the Party of Liberty and Agreement (*Hürriyet ve Itilaf*) was active again in Istanbul. The President was Nuri Pasha, the Head Court Chamberlain of Abdulhamid, and the Secretary General was Ali Kemal Bey.[108] It was this party which mainly organized the pursuit of the culprits.

Vahdettin was not pleased with the Izzet Pasha cabinet. He based his criticism on the fact that the cabinet included supporters of the Party of Union and Progress and that the aforementioned party members were being protected. Meanwhile, two days after the armistice was signed, that is on 1 November 1918, Enver Pasha, Talat Pasha, Jemal Pasha, and the most prominent officials of the Committee of Union and Progress, Bahaettin Shakir Bey, Dr Nazim Bey, Azmi Bey, and Bedri Bey, fled the country. This incident was especially exploited to criticize the government. It was claimed that the escape had been facilitated by the government.

When the Sultan requested from Izzet Pasha that the ministers from the Party of Union and Progress be dismissed, Izzet Pasha resigned on 8 November 1918. Tevfik Pasha was charged with forming a new cabinet. After tumultuous discussions, Tevfik Pasha obtained a vote of confidence from the Assembly on 18 November 1918.[109]

In the Assembly the atmosphere against the Party of Union and Progress was worsening. There were those who desired that members of the war cabinets, Sait Halim Pasha and Talat Pasha, be sent to the High Court of Justice. On 10 November 1918, Fuat Bey, the Representative of Divaniye, submitted a ten-article proposal to the Assembly President. The fifth article began: `Those people who by issuing temporary laws and orders have changed our country from one in which the spirit of our Constitution protected the legal and human rights into a place of tragedy. . . .'[110]

Before this report, which was referred to the Commission, came to the Assembly, the Assembly was dissolved, and the members of the war cabinets who remained in Turkey were sent to the martial law court and later taken to Malta.

The reason for the dissolution of the Assembly was a motion of censure which was submitted. On 21 December, Reshit Pasha, the Minister of Foreign Affairs, read the Government's reply to the motion of censure; immediately afterwards Mustafa Arif Bey, the Minister of the Interior, took the floor and read out the Sultan's order to dissolve the Assembly.

In the meantime, the British had started exerting pressure for the immediate arrest of the offenders, as we shall explain later.

Tevfik Pasha had a special and extraordinary court formed, to try those individuals who would be arrested as war criminals. It was presided over by Mahmut Hayret Pasha, and its members were Ali Nadi Pasha and Suleymaniyeli Mustafa Pasha. (All three were retired army officers.)

'On January 30, 1919, 27 people, including Haji Adil Bey, former Minister and deputy, Huseyin Cahit Bey, Dr Tevfik Rushtu Bey, Mithat Shukru Bey, the general secretary of the Party of Union and Progress, Ismail Canbolat Bey, the former minister of the Interior, Kara Kemal Bey, member of the Central Committee, Ziya Gokalp Bey, deputy Karasu Bey, and Rahmi Bey, the governor of Izmir, were arrested and imprisoned in the Bekiragha Regiment.'[111] The names of most of those who were arrested were submitted by the British.

Meanwhile a most significant incident occurred. Reshit Bey, the Minister of Foreign Affairs, sent a telegram on 18 February 1919 to the governments of Denmark, Holland, Spain, and Sweden, informing them that a commission had been formed to investigate the subject of the relocation, and requested that each state send two legal experts as they envisaged that two members from each neutral country would take part in this commission.

The British tried to prevent the sending of this telegram on the grounds of military censorship.[112] However, when they saw that they were too late and that the telegrams had already been sent, they attempted to prevent the sending of members to such a commission.[113] It is interesting that the British objected to establishing the commission. It is apparent that they did not want anyone else to interfere with this matter but themselves.

But matters did not proceed as rapidly as was desired. The Sultan was not pleased with the Government. Finally Tevfik Pasha was forced to resign. Ferit Pasha formed a new cabinet on 4 March. The members of the new cabinet were from the Party of Liberty and Agreement.

Ferit Pasha established the court known as Nemrut Mustafa Pasha Martial Court, presided over by Mustafa Pasha, and on 10 March sixty more members of the Union and Progress Party were arrested.

We have been unable to determine the exact date when the court martial began to function. We can assume that this court martial, which we know sentenced to death Kemal Bey, the Kaymakam of the *kaza* of Boghazlian, began functioning towards the end of March.

It appears that the trial of the actual members of the Party of Union and Progress began on 27 April 1919. 'The public trial has begun in the presence of the Grand Vizier Sait Pasha Bey, the President of the Legislature Halil, Ahmet Nesimi Bey [Minister of Foreign Affairs], Ibrahim Bey, Shukru Bey, Kemal Bey, Kuchuk Talat Bey, Topchu Riza Bey, Ziya Gokalp Bey, Atif Bey, Colonel Jevat Bey, President of "Teskilati Mahsusu", and the Istanbul Centre Commandant, and in default of Talat Efendi, Enver Efendi, Jemal Efendi, Dr Nazim Bey, Dr Bahattin Shakir Bey, Dr Rusuhi Bey, and the former chief of police, Aziz Bey. Because Enver Pasha and Jemal Pasha had been dismissed from the Army, they were referred to as "Efendi" along with Talat Pasha.'[114]

While this trial was continuing, those individuals whom the British considered to be the most important were taken from Bekir Agha and exiled in Malta. This constitutes the second stage of the pursuit of the offenders. After this, the British were no longer connected with the trial in Istanbul.

On 13 July 1919, the trial, which was continuing in Istanbul, sentenced Talat Pasha, Enver Pasha, Jemal Pasha, and Dr Nazim Bey to death in default, and Javit Bey, Mustafa Bey, and Sherif Bey, who were secondary authors, to fifteen years. These were purely political verdicts.

The Istanbul trial was thus concluded. Talat Pasha and Jemal Pasha, whom the Nemrut Mustafa Pasha Martial Court had sentenced to death, died by Armenian bullets. Falih Rifki says about Jemal Pasha: `Sad Destiny! There are many who still like and miss Jemal Pasha in Syria, where he condemned to death and executed many of the prominent Arab leaders. Jemal Pasha was killed by the Armenians, among whom he had saved tens of thousands with his own hand.'[115]

The Government of Ferit and Vahdettin acted as a tool of the British, exclusively in order to slander the Party of Union and Progress and to get rid of powerful opponents. If the British had not taken those individuals to Malta in order to try them themselves, the Ferit Government might have executed them too.

Before we deal with the second stage of the pursuit of the offenders there is another point we must mention.

It had been decided that the Armenians who had been made to emigrate might return to their previous places of residence,. and that their possessions should be returned to them. This decision was immediately implemented.

The Armenian Patriarch gave the following information about this subject:

The Armenians of Istanbul, and the Armenians in the *sanjak* of Kutahya and the province of Aydin had not been required to emigrate. The Armenians who at the present time are in the *sanjak* of Izmit and in Bursa, Kastamonu, Ankara, and Konya, are those who had emigrated from these areas, and who have returned.

There are many Armenians in the *sanjak* of Kaiseri, and in Sivas, Kharput, Diyarbekir, and especially in Cicilia and in Istanbul, who have returned, but who are unable to go to their villages. The rest of the Armenians of Erzurum and Bitlis are in Cilicia.[116]

The children who had been adopted and the women who had converted were being identified and gathered by a commission. We can make the following observations concerning this issue.

In 1922 in the League of Nations it was claimed that hundreds of thousands of Armenians and Greek children and women were still hidden in the `harems' in Turkey. We quote the following passage from a brochure published by the Ministry of the Interior:

After the Armistice the Ottoman Government spent more than 1,150,000 liras, and employed hundreds of officials to return the Greeks and Armenians to their previous areas of residence from the regions they had been transferred to. The procedures involving the transfer of these people to their homelands, and returning to them their movable and immovable properties, have been carried out through joint delegations formed by British officers appointed by the British High Commission, Ottoman officials, and one   member of each of the interested nations. These delegations, whose number exceeded 62, formed by British and Ottoman officials, which were sent to all parts of the country, acted with the utmost attention and care. Even women who had married Muslim men of their own accord were summoned one by one, and were asked again if they had consented, and those who declared that they were pleased were left to their wishes. In the `harems' or orphanages of Istanbul there were not hundreds of thousands of Armenian or Greek children and women, there are not even two children who remained. While there are no remaining Armenian children, some Muslim children, asserted to be Armenian, are still in Armenian orphanages, even though their mothers and fathers are known to be alive.

Then, how is it possible that thousands of Armenian children, as it is claimed, are still in the presence of Turks? How can the League of Nations, which does not have the legal character of an executive power, and does not have an organization or the means to investigate the actual situation in depth, conceive of the existence of children and women whom the police force, the joint delegation, and the high officials of the Entente Powers in Istanbul were unable to find?

For those who are somewhat aware of the actual situation, the matter is quite simple. Because, if an American historian, who has been in Turkey for more than thirty years, and who is at present a member of the Executive Committee of a Benevolent Society in Istanbul, can try to find (only a week ago) a slave market in Istanbul where girls and women are sold for money, then the report and speech reminding one of the Arabian Night Stories, made by Mademoiselle Vakaresko of Rumania, who does not know Turkey, who constantly looks at Turkey from the perspective of the Armenians and the Greeks, and who is influenced by their exaggeration of violence, must not be considered strange.

How can it be explained that this issue which has escaped the attention and the investigation of the officials, the official and non-official organizations of the Great Entente Powers in Istanbul, was able to be detected only by Mademoiselle Vakaresko who resides in Switzerland?[117]

Halide Edip makes an interesting observation about the children in the orphanages.

. . . Taking the Armenian children from the Turkish orphanages was becoming a tragic sight. . . . A committee was founded, presided over by Colonel Heathcote Smythe, and it was attempting to find the Armenian children and separate them from the Turkish children. They had rented a house in Shishli (a quarter of Istanbul). The majority of the central committee which was to separate the children were Armenians. Nezihe Hanim, General Secretary of the women's branch of the Red Crescent, had been invited to represent the Turks. . . . When children were brought from the orphanages in Anatolia, to Istanbul, they were sent to the Armenian church in Kumkapu, and there they were claimed to be Armenian. Some children tried to escape, but were caught and brought back.

It was a day when I had gone to visit Nezihe Hanim. Two frightened children came into the room, one was limping and the other had been wounded in the head . . . they had come from an orphanage and had been brought to a church. They had strongly resisted being considered as Armenians, as the Armenians had killed their parents. They had been severely beaten, but had succeeded in escaping. They were crying, they were pleading to be protected, not to be sent back. . . . Nezihe Hanim called a few journalists and requested that they be brought to Mr. Ryan, the head translator of the British Embassy. . . . Although it was known how much hatred he had against the Turks, Nezihe Hanim thought that he would be compassionate in the presence of these two innocent and desperate children. . . . I later heard that when these two children were speaking, an Armenian official entered the room to say something to Mr. Ryan. One of the children screamed `this was the man who beat and kicked us'. The man was a member of the delegation in the Church of Kumkapu. . . .

The pain of this little creature affected me very much. For me he symbolized the desperate Turkish nation. He was small and weak.[118]

We can now deal with the second stage of the pursuit of the suspects.

On 3 January 1919, Admiral Calthrope (the British High Commissioner) sent the following telegram to the British Foreign Office: `It appears to me both useless and undignified to continue to make protests to the Turkish Government whilst the present Cabinet gives every evidence of goodwill. Its orders are not obeyed. . . . The situation therefore calls for some fresh form of action and I can think of nothing more likely to be efficacious than to authorize me to demand the immediate arrest and delivery to Allied Military Authorities of persons against whom there appears to be a prima facie case.'[119]

On 24 January, he sent the following telegram: 'Grand Vizier told me the other day that between 160 and 200 persons had been arrested but I think that this must be an exaggeration: some persons however certainly have been.'120

His telegram dated 31 January: `Action taken by Turkish Government in starting to arrest these people is very satisfactory. . . . I intend to supply Minister of Interior with further names though I have not yet presented formal command for surrender of those implicated in cruelty to prisoners, as list is not yet complete.[121]

Telegram dated 11 March: `New Government has commenced making fresh arrests with commendable energy. Over twenty were effected yesterday including large number of those who were Ministers during the war, from ex-Grand Vizier, Said Halim, downwards. . . . Most of those on French list have been seized.'[122]

Telegram dated 29 May: 'British military authorities have now taken over from Turkish authorities sixty-seven persons arrested in accordance with Foreign Office telegram No. 233. They are being sent to Malta with the exception of twelve who will be landed at Mundros for detention there.'[123]

Some persons who were arrested after the occupation of Istanbul on 16 March 1920 were also sent to Malta, and at the end of 1920 the number of arrested in Malta reached 118.[124]

Among these 118 individuals, 55 were guilty of acts in respect of relocation. Among these 55, 16 were blamed with concrete accusations, 17 were blamed because they were in power during the relocation and thus winked at the incidents; 22 were deputies, and it was hard to determine whether these were connected with the so-called massacre.[125]

Those who were arrested before the occupation of Istanbul were divided into three groups: (i) those were arrested by the Turkish authorities (30); (ii) those whose arrests had been officially requested by the British (2); (iii) those whose names were given unofficially by the British to the Turkish authorities. Four such unofficial lists were given, the first on 23 January 1919, and the last on 7 April 1919.[126]

Now the question was to determine who would try these individuals and under what circumstances.

The opinion of the Prosecutor of the Crown was sought, and with this aim a report was sent on 10 July 1919.

In this report those who had been arrested were divided into seven groups based on the following factors: (1) failure to comply with armistice terms; (2) impeding execution of armistice terms; (3) insolence to British commanders and officers; (4) ill-treatment of prisoners; (5) outrages to Armenians or other subject races both in Turkey and Transcaucasia; (6) participation in looting, destruction of property, etc. ; (7) any other breaches of the laws and regulations of war.[127]

The Office of the Prosecutor of the Crown suggested that an article be included in the Peace Treaty concerning crimes connected with relocation.

An interesting point was that, in the report sent to the Prosecutor, it was stated that these individuals had been brought to Malta to be protected, at the request of the Ottoman government.

When the British High Commissioner in Istanbul learned about this later, he was forced to state in a report dated 12 March 1919 that the Ottoman Government had never made such a request, and that the transfer of these persons to Malta had been made by a decision of the British Government.[128]

An article was included in the Sevres Treaty, as requested by
the British Prosecutor. This article was article 230 of the
agreement. But there was more to the question than that. In order
to have these persons convicted by an international or British court,
one needed to have evidence. The Prosecutor of the Crown
requested in his memorandum dated 8 February 1919 that the
evidence be gathered and submitted to him.[129]

The evidence sent from Istanbul was not satisfactory, for
almost all the accusations were based on rumour and hearsay. The
Armenian and Greek branch of the Istanbul High Commissariat
had ordered the arrests, having considered the most trivial
accusation sufficient. Because it had acted in this manner, and had
not carefully investigated each incident, it was now impossible to
determine whether those who were arrested were in fact guilty.
The Prosecutor General of the Crown expressed this point in a
report dated 29 July 1921.

Attention is called to the inherent difficulties with which the
prosecution will be faced, if the Military Tribunals, before which these
persons are to be arraigned, require the production of evidence of a
character which alone would be admissible before an English Court of
Justice. Up to the present no statements have been taken from witnesses
who can depose to the truth of the charges made against the prisoners. It
is indeed uncertain whether any witnesses can be found. . . .

If the charges made are substantially true, it seems more than
probable that the great majority of those who could appear as witnesses
against the accused are dead or have been irretrievably dispersed. . . .

. . . Until more precise information is available as to the nature of the
evidence which will be forthcoming at the trials, the Attorney General does
not feel that he is in a position to express any opinion as to the prospects
of success in any of the cases submitted for his consideration.[130]

Meanwhile Britain turned to one more possibility: to gather
documents from the other powers. On this subject he could only
benefit from the United States of America, because during the war
the American Embassy and Consulates were in Turkey. If the
French had any documents, they would have disclosed them
themselves, in view of their existing engagement.

Instructions were given to the Washington Embassy. The
Ambassador to Washington, Sir A. Geddes, stated in the telegram
he sent on 1 June 1921: 'I have made several enquiries of the State
Department and today I am informed that while they are in
possession of a large number of documents concerning Armenian
deportations and massacres, these refer rather to events connected
with the perpetration of crimes than to persons implicated.,[131] The
items of information given by the American Consuls did not
consist of eye witness reports but were rumours.[131]

As a last resort, the British Foreign Secretary submitted the names of those who were detained at Malta, and requested that a search be made for documentary evidence against them.[132] The British Ambassador replied on 13 June: `I regret to inform Your Lordship that there was nothing there which could be used as evidence against the Turks who are being detained for trial at Malta.'[133]

The truth of it is that the British did everything they could, but the matter was concluded and the Turks who were detained at Malta were exchanged with the British who were detained in Turkey.

The question of whether the British High Commissioner in Istanbul acted objectively or emotionally comes to mind. Of course, the Armenian and Greek branch of the High Commission was receiving its information from the Armenians and the Greeks. It might be expected that they would not take these items of information at face value without investigating them, but is seems that that is exactly what they did.

It also seems that the British High Commissioner in Istanbul had access to the Ottoman Archives. Dr Salahi Sonyel found document No. 9518 E. 5523 among the dossiers in File No. 371 during research that he undertook in the British Archives. This is the original text of a secret order made by Talat Pasha concerning the relocation of the Armenians. This text was enclosed in a letter dated 22 May 1923, written by Mr. Nevile, the then High Commissioner. From this letter it appears that these documents were very probably obtained by the British intelligence service following the Mundros Agreement, that they remained from that time in their safes, and that recently they were sent to the High Commissioner. The last article of the order stated '. . . Because this order concerns the disbanding of the Committees, it is necessary that it be implemented in a way that would prevent the Armenian and Muslim elements from massacring each other.'

In his memorandum about this order, D. G. Osborne of the British Foreign Office says: '. . . the last article of the order states that one must refrain from measures which might cause massacre' (371/4241/170751).

This subject reminds us of Aram Andonian's book entitled *Official Documents Relating to the Deportations and Massacres of Armenians*, which was published in Paris in 1920.[134] If the documents in this book were true and if the Armenians had obtained them when General Allenby entered Aleppo, as is claimed, without any doubt the British would have been the first to hear about them, and to use them to convict those persons detained at Malta. We shall study this book at the end of this chapter.

We shall mention two more points to conclude this subject.

First, the telegram sent by Ferit Pasha to the President of the Paris Peace Conference on 30 June 1919.[135] In this telegram, Ferit Pasha requested the mediation of the victorious powers to ensure the return of war criminals in Germany, including Talat Pasha, Enver Pasha, and Jemal Pasha, in order that they should be tried. At one point the British thought of including an article in the Sèvres Agreement which would make this possible, but it was not done. We have not been able to discover why.

The second point is even more interesting. The British High Commissioner in Istanbul, in a telegram dated 22 April 1920 sent to the British Foreign Office, stated that the Grand Vizier had suggested the arrest of certain individuals, and had implied that it would be preferable that the British themselves arrest these individuals.[136]

Among those whose arrest had been suggested were the following: Mustafa Kemal Pasha, Ali Fuat Pasha, Kazim Karabekir Pasha, Abdulkerim Pasha, Nihat Pasha, Hasan Riza Pasha, Ahmet Izzet Pasha, Ismail Fazil Pasha, Cafer Tayyar Pasha, Selahattin Adil Bey, Ismet Bey.

Bilal Simsir has done extensive research on those who were exiled to Malta, based on the British documents. Those who are interested may refer to his work.137

6. The Sèvres Treaty

The Mundros Truce Agreement was signed on 30 October 1918. The Sivres Treaty between Turkey and the Allies was signed by the Ottoman representatives on 10 August 1920.

The agreements made with Germany and Austria had been prepared and signed much earlier. One may wonder about this delay, as the destiny of the Ottoman Empire had already been determined during the war. One reason is the Turco-Greek war and the disputes which arose with the Arab world, and this is outside our topic of discussion. The other reason is the Armenians.

The problem created by the Armenians was not the question, what would happen to them, but what would happen to the lands relinquished to Russia by the agreements made during the war. The British attempted to give this region to the mandate of the United States of America, and thus create a buffer between Russia and the Arab world, but they were not successful.

Another problem was that although the USA, not having fought against Turkey, did not sign the peace agreement, she had a say in every subject when the agreement was being prepared.

As we know the attitude of France and Britain, let us now attempt to determine the attitude of the USA.

Before the USA entered the war, she had been informed of all the agreements made concerning the division and partition of the Empire. Colonel House, the special envoy of President Wilson, describes a meeting in 1915 with members of the British War Cabinet, including Prime Minister Asquith, Grey, Lloyd George, Balfour, and Lord Reading, in which peace terms were discussed: `We all cheerfully divided up Turkey, both in Asia and Europe. The discussion hung for a long while around the fate of Constantinople.'[138]

The USA was not included in the partition agreements, and had never considered them as a document that was binding on her. However, she did not make any objection, and wanted to remain outside subjects concerning the European powers.

Without any doubt the USA was the country where anti-Ottoman views were most prevalent in that period. The information sent by the Protestant American missionaries in Turkey from the 1890s onward, and `the attitude of the press has poisoned public opinion in the United States with regard to the Turkish people to such an extent that a member of that race is seldom thought or spoken of in this country otherwise than as the "unspeakable". . . . Nor was the government itself impartial in its opinion and attitude concerning the present or the future of the Ottoman state. . . . When Woodrow Wilson was considering the appointment of ambassadors shortly after his election in 1912, Colonel House suggested Henry Morgenthau as Ambassador to Turkey; Wilson replied, `There ain't going to be no Turkey,' to which House rejoined, `Then let him go look for it.'[139]

When the United States entered the war, diplomatic relations with Turkey were severed on 20 April 1917, but no declaration of war took place between the two countries. For this reason there was no question of the United States signing the agreement which was going to be prepared at the Paris Peace Conference.

When war was declared on Germany, the former Ambassador to Istanbul, Morgenthau, met with Lansing, the US Secretary of State, and convinced him, stating that Turkey had become tired of her German masters, and that she might reach a separate agreement with them. President Wilson too, found the idea suitable, and decided to send Morgenthau to Palestine, not to engage in negotiations, but to develop a view of the situation and on the pretext of investigating the condition of the Jews. Since this mission necessitated the cooperation of Jewish leaders, enquiries had been made to the British Government for the participation of Dr. Chaim Weizmann in the mission. Because the subject of Palestine could only be resumed with the defeat of Turkey, Balfour charged Weizmann with the duty of persuading Morgenthau to abandon this project, and he had been successful.

When the Treaty of Versailles was being discussed at the Congress in 1919, Wilson stated that he had been informed of the secret agreements for the first time during the Conference. This was not true; he had been informed much earlier. As a matter of fact, when Balfour, the British Foreign Secretary, came to Washington on 22 April 1917, they had discussed what their war aims would be without making an official discussion of it. Colonel House recorded in his diary: `Constantinople was our next point. We agreed that it should be internationalized. Crossing the Bosphorus we came to Anatolia. It is here that the secret treaties between the Allies come in most prominently. They have agreed to give Russia the region of Armenia and the northern part of Turkey. The British take in Mesopotamia [and the region] which is contiguous to Egypt. France and Italy each have their spheres, embracing the balance of Anatolia up to the Straits. It is all bad and I told Balfour so. They are making it a breeding ground for future war.'[140]

The United States also had their notorious 14 points which Wilson had personally announced on 8 January 1918 and which had been established as the basis for peace. The 12th point concerned Turkey, and stated: `The Turkish part of the present Ottoman Empire must be granted the right of secure sovereignty. The other nations which are now under Turkish rule must be granted the possibility of autonomous development, as well as a right to life which would leave no room for doubt. The Straits will be under an international guarantee, and must always be open to the free passage of ships of all states and for their commerce.'

Such was in summary the attitude of the United States as she took part in the Peace Conference.

We mentioned that Talat Pasha had made attempts for peace through the Spanish Embassy in Washington. Mr. Lansing, the American Secretary of State, replied on 30 October that he would submit this request to the Allies. On the same day the Mundros Agreement was signed.

The Peace Conference began in January 1919. We shall not consider it in detail, even as regards Turkey. We only want to mention briefly the parts concerning the Armenians.

The minutes of the Conference meetings concerning the Turkish Agreement was translated into Turkish by Osman Olcay. It is possible to follow the matters discussed in these meetings, to which the Ottoman Empire representatives had not been invited, from the minutes.[141]

Another interesting source to be referred to, for the general climate of the Peace Conference, would be Lloyd George's book.[142] We shall make a few quotations from this book.

The Armenians took part in the Paris Peace Conference with two delegations. Aharonian presided over the delegation representing the Armenian Republic, and Bogos Nubar Pasha presided over the group called the National Delegation, which in a way represented all Armenians. These delegations gave a note to the Conference on 12 February, and requested that an independent Armenia be established, including the Caucasian Armenian Republic, Cilicia, and seven provinces; that it be given to the mandate of one of the powers; and that those who had taken part in the massacres should be punished.

The Conference listened to them on 26 February. They repeated their demands. In his book, Lloyd George states that the explanations made by Bogos Nubar Pasha were 'fairy tales', and that Aharonian was `as contradictory and confused as Bogos Pasha'.

The Conference was of the opinion that Armenia should be under the mandate of a great power. President Wilson seemed to be inclined to accept this mandate. It is useful to take a look at what Lloyd George wrote about the mandate of Armenia.

But when the question of a mandate over Armenia and the Straits was concerned, the President [Wilson] took a much more sympathetic view of that project. It was obvious that we could not agree to any settlement which would leave the remnant of the persecuted population of Armenia to the cruel mercies of the race which had massacred, outraged, and pillaged it for a generation and continued it through and right up to the end of the War. But Armenia, with its depopulated and dispirited remnants, could not stand alone against the Turks on the one hand, and the Bolsheviks on the other. It was essential therefore that we should find a mandatory Power which would undertake as a humane duty the protection of this harried Christian community in the mountains of Armenia.

It was obvious that neither France, Britain, nor Italy could undertake that task. They were already overburdened with the weight of the mandates they had accepted in Mesopotamia, Palestine, Anatolia, Syria, Africa, and the Southern Seas. So heavy were these burdens that Italy ultimately shrank from undertaking her share in Anatolia. Britain had disembarrassed herself of her task in Mesnpotamia; France renounced the mandate for Cilicia in 1920.

Russia would have been the most fitting choice for a mandatory in Armenia and the Straits. Up to the Revolution her religious sympathies were engaged in a crusade for the protection of the Christian communities in Turkey. It was her military intervention that had emancipated the Christians of the Balkans and a portion of the Christians in the Armenian valleys. Had it not been for our sinister intervention, the great majority of the Armenians would have been placed, by the Treaty of San Stefano in 1978, under the protection of the Russian flag.

When the Sykes-Picot conversations were transferred to Petrograd, the fate of Armenia was one of the subjects of negotiation. It was there decided that the northern half of Armenia should be placed under Russian control, and the southern half under the French.

But the Russian Revolution, and the advent into power of a Government with different enthusiasms and with a totally different view of its aims and responsibilities, had put Russia out of the question as a mandatory even had she been prepared to accept the trust. The secret treaties, by which Constantinople and the Straits and half the province of Armenia were to be placed under the dominion of the Tsars, were promptly repudiated. The minds of the peasants, workers and bourgeoisie alike were concentrated not on reforms in Armenia, or the redress of Armenian wrongs, but on the overthrow of oppression and misgovernment in Russia itself and the reconstruction of a system which had been responsible for reducing the majority of the people of so rich a country to poverty, misery and slavery.

Neither Britain nor Italy was prepared to step into the shoes of Russia, and although France was ready and even eager at that time to secure dominion over the southern part of Armenia, she was by no means prepared to extend her control to the northern part of the province. French, British and Italians alike were driven to the conclusion that America alone was capable of discharging adequately the responsibilities of a mandatory. When the delegates of the Great Powers assembled at the Conference to examine the difficulties, it became clear that America was the only mandatory who would have been acceptable to all alike.

The idea of the annexation of Armenian by a foreign country vanished with the disappearance of Russia from the scene. Since the Sykes-Picot negotiations of 1916, the idea of self-determination had grown considerably in strength, and it now dominated the whole peace policy of the Alliance. The Armenians who, before and during the war, had been quite happy at the prospect of becoming a province in a Christian Empire, had set their minds now on restoring Armenia to its pristine glory as an independent country.[143]

Lloyd George narrates in detail that President Wilson took up this idea seriously, but that on his return to the United States he was unable to persuade Congress to accept it. He goes on to write that the United States did not take part in the conference which was held in April 1920 in San Remo. At this conference the issue of Armenian borders was once again discussed, and it was extensively debated whether Ezurum should be given to the Armenians, despite the fact that its population was entirely Muslim, and whether this city which was under Turkish occupation could be taken by the Armenians. Some observations made by Berthelot, the French representative, and Lord Curzon during this conference are worthy of mention. For example, Berthelot stated that `The United States of America conceives a great Armenia. But this conception does not have a solid basis, and is not in accordance with reality. A more logical approach would be to take Russian Armenia, which had a population of 400-500,000. And this was being threatened from outside. But nevertheless it existed and formed the historical Armenia.' Despite this statement, Berthelot at the same time thought it favourable that Erzurum be given to the Armenians. Curzon made the following observation: `From all points of view, Erzurum is at a dominating position, and to relinquish it to the Turks would make an independent Armenia impossible. A new Pan-Islamic or a Pan-Turanian movement could reappear. The London Conference, which has thought of this possibility, is of the opinion that a barrier, formed by a Christian community, between the Muslims of Turkey and those in the East is desirable for the continuation of world peace. And this barrier will be the new Armenian State.'

It is necessary to look for the reason as to why the United States did not accept the Armenian mandate, in the reports of the King-Crane Commission and the G. Harbord Commission.

The King-Crane Commission was conceived as an Allied commission formed by three states, primarily to examine the situation in Syria. The British at first accepted this offer, which was made by the United States. To begin with, the French had agreed to take part, but later they refused to do so. The British did not take part either, and thus the representatives of the USA were left alone.

The King-Crane Commission stated that it would be appropriate that some Turkish lands be given to Armenia, which would be founded by taking lands from Turkey and Russia, because of the misfortunes which had befallen this nation. It added that the region which would be taken from Turkey should not be too large, and that it would be impossible to suggest an Armenia extending from the Black Sea to the Mediterranean Sea. The Commission emphasized that a powerful mandatory state was necessary [144]

The point which was emphasized in the report of General Harbord was the following:

Very alarming reports had been received from Transcaucasia for several months before its [the mission's] departure from France, particularly as to organized attacks by the Turkish Army impending along the old international border between Turkey and Russia. The itinerary of the mission through Turkey was planned with those reports before it and with the intention of observing as to their truth and if possible to exert a restraining influence. We practically covered the frontier of Turkey from the Black Sea to Persia, and found nothing to justify the reports. The Turkish Army is not massed along the border; their organization is reduced to a skeleton; and the country shows an appalling lack of people, either military or civilian.

The mission believes that the power which takes a mandate for Armenia should also exercise a mandate for Anatolia, Roumelia, Constantinople, and Trans- caucasia. . . . [145]

The United States did not accept the mandate for these reasons. Upon this President Wilson was asked to be the arbitrator in the issue of drawing Armenia's borders. He accepted this task.

As a result of this, Articles 88 and 89, concerning the Armenians, were included in the Sèvres Treaty, along with Article 230 which indirectly concerned the Armenians.

These Articles were:

Article 88. Turkey notifies, as the other states have, that she recognizes Armenia as an independent and free State.

Article 89. Like the other signatories, Turkey and Armenia have decided to submit the task of determining the borders between Turkey and Armenia in the provinces of Van, Erzurum, Trabzon, and Bitlis, to the President of the U.S.A., and to accept his decision on this issue, as well as all the other statutes he may offer concerning Armenia's access to the sea, and the demilitarization of all the Ottomand Lands bordering on the said frontier.

Article 230. The Ottoman Government is responsible for surrendering the individuals, requested by the Allied Powers, who were responsible for the mass killings which occurred during the war in any area which was part of the Ottoman Empire on August 1, 1914.[146]

The Istanbul Government tried to resist so as not to sign the Treaty and to change it. The powers gave the Babiali a deadline until 27 July at midnight to accept the agreement. The Agreement was then accepted and signed on 10 August.

What would have happened if it had not been accepted? In fact, the National Government in Ankara never accepted this Treaty, and Sevres was put away before it came into force. Nothing else would have happened if Istanbul, too, had not recognized it. The country, including Istanbul, was occupied anyway. The victorious powers would not be able to do anything more. If the Istanbul Government had refused to sign, nothing would have changed, but those who refused to sign would have been remembered later with approval. But there was no such person in Istanbul at that time.

7. Tehlirian's Trial and the Book of Andonian

Amongst its various condemnation decisions which aimed at slandering the Committee for Union and Progresss, The Nemrut Mustafa Pasha Military Court which was established by Damat Ferit Government had also sentenced Talat Pasha to death by default.

We had stated within the 5th section of this chapter that on 30 June 1919, Damat Ferit had sent a telegram to the Paris Peace Conference in which he asked for assurance from the Allies that the Criminals of War-amongst whom were also Talat, Enver and Cemal Pashas—who had fled to Germany would be returned to be adjudicated by the court. Nevertheless, because of the fact that this demand was not met by the Allies, there seemed to remain no possibility to execute the death penalty which was issued by

Istanbul Military Court on 14 July 1919. This mission was undertaken by Soghomon Tehlirian, an Armenian terrorist, who shot Talat Pasha to death in Berlin on 15 March 1921.

The Armenian murderer, who was arrested and sent to prison after the murder, was acquitted on 3 June 1921 with no punishment following the court's decision which declared him not guilty of premeditatedly killing a person. Since we have no information concerning the proceeding at German courts, we will not be able to consider whether the acquittal of a murderer on the grounds that he has not committed the crime premeditatedly should be evaluated as something normal or not. As a matter of fact, the main reason as to why this subject has been brought up is not the concerned murder case but a book called "Official Documents Regarding the Armenian Massacre[147]" which was written by Aram Andonian whose name initially started to be quoted in relation with the murder case. We had also referrred to to this book in the 5th section and stated that we would elaborate on it in a separate chapter.

In order to prove that the Ottomans had organized a setup during the war to systematically exterminate the Armenians in the country, this book which was published both in English and in French in 1920, presented copies of approxiamotoly 50 Ottoman Archives documents which were alleged to be official and authentic, and recorded the memoirs of an Ottoman officer Naim Bey—who was claimed to be the person that delivered the abovementioned documents to Andonian—concerning the documents he had delivered.

These documents have been used against the Ottoman nation for 60 years on the grounds that they were accepted as evidence by the German court during Tehlirian's case and hence that their authenticity had been proven in this way. A study which would prove the falsification in these documents had been concluded while "The Armenian File" was going to press. Nevertheless, since it would be impossible to go into details about this subject until the researchers of the abovementioned book publish the results of their study, I would like to complete this issue which was missing in the first edition of the book.

As we have also mentioned in the introduction, although the Armenians are well aware of the falsification in the concerned documents themselves, they have started to refer to this book again for they probably think that after 60 years have passed, the falsification in the documents can no longer be proven. Because this seems to add a new dimension to Armenian allegations, it seems inevitable for us, who aim to determine the real aspects of the issue in this book, to not only lay out the true aspects of the imaginary allegations and underline the falsifity of fake documents but to determine what kind of setups the owners of the allegations recourse to.

Because of this reason, we have included in this book, some of the summarised chapters of the abovementioned book. The chapters we have summarised are from the first 20 pages of the book.[148]

Andonian describes Naim Bey and the story of the documents he obtained from himself as follows:

Naim Bey is the ex-head clerk of the Deportation Administration in Aleppo. Because he held an important post at the General Administration in Aleppo, he had to be knowing a lot, even including the every single thing about what I was interested in. I had thought that the promise of a financial reward would perhaps easily lead him to a long confession. However, during my first meeting with Naim Bey, I realized that I was wrong about what I had thought of him. Although he was not in a very good financial situation, Naim Bey rejected any offer related with money. Because his feeling of being a Turk was very vivid, he was afraid of launching the last strike to his nation who had lost a war and would have to pay the price of the crimes it had committed during the war. It was when I bit by bit narrated the memories of torture and pain which was recounted to me by the visiting Armenian women, and not because he could not resist my requests or insistence that Naim Bey showed willingness to speak. Apart from his personal memoirs, Naim Bey gave us a considerable amount of documents which could be directly useful for history. Some of these documents were recorded when he was writing his memoirs and the photographs of the most important ones were taken during this study. There is no doubt that these documents have been extracted from the files of the office of the Vice president of the Deportation Administration in Aleppo. After he received the orders of the Minister of Internal Affairs which were concerning the Armenians and written in cipher, the governor of Aleppo signed and dated the texts which he had received, wrote a note on the texts stating that the orders written in the texts should be implemented and sent these texts to the office of the vice president of the deportation administration where Naim Bey served as a clerk. When Naim Bey accepted to give us these documents, the Aleppo Armenian National Unity which was an official organization, had the handwriting and signature found on the assignment notes attached to the documents inspected. This inspection took exactly a week. Other documents to which assignment notes written by governor Mustafa Abdulhalik were attached, were also inspected and the smallest details were carefully compared. Consequently, it was clearly understood that the handwriting and signature found on the assignment notes attached onto the document belonged to governor Mustafa Abdulhalik. This was enough to erase any doubt concerning the authenticity of the documents. After the National Unity confirmed the absolute authenticity of the documents, it assigned me with choosing among Naim Bey's documents, those texts which would definitely shed light on the persons responsible from the Armenian Massacre. I chose the documents which were the most important.

Andonian states in his book that the reason why he has written this book was that he at least wanted to collect data for history.

There are issues which Andonian has not mentioned in his book. We find these in a different source. A book was published in Paris in 1981 under the title "Justicier du Genocide Armenian, Le Proces de Tehlirian". Two original letters which were written by Andonian and dated 10 June 1921 and 26 July 1937 are included in this book. There is also information in this book concerning the true nature of Andonian's book. When we gather all this information, it is understood that in order to strengthen the Armenian demands during the peace conference which was held following the defeat of the Ottoman Empire, Kilikya Catholics stated that the preparation of such a book was necessary. There is such a sentence in Andonian's letter dated 1921: As also stated in the travel certificate which I use as a passport and which was issued by the French military authorities in Allepo, I was finally assigned by the Aleppo Armenian National Unity with taking these documents to Europe and submitting them to the Armenian National Delegation at the peace conference.

It is seen that the aim is not to collect data for history but to help the Armenian delegation at the peace conference in the realization of Armenian goals.

These documents which had been prepared with the stated aim in mind were wanted to be submitted to the court as evidence when Tehlirian s case was at stake. Naturally, it was certain that the court would demand that the authenticity of these documents be proven. The information given by Andonian concerning this issue in his letter dated 1937 is as follows:

The matter of the authenticity of the documents had naturally arisen as of the very first meeting which I had with Tehlirian's lawyers in Berlin. On 10 June 1921, I gave them a small note about the origin of the documents. Nevertheless, because the note bore a unilateral value, it was insufficient to solve the problem at hand. Tehlirian's lawyers had presented my book and the documents in my book to the inspection of W. Rossler, an official from the Ministry of Foreign Affairs, who had served as Germany's consul for Allepo during the war.

Rosslers report which was already under my possession was given to me by the late Dr. Lapsius on the condition that I would never reveal it unless I am granted permission by consul Rossler to do so.

This confession which sheds a new light on the character of Dr. Lepsius to whom we had referred before is worth considerable attention . We understand that Rossler wrote in this report that the writer is not objective , the he has been the slave of his obsession, that it was very difficult to determine whether the documents were authentic or not , and that he did not know how this could be done .What Andonian wrote in his letter dated 1937 in relation to this report of Rossler is as follows .

"This report is in German . It consists a lot of criticism about the composition of my book which he finds devoid of any objectivity. Besides , it refutes most of the passages concerning the attitude of the German people who were in Turkey during the war .there is doubt that he is right at most of the issues he raises . However , he forgets that my book is not a historical study but a work aiming to propagandise .Naturally , my book could not have been purified from errors that are peculiar to these kind of publications . I also wish to add that for the sake of the case they support , the Armenian Bureau in London and the Armenian National Delegation in Paris have used the text, which I wrote during the publication of my book , freely in the way they liked to use it .

Now we clearly understand why this book has been written. the aim is to propagandise. Andonian wrote a book oriented towards this aim which could not have been thought to be "purified from errors" .

What is more , while the book was published ,the Armenian organizations in London and Paris had used "the text freely in the way they like",i.e.,it is understood that their distortion of the texthad reached such a dimension that even Andonian was reluctant to accept his own text.

The information given in Andonian's letter dated 1937, concerning Naim Bey and the information he gave about the documents is even more interesting :

"Allepo was about to fall and the British were very close to Damascus .I told Naim Bey that he could sell Armenian offices which would be established when the British entered Allepo , every kind of document concerning the Armenian massacre at a very high price .I also encouraged him to write his memoirs about the Armenian issue.....Because of this , he stayed in Allepo .There were things which I would not be able to explain whether in my book nor to Tehlirian's lawyers ,so as not to give any harm to the personality of Naim Bey which was not completely flawless . He was addicted to alcohol and gambling. These were the flaws which actually led him to treason. The truth is that we bought ever document which he gave to us.

I drew on entirely different Naim Bey portrait in my book, for it will be of no use to put forth the genuine thruth about him. Naim Bey was a completely immoral creature. The Armenians founded National Union in order to purchase the documents stolen by Naim Bey . The National Union established by the Armenians bought the documents stolen by Naim Bey following a lot of inspections that were carried out ."
And now emerges an entirely different Naim Bey character .
What the Berlin prosecutor said when these documents were desired to be presented at the court was recorded in the case minutes and is exactly as follows:

"The usage of fake documents cannot lead me to error, either. As a prosecutor, I know well how during the turmoil caused by the revolution, documents bearing signatures of very important persons had emerged just to be proven later to become false and devoid of any authenticity".

As a result of the study carried out on these documents, the fraudulent distortion in the documents has been proven in various ways in a book titled "The real story behind the telegrams attributed to Talat Pasha by the Armenians".

First of all , the analysis made on the then used cipher coder and cipher record book has revealed that the cipher wires whose photocopies are given , can by no means be correct in terms of the used encoder , date or number.

When the signature and handwriting which were found on the decoded texts and which allegedly belonged to Abdulhalik's, were compared with Abdulhalik's own signature and handwriting, it was clearly revealed that this handwriting and signature were fake .Furthermore, the differences between the Roman calendar and the Gregorian calendar and the signs that were used to denominate the formula Bismillahirrahmanirrahim in previous correspondences also attest to the falsity of these documents.

When the totality of the allegedly authentic documents inherent in Andonian's book, which originally aimed to propagandise and was incredibly distorted by the Armenian organizations in Paris and London, turned out to become fake, the whole book is revealed to be a document of international forgery.

Andonian writes in his letter dated 1937, that Naim Bey was a completely immoral person and that the Armenian organizations had bought the concerned documents from him. One wonders whether these fake documents were prepared by an "immoral" Naim Bey which were then scrutinized by the Armenian organizations which thought these documents were authentic and thereafter purchased these documents . We will never be able to learn this .

However , one could also think that a person called Naim Bey was an imaginary figure made to live merely in dreams and that these fake documents were arranged by Andonian himself.

The revelation of the falsity of these documents renders one of the most important trumps of Armenian organizations useless and deprives them of the chance to reiterate their genocide claim.

CHAPTER SIX

The War of Independence

1. The beginning of the National Struggle and its aims

Following the signing of the Mundros Truce Agreement the process of discharging and disarming the Turkish Army began, in accordance with the conditions of the treaty.

The duration of the Truce can be considered as having been between 30 October 1918 and 15 May 1919. During this period, the French occupied the province of Adana, and the British occupied Urfa, Marash, and Antep (later they would be transferred to the French). Italian soldiers were present in Antalya and Konya, and British soldiers were in Merzifon and Samsun. We no longer consider the provinces of Mussul and Syria, for they had been relinquished before the treaty.

We have previously examined the situation in the eastern front when the treaty was announced, and the new situation which arose following the treaty when the Turkish Army retreated behind the borders of 1914.

When the Greeks occupied Izmir on 15 May 1919, the period of the Armistice came to a *de facto*, if not *de jure*, end.

Mustafa Kemal Pasha (the name Ataturk had not yet been adopted) landed in Samsun on 19 May 1919, and thus began the period which we call the National Struggle.

The aims of the National Struggle were announced to the world for the first time with the resolutions adopted by the Sivas Congress on 11 September 1919. We quote below some articles of this decision, which are of interest to our topic by virtue of their historical importance:

1. The Ottoman Empire which is within the borders of October 30th, 1334 [1918], the date when the truce between the Great Ottoman State and the Allied States was signed, and every part of which has an overwhelming majority of Muslims, constitutes a whole, which will not be divided for any reason. . . .

2. It is necessary that National Independence is made effective, and the will of the nation is made sovereign in order to ensure the integrity of the Ottoman community, the independence of our nation, the protection of the sublime office, and the inviolability of the Sultanate.

3. The principle of united defence and resistance to any interference and especially invasion of any part of the Ottoman Empire, and to any movement directed especially to the establishment of an autonomous Greece or Armenia within our country, as in the national struggle along the fronts of Aydin, Manisa, and Balikesir, has been accepted as legitimate.

4. Because all rights of the non-Muslim elements with whom we have been living for a long time in the same country are entirely protected, these elements will not be given privileges which infringe our political sovereignty and internal order.

Later, these principles were codified by a regulation during the last Ottoman Assembly which met in Istanbul on 28 January 1920. Because of its historical importance, we quote below the first article of this regulation, which is known in Turkish history as the National Pact.

1. Because it will be necessary to determine the fate of the areas of the Ottoman State, which are exclusively inhabited by an Arab majority, and which were occupied by the enemy armies at the time of the conclusion of the truce dated 30 October 1918, through the votes of the inhabitants of these areas, the area inhabited by the Ottoman Muslim majority, within the aforementioned trucial border, united in religion and customs, saturated by feelings of sacrifice and reciprocal respect towards one a nother, and entirely respectful of their social rights and the conditions of their surroundings, is a whole which cannot be separated for any reason.

After Istanbul had been occupied by the Allies on 16 March 1920, the Assembly dissolved, and the deputies who had been arrested exiled to Malta, the Grand National Assembly which opened on 23 April 1920 in Ankara elected Mustafa Kemal Pasha as its President at its first session, and from that date onward the centre and nucleus of the National Struggle was Ankara.

Let us hear from Ataturk himself about the condition of the army within the borders of the truce when the National Struggle began.

. . . . Mainly two army inspectorships had been established in Anatolia. As soon as this truce became effective, the troops had been discharged, their weapons and ammunition had been taken away from them, some cadres lacking combative value had been formed. The situation of the troops belonging to the 2nd Army Inspectorship, whose base was in Konya, was as follows:

The 12th Army Corps Headquarters were in Konya; one division (41st division) was in Konya, and one division (23rd division) was in Afyon Karahisar. The 57th division in Denizli of the 17th Army Corps which surrendered in Izmir had been added to this Army Corps.

The 2nd Army Corps Headquarters were in Ankara, one of its divisions (24th division) was in Ankara, one division (11th division) was in Nigde; the 1st division which was in Izmir had been added to the 25th Army Corps in Istanbul. The 10th Caucasus division was in Istanbul.

The 61st and the 56th divisions, which were in the vicinity of Balikesir and Bursa, formed the 14th Army Corps, whose headquarters were in Bandirma, and which depended on Istanbul.

I was the Inspector of the 3rd Army Inspectorship. I had landed in Samsun with my headquarters. I would have directly under my command two Army Corps. One of them was the 3rd Army Corps, whose base was in Sivas . . . the base of a division (5th Caucasus division) belonging to this Army Corps was in Amasya, the base of the other division (15th division) was in Samsun. The other was the 15th Army Corps which was based in Erzurum. . . . One of its divisions (9th division) was based in Erzurum, and the other (3rd division) was based in Trabzon. Of the other two divisions of the Army Corps, the 12th division was at the border near Hasankale, and the 11th division was in Beyazit.

The 14th Army Corps which had two divisions in the vicinity of Diyarbekir was independent. It was attached to Istanbul. One of its divisions (2nd division) was in Siirt, and the other (5th division) was in Mardin.[1]

In his memoirs, Kazim Karabekir Pasha, the Commander of the 15th Army Corps, has stated that this Army Corps, which would execute the operation in the east, totalled 17,860 soldiers.[2]

The National Struggle began with these forces at hand. First the eastern front was cleared, followed by the southern front. Subsequently the western front was cleared, the enemy soldiers were driven out of the country, and the Struggle ended with the signing of the Mudanya Truce on 11 October 1922.

The Struggle, which began on 19 May 1919, and whose aims were announced on 11 September 1919, lasted, for 3 years, 4 months, and 22 days. We shall now examine these three fronts in turn.

2. The eastern front

In my opinion the person who best knew the eastern front operation in Turkey was the late Kazim Karabekir Pasha, who led this operation from the first day to the last as a responsible commander. Because of this, the best way to explain this subject would be through quotations from his book entitled *Our War of Independence*. The documents which would leave no doubt in one's mind would be the orders of the front. (We do not refer to communiqués, but rather to orders given to the units.)

Colonel A. Rawlinson, of the British Army, had been charged with supervising the implementation of the truce conditions in the eastern front. We shall also quote from Rawlinson, who later published an account of his activities in the region.[3]

After the truce had been signed, Kazim Karabekir Pasha went to Istanbul. For some reason it was decided that he should return to lead his Army Corps, and he left Istanbul on 12 April 1919, arriving in Erzurum on 3 May, to resume his duty. On the day he arrived, Rushtu Bey, the Commander of the 9th division, who assisted him, showed him an order sent by Rawlinson. In this order it was stated that Lieutenant-Colonel Halit Bey, the Commander of the 3rd division was to be arrested and sent to Trabzon, because he had retaliated against the Georgians.

The first meeting between Karabekir Pasha and Rawlinson was interesting. We quote from p. 23 of his book. This meeting is significant in that it shows just how limited, in practice, was the power of an army corps commander in the east during the period of the truce.

Today Rawlinson, the British colonel, came to visit me. A summary of our discussion is as follows: I asked him what his duty was. He said that it was to supervise the implementation of the treaty conditions in the East. I asked why in that case he had written as if he was giving orders to the divisions and the Army Corps. We were speaking in French. He said that such situations would not recur from now on. Communicating through an interpreter was creating misunderstandings. I said, from now on you will tell me your wishes, but any decision will be implemented absolutely by an order from the Ministry of War. Your note stating that if Halit Bey, the Commander of the 3rd Army Corps, is not arrested, the Assistant to the Army Corps, Rushtu Bey, would go, created very negative reactions among the people. I only arrived yesterday, and many people and officials came to see me. I stated, if the situation is out of control on the first day, we both can be in danger. Rawlinson reflected for a while, and thought that my statements were reasonable. He said that from now on he would act more politely. I said "Mr. Lieutenant-Colonel, if you wish, let me send an officer to accompany you. However, we do not have someone who speaks English. I will find someone who speaks French. Rawlinson was very pleased. (I sent an officer who also spoke English, with the instruction that he did not disclose that he spoke English, and I benefited a great deal from this. I would have been informed much earlier of the conversations and correspondence in his office.)

The next day he acted very sincerely when I returned his visit. He brought the conversation to the Bolsheviks. He stated that the situation was a difficult one because their administration was now in order. I mentioned that there was no reason to be concerned about the Caucasus, because the Cossacks supported the Czar. He said, unfortunately they, too, have changed. When I stated that the opposition would take care of the situation with a strong army, he said impossible, impossible, it is impossible to summon new forces, besides, the Bolsheviks have many armies, the thing to do is to prevent Bolshevism spreading to other countries, they are sending their propagandists everywhere. Today, Rawlinson did not mention Halit Bey or the arms. I felt that he was trying to push me to take action, claiming that the Bolsheviks were in the Caucasus, when I was making plans so as not to hand over a Commander or arms.

Rawlinson and Karabekir Pasha met again on 29 June 1919. We shall also quote this meeting (pp. 62-3):

June 29th was the Ramazan holiday. Rawlinson, a Russian lieutenant-colonel from the Denikin Army, and an American lieutenant (he was one of the councillors of Admiral Bristol in Istanbul) came to visit me. It is apparent that the Russian lieutenant-colonel is searching for the materials of Russian armies, but emotionally he is very weak. When I returned the visit, the American was in Rawlinson's room. At one time, Rawlinson, as a joke, touched slightly the American's side pocket, and said: `The concern of Americans is to fill their pockets with dollars.' The American replied somewhat seriously: `And the concern of the British is to swallow the entire world, what are you doing here?' Rawlinson became angry, he stopped talking French, and said something in English. And the American replied. Their attitude made me think that Rawlinson said `You have acted improperly,' and that the American replied: `You acted improperly in the first place.'

I also invited the foreigners to the Gymnastics Day at the Kars Gate on June 30th. The cheerfulness and agility of all Erzurumites filled our hearts. The foreigners watched with awe. After a while, the American requested permission to leave, stating `I will go tomorrow'. He was followed by Rawlinson who did not leave the American alone. We were alone with the Russian officers. The Russian colonel approached me. He stated that the Bolsheviks had also successfully occupied Lengeran (to the south of Baku on the shores of the Caspian Sea), and that it was true that Enver had arrived at Kerus. He seemed quite sincere. I realized this truth: the American and Russian officers were not pleased with the sovereignity of the British, especially in the East, and described the general situation to us in glowing terms. From this point I probed the Russian officer's thoughts and I told him: `It is of no importance to us whether the Bolsheviks have come or not, whether Enver has come or not. The nation has made its decision. Turkey shall live independently. These areas, too, belong to the Turks. No one else may reside here.' The eyes of the Russian colonel sparkled. His speech became more agitated. He aid: `What are these British doing here? Our governments are responsible for the mistakes. The sincere agreements between the Russians and the Turks should not have allowed these misfortunes to happen. At least from now on, this must be ensured and these men must be driven away. The British are very much afraid of the Bolsheviks, and they are gathering their soldiers from everywhere to Iran.'

The Russian officers have made statements here and there against the British. Rawlinson was informed, the men could not stay for more than one or two days, they went outside the borders. A few days later, when Rawlinson mentioned this, he grumbled and said, `Are these rascals also Bolsheviks? I brought them in order that they might do a useful job; that they find ammunition for the Denikin Army, but they are doing other things. The officers of the Denikin Army are only for show, they are not an army but a herd, the Bolsheviks are better then they are.' It was stated in the information which arrived from the Beyazit Commander on June 30th, that because the Armenians had occupied the area of Nahjivan, and they wanted the Muslims to hand over their arms, the people had sent men asking what we can do. I had protested to Rawlinson. He had stated that there were no British troops left in the Caucasus, and that there was nothing he could do. I wrote the following coded order to the 11th division command in Van in Beyazit, to which he belonged:

'The atrocities which the Armenians have begun in the area of Nahjivan are the result of their enraged actions, as they realize these are their last days. Consequently, they will gain time if the intelligent people of Nahjivan mediate and suggest to those Armenians who are reasonable, the point of view regarding the reconciliation of the Armenians and the forces which have come to Shush and Kerusi, and which includes Armenians. This would be very beneficial. However, the principle of any agreement should be not to hand over arms, and not to relinquish strong positions. This has been written to the Commanders of the 11th division and Beyazit. July 1, 1335, Kazim Karbekir.'

The American to whom Kazim Karabekir referred was Robert Dunn. He too, has written his memoirs.[4] The passage concerning the above-mentioned conversation is on p. 311 of his book. It is useful to record a conversation which took place before these two individuals arrived at Erzurum. Robert Dunn gives the account of this conversation on p. 309 of his book:

. . . Next I was drinking Scotch with British officers in Erzurum, in what had been an American mission school for girls. Now it housed Colonel Toby Rawlinson from Donsterville's hush-hush army. They put me up and I heard, in Oxford English, more stories of Armenians murdering Turks when the Czarist troops fled north. My hosts told me of their duty here: to keep tab on brigands, Turkish troop shifts, hidden arms, spies - Christian, Red or Tartar - coming in from Transcaucasus. Then they spoke of the hell that would break loose if Versailles were to put, as threatened, the six `Armenian' vilayets of Turkey under the control of Erevan.
'We sit on the edge of a volcano, Dunn,' said Rawlinson.
'So you want us to take a mandate over it all,' I said, 'as buffer to your Iraq.' 'America had never been so mad. I've been in America. Your people are too damned level-headed.'
'If the President's behind it.'
'An Armenia without Armenians! Turks under Christian rule?' His lips smacked in irony under the droopy red moustache. `That's bloodshed - just Smyrna over again on a bigger scale. If you touch that business you're bigger fools than I've ever taken you for.'

There are many interesting passages in Dunn's book about the atrocities committed in the east by the Armenians. We shall not mention them, remaining loyal to the principle we have started at the beginning of our book.
On 3 June, Karabekir wrote as follows (p. 66):

Today the Information Department of the General Staff reported the following summary of the Istanbul newspapers: an Armenian delegation of twelve members has returned to our city from the Caucasus where they examined the Armenian demands and assertions. The said delegation will submit to the Peace Conference the report it has prepared based on documents whose rejection is unacceptable.
Summary of the report:
1. Because there is no Armenian population left, it is impossible that an important and extensive Government, as conceived by the Armenians, be formed.
2. The lack of money in Armenia is perceptible in that proportion. If there is no financial aid, the Government will not be able to survive for long.
The information we have received from Armenia is the following:
`On July 5th and 6th, the Armenians attacked the town of Buyuk Vadi (a large Turkish village) in the vicinity of Erivan, but retreated when they were defeated. It seems there were 800 dead and 1,200 wounded. The Turks seized much, including two cannons and six machine guns. A secret

order given by the general charged with the operation was also obtained. It states that the Muslims will be destroyed and thrown into the Aras river. The Commander of the force which attacked was General Mayor Sholkonikof, who signed the order.'

Following the incident, two British officers came from Erivan. They stated that they would reconcile the Armenians and the Muslims, and that the cannons belonged to the British. They took the cannons and left. The Muslims later realized that these officers were two Armenians wearing British uniforms. The Armenians obtained reinforcements and again surrounded the town. This shows that despite the fact that Armenia, which has no money or population left, and has occupied the three provinces with the guidance of the British, is uncontrollably ambitious. The Armenians who are very much covered with the support of America, England, and France, became almost intoxicated with their own dream of conquering Sivas. It seems that the Armenians who have previously occupied our three provinces with the same trick wish to shake hands in Kizilirmak with the Greeks who have occupied Izmir, and that they dream of making the Kizilirmak flow red with Turkish blood. It seems that the Armenians and Greeks have sworn and are swearing in churches that they will drown the Turks. It seems that the civilized world will celebrate this red day.

The record for 8 July (p. 71):

On 8 July we received some information about the Armenians. Apparently they have begun to pillage and massacre the Muslim villages all along the border. Tonight Rawlinson was in Hasankale. The information was documented. Without any doubt, these attacks by the Armenians occurred with the order of the British. I told him on the telephone that he should immediately go to Sarikamish and see the situation for himself. I wrote to him as follows:

'To His Excellency Rawlinson, the British Representative,

1. Those individuals who have escaped in order to save their lives, have reported that the Armenians have begun to destroy by massacres the Muslim inhabitants of Kaghizman and its vicinity.

2. The Armenians have attacked Kurudere, have killed 5 men and 3 women, and have taken along 33 men, 1 bride, 1 girl, and 440 head of cattle.

3. It is known that on July 4th, they attacked four villages under the jurisdiction of Akchakale between Kars and Oltu, and have killed all the inhabitants of one, and have taken 60 men from each other village, and butchered them. The Armenians who attacked these villages made use of five cannons, and seven machine guns. The Commander of this force was someone named Arshak.

4. In the village of Yüzkush, the Armenians abducted the sister, wife, and daughter of a Muslim.

5. The Armenians are continuing to massacre Muslims in the vicinity of Karakut. I request that this distressing situation, which is occurring outside the border, and which is creating deep effects on the people in general, be stopped, that the responsible ones be punished, and that we are enlightened on this matter. Respectfully, Kazim Karabekir.'

On 26 July, Kazim Karabekir received the following telegram from Rawlinson (p. 85):

To the Commander of the 15th Army Corps.

You are not doing your best. The train is held in Sarikamish guarded by gendarmerie. The field train came to the border with the British guard officers. Your gendarmerie does not allow the passage of the train so it can pick up the cannon parts. The Commander in Ziyon does not assign soldiers to transfer the cannon parts through quarters where the road has been destroyed. Recently the individuals at hand have proved insufficient to clear the road. For this reason, if there is no other prompt means by which they may be transferred, it is my duty to inform the High Commission in Istanbul that the transfer of spare cannon parts they requested is being intentionally delayed by you.

Karabekir Pasha writes as follows concerning this telegram: 'The Armenians are firing guns at the border. They are screaming "to Sivas". At a time when everywhere there are attacks on my area, any person other than Rawlinson would realize the foolishness of his acts.'

On 27 July the Ministry of War in Istanbul requested information about the situation. The following correspondence took place (p. 94):

To the office of the Acting Inspector of the 3rd Army.

The General Gendarmerie Command informs us, basing on the communication of the Erzurum Gendarmerie Regiment Commander, that the Armenians in Sarikamish are gathering large forces, weapons, and ammunition, that they will attack with this force from the direction of Chakirbaba-Soghanli, and that they are destroying the Muslims in the area of Kars by seizing and arresting them. I request that I be informed of the situation.

To the Ministry of War.

The Armenians are inflicting all sorts of cruelties on the Muslims in the Caucasus, and are sending forces to quarters which resist them. To achieve this aim, they are sending forces to the areas of Nahjivan, Sherur, and the vicinity of Kaghizman and Oltu, and are constantly following the policy of destroying Muslims. We have been informed that recently approximately five hundred cavalrymen and infantrymen and four cannons have arrived in Sarikamish, as part of the reinforcement troops of the Armenians, that the Armenians are requisitioning from the inhabitants of Sarikamish and its western district military taxes together with carts and vehicles; and it was not assumed that they will engage in any operations against the Muslims in the direction of Oltu. The rumours spread by the Armenians that they will occupy the six provinces and that they will soon go to Sivas, and their activities and operations near the border, are having adverse effects on the people who are uninformed of the general situation and the political conditions, and are spreading all sorts of rumour and increasing existing fears. As long as we possess the arms which we have today, we are in a secure position against any attacks of the Armenians. Kazim Karabekir.

There are successive reports about the attacks made by the Armenian bands in the three provinces outside the Truce borders. It is of course impossible to record every one of them. During this time, Kazim Karabekir Pasha was making preparations against any possible attack against the Truce border. He gives an account of the situation on 23 September (p. 284):

I was ready with my four divisions against an attack from any direction. One division (3) was aligned against the Pontic Greeks along the shore in the vicinity of Trabzon; two divisions (9 and 12) were against the Armenians in the valley of Pasinler, and ready against all sides; another division (11) was against the Armenians in the area of Van-Beyazit-Karakose. My main plan was to attack the Armenians, in the event of the beginning of an attack, and thus eliminate the danger. I am spreading the rumour that my forces have a hundred thousand bayonets. The foreigners who come and go, the British officials, and even Rawlinson believed that I could gather such a force and that the people had this quantity of arms in their possession.

On 24 September the delegation of General Harbord came to Erzurum. On 25 September, Karabekir Pasha submitted a report to Harbord about the situation. The following passage concerns the Armenians (p. 292-304):

The weapons of the army which we had demobilized in Batum were placed in warehouses in Batum, guarded by officers and soldiers. These weapons have all been taken and given to the Armenians, the Greeks, and the Russians. They have confiscated the gasoline, kerosene and fuel oil we had purchased from the Government of Azerbaidjan in Batum, and they have seized the provisions and the railway cars brought by our troops. . ..
After the Ottoman soldiers had retreated from the areas of Kars, Ardahan, and Kaghizman on January 1, 1335 [1919], following the truce, the Muslims, who constituted the great majority of this region, formed a national council in Kars. They began to administer the area. The council administered the said region and maintained public security and order in a praiseworthy way. During the administration of the council no incidents occurred. Peace and order were excellent. When the Ottoman soldiers had retreated, British soldiers arrived in Kars. The British representative accepted and approved the council and was pleased with the administration of the council. The council's efficiency in maintaining public order was appreciated.
However, after a short period of time, the British occupied the Council in April 1335 with the troops they had brought, and exiled or arrested some of its members. They took control of the administration and one night they brought Armenian soldiers from Gumru to Kars without the knowledge of the Muslims. They increased the Armenian forces with the influence of the British, and handed power over to the Armenians. After the Armenians had settled in this manner in all parts of the region with the support of the British, they began to destroy the Muslims and thus were in a majority. They began to inflict much cruelty and oppression. For this reason tranquility and order in the area disappeared.

Every day, the blood of hundreds and thousands of Muslims was shed. The support and protection of the British spoiled the Armenians, and increased the cruelties of the Armenians against the Muslims. The Armenians obtained Sarikamish, Kaghizman, and Ardahan from the British. They settled in this region with the support of the British. On September 5th 1335, a British officer, accompanied by Ahmet Bey, a member of the Kars National Council, and two Armenian officers, as well as eight Armenian gendarmes, visited Eyyup Pasha, the leader of a tribe in the vicinity of Bardiz, offered him the opportunity to surrender to the Armenians and threatened that they would be punished severely, because working against the British Government was a serious crime. Although they made suggestions that they submit to the Armenians, they did not say anything as they listened to the atrocities inflicted by the Armenians. As the Armenians attacked on July 5, 1335 several Muslim villages near Karakurt and engaged in massacres, the Muslims united and put up resistance. On July 7, 1335, a British officer came and ordered that cannon shots be fired on the Muslims (it is possible that this man was an Armenian officer wearing a British uniform). The British representative in Erzurum, Rawlinson, on the basis of the information he received on July 4, 1335 from the Kars representative, that 40,000 Muslim refugees had gathered in the area, and that it was possible for an incident to occur, stated that he was going to go to the area to examine the situation. And he went. As a result, he confirmed that the Armenians had committed atrocities and massacres against the Muslims in Kars, Sarikamish, and Kaghizman. On June 5, 1335, a British lieutenant came from Ighdir to Beyazit, accompanied by an Armenian interpreter, and met with the governor of Beyazit. They communicated that the area of Beyazit was given to the Armenian Government which was formed under the protection of the British Government, they notified that the Conference possessed this communication, that they would be bringing 15,000 Armenians, protected by Armenian soldiers, within one month. On the same day they left for Baku and Iran. The British representative Rawlinson has confessed that this officer wearing a British uniform was in fact an Armenian, and that this offer had no real basis.

Confirmation of these passages we have quoted from Karabekir Pasha's report may be found on pp. 198-216 of Rawlinson's book.

On 22 October news was received that the Armenians were preparing to occupy Oltu, and correspondence was found concerning Armenian preparations to unite with the tribes of the region. An Armenian named Hatchador Agha had sent letters to various tribal leaders, Hamit Bey, Ali Merze Bey, Ahmet Hasan Bey, and Yusuf Bey (pp. 344-S).

The following message sent by Mustafa Kemal Pasha to Karabekir Pasha on 22 January 1336 (1920) is important, as it concerns the Malta exiles (p. 426):

Should the British in Istanbul continue to fail to observe the truce, and arrest some persons among the ministers and deputies, particularly Rauf Bey, in retaliation, the British officers present in Anatolia will be arrested. Consequently, I request that measures be adopted to prevent the escape of Rawlinson in Erzurum. Mustafa Kemal.

Istanbul was occupied on 16 March. At that time Rawlinson was in Erzurum. We give below the texts of the order sent by Karabekir Pasha to the Commandant of the Erzurum Fortress, and the message he received from Rawlinson (p. 502):

To the Commandant of the Fortress.

It is possible that the people of Erzurum will become agitated and mistreat Rawlinson, the British representative here, because of events such as the seizure of the Istanbul Government by the British, and their arresting various persons. Consequently it is necessary that the residence of the aforementioned man be protected by soldiers and an officer, that the weapons and arms in his possession and in the possession of his staff are taken and placed temporarily in a suitable place, and that the attention of the said man is called to the fact that this procedure has the aim of protecting his life and honour. Kazim Karabekir.

The reply of Rawlinson:

My Pasha: I express to you my deepest regrets as I have been informed by you of the events. At the same time, my staff and I are at your orders. I regard it as a duty to present my gratitude in the face of your courtesy and your gracious and well thought treatment you have considered in the presence of this sinister situation. I request the acceptance of my feelings, my Pasha. Rawlinson.

Rawlinson was freed in exchange for the Malta exiles.

The occupation of Istanbul, and the fact that the Assembly was closed, and the deputies were arrested, necessitated a different strategy. On 16 March, Mustafa Kemal Pasha sent the following telegram to Karabekir Pasha (p. 505): 'We request, Sir, that we be informed about the time and place of the implementation of the idea which has been discussed for a long time concerning an attack in the East. In the name of the Representative Delegation, Mustafa Kemal.'

On 16 March, Kazim Karabekir Pasha replied to the telegram (p. 505):

The situation in Istanbul and the form the Government will take have not been entirely determined. The Bolshevik armies did not arrive in the Caucasus mountains, and no communication has arrived from any front. The Bolsheviks will not be able to bring their fleet into the Caspian Sea via the Volga river before the end of April, and will not be able to begin any operations before that time. Because there is much snow within my area, and especially between Erzurum and Sarikamish, the realization of the serious operation will be quite difficult at the beginning and even before the middle of April. Kazim Karabekir.

Kazim Karabekir Pasha wrote on 22 March (p. 523):

With the occupation of Istanbul, the Armenians have increased their audacity. In the days preceding the occupation, the British were engaged in a world-wide propaganda effort claiming 'the Armenians are being massacred everywhere'. Taking this as a good pretext, massacres of the

Muslims began. I thought it was necessary that I write an official protest to the military commander of the Armenian Republic, and that the Representative Delegation send a letter of protest to the civilized states. I sent their texts to the Representative Delegation. It was considered appropriate and it was done. The letter I wrote to the Armenians:

'The atrocities and massacres which have been committed for a long time against the Muslim population within the Armenian Republic have been confirmed with very accurate information, and the observations made by Rawlinson, the British representative in Erzurum, have confirmed that these atrocities are being committed by the Armenians. The United States delegation of General Harbord has seen the thousands of refugees who came to take refuge with us, hungry and miserable, their children and wives, their properties destroyed, and the delegation was a witness to the cruelties. Many Muslim villages have been destroyed by the soldiers of Armenian troops armed with cannons and machine guns before the eyes of our troops and the people. When it was hoped that this operation would end, unfortunately since the beginning of February 1336 (1920) the cruelties inflicted on the Muslim population of the region of Shuraghel, Akpazar, Zarshad, and Childir have increased. According to documented information, 28 Muslim villages have been destroyed in the aforementioned region, more than 2,000 people have been killed, many possessions and livestock have been seized, young Muslim women have been taken to Kars and Gumru, hundreds of women and children who were able to flee their villages were beaten and killed in the mountains, and this aggression against the properties, lives, chastity and honour of the Muslims is still continuing. . . . It is the responsibility of the Armenian Government that the cruelties and massacres be stopped in order to alleviate the tensions of Muslim public opinion due to the atrocities committed by the Armenians, that the possessions taken from the Muslims be returned and that indemnities be paid, that the properties, lives, and honour of the Muslims be protected. At a time when we were most threatened and weak, our Government and nation provided the Armenian nation, like all nations, with the right to exist, and with administrative freedom and self-determination. As you will remember the justice and compassion I showed to the existence of your nation when I was there with my troops during the operation which followed the recovery of Erzurum two years ago, I hope that this expression of my good faith will be received with sincerity. I present my respects. Kazim Karabekir.

On 28 March Kazim Karabekir Pasha sent the following telegram to Mustafa Kemal Pasha (p. 549):

1. The information is documented. The Armenians, who were very much confused during the recent victories which put an end to the survival of the Denikin Army in the Caucasus, have engaged in surprise attacks against the Muslims in the areas of Ordubad, Nahjivan, and Vedibasar since March 19th. These Armenian attacks have been repelled in these three Muslim areas, determined to defend their rights and honour with much courage and sacrifice, and the Armenians suffered many casualties. The Muslims in the area of Vedibasar have defeated the enemy of superior strength who attempted to attack them without any reason, and took as war booty four machine guns and other weapons. Later, they

followed the defeated Armenians up to the mountain 7-8 km to the east of the city of Revan, which is the capital of Armenia, and approached the barbed wire on this mountain which the Armenians have fortified to protect Revan. The Muslim forces which demonstrated their determination as they stayed one night on this mountain and cut the barbed wire with daggers and knives, returned victorious to their area. Kazim Karabekir.

Karabekir Pasha had prepared the operation plan on 26 April.
Karabekir Pasha, in the telegram he sent on the same day, 26 April, to Mustafa Kemal, stated this situation and requested instructions:

The concentration of the Army Corps has begun. It is expected that it will be completed in two weeks. Our food supplies will not enable us to stay longer after the completion of the concentration. . . . I request permission again that military instructions be sent immediately. If it is considered inconvenient for the decision to be made by the National Assembly at such short notice, or if the National Assembly is unable at this time to take such a decision, I request that we have freedom of operation in order not to lose this last opportunity.

On 28 April he received the following answer (p. 627):

The message dated April 26, 1336 has been received. The copy of the instructions you have requested has been presented on April 26, 1336 after modification. We request that the situation be maintained. It is certain, Sir, that in any case the decision about the border operation will be communicated from here. M. Kemal.

The reason why the order to begin the operation was not given is found in this telegram to Karabekir Pasha, dated 10 May:

1. The point of view of the National Assembly is that a military operation outside the borders must not begin before contact has been made with the Bolsheviks and before a concrete agreement has been reached. For this reason, as has been communicated before, it is necessary that the operation is postponed until an agreement.
2. Bekir Sami Bey and Yusuf Kemal Bey will leave Ankara tomorrow in the direction of Erzurum. I request that the soldiers who will join them there are summoned. The president of the Grand National Assembly. Mustafa Kemal.

After this date extensive correspondence took place concerning the beginning of the operation. It appears that Ankara did not consider it suitable to invade the borders of Brest-Litovsk again before making contact with the Russians. With this aim, the delegation of Bekir Sami Bey went to Moscow.
Finally, on 6 June, the following instructions for Karabekir Pasha arrived from Ankara (p. 727):

The suggestion dated June 4, 1336 of the Commander of the 15th Army Corps concerning the advance of the troops to invade the Soghanli passes in order to improve our defensive position, has been examined and approved by the Council of Ministers. Because the right to occupy the three provinces has been given by the Grand National Assembly to the Executive Committee, the Council of Ministers has decided that the suggestion be implemented, based on this authority. The necessary documents for the administration and announcement of the political aspect of the decision will be communicated to your Excellency. It is requested that until then no political attempt be made, and that we are informed as to when this operation may begin. Mustafa Kemal.

The following is Karabekir Pasha's reply dated 7 June (p. 728):

I gave the order to mobilize the 305th through the 316th detachments of conscripts in order to double the forces available for the military operation. This mobilization will not affect all areas of the Army Corps, and is restricted to the areas of the provinces of Erzurum, Van, and the sub-district of Erzincan. On June 12th the rest of the headquarters will be transferred to the hills of Horum. I am having explorations made. It is requested that the operation begin according to the situation, not before the 16th of June. Kazim Karabekir.

As Karabekir Pasha was about to begin the operation, the operation was postponed by instructions that he received on the night of 22 June.

On 27 June, the Armenians attacked Tuzca near Oltu, but retreated because these areas were held by troops. On 30 June the Armenians fired cannons at Oltu. On 1 July there was an Armenian attack in the region of Bardiz; eight private soldiers died. On 8 July the Armenians organized two attacks on Dughun Tepe.

The Armenians developed their operations in the region of Nahjivan. On 22 and 23 July they attacked the area of Kaghizman, and on 9 September they began to invade the area of Kulp.

Finally, on 20 September 1920 Karabekir Pasha was given permission to begin the operation. He instructed the troops with an order dated 26 September 1920 that the operation would begin on 28 September 1920 at 3 a.m.

The matters we have recorded here in detail, which can be considered as unnecessary, were aimed at emphasizing one point: the Armenians often spread rumours that the Turks had in fact attacked them in the east throughout the two-year period from the time the truce was signed until 28 September 1920, when the actual offensive began. We can find a typical example of this in the French Archives. Aharonian, who went to Paris for the Peace Conference, stated in a letter dated 11 September 1919 which he sent to Clemenceau, the French Prime Minister, that:

The regular troops of Mustafa Kemal Pasha, the Turco-Tartar bands and the Kurdish hordes have begun to surround the Armenian Republic.

Our troops were forced to abandon the province of Nahjivan, after a fierce battle, because of a lack of ammunition, and retreat before the enemy forces which are numerically far superior.

Two divisions of Mustafa Kemal Pasha are attacking Sarikamish and Kaghizman. . . .

In the presence of the advancing Turkish troops, the Armenian population of the Kars area and the Armenian refugees are escaping towards Erevan.

The occupation of this district by the Turks is imminent.

The letter ended with a request for intervention.

How can one reply to such a flagrant lie?

As can be seen, Karabekir Pasha did not find it appropriate to engage in an operation before the middle of April 1920, and waited until 28 September because he did not receive the order before then, and the Turkish soldiers did not attack the Truce border. On the other hand, the Armenians created many sad incidents on the other side of the border.

We can now summarize developments after the beginning of the operation.

On the morning of 29 September, Sarikamish was recovered; in the evening Chalak, Divrik and the Bezirgan Pass were recovered. Merdinik was taken on 30 September. On 1 October Kaghizman was taken.

On 13 October the Armenians began their counter-offensive. They were driven away. Bashkaya and the outer localities were taken.

On 24 October, Karabekir Pasha announced the order to attack Kars. On 27 October the offensive began. The hills of Yahniler and the hill of Vezirkoy-Üçler were taken. On 30 October, the day when the offensive against the Kars fortress was begun, the fortress and the city were recovered. Karabekir Pasha recorded the number of individuals who were captured on that day (p. 841):

The number of prisoners who were gathered in the station in my headquarters until the evening included: 3 generals, 6 colonels, 12 majors, 16 captains, 59 lieutenants, 16 civilian officials, 12 officers, 4 cadets. The number of captured soldiers was 1,150. The number of confirmed Armenian casualties was 1,100. There were 337 cannons, 339 cannons which needed repair, an abundant number of machine guns, all kinds of bullets and other war equipment, projectors, etc. Among the prisoners were Vekilof, the President of the General Staff, Aratof, the Minister of War, Primof, the commander of the Kars fortress, and a civilian minister.

The offensive I organized, using counter front strategy, gave us a great victory, and resulted in the defeat of an important part of the enemy army, and in return for taking a modern fortress we had few casualties: 9 dead and 47 wounded.

In my order to attack Kars, I had stated that 'The aim of the offensive operation is to destroy the Armenian army within Kars and by pursuing them after Kars.' As a matter of fact, my soldiers had showed that the Turkish Army was far superior in force to the most civilized armies, and more humane. Despite the fact that they attacked like lions such a modern fortress as Kars, they did not commit even the smallest cruelty against the Armenian inhabitants. This was witnessed also by the American delegation there and stated in the telegram they sent to Admiral Bristol on 31 October: 'All the Americans in Kars are well and the Turkish Army gives us excellent protection and all consideration. We have permission as before to continue our organisation. The Turkish soldiers are well disciplined and there have been no massacres. Edward Fox, District Commander, Near East Relief. Kars.'

On 3 November the Gumru operation was begun. On 6 November the Armenians requested a Truce. They were notified that their request would be accepted if they relinquished Gumru. On 7 November Gumru surrendered. On 8 November the terms of Truce were communicated from Ankara to Karabekir Pasha, as follows:

1. The delimitation of the Turkish-Armenian border will be a simple matter of statistics and general vote. All inhabitants of the disputed areas will be invited to determine their own political destiny according to the principles announced by the Bolsheviks and by President Wilson, which stipulated that nations should determine their own destiny. This population will vote in full freedom for their right to form an independent government or to be subject to one government. We agree that the gendarmes of various governments shall be employed until the completion of the voting in disputed areas in order to ensure that the votes are given in absolute freedom. Of course the collection of the votes must be done as soon as possible. The Ankara Government is convinced that this solution is just, that it is in the interests of humanity and consequently conforms to the interests of the Turkish and Armenian groups and of the people who reside in the disputed areas.

Unfortunately we are afraid that the Erevan Government refuses this solution in order to present a good image to the Western imperialist and especially to England. This situation will be in contradiction to the political principle applied by their western protectors to the people of Asia and Africa.

2. Turkey engages itself to take all steps within its power in order to provide the secure development and the complete independence of its neighbouring community. Within our powers, we shall help Armenia and the establishment of the economy of that country.

3. The Governments of both sides agree that they will not prevent the passage in absolute freedom of persons and possessions belonging to the other side, using their roads, and will in no way prevent transfer between any country or population centre of the other side.

4. Turkey is engaged to ensure that the Armenians who left their lands during the World War may return and resettle in their original places of residence, and that these people shall enjoy the same rights as minorities in the most civilized countries.

5. Turkey demands that Armenia gives a guarantee for its security.

Our delegates expect the Armenian delegates authorized to take part in and sign the peace negotiations in Gumru.

6. The Commander-in-Chief of our eastern front will communicate to you the terms of truce which will end hostilities during the peace negotiations.

The Armenians announced on 10 November that they refused the armistice terms. On 11 November the operation began again. On 15 November, the Armenians were defeated in Shahtahti, and once again requested an armistice. A cease-fire was declared on 18 November, and on 25 November peace negotiations began in Gumru. Hatissian presided over the Armenian delegation. The Gumru Agreement was signed on 30 November.

Later, the regions which the Georgian had occupied after the Mundros Treaty were recovered. Ardakhan was taken on 23 February, Ahiska on 9 March, Batum on 11 March and Ahilkelek on 14 March.

On 16 March 1921 the Moscow Agreement was made with the Russians in Moscow. The first article of the Moscow Treaty determined the Turkish- Russian border. We give below the 1st, 2nd, 3rd, and 15th articles.

Article 1. Each of the contracting parties accepts as a principle not to recognize any peace treaty or any international contract which may be forced on the other party. The Federated Soviet Republics of Russia recognize by the term `Turkey' all the areas which were announced on January 28th 1336 [1920] by the deputies of the Istanbul Assembly [National Pact] and which has been communicated to all the Governments and to the Press. Turkey is represented by the Grand National Assembly. . . . [Then the border line is designated as the present-day border.]

Article 2. Turkey agrees to relinquish to Georgia the right to rule over the city and harbour of Batum and the area which is to the north of the border set forth in the First Article of this Treaty, and which is part of the *kaza* of Batum, with the conditions set below. . . .

Article 3. Both sides . . . agree that the area of Nahjivan constitutes a sovereign region under the protection of Azerbaijan, on condition that Azerbaijan does not, relinquish this protection to a third state.

Article 15. Russia engages itself to ensure that the Caucasus Republics accept the articles which concern them in this Turkish-Russian Agreement, and in the agreements to be made between Turkey and these said Republics.

The Moscow Agreement was approved by the Grand National Assembly on 27 March. The certificates of this agreement, which was also approved by the Russians, were exchanged in Kars on 22 September 1921.

On 26 September the Kars Conference began, concerning the agreements to be made with the Caucasus Republics. The chief delegates were: Ganetzki (Russian Soviet), Behhud Shahtahtinski (Azerbaijan), Ilyava and Shvanidze (Georgia), Muravian and Makinzian (Armenia).

We wish to record the speech made by Muravian, the Minister of Foreign Affairs of Armenia, when the Conference began (p. 943):

The Republics of the Caucasus have entrusted me with the responsibility of submitting to you the feelings shared by our population and us, delegates, on the occasion of the first Conference in Kars between the delegates of the Government of the Grand National Assembly of Turkey and the delegates of the sister Soviet Republics of Azerbaijan, Armenia, Georgia of Transcaucasus.

We have not come here with antagonistic feelings, and we have no intention of presenting here the controversial issues which have been rejected because they created arguments, and which we have inherited from the former nationalist governments. No, now we are not concerned with these matters, and feelings of antagonism. We are only admirers of the brave struggle which the persevering people of Turkey engaged in. We carry a sincere wish, and we are absolutely convinced that a nation which defends its country will be victorious and the enemy will be defeated.

We are certain that this conference will strengthen the feelings of friendship of the Republics of the Caucasus in regard to Turkey, and that Turkey will learn that there are no enemies behind her, and that her neighbours are inclined to her in the struggle she engaged in against the imperialism which wanted to destroy the aspirations of the Turkish nation.

Honourable delegates! We have not come to this conference as victorious, or as vanquished. We have come to you, who are the representatives of a nation which has defeated Imperialism, and we are happy to give you the good news that our country will come victorious out of the struggle.

Great Russia was able to defeat her enemies, because the workers and the peasants who are interested in protecting the victories of the great November Revolution rose with great zeal in order to defend Russia. We are absolutely convinced that the revolutionary combat of the Russian nation constitutes a great example to the Turkish nation who will be able to defeat the paid mercenaries of the Allied Powers which fight now on Anatolian lands to serve their own interests and in order to destroy the Turkish nation.

The nations of the Caucasus are certain that this conference will prepare a solid foundation for friendship and sisterhood with the Turkish nation, and will be able to settle easily the disputed matters which are easily settled between the Soviet Republics. The Delegates of the three Soviet Republics who have deep and noble feelings for the Turkish nation salute the Conference.

The treaty negotiations ended on 10 October. The agreement was signed on 13 October at 2 p.m. The 1st, 2nd, 4th (only the first paragraph), 5th, 6th (only the first sentence), and 15th articles of this agreement were:

1. The Government of the Grand National Assembly of Turkey and the Governments of the Socialist Republics of Armenia, Azerbaijan and Georgia have annulled the agreements which were concluded between the governments which previously exercised their right of sovereignty in the area of the governments of the agreement, and which concerned the said area, and the agreements which were concluded with the three states concerning the Trans-Caucasian Republics. It is clear that the Turkish-Russian agreement which was concluded in Moscow on March 16, 1337-1921, is an exception to the content of this article.

2. Each of the signatory governments accepts the fact that they will not recognize any peace agreement or international contract which is forced upon the other. In accordance with this agreement, the Soviet Socialist Republics of Armenia, Azerbaijan and Georgia accept that they will not recognize any international contract which the National Turkish Government represented by the Grand National Assembly does not recognize.

3. The Government of the Grand National Assembly of Turkey accepts that it will not recognize any international contract which conerns Armenia, Azerbaijan and Georgia but which is not recognized by the Governments of the countries represented by the Councils of Armenia, Azerbaijan and Georgia.

4. The border of North-Eastern Turkey is the border (according to the 1:210,000 verst scale map of the Russian War Staff) which begins in the village of Sarp on the shores of the Black Sea, which goes through the mountain of Hedismena and Shavshat mountains and the waters of Kanlidagh, and which continues until the former northern border of the sunjaks of Kars and Ardahan, and until the estuary of the rivers of Nijni Karasu Ashagi Karasu and Arpachay, and which follows the thalweg of the river of Aras.

5. The Governments of Turkey and Azerbaijan agree that the area of Nahjivan is an autonomous area, defined by enclosure No. 3 appended to this agreement, and protected by Azerbaijan.

6. With the conditions stated below, Turkey agrees to relinquish to Georgia the harbour and city of Batum, and the area which is to the north of the border which is set forth in the fourth article of this agreement, and the rest of the kaza of Batum.

15. The Governments signatory to the agreement are engaged in declaring a general amnesty restricted to the citizens of the other side about the murders and atrocities committed as part of the war in the Caucasian front, following the signing of this agreement.

The eastern front was thus eliminated.

Kachaznuni reports as follows about the conclusion of this front.

The Turkish-Armenian war began at the beginning of autumn and ruined us totally. Probably it was impossible for us to escape this war. In 1918 Turkey was left alone for a period of two years. Measures which would take into consideration the fact of its defeat, and which would introduce new systems, were not taken. During these two years the Turks had been relieved. Their wounds had healed. Young, patriotic, enterprising officers appeared, and began to reorganize the Army in Anatolia. . . . Something cannot be refuted, that is we did not make any effort to avoid the war. There was a simple and inexcusable reason for this. We had no idea of the strength of the Turks, and we were too sure of our own strength. This was the main error. We were too sure of our own strength. This was the main error. We were not afraid of the war, because we were sure that we would win. Just as we had no idea of the strength of the Turks with the insensitivity peculiar to ignorant and inexperienced people, no preventive measures had been taken at the border. On the contrary we invaded Oltu, as if we were engaging in a duel. It was as if we wanted war. When confrontations at the border began, the Turks offered peace negotiations. We refused in a haughty manner. This proved to be a great error. The reason was not only that we were sure of our victory, but the fact that it was impossible for us to be reconciled. It might not have been realized, but it was not impossible. In spite of everything, we did have an opportunity to agree with the Turks. . . . We did nothing to avoid the war, on the contrary we gave a reason for the war. The fact that we had been unable to estimate Turkish strength and that we did not have a clear idea of our own strength were inexcusable errors. Our army, which was well clad, well fed and well armed, did not fight, it retreated constantly; it left its fortifications, it abandoned its arms, and scattered to villages. . . . When Karabekir Pasha arrived at Alexandropolis in the second half of November, the Bureau-Government submitted its resignation to Parliament. It had been defeated and humiliated, it could no longer stay in power. The peace negotiations would begin, and it was preferable that these negotiations be made by new individuals. After a short period of indecision, it was decided that a government should be formed with the social revolutionaries and the Dashnaks, under the leadership of U. Vrassian. . . . The Turks had occupied Alexandropolis. At the same time the Armenian Bolsheviks entered Ichevan and Telijan in the direction of Aghistaf led by the Red Army. Was there an agreement between the Turks and the Bolsheviks? At the beginning we believed such a possibility. But now I think that we were wrong, because no evidence to this effect has been found. It was probable that the Bolsheviks wanted to destroy our army from within, and an agreement with the Turks was not necessary for this. . . . On December 1st or on November 30th, our representatives signed an agreement with the Turks in Alexandropolis. The articles of this agreement were as harsh as in Batum. Again on December 1st, the Vrassian Government resigned and transferred power to the Bolsheviks.[6]

Because the events which occurred in the Republic of Armenia are outside our topic of discussion, we shall not report them.

3. The southern front

The Mundros Truce stipulated a withdrawal in the east of Turkey behind the pre-war borders. However, in the south it did not give the victorious powers the right to occupy areas to the north of the armistice line. It only stipulated the occupation of the Taurus tunnels, with article 10.

The fifth article of the Truce stated that 'The troops which are in Hejaz, Assyria, Yemen, Syria, and Iraq will surrender to the nearest Allied Commander, and parts of the forces in Cilicia, which are more than the required amount for the maintenance of order, will be discharged.'

Mustafa Kemal Pasha, in the second article of a telegram dated 3 November 1918 which he sent to the Commander-in-Chief, stated that 'While we recognize as the border of Syria, the north of the border of the province of Syria, it is necessary that we are informed if there is another point of view. There are no troops we have left in Syria, and with which we have contact. We have a campaigne force in Hejaz. But we do not even have radio contact with it. Despite the fact that the region of Cilicia contains an important part of the province of Adana, its borders are unknown. It is necessary for this, too, to be specified.'

In the answer of the Commander-in-Chief dated 5 November 1918, it was stated that the border of Cilicia would be announced should it prove necessary.

The answer of Mustafa Kemal Pasha of the same date is a very clear example of far-sightedness:

. . . My humble intention in asking about the border of Cilicia was to explain that in the British map which officially recognized its border, Syria lies to the east of the region of Cilicia, while its northern border passes through the north of Marash, because there is no doubt that the British Government, which puts the name Cilicia instead of Adana, considers that the Syrian border extends to the east of the northern part of the Cilicia border. . , , For a few days the British have been talking about landing soldiers at Iskenderun, because in the map which shows the area of Cilicia, Iskenderun is on the borders of Syria and Cilicia. The aim is to invade Iskenderun, and to cut the line of retreat of the 7th Army which is on the Antakya-Diricemal-Ahterin line, by moving on the Iskenderun-Kirikhan- Katma line, and to put this army in a position which would not enable it to refrain from surrendering, just as was done in Mussul. The fact that the British have incited Armenian bands to act today in Islahiye strengthens this opinion. . . . I ordered that the British, who may attempt to send soldiers with whatever reason and pretext to Iskenderun, are opposed with fire, that the equipment of a very weak advance outpost be left to the 7th Army, and that it draw the main part within the Cilicia border in the direction of Katma-Islahiye.

The answer sent by the General Staff, again on 5 November, stated: 'Although the Armistice provisions do not give the British the right and authority to invade Iskenderun. . . . the fact that they wish to use the harbour of Iskenderun is a justifiable request. . . .'

Thus the British were granted the right to land on Iskenderun.

After this, the French and the British did not pay any attention to the Armistice conditions, and began to occupy the south.

On 11 December 1918, a French battalion formed of 400 Armenians entered Dortyol. . . . 'On December 17, 1918 a French unit led by Lieutenant Colonel Romieu landed in Mersin. In the 1,500 man unit there were only 150 French soldiers. The others were Armenian legions. On December 18, 1918 General Hamlin, the Commander of the French Occupation Army of Syria, entered Adana in great pomp.'[7]

The British occupied Antep on 1 January, Marash on 22 February, and Urfa on 24 March. These areas were actually areas which had been given to the French through secret agreements. Because of this, serious disputes arose with the French, and finally an agreement was reached and these provinces were given to the French on 15 September 1919. We shall not dwell on the British-French disagreements. The interested reader may refer to the books mentioned in the previous chapter by Lloyd George and Evans.

Let us summarize how and for what reasons the southern front appeared from the work of Kasim Ener, who has written the history of this front (pp. 30-40):

The Turkish people were left face to face with the Armenians under the administration of an administrator without any influence, because the Ottoman Government had not sent someone to replace the governor Nazim Bey, who had resigned. However, General Hamlin, too, was worried about the situation of the legions and the revolutionaries, because the French soldiers, who were numerically few, had succumbed to luxury. Armed confrontations occurred first in Iskenderun, then in Belen, because of the Armenians' exuberances and their harmful activities. The Armenian detachments who were on leave were attacked by the Turks in Ozerli on January 1, 1919. The Armenians began to kill any Muslims they could lay their hands on, to avenge those who were killed. On January 10, 1919 they attacked the farm of Abdo Agha near Kahyaoglu (Shehitlik). They killed Abdo Agha and 14 of the workers. During the confusion, one of the workers hid inside an oven, and escaped death. The next day he came to the city and told of the atrocity. A few Armenian soldiers were arrested, but were later freed. On February 10, 1919 the Armenians pillaged the Turks' shops. On February 25, the house of a money-changer named Vanli Ahmet Efendi in the Saracan quarter was pillaged during the night by his neighbour Agop and Kamvorlar. The poor man's body was full of bayonet wounds. The Muslims were agitated. Suphi Pasha, the former deputy of Adana, went to the Government, and was promised that the aggressors would be punished. Although Agop and his companions were jailed, they were pardoned as it was claimed that they were innocent. On March 14, 1919 Dellal Ahmet was found dead in his house in the orchards. Of course the assailants were not found. Similar incidents occurred in our other bujaks, counties and villages. Facing this situation, the Turks began a guerilla war beginning from the area of Kirikhan-Kilis, following the cities which began to implement defensive measures. Upon this, Commander-in-Chief General Allenby divided the areas under French occupation in two. He gave the civilian administration to the French, and the military control to the British. He appointed Colonel Bremond as the governor-general of the Northern area, its centre being Adana. . . . The attitude of Bremond, who told the Armenians that he brought the greetings of Bogos Nubar Pasha, encouraged the revolutionaries further: . . . According to Allenby's instructions, the officials who were appointed would have to be approved by the British general headquarters. For military aid, one would refer to the Cilicia occupation command. But Bremond went even further and:

1. He appointed officers who were not on the permanent staff to the gendarmerie, he confiscated the depots.

2. He dismissed the Turkish teachers, officials whom he considered patriotic.

3. He changed the uniform of the police and the gendarmerie. The crescent on the caps was removed. .

4. Teaching of the German language was forbidden in schools. The command language was changed to French.

5. He forced travellers to obtain a travel document, and to pay for their train tickets with silver and gold coins.

6. He had the Cilician seal put on the Ottoman postage stamps.

7. He subjected letters and telegrams to severe censorship.

8. He transferred the sentences given by the Adana courts to the court of appeal in Beirut.

9. He forced the Turkish people to obey his orders. He severely fined those who did not.

10. He gave all the contract rights to the French. In this manner he tried to enrich even the lowest-ranking French officers through official and private means. The Armenians who were encouraged by Bremond's attitude increased their pillages and aggressions. . . .

On February 15-18, 1919, 3 infantry regiments, 1 Indian cavalry regiment, and 1 British regiment arrived led by the British General W. S. Leslie, and fears were dissipated. On February 19, 1919 the war committee met and decided that part of the Armenian legions should be discharged. In return, General Leslie, in response to Bremond's insistence, had Hashim Bey, the Gendarmerie Commander, arrested with the approval of Marshal Allenby, in his office on March 3, 1919. Hashim Bey was sent to Egypt. . . . Captain Luppé was appointed as the gendarmerie inspector. Armenians were brought in to replace the Turkish gendarmes. On March 8, 1919 Captain Taillardat and First Lieutenant Suby were sent to Kozan, and Captain Arrikhi was sent to Ceyhan. They were followed by the forces of occupation. The Armenian refugees were encouraged by this, and began to torture the Muslims of that area. They shot Yunus Hoca in Ceyhan, as he was reciting the ezan [call to prayer]. On April 28, 1919; Bremond announced this communication: `Within the next 24 hours, everybody will surrender their weapons to the Government. At the end of this deadline, all the houses will be searched, and if we find any arms, the owner will be hanged.'

A day after the announcement was published, the houses were searched. Sherif the quilt-maker, Mustafa the police-man, and Imam Ziya were beaten because meat knives were found in their houses. . . . During those summer months the Turks were able to go to their orchards and summer camping grounds, thanks to the Muslim Indian soldiers, but then the scene changed. . . . During the discussion which took place in London, it was decided that French soldiers should replace the British. As a result, two infantry battalions arrived in Adana on July 13, 1919 led by First Lieutenant Thibault. Other French troops landed in Iskenderun. Thus the French forces had settled in Cilicia, the command of Colonel Piepapé was established, and trust began to disappear again, because many soldiers of these two infantry battalions were Armenians wearing French uniform . . . . Marshal Foch reserved the 156th division led by General Dufieux for Cilicia, in accordance with the agreement of September 15, 1919. Major Hassler was the Chief-of-Staff of the division. . . .

When the British forces left Chukurova, the French had three infantry battalions and two cavalry detachments there. The situation was critical for the French administrators, owing to the fact that they had few forces. Their situation was improved when the Algerian soldiers led by General Dufieux arrived in Adana on November 1, .1919. They were followed by the Senegalese regiment. Thus the Eastern First Division led by General Dufieux was modernized in regard to weapons and equipment. The headquarters, the band company of this division, 'its 21st and 22nd regiments, its cannon regiments, its heavy cannon battalions, and its fortification battalions were in Adana. Moreover, the headquarters of the 7th cavalry regiment, and the cavalry, tank, and aeroplane detachments were also there. They had also armed the legions as well as the civilian Armenians.

After having ensured absolute security in the centre, the French began to organize their activities. Colonel Piepapé was entrusted with replacing the British units in Urfa, Antep, and Marash.

General Gouraud, who was appointed Commander-in-Chief in the Near East, came to Adana on December 11, 1919. When he was passing through the Turkish quarters, he asked `Doesn't anybody live here?' as he saw that everything was closed. Bremond then replied, `My General, the Turks live in these quarters, but they do not leave their houses as they are wild in comparison with the Christians.' The shrewd general realized the situation when he saw that the students refused to applaud for him when he visited the Boys' High School, and they refused to sing the French national anthem in spite of pressure to do so, and at that time he understood that the situation in Chukurova was a hopeless one for them . . . . On November 12, 1919 General Gouraud concluded his inspection and left Adana, and, as Du Véou stated in his work *La Passion de la Cilicie*, `he left Bremond alone with the hundred thousand Armenians he had settled in Chukurova'. Again Du Véou informs us that of these Armenians, 70,000 had been settled in Adana and in its villages, 12,000 in Dortyol, 8,000 in Saimbeyli, and the rest in Osmaniye, Kadirli, and Kozan. Moreover, 50,000 Armenians were brought in from Istanbul and Anatolia to Antep, Marash, and Zeitun.

Before we give any information about the strength of the southern front, it is necessary to look at the French documents.

G. Picot, the French High Commissioner who was in Cairo at that time, sent the following telegram to his Ministry on 19 November 1918: `The commander-in-chief to whom I insisted, on the instructions of Your Excellency, that the Armenians be entrusted with ensuring the occupation of the Taurus passages, assures me that his intention was to send them to this area as soon as possible. The measure seems to me very urgent as they have recently provoked most unfortunate incidents in Beirut.[8]

The following note submitted by the French Minister of Foreign Affairs to his Prime Minister on 19 November 1918 is also significant.

. . . I consider, like you, that there is good reason to anticipate that the Armenian forces which are at the present time in Persia will be gathered in Armenia, or more exactly in the three Turkish provinces of Bitlis, Van, and Erzurum. However, one must take into account the fact that among the Armenian volunteers who are under Andranik's command a large part are originally from little Armenia, that is from the northern districts of Cilicia. As this region is within the French sphere of influence according to our agreement with Great Britain, it would be advantageous if the volunteers who are from Cilicia can be sent to Antep and incorporated in the Armenian battalions of the Eastern Legion.

There is good reason for these contingents to be officered by energetic European officers, in order to prevent the hatred which has accumulated by their sufferings driving the Armenian volunteers to make reprisals. If they feel that they are under surveillance, it is probable that they will behave as civilized men.

It is not possible to determine as of now the boundaries of an Armenian nation. Even before the massacres of 1895, the Armenians were not in a majority in the so-called Armenian provinces. In the provinces of Bitlis and Van, they formed compact communities, but the statistics, which were not based on any serious census, varied from the real numbers to double the actual total, in accordance with the inclinations of their authors. In the three other provinces of Diyarbekir, Elaziz, and Trabzon, the Armenian population was much less dense, and constituted only a meagre percentage of the population.

We can therefore conceive of the unification of the provinces of Van, Bitlis, Erzurum and Trabzon, with the districts separated from Elaziz, and Diyarbekir, and maybe also the district of the Russian Transcaucasus around Mount Ararat, in order to found a state of mixed nationalities, which would enjoy autonomy under the guarantee and supervision of the Allies. . . .

As the region of Ottoman Turkey, which has fallen under French influence, will extend up to the borders of this heterogeneous state, it would be natural that France should receive the mandate from the Allied Powers to ensure the maintenance of order and good relations. The French possessions would then border the petroliferous regions of the Caspian Sea, where French capital has already been invested, and Persia, in order to attain the districts of the Transcaucasus and profit from their diverse resources.[9]

As can been seen, the French did not conceive of establishing an Armenia in Cilicia, but were planning to border with an Armenia which would be established in the east (that is in regions which were once relinquished to Russia), and to exert their influence in that area. In 1920, when the Armenians claimed that they were promised an Armenia in Cilicia, referring to Bogos Nubar Pasha, the French openly accused Bogos Nubar of lying. Let us look at the following letter sent by the Ministry of Foreign Affairs to the President of the Foreign Affairs Commission of the French Senate on 28 December 1920:

. . . You have asked me whether in 1916, or since that date, the French Government had engaged itself in regard to Armenia, to constitute an autonomous Cilicia.

. . . I have the honour of informing you that no engagement of this nature ever took place.

. . . Bogos Pasha claims that M. Geroges Picot assured him in London that France had engaged herself to give, after the victory of the Allies, autonomy to Cilicia under her protection.

This so called engagement was apparently the counterpart of the recruiting of the Armenian legion, which had been formed at the suggestion of M. Georges Picot, to help to drive the Turks from Cilicia.

To strengthen his claim, Bogos Pasha cites a telegram he sent to his son in Cairo, through the mediation of the Ministry of Foreign Affairs, in order to take the necessary measure for the establishment of the Armenian legion. He adds that Commander Romieu, charged with this formation, confirmed to the Armenian notables the agreement reached in London, and read them a letter written by M. Briand, who was then the President of the Council, in which he declared that he was in agreement with the national Armenian delegation.

M. Georges Picot has never informed the Ministry of the discussion he had with Bogos Pasha in London. As a matter of fact, he had no authority which would permit him to engage the French Government.

The telegram sent by Bogos Pasha to his son only states 'the official assurance that the national aspirations of the Armenians be satisfied when the Allies are victorious'. The department would not have sent this telegram if it had concerned Cilicia. Cilicia was not mentioned in this telegram. The sentence which is quoted could only refer to the establishment of an Armenian state within the limits determined by the Powers. This is exactly what was done by the Treaty of Sevres.

There is no evidence in the Archives of the Foreign Affairs indicating that M. Briand wrote a letter to Commander Romieu.

There is no document of any kind which confirms the claim made by Bogos Nubar Pasha that M. Georges Picot assured him that 'France would create an autonomous Armenia, after she conquers Cilicia, within the limits of the 1916 agreement'. . . . [10]

This letter continues by proving that Bogos Nubar Pasha made unfounded claims. We have included this letter here, in order to indicate to what extent Bogos Nubar Pasha, who took upon himself the right to speak on behalf of Armenia, can be trusted.

Let us now continue our topic of discussion. High commissioner Picot, in a telegram he send on 26 December 1918, stated that 'The best way for us in order to found our influence among the Armenians on solid grounds, is to form the nucleus of their army under our flag.'[11]

Picot ended his telegram dated 30 January 1919 with the following statement: 'As to the indiscipline of the Armenians, it is nearly impossible to remedy.'[12]

The report dated 27 June 1919 sent by General Hamlin to the Ministry of War is even more interesting. This report concerns nineteen non-commissioned officers, corporals, and privates, belonging to the Armenian legion, who were sent to the military court because of their undisciplined behaviour. General Hamlin wrote:

Two death sentences have been announced. The execution of the decision has been postponed, because the two convicts submitted a petition for appeal and a petition for pardon.

But it seems to me necessary to point out to you once again on this occasion, the inauspicious action exerted by the Armenian committees on the legionaries who are serving under our flag.

The report of the Commissioner Reporter mentions this action, of which my information service was already informed.

My telegrams of 166/G dated February 3rd, and 378/G dated March 10th, pointed out to you the difficulties which the Armenian committees had created for me.

On April 13th in 514/G I informed you that Armenian indiscipline in Cilicia was partly caused by provocation by the Committee of the National Armenian Union, and also by letters sent from Egypt.

This state of affairs had driven me to lay the matter before the British General Headquarters, which had intervened to the Armenian committee in Egypt, in order to put an end to this situation.

Since then the Commander of the 1st battalion of the Armenian legion wrote on May 1st that M. Epremian, the delegate of the Committee in Cairo, had visited his unit. Further, very recently, on May 29th, the colonel, commander of the French troops in Cilicia, sent me a copy of a telegram sent by the committee in Paris, signed by 'Nubar' to Epremian. In the telegram information was requested about the legionaries who were freed'; this showed that the mission of the delegate of Cairo had been sent in agreement with the committee in Paris.

Finally, examination of the correspondence sent to the Armenian legion continues to reveal provocations to indiscipline and against France, directed to the legionaries by the Armenian notables in Egypt, and even by various members of the Armenian National Union.

It is indisputable that there was a time when we benefited from the Armenian committees, but at the present time their influence is pernicious, because it feeds political agitation among the troops, whom it encourages to indiscipline. . . .[13]

Picot's telegram dated 16 July 1919: 'Colonel Bremond informs me that various Armenian elements which were recently still favourable to France, have now turned against us. The Protestant American propaganda of M. Damadian against France has increased. . . .[14]

The situation indicated by these telegrams was as follows.

First of all, the Armenians' aggressive behaviour towards the Muslim community continued. This was expected by the French, who thought they could nevertheless prevent it. As to the actions against France, the Armenians were aware that if this region were to fall into French hands, they would not be given autonomy. This period covers the days when the negotiations concerning the transfer of the region from the British to the French were continuing. For this reason, attempts were made to create an anti-France climate. Were the British involved in this? We cannot affirm anything. Moreover, the Istanbul Patriarchate was making great efforts to concentrate as many Armenians as possible in the region. This was because there was no Armenian population left in the east, and even if an autonomous Armenia was established there, it would be quite difficult to gather the entire population, which had dispersed, owing to the difficult living conditions. Furthermore, as there were no occupation forces in the east, the Armenians would not be able to move about freely.

On the contrary, Cilicia was a comfortable and secure region for various reasons. In addition, an Armenian concentration here increased the possibility of autonomy in this region.

Proof of our statements may be found in the French Archives.

The report sent by the French High Commissioner in Istanbul to M. Pichon, the Minister of Foreign Affairs, on 27 September 1919[15] stated the following points:

During the journey which he has just completed, Lieutenant Dubreuil has established that the Armenians of the region of Kayseri are leaving the region; this exodus was not motivated by any sudden fear felt by the Armenians, as they have attested to the security which reigns at least at the present time in the province, but rather by the advice and exhortations which are given to them by their co- religionists and by their bishops who reside in Constantinople, in other cities of Turkey, and even in Europe. . . .

In the enclosed report Lieutenant Dubreuil stated the following:

I have the honour of informing you that the Christians of the region of Kayseri are abandoning their region en masse . . . at the present time, the Catholic bishop of Kayseri, who is in Istanbul, is one of the main organisers of this exodus, through the advice he provides. The policy followed in Cilicia which aims at making Adana a province solely populated by Armenians, is certainly one of the factors behind this departure en masse. . . .

Colonel Bremond, affected by this exodus which he did not understand, which I think may be one of the involuntary factors, has suggested the immediate occupation of Kayseri by the Allies. After having listened to me, Colonel Piepapeé, commander of the Cilician troops, sent a telegram to Beirut concerning the exaggeration of the interpretation of this situation. I hope that Colonel Bremond's request will not be approved.

As can be seen, the explanations given by the Church and Bremond for this exodus stated that the Armenians were being oppressed there.

Finally, a telegram dated 21 October sent by Picot ends like this: 'It is agreed that our troops will arrive in Urfa, Marash, and Antep, before the departure of the British troops, in order to avoid the return of the 11,000 Armenians to Adana, whose arrival would further complicate a situation which is already complex.'[16]

These quotations that we have taken from Turkish and French sources as to how and why the National Struggle in Cilicia began make the same point.

Now let us examine the forces which took part in this struggle. In the above discussion we have seen the condition of the Turkish forces on 19 May 1919, as narrated by Ataturk himself. The strongest of the units at hand was in the east. The others had been weakened. It was impossible even to conceive of sending soldiers to this region. The issue was discussed first in Sivas. Kazim Karabekir Pasha wrote:

Today, Mustafa Kemal Pasha, Ali Fuat Pasha, Selahhatin Bey and I read, in the office of the 3rd Army Corps Command, the drafts of instructions concerning the national operation in the regions of Adana, Marash and Antep. The government which followed the Armistice made the mistake of evacuating the province of Adana, and the subdivisions of Antep, Marash and Urfa. Taking advantage of this, the British occupied this area. Recently it has become apparent that in that area which the French settled in as the British left, attempts were made to bring about a substantial Armenian population. The activities and the British Press indicated that the intention of the French was to establish a great Armenia in Cilicia, united with the actual Armenia. The British newspapers mentioned that this was impossible. Thus in order to free our people who were conquered unjustly, and whose future appeared hopeless, the national struggle would begin with the assistance of the 20th, 13th, 3rd, and 12th Army Corps.[17]

Of the Army Corps which would assist, the 20th was in Ankara, the 13th was in Diyarbekir, the 12th was in Konya, and the 3rd was in Sivas. The divisions of these Army Corps were in various provinces. Assistance was limited to sending a few officers who would be able to set up a resistance organization which would be formed locally. Because equipment aid was only furnished by the 41st division of the 12th Army Corps in Konya, the national forces in the south were considered as part of this division.

According to Kasim Ener, the total of the national local forces was 1,500 men. He provides us with the following information with regard to this: 'We are informed by the dossier No. 5/801 and No. 8 and file no. 706 of the Archives of the War Department, that on July 2, 1920, the National Forces had in their possession, during the siege of Pozanti, a mountain cannon which was left by the 11th division, and 2 small cannons of 5.5 obtained from the French as war booty in Karboghazi. There were 10 usable machine guns. Most of them were again obtained from the French as war booty. On August 11, 1920, two cannons of 10.5 were brought to the Kurttepe front. But the cannons had little ammunition or gun powder.'

The condition of the French forces during the same period was as follows:

According to information received from the 41st division on August 13, 1920, the French units were formed in the following manner: One division, four regiments; each regiment had four battalions; one was motorized and the other three were infantrymen. Each infantry battalion had four companies, one of them equipped with an automatic machine gun.

Each cavalry battalion was formed of four companies, three of which were armed with sabres and the fourth with automatic rifles.

Although no information was received about the battalion which was equipped with a machine gun, it appeared that there were four companies according to the number of arms.

The total of each infantry company was, on average, 140 soldiers and 11 automatic guns.

The total of each company equipped with a machine gun was 150 soldiers and 8 machine guns.

In Adana there were 4 infantry regiments and a fortifications company with the headquarters of the cavalry regiment. One infantry battalion had been reserved to defend Misis. General Dufieu had under his command 20 cannons, a large number of machine guns, 5 armoured cars, tanks and aeroplanes. Moreover, they were assisted by the thousands of Armenians who had been armed.[18]

The struggle on the southern front occurred between these two forces. On 7 January 1920, Mustafa Kemal Pasha sent the following telegram to Karabekir Pasha:

Georges Picot, the French High Commissioner of Syria and Armenia, who has left Syria to attend the Paris Peace Conference, has arrived in Sivas in order to acquire information about our national actions, and in order to exchange views with the Representative Delegation. In the special meeting which took place, it was explained to him that the nation's goal is included in the declaration of the Sivas Congress, and the occupation of Cilicia, Urfa, Marash, and Antep, which was contrary to the armistice, was objected to strongly. The brutalities inflicted by the Armenians in these areas and the insulting treatment of Ottoman officials by the French Government was strongly denounced, and he was informed that the nation demanded the annulment of these unjust occupations, and that it was determined to recruit all its material and spiritual forces with this aim. Picot's reply: he had ordered before he left that the Armenian troops retreat from the areas which had recently been occupied. He stated that the French recognized the independence of the Ottoman Empire, and that they wished to ensure it. He said that it was probable that the French would evacuate Marash, Urfa, Antep, and Cilicia in return for obtaining economic concessions in Adana. It was also probable that attempts would be made at the Peace Conference to annul the occupation by the other powers. He brought these points forward for discussion on condition that they were his personal observations and that they be confidential. And he requested from us that no rebellion occur against the French, while we continued with establishing our national organization in Adana, Urfa, Marash, and Antep. We told him that we would take steps to ensure that the Muslim community did not commit any aggression as long as the Armenians did not provoke them, but that the responsibility would be theirs, should they provide any reason for it. It is very important that this detailed request be confidential. Based on the above discussion, we are convinced that the French consider an action in favour of Turkey in the east, for their interest. Georges Picot's intention was to gather definite information about the national point of view when he went to Paris. Consequently it is necessary to make efforts with even greater ardour for the development of our national organization in the occupied areas and that any armed attacks are prevented until further notice. Strong protests by the Government, as well as the people, at any actions contrary to the treaty, such as interference by the police and the gendarmerie with our internal affairs, will be most favourable to our political aims today. Mustafa Kemal.[19]

However, this conversation did not produce any results, In the south the national forces began their activities through hit-and-run band fights. But the most significant confrontations began in Marash on 20 January 1920, and the French were forced to evacuate Marash.

Because the southern front was not a regular battle ground, but was the scene of isolated confrontations with the occupation forces in Marash, Urfa and Antep, we shall not examine each one of them. However, this first confrontation was reported in Europe with such exaggerations that we think it is necessary to record it. First of all, on 6 February, Zaven, the Armenian Patriarch in Istanbul, sent a telegram to Nubar Pasha, stating that 2,000 Armenians had been massacred in Marash.[20] On 25 February, the Reuter news agency announced this figure as 70,000.[21]

At that time the peace negotiations were being held in London. During the session on 18 February 1920, Lord Curzon stated that, according to the information he had received from Bogos Nubar Pasha and from the British admiral in Istanbul, 20,000 Armenians had been massacred by the forces of Mustafa Kemal Pasha. Suggestions such as deposing the Sultan and arresting the Grand Vizier and ministers were discussed.[22]

As a result, information was requested from Istanbul. The following reply came from General Gouraud, the military commander in Beirut:

Study of the Marash incidents and examination of all the information which I received concerning the organization of the movement which continues to threaten Cilicia, confirm that the aggression of the nationalist Turks was caused mainly by the protection we have granted to the Armenians. In some cases, this protection of an entity, which is itself aggressive and more capable than the Turks of circumventing European officers and agents, has been too conspicuous.

Your Excellency may have been aware of my concern to stop this grief of the Turks through many of my telegrams, and through the instructions sent to General de Lamothe by courier.[23]

This following telegram sent by Millerand, the Prime Minister and Minister of Foreign Affairs, to London is even more interesting:

. . . . I am surprised that London should possess information which no one here is aware of, and is able to document.

As a result, it has been impossible until now to determine exactly that Armenians have been massacred in any area. There is much talk about it, but no one was able to give me certain and exact information. In particular the Armenian losses in Marash appear to be absolutely false. Apparently, the Armenians took part in the struggle of our troops in this city, and had casualties like all the fighters.

A serious study of the figures shows that these Armenian casualties do not exceed 1,000. . . .[24]

The following telegram dated 12 March, sent by General Gouraud, is worth mentioning:

. . . . The total of the Armenian legion includes 1,496 soldiers. . . . Increasing these units would only increase trouble and difficulties, and would constitute a most inauspicious political measure. We can consider employing these Armenian units only in an area where they would not be in contact with the Turks. Syria would be the only place. However, the Armenians have inflamed such hatred in that area, that they asked the General to save them from these people. . . .[25]

It would be very useful to evaluate the claims of the Armenian massacres, keeping in mind the telegrams of General Gouraud, and especially of Millerand.

Atatürk reported the Marash incidents during the 1 May 1920 session of the National Assembly:

With your permission, let me talk about the Cilicia front. When we discuss this front we can talk about Antep, Marash, Urfa, the so-called three provinces. Gentlemen, like everywhere else, the Entente powers have occupied this area contrary to the armistice. Later, they made an agreement among themselves, and England broke it. England left Cilicia, Antep, Marash, Urfa, and the whole of Syria to the French, and the French occupied these areas.

The central Government took no measures against this aggression, it did not even protest. You are all aware of this.

However, these areas are included within the borders we have drawn in the main programme we have accepted, and it is necessary that these areas are freed from the enemy.

However, at the same time, we were always careful not to give cause for any confrontations so as not to force the enemy to fight. But the French, after they unjustly occupied this area, acted very aggressively, and committed harmful acts against the Muslim community, and they entrusted the Armenians wearing French uniforms with these actions. It can be stated that, for whatever reason, various bloody incidents have occurred in this country between the Armenians and our nation. These two nations have against each other, and especially the Armenians have against our nation, a great deal of hostility. Consequently, to incite the Armenians to attack us, to attack the Muslim community, was a great error, because the intention of the Armenians is to destroy the Muslim people in Cilicia, Antep, Marash, Urfa, and wherever they are present; especially since they have been protected. Our poor brothers living in those areas were subject to great atrocities. They ask the help of the entire nation for the protection of all sacred things. But they remain unheard. Unfortunately the central government has given no assistance. For many reasons, it was unable to take any definite steps.

Thus the inhabitants of Cilicia and other areas, who abandoned all hope and who were convinced that they were sentenced to die, were driven to rush forward in order to protect their own existence. It would not have been right to be a mere spectator of these people, especially for the neighbouring Muslim community.

In fact, within the country and especially from Sivas, conscientious patriots rushed forward, entered these occupied areas, united with their brothers there, ' and were in the same ranks with them in their struggle for honour, sacredness, and existence.

The struggle is continuing. The first confrontation occurred in Marash, and the result has been to the advantage of the righteous.

After this, confrontations occurred in Urfa and in the Silifke region. Here too, we were the victorious ones; at the present time the enemy is being chased in the direction of Arappinari.

In Antep the skirmishes which were caused by the Armenians' aggression are continuing. From various sides troops have arrived to reinforce the enemy forces. But they were paralyzed by the national forces. Enemy forces have remained only in Misis and in some other localities.

If we are to go more to the West, the enemy forces have been defeated near Bozanti, and that area too is controlled by the national forces.

During the Cilicia incident, the inhabitants of Silifke showed great courage and patriotism. Some of our forces, which we can call the Silifke forces, have recovered the area up to Mersin, with the exception of Mersin itself.

In Mersin too, they are superior to the enemy. Just a few days ago some of our companions arrived from Mersin. They state that the French forces in Mersin are few and nervous. I have presented the last stage of the operation in the Cilicia front.

Until we determine the policy we shall adopt together, we thought that to wait was a more favourable measure, and in the last instruction it was ordered not to go any further, and for this reason the city of Mersin was not occupied. However, we control it and we can conquer it whenever we wish to.

Now gentlemen, the French, as a result of this pressure, have felt the necessity to come into dialogue with those people who have put this pressure.

Today an individual named Monsieur Albert Sarrault has arrived here from France in order to discuss with us.[26]

Atatürk included the meeting which took place with the French in his great speech:

National forces had been organized in the area of Adana against the French, in the areas of Tarsus, Mersin, Islahiye, and in the vicinity of Silifke, and they had begun a most courageous operation. The heroic acts of Captain Osman Bey who operated in the region of southern Adana, under the title Tufan Bey, are worthy of recording. The national detachments have secured their control up to the gates of the cities of Mersin, Tarsus and Adana. In Pozanti they defeated the French and forced them to retreat.

Serious combats occurred in Marash, Antep, and Urfa. As a result, the occupation forces were forced to retreat from these areas. I regard it as a duty to mention here the names of Kiliç Ali Bey and Ali Saip Bey who were the dominant figures in obtaining this victory.

The national forces were being more and more organized in the areas of French occupation and its fronts. The national forces were reinforced by the regular troops. The forces of occupation were pressed strongly from all directions.

Gentlemen, since the beginning of May 1920, the French have sought negotiations and dialogue with us. First of all, a major and a civilian arrived in Ankara from Istanbul. These persons had first gone to Beirut from Istanbul; Haydar Bey, the former Van deputy acted as a guide for them. No significant result came out of our discussions. However, towards the end of May, a French delegation, presided over by Monsieur Duquais who was acting on behalf of the High Commissioner of Syria, arrived in Ankara. We made an armistice for twenty days with this delegation. By temporarily ending hostilities, we were aiming at beginning the evacuation of the region of Adana.

Gentlemen, the impression I had of these discussions was that the French would evacuate Adana and its vicinity. I presented my opinion to the Assembly. As a matter of fact, although the French attempted to show that the ceasefire was limited to the region of Adana, by occupying Zonguldak before the end of the armistice, we considered this action as the annulment of the armistice. Our agreement with the French was delayed for some time.[27]

The struggle with the French continued until March 1921. On 4 September 1920, Bremond, who had been acting as a symbol of wickedness, was dismissed from office. The southern front was concluded legally with the Ankara Agreement of 20 October 1921. Ataturk described the making of this agreement in his great speech.

Gentlemen, the Ankara Agreement constitutes our positive relations with the west after the victory of Sakarya. This agreement was signed in Ankara in October 1921. Let me explain a point here, in order to give you a general explanation.

For various reasons, it was clear that the French, who occupied, besides Syria, these provinces I have mentioned, were inclined to reach an agreement with us. Despite the fact that the agreement which was made between Bekir Sami Bey and Monsieur Briand, and which was unacceptable to our nation, had been rejected, neither the French, nor we, wanted to continue the confrontation. For this reason both sides sought an agreement. France had sent Monsieur Franklin Bouillon, a former Minister, first unofficially, to Ankara. I negotiated with M. Bouillon, who arrived in Ankara on 9 June 1921, for two weeks, in the presence of Yusuf Kemal Bey, the Minister of Foreign Affairs, and Fevzi Pasha.

I stated that our starting-point was the contents of the National Pact of 1920.

M. Bouillon stated that it would be difficult to discuss principles, and that the Sèvres agreement existed as a *fait accompli*. He added that it would be favourable to accept in principle the agreement made in London between Bekir Sami Bey and M. Briand, and to discuss the contents of this Agreement where they were in conflict with the National Pact. In confirmation of this suggestion he remarked that our representatives who had gone to London had not mentioned the National Pact, and that the National Pact and the national movement had not even been approved in Istanbul, let alone in Europe.

I replied: 'A new Turkey was born of the old Ottoman Empire. This must be recognized. This new Turkey will have its legality recognized, like every independent state. The Sèvres Agreement is such an inauspicious death sentence for the Turkish nation, that we prefer not to hear it from a friend. Even during our discussions I would not wish to mention the Sèvres Agreement. We cannot engage in negotiations based on the principle of trust, with nations who do not erase the Sèvres Agreement from their minds. In our view, this agreement does not exist. If the President of our delegation, which went to London, did not mention this, then he did not act on the instructions we gave him. He did wrong. It appears that this error gave rise to adverse effects on European and especially French public opinion. If we were to act like Bekir Sami Bey, we would commit the same error. It is impossible that Europe is not aware of the National Pact. It is possible that Europe has not understood the meaning of the term, National Pact. However, Europe and the entire world who saw that we have been shedding our blood for years must certainly reflect on the causes of our bloody struggle. The statement to the effect that Istanbul is unaware of the National Pact and the national struggle is not accurate. The population of Istanbul, like the entire Turkish nation, is aware and supportive of the national movement. The individuals and citizens who stand against the national movement are few and are known to the nation.'

When I stated that Bekir Sami Bey had acted without authority, Franklin Bouillon asked whether he could mention this. I told him that he could mention my statement wherever he wanted. Bouillon gave many excuses so as not to be removed from the agreement of Bekir Sami Bey, and repeated that Bekir Sami Bey had not mentioned the existence of a National Pact, and that he could not go beyond its boundaries; that if he had mentioned it, it would have been possible to act and discuss accordingly, but that now the matter was complicated. The public will ask, why haven't the Turks mentioned this before through their representatives? Now they are creating more complications.

Finally, after much negotiation and discussion, Bouillon suggested postponement of the discussions, until he had read and understood the National Pact. Following this, the discussions were begun, as we read the articles of the National Pact one by one from beginning to end.

Gentlemen, we exchanged views for days with M. Bouillon on these important matters. I think that, as a result, we were able to understand one another. However, it was necessary that more time had pass in order to to be able to determine definite points of agreements between the French Government and the national Turkish Government. What was expected? Very likely the confirmation of the national Turkish existence with a greater victory after the victories of the First and Second Inonu battles. In fact, the Ankara Agreement, which M. Bouillon approved and signed, is a   document which was established on 20 October 1921, thirty-seven days after the bloody battle we won at Sakarya.

With this agreement, we have liberated the valuable parts of our country from occupation, without sacrificing any part of our independence from an economic, political, or military standpoint. With this agreement, our national aspirations were approved by a member of the Western states.

Following this, M. Franklin Bouillon came to Turkey a few times more, and sought opportunities to manifest the feelings of friendship which were established in Ankara during the first days of our discussions.[29]

The text of the Ankara Agreement was as follows:

Article 1. Both sides will announce that the war between them has ended, after they have signed this treaty. The armies, the civil servants and the population will immediately be informed of the state of affairs.

Article 2. After this treaty has been signed, all the prisoners of war of both sides, all Turkish and French individuals who were arrested or imprisoned, will be freed; each side will pay the travel expenses of these individuals and will send them to the nearest designated place.

Article 3. At most within two months after this treaty has been signed, the French troops will retreat to the south of the line established in Article 8, and the Turkish troops will retreat to its north.

Article 4. During the period mentioned in the 3rd article, a joint commission will be formed, which will determine the procedure for the implementation of this article.

Article 5. Both sides will announce a general amnesty in the evacuated area, following the occupation of this area.

Article 6. The Government of the Turkish   Grand National Assembly announces that it will support the rights of minorities, as openly recognized in the National Pact, based on the principles included in the agreements which were made concerning this matter, between the friends and the enemies of the allies.

Article 7. A special administrative system will be instituted for the area of Iskenderun (Hatay). The Turkish inhabitants of this area will enjoy all kinds of organizations for the development of their culture. In that area the Turkish language will be the official language.

Article 8. The line which was mentioned in article 3 will begin in Payas in the Iskenderun bay, will go to the Meydani Ekbez-Kilis-Choban station, and will reach Nuseybin from Choban Beyli, on condition that the railway remain within Turkey. Payas and the stations of Meydani Ekbez and Choban Beyli will remain in Syria. Within one month of the signing of this treaty, a commission formed by members of the two sides will determine the aforementioned line, and will supervise the procedure of determining.

Article 9. The mausoleum of Suleiman Shah, the grandfather of Sultan Osman, the founder of the Ottoman dynasty, which is located in the Caber castle, and which is known by the term Turkish tomb, together with its annexes, will be the property of Turkey, and Turkey will place guards there and will raise the Turkish flag.

Article 10. The Government of the Turkish Grand National Assembly accepts that it will give the right to operate the departments in the province of Adana, of the Baghdad railway line between Pozanti and Nuseybin, to a French group designated by the French Government, as well as all matters concerning the commercial and transportation affairs of this railway. The Government of Turkey will engage in military transportation by railway in Syria from Meydani Ekbez to Choban Beyli.

Article 11. After this agreement has come into effect, a joint commission which will be chosen will put in order matters concerning customs between Turkey and Syria, and until this operation has been completed, both countries will act freely.

Article 12. Turkey and Syria will equitably benefit from the Kirik stream. The Syrian Government will be able to take water from the Turkish part of the Euphrates, and the expenses will be met by the Syrian Government.

Article 13. The sedentary and semi-nomadic people residing on both sides of the line established in Article 8 will benefit from the pastures in this area, and those who possess lands and immovable property will continue to use their rights as hitherto. These persons will be able to transport their animals, tools, seeds, and plants freely, without giving any pasture toll, customs, or any other fee. It has been decided that they shall pay the corresponding taxes to the country they reside in.

Kasim Ener has written about the subject of the evacuation of the south by the French.

In response to the signing of the Ankara Agreement, the Armenian community in Adana organized a demonstration. The Armenians closed their shops. But the French military administration re-established order. General Dufieux invited prominent Christians to the government office, explained the principles of the agreement, and stated that martial law was in operation. He added that no excessive acts must be committed, no flags raised, and that there was no reason for any one to be afraid. Meanwhile Ferit Bey, our representative in Paris, arrived in Tarsus. He was met by Lieutenant-Colonel Sarrous, and they both went to Mersin. There Sarrous stated that he did not doubt that the Grand National Assembly of Turkey would act justly, and that individuals who disrupted public order during the process of evacuation would be delivered to the Ankara Government.

General Dufieux was not pleased with the Ankara Agreement. His military pride could not accept the fact that the French had delivered Cilicia to the Turks. Because of this he avoided the discussions, and did not want to be present during the evacuation. As a result, on 24 November 1921 he left Adana with his headquarters, and before he left, he visited the French cemetery. He expressed his grief in his speech, which began: 'O French soldiers, we shed your blood for nothing.'

The Armenian revolutionaries were very worried because of the unbelievable atrocities they had committed during the occupation. We have included the letter written by the Sis Catholicos on 29 November 1921 in Iskenderun, to the national Armenian delegation in Paris, in order to elucidate this subject further.

The Catholicos stated: 'No decision was taken in the discussions which occurred with the representatives of the cities of the entire occupied region, as the Armenians panicked after the Franklin Bouillon Agreement. The reason for this is that people are afraid of a massacre should the Kemalists arrive. We discussed the subject that the Armenians must not be miserable, thinking where they would go and what they would do. However, the Kemalists did not expect and wish an emigration *en masse*. Thus they informed us from Bozanti, through their representatives in Adana, that they wished to meet our religious leaders. The Kemalist representatives in Adana were the following: Suleyman Vahit Efendi, Gergeli Ali Efendi, Müçteba Ramazanoghlu Efendi, and Mustafa Efendi. These representatives brought to our leaders a letter signed by Suphi Pasha of Adana and Mehmet Fuat Diblan, the mayor. In this letter Suphi Pasha and Fuat Diblan Bey wrote that they wanted to discuss with us in Kelebek or Dikili, and invited us there. The French authorities wanted us to accept this invitation, and they provided cars for our representatives to go there. Monsignor Elyse, Monsignor Keklian, Haruttionian, the Protestant priest left. They took with them an Armenian, a Greek, and a Turk (Assyrian) named Chukur Aslan, and on 15 November, 1921 they were taken to Kelebek by Kemalist agents.

After a while the Kemalists arrived. Suphi Pasha was the first one to talk. He stated that he could not speak on behalf of the Ankara Government as he had no official title, and that he considered it as a duty to meet and discuss here, because he was a child of the country and had feelings towards his fellow countrymen. He added that he thought of taking a decision to prevent the migration of the Armenians. He continued, and stated that the Kemalist Government was a very just and good government, and that Turkish laws would be equally implemented for Muslims and Christians. Dr. Eshref Bey and Diblan Bey repeated this. Our spiritual leaders stated that the Turkish-French Agreement did not have a clause which protected Christians' lives, and that, as the Turkish delegation did not have an official title, it could not constitute a guarantee, despite the fact that they believed in their honesty. They promised that they would do everything possible, and left. As to the Armenians they prepared their evacuation.

Facing this situation, the French, at the insistence of Hamit Bey (he was the Kemalists' governor in Adana at that time), Muhittin Pasha, and especially Colonel Sarrous, invited our representatives to meet the Turkish delegates in Yenice, on 22 November. On the same day Franklin Bouillon and the representatives of Tarsus and Mersin arrived there. A meeting was held, at which he presided. Hamit Bey and the new French Consul Laporte took part in this meeting. The same statements were made and again it was insisted that the Armenians should not leave.

On 23 November, Franklin Bouillon invited our spiritual leaders to his house (in the old station) and told them that the Kemalist Government had very good intentions and that it would protect all our rights; however, this was not an official guarantee. Because of this, the Christian community (Armenian-Assyrian) lost hope, and fled to the harbours using every possible means of transportation. Only officials and the sick remained in Adana. The schools were closed.

As we were unable to help the Armenians, a telegram was sent to General Gouraud through General Dufieux. We requested that the French transfer the orphans and the sick, and that the rest be transported from Dortyol to Iskenderun. On 23 November, we received an answer from General Dufieux. He notified us to conclude our preparations in order to leave on 25 November and said that he would meet us.

On 29 November 1921, Franklin Bouillon sent the French Consul to Iskenderun. We had a long meeting with the Consul. A summary of our discussion is as follows. The Government which will be formed will be a just one, and will protect the rights of minorities. For this reason, we must save the emigrants from misery and from endangering their properties. Because of this, those who have left must return. Your desire to leave this area will destroy the Armenian community's trust in the Turkish-French Government. At the same time your action will be considered disloyal to the French Government. He stated, the French sacrificed 5,000 of their children on this land for you. And he mentioned the honesty of Hamit Bey. In answer to these statements made by the Consul Laporte, I said: "Yes, when he was in Diyarbekir, Hamit Bey really acted honestly. I know him and I trust him. However, we should not endanger the Christians' lives by trusting a man. We remember in gratitude what the French did for us. But since the armistice 30,000 Armenians have died for the French." Thus I concluded the subject.' (The Catholicos left Adana on 25 November to go to Iskenderun.)

When the above statements are examined carefully, it will be seen that the fact that the Armenians fled in spite of all the promises was due to their fear of the innumerable murders committed by the revolutionaries called Ganavors, as we have mentioned previously. As a matter of fact, the Greeks remained like the Jewish minorities, as they did not take part in such occurrences. In the meantime, General Gouraud had sent a message to the Armenians through General Dufieux, and had advised them that they should stay in Adana, and that they should trust Turkish justice.[30]

On Wednesday, 1 December, 1921, the ceremonies of handing over the administration took place in Adana with the French, and the front was concluded. In his work *Hatiralarim*, Damar Arikoglu gives interesting information about this front (pp. 72-86, 103-35).

4. The Western Front

During the War of Liberation the western front was the Greek front, in which the Armenians acted with the Greeks. We are informed by the Bristol report that the Armenians even took part in the excesses which occurred on the day Izmir was occupied by the Greeks, and which resulted in the death of many Turks.[31] In the 22nd paragraph of the chapter of this report entitled `Exposé des Faits survenus depuis 1'occupation qui ont été établis au cours de 1'enquête entre 1e.12 août et le 6 octobre 1919' we see that there were two Armenians among the people who were sentenced by the military court established by the Greek Command in Izmir, because of the incidents of 15-16 May. We also find the following statement in the report dated 23 May 1921 of the commission formed by the commission of the allies for the incidents of Yalova and Gemlik: 'The members of the Commission consider that, in the part of the *kazas* of Yalova and Gemlik occupied by the Greek army, there is a systematic plan of destruction of Turkish villages and extinction of the Moslem population. This plan is being carried out by Greek and Armenian bands, which appear to operate under Greek instructions and sometimes even with the assistance of detachments of regular troops.[132]

It is known that from the beginning of 1921 the Greeks recruited Christians who were Turkish citizens, and of course Armenians too, in the regions they occupied. Because of this, when the Greeks retreated from Anatolia, the Armenians of that area left with them. During the Lausanne Conference, Ismet Pasha openly stated this fact, and no one offered any objection. We shall quote Ismet Pasha's statement when we discuss the Lausanne Conference.

For these reasons we thought it necessary to mention the western front briefly.

As a matter of fact, it would also have been useful to talk about the Istanbul Front, and mention the relations of the Patriarchate and the Armenians, and also of some untrustworthy Turks with the British Embassy and especially with Mr. Ryan, the chief interpreter of this Embassy, who was famous for his hostility to the Turks. But we do not think this is necessary.

5. The Treaty of Lausanne

The War of Independence ended on 11 October 1922 with the Mudanya Armistice. The peace negotiations began on 20 November 1922 in Lausanne.

Just as there was not one word in the Mudanya Agreement about the Armenians, neither did the Lausanne Agreement mention them.

When the War of Liberation was still in progress, the Allied Powers made two proposals for peace. In both there was a clause about the Armenians. The first came after the Inonu victory, and a meeting was held in London on 21 February. During this meeting it was suggested that the stipulations of the Sèvres Agreement be improved to some extent, and concerning the Armenians it was requested that Turkey accept the right of the Armenians to establish a homeland on the eastern borders of Anatolia, whose borders would be determined by a commission chosen by the League of Nations. The second proposal came in written form in March 1922. In this the Sèvres conditions were further improved, and it was requested that an Armenian homeland be established in the East, and that the League of Nations intervene in this matter. This proposal, too, did not bear fruit.

When it became clear that a conference was to be held in Lausanne to reach a peace agreement with Turkey, the spokesmen of the Armenian cause began a campaign with the aim of being invited to this conference or of having their opinions heard. Among those spokesmen were such individuals as Aharonian, Hadissian, Noradukian, and Leon Pashalian.

Hadissian sent a letter to each of the governments of France, Italy and Britain, on 18 August 1922, asking whether he could take part in a preliminary commission which would organize the eastern issues; he was informed on 21 August that his request had been refused.

On 18 November 1922, Hadissian sent another letter and repeated his request. Despite the fact that, as a result of these efforts, the four individuals mentioned addressed the Subcommittee for Minorities in Lausanne, they did not take part in the discussions.

Aharonian and Hadissian had come on behalf of the Armenian Republic.

However, the Kars Agreement had been made with Armenia, and this issue had been concluded. But it was of no consequence whether the agreement existed or not. What was important was to take advantage of opportunities when they arose.

Surprisingly, this time the Armenians did not claim that they had been belligerents during the war and that this aspect should be recognized. They had asserted this point of view in order to be able to attend the Sèvres negotiations. They had proved that during the war they had been combatants, but they had not abandoned their accusations against the Turkish Government of massacres, concerning the justifiable measures taken against a combatant community.[33]

When the Conference met, the Armenians presented a note. In his book, Esat Uras has quoted this note from Hadissian.

. . . . This war has taken a very heavy toll of the Armenians.

Of the 2,250,000 Armenians of Turkish Armenia, 1,250,000 have been destroyed. 700,000 have emigrated to the Caucasus, to Iran, to Syria, to Greece, to the Balkan States, and to other places. At the present time there are only 13,000 in the villages of Turkish Armenia, and 150,000 in Istanbul. And these are constantly ready to emigrate. . . .

Three different decisions for the establishment of the national home had been taken:

1. The decision taken by the honourable President of the USA, acting as an arbitrator, which concerns the setting apart of an area of land for the Armenians.

2. To extend the borders of the Erevan Republic, by extending some parts of the Eastern provinces, and by providing a harbour at the sea.

3. To add to this homeland part of Cilicia which had been relinquished to Syria with the Sèvres Agreement, and which was later given to Turkey with the Ankara Agreement.[34]

The United States of America took part in the Lausanne Conference as an observer. Because there had been no war between the U S A and Turkey, there was no need for peace between them. The written instructions of the U S A delegation to the conference included the following point about the Armenians: `The question of the homeland of the Armenians may be raised. It is possible that upon the return of more settled conditions in Russia, the Russian Caucasus may offer the best refuge for Armenians from Turkey.'[35]

In the general session of the First Commission of the Lausanne Conference about minorities on 12 December 1922, chairman Lord Curzon brought forward the Armenian question and said:

It is necessary to bear these in mind, especially because of the promise given to them concerning their future. Now, in the old Russian province of Erevan, which is now a Soviet Republic, there is a so-called Armenian State, which, according to what they told me, has a population of 1,250,000, which is saturated with emigrants who have come from all directions, and which is unable to accept a larger population.

On the other hand, the Armenian population of Kars, Ardahan, Van, Bitlis, and Erzurum has been nearly destroyed. When the French evacuated Cilicia, the Armenian population of this province panicked, and left with them. Now they are dispersed in the cities of Iskenderun, Aleppo, Beirut, and all along the Syrian border. I believe that of the Armenian population of nearly 3 million, in Asiatic Turkey, a mere 130,000 has remained. Hundreds of thousands of them have scattered and taken refuge in the Caucasus, Russia, Iran, and neighbouring regions. . . .

And thus, as it was often affirmed, Turkey must find a region within which to settle the Armenians, in one part of its land in Asia, be it in the north-eastern provinces, or in the south-eastern part of Cilicia and on the Syrian borders.[36]

Ismet Pasha, who gave a speech about the minorities in Turkey at the same meeting, also mentioned the Armenian question. After he had given a general account of the history of this issue, he focussed on the present-day situation:

. . . . It would be correct to state that there is no longer a minority which is capable of establishing an independent state within the Ottoman Empire which is now formed of only Turkish provinces. Until such time as the principle of nationalities is equitably applied everywhere, the trend to give independence to those parts of the Ottoman Empire which include significant non-Turkish elements, the existence of separatist trends, might have been shown as justifiable. At the present time the situation is entirely different. Just as it cannot be conceived logically that the Greeks who have settled in Marseilles should establish an independent Greek state there, or that they should annex this city to their mother land, the Greeks or the Armenians of Turkey will not have the right to make similar demands.
. . . . In fact the friendly and good neighbourly relations which were reinforced by the agreements made between Turkey and Armenia have removed the possibility for the Armenian State to engage in any kind of provocation. On the other hand, among the Armenians, those who have decided to remain in Turkey must have realized the necessity of living as good citizens. . . .

After Ismet Pasha, M. Venizelos spoke, and as he talked about the Greek minority, he also mentioned the Armenians. Later, Mr. Child, the USA representative, spoke, and indirectly talked about the subject of the Armenian homeland.

The last to speak at the meeting was Ismet Pasha; he stated that he reserved the right to reply to the statement by Lord Curzon, and replied to Venizelos, making the following remarks:

. . . . Without any doubt, M. Venizelos pretends not to see that the occupation of Asia Minor has been a source of new miseries for the Armenians. This poor community was forced to enlist and to join the ranks of the Greek army. . . . The Armenians were sent to the front and were forced to shoot at the Turks. After the defeat many pillages occurred. Moreover, the Greek authorities engaged in propaganda to attribute these offences to the Armenians. Later, when the Greeks left Asia, they dragged the Armenians along. It is necessary to accept that the last government in the world which can have the audacity to pity the Armenians in front of everybody is the Greek Government which has directly created these misfortunes for the Armenians.

During the meeting which took place on 13 December, Ismet Pasha stated that there was not one inch of land in the Turkish motherland to be given to the Armenians. He added, 'today there is no obstacle for the Armenians who are in Turkey to live comfortably, in harmony with their fellow citizens'. During this meeting Lord Curzon spoke again, and asked how the Armenian population of 3 million in Asia Minor had been reduced to 130,000 and why 60-80,000 Armenians had fled after the French, when the French left Cilicia.

The meetings continued on 14 December. This time, Ismet Pasha stated that in no period of Turkish history were there 3 million Armenians in Turkey, and that even in the whole world, according to foreign statistics, there were not so many Armenians. After he had asserted that the Armenians who left Cilicia had been forced to flee by the threats of the agents of revolutionary committees, and that this was known to the whole world, he said: '. . . . What happened to the Armenians who are missing today should be sought in recent wars and in the wars which were forced on Turkey. The Muslim population in the eastern provinces which was 4 million has fallen below 3 million, in the western provinces from 3.5 million to 2 million. Those who are missing, that is 2.5 million people, are the victims of the war years. Lord Curzon asked whether a place could be reserved for the Armenians in such a large country as Turkey. I remind you that there are States much larger than Turkey.'

After this the Armenian question was discussed in the 15 December meeting of the Subcommittee for Minorities. The Italian Montagna, chairman of the commission, said that the Subcommittee could examine the issue of the Armenian homeland, but Riza Nur Bey stated that he refused to discuss such an issue. During the 22 December meeting of the Subcommittee, M. Montagna suggested that they should hear the representative delegation of minorities. Riza Nur Bey replied that sessions in which such delegations were heard would not be considered official sessions of the Subcommittee, and that the Turkish delegation would not attend such sessions.

The Armenian delegation spoke on 26 December, in the Subcommittee, which was not attended by the Turkish delegation. The Armenian delegation included Noradukian, Aharonian, Hadissian, and Pashalian. The delegation made the same statements as those which had been expressed in the note they had submitted previously. In his speech, Noradukian suggested that it should be permitted to enlist soldiers in the Armenian land, that every Armenian should be allowed not to do his military service, and that the Patriarchate should be independent. He stated, 'His Excellency Ismet Pasha does not see the necessity for us to form an Armenian land, he thinks it is sufficient for peace to allow the return of our refugees who are in foreign countries.' The other new point was the following statement made by Aharonian: 'They tell us that the Armenian Movement of Liberation occurred because of influences which came from Great Britain and Tsarist Russia. I will affirm here that the government of Tsarist Russia and the Sultan were of the same opinion, to destroy all movements which aimed at abolishing the absolutist regime. All the Caucasian bands who were formed so that they could rush to the help of their brothers in Turkish Armenia were destroyed along the border by the Russian Army, because the Tsarist Government did not want to create a Bulgaria in the southern part of its borders.'[37]

During the 30 December session of the Subcommittee, the American representative read a note with regard to the establishment of a national homeland for the Armenians.

The Subcommittee held its last session concerning minorities on 6 January 1923. When the procedures were concluded in this meeting concerning the articles which would be included in the agreement about minorities, M. Montagna spoke and read a note on the subject of the Armenians. He expressed his wish for the establishment of an Armenian land. Then Sir Horace Rumbolt, the British representative, spoke and read a note on the same subject. Although it was the turn of the French representative to speak, Riza Nur Bey spoke, stating: 'The Allied States had the right to be present to listen to the notes which were just read, because they have taken upon themselves a moral obligation in regard of the Armenians. In fact, it was the Allied Powers who used these people as a political tool to have them attack Turkey. Under these conditions the Turkish representative delegate considers these notes as invalid. The Turkish Delegation is of the opinion that it is better to leave the session, instead of listening to such statements',[38] and left the meeting without listening to the French representative.

The U S A representative, Joseph Grew, reports this scene as scandalous in his memoirs, and adds: 'As regards the National Armenian Home, the privately expressed views of the Allied representatives are that it is not possible to formulate any concrete plan which will be wise even for the welfare of the Armenians themselves. The creation of these little new segregative areas, autonomous or otherwise, is not regarded favourably, and confidentially Curzon, Barrere and the Italian delegates say so.'[39]

It is useful to read Riza Nur's own account of the incident which occurred in the Subcommittee:

Towards the end of the sessions of January 6, 1923, Montagna turned to the question of the Armenian homeland. He began to read what he had written on this subject. I saw that it was quite long. I had never been wrong about Montagna. It was as if I knew what he was going to say. I saw that he was adding things that had not come to my mind. For example they had previously heard the Bulgarians. We did not go to that session. Their statements were not included in the minutes. He said, 'Unfortunately the Turks did not attend the session. I will communicate their demands by proxy to the Turkish delegation.' That was the last straw. I objected, he would not listen. I said 'We cannot listen, was it supposed to be like this?' He didn't care. . . . He just continued. As if the man was deaf from birth. . . . He finished, Rumbolt began to speak. I objected again. I requested to speak. They did not listen. . . . They continued. . . . They read for a long time, their faces were red, they were worried. Apparently they were afraid that an impropriety would occur. I requested to speak. He finished, the French delegate began to speak. This time I repeated my request more harshly. I got up. Like Montagna I said, 'I will say a few words.' I began to speak before the French.

I said: 'The Allied Powers made the Armenians a political tool for them, and forced them to open fire. They made them rebel against their government. As a result they were punished. They were destroyed as a punishment with epidemics, famine, and emigration. The entire responsibility for this does not fall on us, but on the Allied Powers. If a reward must be given to the Armenians, you give it. . . .

'That the Armenians were unfortunate. That they must be given a home land, independence. We are certain of this. However, there isn't only one unfortunate nation in the world. Egypt so many times, and only yesterday, has been bathed in its blood for its independence. India, Tunisia, Algeria, Morocco want their independence, their home land. For how many centuries, how much blood have the Irish shed for their homeland, for their independence? . . Give these people their homeland, their independence. . . What you have read is out of order. Under these conditions we cannot stay here. I am leaving the session.'

I got up. My statements were harsh. They were all red as beets. Rumbolt especially was now red, then purple.

In my opinion, England had never heard such harsh and accusing statements in diplomacy. At a time when they were at the apogee of their might and power, it was very hard for these proud British to hear these statements from a Turkish delegate.

They did not include in the minutes these last parts of my statements. They falsified the minutes as they pleased. What forgery. . . . However, my statements were reported exactly by the newspapers of the time. A few days later the Irish revolutionaries wrote me a letter and said: 'We thank you for having included the Irish among the oppressed nations who want their independence.'[40]

The Subcommittee brought the report to the 9 January 1923 meeting of the First Commission. Lord Curzon mentioned the subject of the national homeland, and Ismet Pasha stated that there was nothing he would add.

After this date the Armenian question was not discussed during the Lausanne talks and no article was included in the agreement.

The Armenian representatives again sent letters to the powers, but received no answer. A significant point here was that a telegram was sent to Chicherin, Soviet Minister of Foreign Affairs, on behalf of the Union of Armenian friends, and that the following remarks were made:

The Union of Armenian Friends knows that Soviet Russia saved the Armenian Republic of Caucasus. . . .

The Russians may make a special agreement with the Turks, concerning the extending of the border of the Caucasus Armenia towards the areas of Van and Bitlis. In this way the Russians will have solved the Armenian question with the Turks and with the Allied powers who were put in a difficult position as the Turks opposed the attempts to establish an independent Government within their borders.

After the anti-Russian declaration in the Subcommittee, this letter is naturally quite interesting, but even more interesting was Chicherin's answer dated 25 January: '. . . . Now I inform you that the Governments of Russia and Ukraine have proposed to take within their borders the Armenian deserters, whose number will be correctly determined. I request that my information be communicated to the authorities.'

Esat Uras has included these telegrams on pp. 740-1 of his book, as quoted by Hadissian.

This exchange of telegrams is also reported by Kachaznuni. We summarize below what he has written on this subject:

In 1922 the cause of the Turkish Armenians was in its death-throes. At the London Conference the term "Homeland" was used officially for the first time. The Sèvres Agreement had been entirely forgotten. Neither the independent Armenian State nor the independent provinces were any longer a matter of discussion. There was talk of a disputable national homeland in some other's home.

This was the last concession given by Ankara for the sake of peace. The demand for a homeland would be obligatory for Turkey, and the homeland would be independent from the administration of Turkey. This was the situation in March.

At the end of the year, the situation in Lausanne had somewhat changed. The demand for a homeland was not made. It was presented as a simple matter, as a favour of the friendly feelings and good intentions of the Turks. A dialogue, worthy of operettas, was established. The Turks stated that they were quite sad, but that they could not accept this friendly offer, the Allied Powers asserted that there was nothing else they could do for the poor Armenians. . . . Then they went on to the matter of 'Coupons'.

But here, comrade Chicherin spoke on behalf of Soviet Russia, and suggested that an area be given to the Armenians in Crimea, on the banks of the Volga, and in Siberia. The State changed into the homeland, and the homeland was modified into colonies. . . .[41]

The Armenian delegation, who could do no more in Lausanne, left the city, after having submitted a letter of protest to the Powers, on 2 February 1923.

The Lausanne Agreement was signed on 24 July 1923. There was no clause in it concerning the Armenians. Articles 37-44, which concerned minorities, would naturally apply to the Armenians as well. When the Turkish Civil Law was published, the Armenian community officially declared that they did not want to have for themselves the status of a minority. They preferred to live in Turkey like any other citizens. Since that day, not the slightest harm has been inflicted on the Armenians.

With the 'Declaration and Protocol' concerning the general amnesty annexed to the Lausanne Treaty, a general amnesty was declared for individuals who could be considered as having committed offences by their activities during the war. It was declared that of these individuals, only 150 would not be allowed to reside in Turkey, and the list of these 150 persons was announced. (Later, they were pardoned.)

It was decreed that people who resided in those countries that were separated from Turkey by the 31st article of the Lausanne Agreement, and who had automatically gained citizenship of that country by article 30, would have the right within two years to choose Turkish citizenship. Through these decrees, all the Armenians who were at that date outside Turkey, and who had retained Turkish citizenship, and those Armenians who were in those countries which separated from Turkey, obtained the right to return to Turkey if they wished.

We do not know whether any Armenians have returned to Turkey. But if they have, they are included in the community which lives in Turkey today.

Let us report here the answer given by Ataturk to a question asked by the American journalist Clarence K. Streit, on behalf of his newspaper, about the Armenians, on 4 February 1921:

Aside from the exaggerations claimed by those who are making antagonistic accusations, the question of the relocation of the Armenians actually consists of this.

When the Russian Army had begun its great offensive against us in 1915, the Armenian Tashnak Committee, which was at the service of the Czarist regime, drove the Armenian community, which was behind our military units, to rebellion. Because we were forced to retreat, in face of the superiority in numbers and equipment of the enemy, we considered ourselves constantly as being between two fires. Our convoys of supply and wounded were massacred without mercy, the bridges and roads behind us were destroyed, and in the Turkish villages terror reigned.

The bands who committed these murders, and who took all the Armenians capable of bearing arms into their ranks, took advantage of the immunities given to them since peace time, though the capitulations, by some great powers, and they made all their transfers of arms, ammunition, and supplies, of which they had been successful in collecting large stocks, through the Armenian villages.

World public opinion, which was quite indifferent to the treatment of Ireland by Great Britain during peace time, and away from the war area, cannot make a justifiable accusation against us concerning the decision we were obliged to take regarding the relocation of the Armenian community.

In refutation of the accusations directed to us, those who were relocated are alive, and most of them would have returned to their homes, if the Allied Powers had not forced us to engage in war again.[42]

Article 6 of the general amnesty declaration which was signed in Lausanne stated: 'The Turkish Government, which shares the desire for general peace with all the Powers, announces that it will not object to the measures implemented between 20 October 1918 and 20 November 1922, under the protection of the Allies, with the intention of bringing together again the families which were separated because of the war, and of returning possessions to their rightful owners.' It is apparent that this article concerned the individuals who had been forced to emigrate, and who returned to their homes during the period of armistice and occupation. At that time, Turkey announced that these procedures, which were made under the control of the occupation powers, would be maintained without modification.

The 65th article of the Lausanne Agreement stipulated that the possessions of individuals who had foreign citizenship when the war started, and whose possessions in Turkey had been confiscated, would be returned to them. The 95th article gave a deadline for inquiries on this matter.

Finally, articles 46-63 stated the liquidation of the debts of the Ottoman State. (The process of liquidation has ended.)

Today, no one has the right to make any kind of demand from Turkey about the events occurring before the signing of the Lausanne Treaty.

Conclusion

After Lausanne, the European Powers and Russia turned their attention to internal matters. The Armenian files in these states were closed.

Actually the Armenians were in conflict among themselves. The Tashnaks and the Hunchaks, the Antilyas Church and Etchmiadzin, were in open conflict. This struggle among the Armenians is outside our topic. (The details may be found in Papazian's work entitled *Patriotism Perverted.*

In the United States of America the situation was a little different. The climate created by the missionaries in this country, which only had contact with the Ottoman Empire through the missionaries, had aroused antagonistic feelings against the Turks, at least among certain sections of society. The Protestant Church also had a very important influence on public opinion. The Armenians who took advantage of this, and who were almost entirely emigrants from Turkey, formed a lobby.

The U S A had not signed the Lausanne Treaty, because it had not been at war with Turkey. However, as diplomatic relations had been severed, an Agreement of Friendship and Commerce had been signed in Lausanne on 6 August, 1923 between the U S A and Turkey. The Armenian lobby in the U S A engaged in a campaign to prevent the passage of this agreement through Congress. The Democratic Party even included this issue in its election campaign. As a result, in the vote which took place in the Senate in 1927, there were six votes fewer than were necessary to obtain a two-thirds majority, and the agreement was rejected.

A new agreement with the U S A was not made until 1930.

The economic crisis which arose after the 1930s left the U S A with its own problems, after a short time the developments which eventually led to the Second World War began, and in the U S A too the Armenian file was forgotten.

The subject of Kars-Ardahan was brought up at the meeting held by the world Armenian organizations in Erivan, on the occasion of the election of the new Armenian Catholicos, in June, following the end of the war in 1945. Attempts were made to direct the subject to the peace conference. However, the division of the world into two spheres, and especially the warm feelings and friendship which developed between Turkey and the U S A during the Korean War which occurred some time later, did not make it possible for antagonism towards the Turks, which was isolated within the Armenian communities in some countries, to reach significant levels.

Starting from the 1960s, when the period of détente began between the Eastern and Western blocks, the isolated attempts began to be unified, demonstrations were held in an increasing number of countries on 24 April, monuments were constructed. In

1966 there was an attempt to bring the issue to the United Nations.

When the Cyprus crisis occurred, cooperation was established between the Armenians and the Greeks, which was not even concealed, and which recalled the cooperation during the War of Independence.

Kachaznuni wrote:

The European Powers have abandoned our Cause. Half of the Armenian nation has been destroyed or has been dispersed around the world. The other half has had its sap drawn, its house destroyed, it needs a long rest. The Armenian Republic is a sovereign state of Russia. Even if we wanted to, we could not separate our state from Russia. The Party has been defeated and has lost its efficiency. It has been thrown out of the country. It cannot return to the land. It cannot achieve anything outside. This is the situation today. There is nothing else the Tashnaks can do now.

However, it appears that Kachaznuni was wrong, and what the Tashnaks are able to do, which is to commit murder, is being done. But, this time, the Powers have not opened the old dusty Armenian Files, but the murder files in the records of the police.

Notes

The following books and archives have been cited in abbreviated form.

AAEF - Archives des Affaires Etrangéres de France
Bayur - Yusuf Hikmet Bayur, *Türk Inkilabi Tarihi*, 3 vols (Ankara, 1940-67)
Die Grosse Politik —Die Grosse Politik der Europaischen Kabinette 1911-1914, ed. Lepsius (Berlin, 1922-7)
F. O. - Foreign Office Papers, Public Record Office
Gatteyrias (1882) - J. A. Gatteyrias, *L'Arménie et les Arméniens* (Paris, 1882) Genelkurmay - Turkish General Staff
Morgan (1919) - Jacques de Morgan, *Histoire du Peuple Arménien* (Paris, 1919) Nalbandian (1963) Louise Nalbandian, *The Armenian Revolutionary Movement* (Berkeley and Los Angeles, 1963)
Pastermadjian (1949) - H. Pastermadjian, *Histoire de l'Arménie* (Paris, 1949) Price (1923) - Clair Price, *The Rebirth of Turkey* (New York, 1923)
Sanjian (1965) - Avedis K. Sanjian, *The Armenian Communities in Syria under Ottoman Dominion* (Cambridge, Mass., 1965)
Turkey - British Blue Books on Turkey
Uras (1976) - Esat Uras, *Tarihte Ermeniler ve Ermeni Meselesi* (Istanbul, 1976) USNA - United States National Archives

Introduction

1 As this information can be found in any general 'Armenian History' it has not been deemed necessary to cite a reference for it.
2 Morgan (1919), p. 304.
3 Gatteyrias (1882), p. 77
4 Morgan (1919), p. 310.
5 Pastermadjian (1949), p. 113 n. 2.
6 David Marshall Lang, *Armenia, Cradle of Civilization* (London, 1980), p. 268.
7 August Carriere, *Moise de Khoren et les Genéalogies Patriarcales* (Paris, 1891).
8 Morgan (1919), p. 309
9 Descriptions of these two works are found in M. F. Brosset, *Collection d'Historiens Arméniens* (reprint, Amsterdam, 1979).

1. Armenia and the Armenians

1 A. J. Toynbee, *A Study of History* (Oxford University Press, 1963), Vol. VII, p. 661
2 Gatteyrias (1882), pp. 12-15.
3 Morgan (1919), pp. 43-4.
4 Frédéric Macler, *La Nation Arménienne, son passe, ses malheurs* (Paris, 1924), pp. 18-19.
5 Pastermadjian (1949), p.23.

6 Nalbandian (1963), p. 4.

7 Richard Hovannissian, *Armenia on the Road to Independence.* (Los Angeles, 1963), p. 2

8 René Grousset, *Histoire de l'Arménie* (Paris, 1973), pp. 67-8.

9 David Marshall Lang, *Armenia, Cradle of Civilization* (London, 1980), p. 94.

10 Grousset, op. cit. , p. 42.

11 Bedrich Hrozny, *Histoire de I'Asie Anterieure* (Paris, 1947), pp. 191-7.

12 Herodotus, *The Histories* (Penguin Books, 1972).

13 Xenophon, *The Persian Expeditions* (Penguin Books, 1979).

14 Xenophon, *Oeuvres Completes,* Vol. 2 (Anabase) (Garnier-Flammarion, Paris, 1967), p. 249.

15 Ruppen Courian, *Promartyrs de la Civilization* (Yverdon, Switzerland, 1964), p. 27.

16 Grousset, *op. cit.,* pp. 287-95.

17 Sanjian (1965).

2. The origins of the Armenian question

1 A. J. Toynbee, *A Study of History* (Oxford University Press, 1963), Vol. VII, p. 381.

2 Francesco Gabrieli, *Muhammed and the Conquest of Islam,* p. 110.

3 *The first genocide of the 20th century.* Compiled by James Nazer (New York, 1968), p. 15.

4 Dickran H. Boyajiyan, *Armenia* (New Jersey, 1972), p. 87.

5 Sanjian (1%5), p. 21.

6 Morgan (1919), p. 364.

7 Pastermadjian (1949), p. 290.

8 Nalbandian (1963), pp. 30-1.

9 Boyajiyan, *op. cit.,* p. 84.

10 Samouel d'Ani, *Tables chronologiques,* in M. F. Brosset, *Collection d'Historiens Armeniens* (Amsterdam, 1979), p. 345.

11 Morgan (1919), p. 102.

12 Gatteyrias (1882), pp.46-55.

13 Boyajiyan, *op. cit.,* p. 86.

14 Edwin M. Bliss, *Turkey and the Armenian Atrocities* (Philadelphia, 1896), pp. 1-2.

15 Felix Valyi, Revolutions in Islam (London, 1925), pp. 27-8.

16 E. Alexander Powell, *The Struggle for Power in Moslem Asia* (New York, 1925), p. 120.

17 Ernest Jackh, *The Rising Crescent* (New York, 1944), p. 37.

18 Valyi, *op. cit.,* pp. 48-9.

19 Pastermadjian (1949), p. 274.

20 Talcott Williams, *Turkey, A World Problem of Today* (New York, 1922), p. 194. 21 Powell, *op. cit.,* pp. 27-8.

22 Price (1923), p. 79-80.

23 Valyi, *op. cit.,* pp. 31-8.

24 Bliss, *op. cit.,* pp. 302ff.

25 Cyrus Hamlin, *My Life and Times* (Boston, 1893), p. 284.

26 Price (1923), pp. 65-6.

27 Elie Kedourie, *The Chatham House Version and other Middle-Eastern Studies* (New York), pp. 287-9.

28 Sydney Whitman, *Turkish Memories* (London, 1914), pp. 120-1.

29 Rev. Henry Fanshawe Tozer, *Turkish Armenia and Eastern Asia Minor* (London, 1881), p. 230.

30 Powell, *op. cit.*, p. 22.

31 Ibid, p. 30.

32 Whitman, *op. cit.*, p. 29.

33 Ibid, pp. 70-94.

34 Price (1923), p. 189.

35 A. J. Toynbee, *The Western Question* (New York, 1970), p. 80.

36 F.O. 371/3404/162647, p. 2.

37 Lucy Masterman, C. F. G. *Masterman* (London, 1968), p. 272.

38 Ibid, p. 298.

39 Ibid, p. 273.

40 *Third Report on the work conducted for the government at Wellington House*. British documents, 37/156/6/22234.

41 A. J. Toynbee, *Armenian Atrocities: The murder of a nation* (New York, 1975). 42 Arthur Ponsonby, *Falsehood in War-Time* (New York, 1971).

43 Cate Haste, *Keep the home fires burning* (London, 1977).

44 C. F. Dixon Johnson, *The Armenians* (Blackburn, 1916), p. 61.

3. The Armenians in the Ottoman Empire and the policies of the great powers

1 M. F. Brosset, *Collection d'Historiens Armeniens* (Amsterdam, 1979), pp. 286, 297.

2 Sanjian (1965), p. 34.

3 W. E. D. Allen, *Caucasian Battlefields* (Cambridge, 1953), p. 18.

4 Ismail Hami Danismend, *Izahli Osmanli Tarihi Kronolojisi* (Istanbul, 1972), Vol. IV, p. 65.

5 Richard Hovannisian, *Armenia on the Road to Independence* (Los Angeles, 1963), p. 9.

6 W. E. D. Allen, *op. cit.*, p. 43.

7 Hovannisian, *op. cit.*, pp. 10-11.

8 Danismend, *op. cit.*, IV, p. 174.

9 Ibid, pp. 176-7.

10 C. Oscanyan, *The Sultan and His People* (London, 1857), pp. 353~.

11 Gatteyrias (1882), p. 136.

12 M. B. Dadian, `La Societe armenienne contemporaine', *Revue des deux Mondes* (June 1867).

13 Gatteyrias (1882), p. 139.

14 Pasdermadjian (1949), p. 312.

15 Mikail Varandian, *L'Arménie et la question armenienne* (Laval, 1917), pp. 42-6.

16 E. Aknouni, *Les Plaies du Caucase* (Geneva, 1905), pp. 117-19.

306

17 Ibid, pp. 1ts 14.

18 Rifki Salim Buçak, *Turk-Rus-Inqiliz munasebetleri* (Istanbul, 1946), p. 9.

19 Jacques Ancel, *Manuel Historique de la question d'orient*, p. 143.

20 Pastermadjian (1949), p. 353.

21 Marcel Léart, *La Question armenienne à la Iumière des documents* (Paris, 1913)" 'PP. 65ff.

22 Dadian *op. cit.*, p. 915.

23 Uras (1976), p. 179.

24 F.O. 424/46, No. 336.

25 F.O. 424/51/Conf. No. 588.

26 F.O. 424/63, No. 277.

27 F.O. 424/63, 352.

28 Hovannisian, *op. cit.*, p. 37.

29 Pastermadjian (1949), p. 374.

30 Morgan (1919), p. 297.

31 Léart, *op. cit.*

32 F.O. 96/205.

33 H. F. B. Lynch, Armenia, *Travels and Studies*, Vol. II, (Beirut, 1965), p. 427. 34 F.O. 424/107, No. 104, Enclosure I.

35 Lynch, *op. cit.*, II, p. 427.

36 F.O. 424/106, No. 273, Enclosure I.

37 F.O. 424/107, No. 135, Enclosure I.

.38 F.O. 424/106, No. 200.

39 F.O. 424/132, No. 46, Enclosure I.

40 F.O. 424/107, No. 104, Enclosure I, p. 2.

41 F.O. 424/132, No. 46, Enclosure 5.

42 Ludovic de Constenson, *Les Reformes en Turquie d'Asie* (Paris, 1913).

43 Viconte de Coursons, *La Rebellion Armenienne, son origine, son but* (Paris, 1895).

44 Christopher Walker, Armenia. *The Survival of a Nation* (London, 1981), p. 230. 45 Rev. Henry.F. Tozer, *Turkish Armenia and Eastern Asia Minor* (London, 1881), p. 194n.

46 Price (1923), p. 78.

47 Alexander Powell, *The Struggle for Power in Muslim Asia* (New York, 1923), p. 114.

48 Lynch, *op. cit.*, Vol. II, p. 428.

49 Vital Cuinet, *La Turquie d'Asie* (Paris 1892-4), 4 vols.

50 *Documents diplomatiques, Affaires arméniennes, Projet de Reforme dans l'Empire Ottoman, 1893-1897*, pp. 2-8.

51 Kemal H. Karpat, 'Ottoman Population Records and the Census of 1881/82- 1893, *International Journal of Middle East Studies*, 9 (1978), pp. 237-74.

52 Lynch, *op. cit.*, II, p. 408

53 F.O. 424/106, No. 273.

54 F.O. 424/107, No. 135, Enclosure I.

55 Lynch, *op. cit.*, II, p. 206.

56 *Turkey*, No. 8 (1896), No. 109.

57 F.O. 424/107, No. 104, Enclosure 3.

58 Lynch, *op. cit.*, II, p. 412.

59 Lynch, *op. cit.*, II, p. 151.

60 Uras (1976), pp. 200ff.

61 Paragraph 16 of Ayastefanos is: 'Comme l'evacuation, par les troupes russes, des territoires qu'elles occupent en Arménie et qui doivent etre restitués à la Turquie, pourraity donner lieu à des conflits et á des complications prejudiciables aux bonnes relations des deux pays, la Sublime Porte s'engage á realiser sans plus de retard les ameliorations et les reformes exigées par les besoins locaux dans les provinces habitées par les Arméniens et à garantir leur securité contre les Kurdes et les Circassiens.'

62 F.O. 424/68, No. 639.

63 F.O. 424/68, No. 644.

64 F.O. 424/69, No. 214.

65 Uras (1976), pp. 227-35; Léart, op. cit., pp. 28-30.

66 F.O. 424/72, No. 10.

67 F.O. 424/72, No. 99.

4. The Armenian question

1 F.O. 424/76, No. 23 enclosure.

2 F.O. 424/73, No. 261.

3 F.O. 424/74, No. 388.

4 Uras (1976) pp. 256-66.

5 F.O. 424/74, No. 503.

6 F.O. 424/76, No. 554.

7 F.O. 424/98, No. 67.

8 F.O. 424/106, No. 246 enclosure.

9 F.O. 424/107, No. 2.

10 The note was submitted in French. The French text may be found on pp. 32-7 of Marcel Léart's book, its Turkish translation on pp. 287-93 of Esat Uras' book.

11 F.O. 424/107, No. 194.

12 F.O. 424/123, No. 6.

13 F.O. 424/123, No. 104, enclosure 2.

14 F.O. 424/123, No. 75.

15 F.O. 424/123, No. 113.

16 F.O. 424/123, No. 126.

17 F.O. 424/123, No. 180.

18 F.O. 424/123, No. 215.

19 F.O. 424/132, No. 22.

20 *Die Grosse Politik*, Vol. 9, No. 2183.

21 Ibid.

22 F.O. 424/107, No. 194, enclosure 1.

23 F.O. 424/107, Nos. 185 and 212.

24 F.O. 424/107, No. 213.

25 F.O. 424/122, No. 1 enclosure.

26 F.O. 424/122, No. 35.

27 F.O. 424/122, No. 54, enclosure.

28 F.O. 424/132, No. 36.
29 F.O. 424/132, No. 101.
30 F.O. 424/132, No. 143.
31 Nalbandian (1963), p. 71.
32 Uras (1976), p. 421.
33 Nalbandian (1963), p. 94.
34 Ibid, pp. 97-9.
35 The Hunchak programme and organizational regulation may be found on pp. 432-9 of Uras' book, as translated from the text published in Armenia in 1887 in London.
36 Uras (1976), p. 441.
37 Nalbandian (1963), p. 152.
38 K. S. Papazian, *Patriotism Perverted* (Boston, 1934), p. 11.
39 Nalbandian (1963), p. 155.
40 Papazian, *op. cit.*, p. 14.
41 Nalbandian (1963), p. 168.
42 Uras (1976), pp. 446-9.
43 Papazian, *op. cit.*, p. 17.
44 See page 38, note 33.
45 Price (1923), p. 77.
46 William A. Langer, *The Diplomacy of Imperialism*, pp. 157-8.
47 David G. Hogarth, *A Wandering Scholar in the Levant* (New York, 1896), pp. 147-50.
48 Sir Mark Sykes, *The Chaliph's Last Heritage* (London, 1915), pp. 409 and 416-18. 49 Sir Edwin Pears, *Forty Years in Constantinople* (London, 1915), p. 155.
50 C. F. Dixon-Johnson, *The Armenians* (Blackburn, 1916) pp. 24-5.
51 Avetis Aharonian, 'From Sardarapat to Sèvres and Lausanne, *The Armenian Review*, September 1963, p. 53.
52 See p. 119.
53 Nalbandian (1963), p. 87.
54 F.O. 424/145, No. 36.
55 Nalbandian (1963), p. 100.
56 *Turkey*, No. 1 (1889), No. 85, enclosure 3.
57 Ahmet Hulki Saral, *Ermeni Meselesi*, pp. 78r-9.
58 Hazinei Evrak, Carton 312, File 64, circular dated 6/26/1890 of the Ministry of Foreign Affairs.
59 *Turkey*, No. 1 (1890-1), No. 66.
60 Ibid, No. 106, enclosure.
61 Nalbandian (1963), p. 118.
62 Uras (1976), p. 463.
63 Hazinei Evrak, Carton 310, File 56.
64 *Die Grosse Politik*, Vol. 9, No. 2175.
65 Nalbandian (1963), p. 119.
66 *Die Grosse Politik*, Vol. 9, Nos. 2177 and 2178.
67 Ibid.
68 *Turkey*, No. 1 (1892), No. 3.
69 F.O. 424/162, No. 54.

70 *Turkey*, No. 3 (18%), No. 82.
71 Nalbandian (1963), p. 120, n. 40.
72 Edwin M. Bliss, *Turkey and the Armenian Atrocities* (Philadelphia, 1896), p. 337.
73 Ibid, p. 344.
74 Nalbandian (1963), p. 120.
75 *Turkey*, No. 1 (1895) Part I, No. 252, p. 135.
76 Hazinei Evrak, Musir Zeki Pasha's report, box 321, file 89.
77 Rev. A. W. Williams, *Bleeding Armenia* (Publisher's Union, 1896), p. 331.
78 Bliss, *op cit.*, pp. 370, 371.
79 Pastermadjian (1949), p. 384.
80 F.O. Turkey No. 1 (1895), No. 252, pp. 155~1.
81 Ibid, No. 267, enclosure, p. 203.
82 Nalbandian (1963), p. 123.
83 AAEF-CP-Turquie, Vol. 524, Folio 39 and following.
84 F.O. 424/184, No. 36.
85 F.O. 424/184, No. 3.
86 F.O. 424/184, No. 5.
87 Hazinei Evrak, Carton 321, File 89, report dated September 21, 1311.
88 Johannes Lepsius, *L'Arménie et l'Europe* (Lausanne, 1896), pp. 243ff.
89 *Die Grosse Politik* Vol. X. No. 2428.
90 *Turkey*, No. 1 (1896), p. 359.
91 Hazinei Evrak, Carton 314, File 76, report dated 11/4/1895, No. 16214/183.
92 Hazinei Evrak, Carton 312, File 64, telegram dated October 9, 1311 of the gubernorate of Erzurum.
93 Hazinei Evrak, Carton 314, File 76.
94 Hazinei Evrak, Carton 312, File 68, circular dated 11/4/1895 No. 16225.
95 Hazinei Evrak, Carton 321, File 89, telegram dated October 18, 1331 of the province of Erzurum, and Carton 312, File 64, circular No. 16336 dated 11/12/1895 of the department of Foreign Affairs.
96 Hazinci Evrak, Carton 313, File 70, telegram dated 10/28/1311 of the province of Diyarbekir.
97 Hazinei Evrak, Carton 302, Number 111, File 6, No. 74.
98 Uras (1976), p. 488.
99 Nalbandian (1963), pp. 68-9.
100 Aghasi, *Zeitoun, traduction d'Archag Tchobanian* (Paris, 1897), p. 186.
101 Lepsius, *op. cit.*, p. 243.
102 F.O. 424/184, No. 426.
103 F.O. 424/184, Nos. 21 and 4.
104 General Mayewski, *Statistique des Provinces de Van et de Bitlis*, pp. 33-9.
105 *Turkey*, No. 8 (1896), No. 117, enclosure 1.
106 Hazinei Evrak, Carton 313, File 69, circular dated 7/23/1896. (The dates refer to the old calendar; 13 days must be added.)
107 F.O. 424/188, No. 174, enclosure 4.

310

108 Uras (1976), pp. 509-11.
109 Nalbandian (1963), pp. 176~7.
110 F.O. 424/188, Nos. 149 and 169.
111 F.O. 424/188, No. 190, enclosure 1.
112 Papazian, *op cit.*, p. 22.
113 Uras (1976), pp. 523-4
114 Papazian, *op. cit.*, p. 24.
115 D. M. Lang, *The Armenians, A People in Exile* (London, 1981), p. 10.
116 Pastermadjian (1949), p. 388.
117 J. Missaskian, *A Searchlight on the Armenian Question* (Boston,.1950), p. 16.
118 *Turkey*, No. 1 (1896), Nos. 1 and 2.
119 *Turkey*, No. 1 (1896), No. 45 and enclosures.
120 *Turkey*, No. 1 (1896), No. 65.
121 *Turkey*, No. 1 (1896), No. 71.
122 *Turkey*, No. 1 (1896), No. 94.
123 *Die Grosse Politik*, Vol. X, No. 2394.
124 Ibid, No. 2396.
125 *Turkey*, No. 1 (1896), No. 130, enclosure.
126 *Turkey*, No. 1 (1896), No. 204 and enclosures.
127 F.O. 424/189, No. 75.
128 F.O. 424/189, No. 80.
129 F.O. 424/189, No. 111.
130 F.O. 424/189, No. 230.
131 F.O. 424/220, No. 48, enclosure.
132 Jemal Pasha, *Hatiralar* (Istanbul, 1959), pp. 345--6.
133 F.O. 424/219, No. 83.
134 USNA, 353/43, No. 87, 4016/13.
135 F.O. 424/237, No. 8.
136 Bayur, Vol. II, Part III, p. 31; Die Grosse Politik, Vol. 38, document 15284.
137 Bayur, p. 33; *Die Grosse Politik*, Vol. 34, Part I, document 12737.
138 Bayur, p. 35; *Die Grosse Politik*, Vol. 34, Part I, document 12725.
139 Bayur, p. 37; *Die Grosse Politik*, Vol. 34, Part I, document 12744.
140 F.O. 424i237, No. 38.
141 Bayur, p. 108.
142 Bayur, p. 116; *Die Grosse Politik*, Vol. 38, document 15344.
143 Bayur, p. 169.
144 Ibid, p. 178.

5. The First World War

1 The Turkish text of this telegram may be found in Bayur, Vol. II, Part IV, p. 633, the German text in the German Archives, First World War, document 117, the English text in Ernest Jackh's book, *The Rising Crescent*, p. 12.
2 Uras (1976), pp. 576-7.
3 Ibid, p. 581.

311

4 Price (1923), p. 85.
5 F.O. 371/3404, No. 162647, p. 4.
6 K. S. Papazian, *Patriotism Perverted* (Boston, 1934), pp. 37-8.
7 Hovhannes Kachaznuni, *The Tashnaks Have Nothing More to do.* paragraph 1. (It is known that this book, which was published in Armenia in 1923 by the Mekhitarian Printing Press in Vienna, was translated into English. Its record has been found in investigations made in the national libraries of various countries, but it has been determined that both the English and Armenian versions of the book had been checked out and not returned. Finally, the copy in Armenian present in Turkey has been translated into Turkish, but we are unable to give the pages, as it is still in manuscript. Therefore we give the number of the paragraph.)
8 Uras (1976), pp. 583-5.
9 Aram Turabian, *Les Volontaires Armeniens sous les Drapeaux Français* (Marseilles, 1917), p. 6.
10 Rafael de Nogales, *Four Years Beneath the Crescent*, English translation by Muna Lee (New York, 1926), p. 45.
11 M. Philips Price, *A History of Turkey* (London, 1956), p. 91.
12 Philippe de Zara, *Mustapha Kemal, Dictateur* (Paris, 1936), pp. 159-60.
13 Price (1923), pp. 86-7.
14 Felix Valyi, *Revolutions in Islam* (London, 1925), pp. 233-4.
15 Genelkurmay, 1/131, KLS 2287, File 12, F. 1-10.
16 USNA M-353/6, 867.00/761, p. 196.
17 Genelkurmay, 4/3671, KLS 2818, File 59, F. 2-5.
18 Ibid, 4/3671, KLS 2818, File 59, F. 2-10.
19 Ibid, 4/3671, KLS 2811, File 26, F. 28.
20 Ibid, 4/3671, KLS 2811, File 59, F. 2-19.
21 Ibid, 4/3671, KLS 2818, File 59, F. 2-23.
22 Ibid, 4/3671, KLS 2811, File 26, F. 15-1.
23 Ibid, 4/3671, KLS 2818, File 59, F. 2-35.
24 Ibid, 4/3671, KLS 2818, File 59, F. 2-36.
25 Ibid, 4/3671, KLS 2818, File 59, F. 2-37.
26 Ibid, 4/3671, KLS 2818, File 59, 2-43.
27 Ibid, 4/3671, KLS 2820, File 69, F. 1-7.
28 Ibid, 4/3671, KLS 2818, File 59, F. 2-54 and 2-55.
29 Ibid, 1/2, KLS 4, File 23, A, F. 4.
30 Ibid, 1/2, KLS 520, File 2024, F. 5.
31 Dahiliye Nezareti Sifre Defteri, No. 48, 846-151214.4.
32 Genelkurmay, 1/1, KLS 4, File 23, A, F. 5.
33 Ibid, 4/3671, KLS 2820, File 69, F. 2-5 and 5-1.
34 Ibid, 1/131, KLS 2287, File 12, F. 6-2.
35 Ibid, 1/2, KLS 520, File 2024, F.11-1.
36 Ibid, 4/3671, KLS 2818, File 59, F. 1-5.
37 Ibid, 4/3671, KLS 2818, File 59, F. 1-17.
38 Ibid, 4/3671, KLS 2818, File 59, F. 1-19.
39 Ali Ihsan Sabis, *Harp Hatiralarim* (Ankara, 1951), Vol. 2, pp. 218, 219 and 205. 40 Genelkurmay, 4/3671, KLS 2820, File 69, F. 3~.
41 Ibid, 1/1, KLS 44, File 207, F. 2.

312

42 Ibid, 1/1, KLS 44, File 207, F. 2-1.

43 Ibid, 1/2, KLS 13, File 63, F. 7.

44 Ibid, 1/131, KLS 2287, File 12, F. 6.

45 Ibid, 1/131, KLS 2287, File 12, F. 6-4.

46 Ibid, 1/131, KLS 2287, File 12, F. 8.

47 Ibid, 4/3671, KLS 2818, File 59, F. 1-37.

48 Ibid, 1/131, KLS 2287, File 12, F. 6-16.

49 Ibid, 4/3671, KLS 2820, File 69, F. 3-45.

50 Ibid, 4/3671, KLS 2820, KLS, File 69, F. 3-82.

51 F.O. Dossier 2484, document 22083.

52 Oden Hedin, Bagdad, Babylon, Ninive (Leipzig, 1918), p. 70.

53 USNA M-353/43, 867.4016/591/2, p. 658.

54 Ibid,867.4016/58,p. 651.

55 Ibid,867.4016/580, p. 655.

56 Dahiliye Nezareti Emniyet Umum Mudurlugu, File 44, 844/51.

57 Genelkurmay, 1/131, KLS 2287, File 12, F. 9.

58 Ibid, 1/2, KLS 401, File 1580, F. 1-3.

59 Ibid, 1/131, KLS 2287, File 12, F. 12-1.

60 Ibid, 1/1, KLS 44, File 207, F.2-3.

61 Bayur, Vol. III, Part 3, p. 37, taken from the minutes dated 30 May
1915 (17 May 1331) of the Council of Ministers.

62 Ibid, p. 40.

63 Ibid, pp. 40-2 (taken from the minutes of the Council of Ministers of
30 May 1915) (17 May 1331).

64 Ibid, p. 46.

65 Dahiliye Nezareti Evrak, Oda, Sif, Kal, File 53, 854/54.

66 Ibid, File 53, 856/56.

67 Ibid, File 53, 855/55.

68 Ibid, File 53, 858/58.

69 Ibid, File 53, 863/61.

70 Ibid, File 53, 879/71.

71 Ibid, File 53, 893/77.

72 Ibid, File 54, 864/62.

73 Ibid, File 54, 887/72.

74 Ibid, File 54, 892/16.

75 Ibid, File 54, 895/19.

76 Ibid, File 54, 904/83.

77 Ibid, File 54, 915/20.

78 Ibid, File 54, 917/88.

79 Ibid, File 54, 920/90.

80 Ibid, File 54, 925/92.

81 Ibid, File 54, 932/94.

82 Ibid, File 54, 930/25.

83 Ibid, File 69, 952/101.

84 Ibid,972/105.

85 Hazinei Evrak, Box 178, File 23, memo No. 42746/146 of the Dahiliye
Nezareti. 86 Bayur, Vol. III, Part 3, p. 43.

87 Genelkurmay, 1/2, KLS 361, File 1445, F. 15-22.

88 Turabian, op cit., pp. 38-42.

89 Uras (1976), p. 621.
90 Hassan Arfa, *The Kurds* (London, 1968), pp. 25-6.
91 Georges Boudiére, `Notes sur la Campagne de Syrie-Cilicie, L'Affaire de Maras', *Turcica*, Vol. IX/2-X (1978), p. 160.
92 F.O. Hc. 1/8008, XC/A-018055, p. 651.
93 F.O. 371/65561E.2730/800/44.
94 Frank G. Weber, *Eagles on the Crescent* (Cornell University Press), pp. 150-2, 187.
95 Bayur, Vol. III, Part 3, p. 22.
96 Harry N. Howard, *The King-Crane Commission* (Beirut, 1963), p. 1.
97 Bayur, Vol. III, Part 4, pp. 1-14.
98 Harry N. Howard, *op cit.*, p. 4.
99 Bayur, Vol. III, Part 4, p. 121.
100 To understand the Russian attitude on this subject, see *Soviet Foreign Policy* (Moscow, 1980), Vol. I, pp. 48-66.
101 Bayur, Vol. III, Part 4, pp. 136-7.
102 Kachaznuni, *op. cit.*, paragraph 12.
103 Twerdo Khebof, *Journal de Guerre du 2ᵉᵐᵉ Regiment d'Artillerie de forteresse Russe d'Erzeroum, et Notes d'un officier Superieur Russe sur les atrocites d'Erzuroum, Traduit du manuscrit original russe*, 1919.
104 Bayur, Vol. III, Part 4, p. 250.
105 Celal Bayar, *Ben de Yazdim* (Istanbul, 1965), Vol. I, p. 14.
106 Kazim Karabekir, *Istaklal Harbimiz* (Istanbul, 1969), p. 1.
107 Celal Bayar, *op. cit.*, Vol. I, p. 24.
108 Ibid, Vol. 4, p. 1346.
109 Ibid, Vol. 5; p. 1429, n. 1.
110 The original text of the order may be found in Celal Bayar, *op. cit.*, Vol. 5, p. 1653.
111 Ibid, Vol. 5, p. 1507.
112 F.O. 371/4172, X/M 09394-29498.
113 F.O. 371/4173, X/M 08936~7913.
114 Celal Bayar, *op. cit.*, Vol. 5, p. 1510.
115 Falih Rifki Atay, *Zeytindagi* (Istanbul, 1938), p. 50.
116 F.O. 371/6556/E.2730/800/44.
117 *Cemiyeti akvam ve Türkiye'deki Ermeni ve Rumlar, Dahiliye Nezareti* Muhacirin Kalem Md, Nesriyat No. 6 (Istanbul, 1922), p. 14.
118 Halide Edip, *The Turkish Ordeal* (London, 1928), pp.16-18.
119 F.O. 371/4172, X/M 09394/2391.
120 F.O. 371/4172, X/M 09394/13694.
121 F.O. 371/4172, X/M 09394/17682.
122 F.O. 371/4172, X/M 09394/41632.
123 F.O. 371/4173, X/M 08936/81368.
124 F.O. 371/6504/09697/C.P. 3269.
125 F.O. 371/4175, X/M 08794/163689.
126 F.O. 371/4174/08992/118377.
127 F.O. 371/4174/08992/129560.
128 F.O. 371/6500/9456/E.3552.

314

129 F.O. 371/6499/9558/E.1801.
130 F.O. 371/6504/9697/E.8745.
131 F.O. 371/6503/9647/E.6311.
132 F.O. 371/6503/9647/E.6311/132/44.
133 F.O. 371/6504/9697/8519.
134 F.O. 371/7874/20769/E.5516.
135 F.O. 371/4174/08992/98910.
136 F.O. 371/5090/9632.
137 Bilal Simsir, *Malta Sürgünleri* (Istanbul, 1976).
138 Laurence Evans, *United States Policy and the Partition of Turkey, 1914-1924* (Baltimore, 1965), p. 30.
139 Ibid, p. 29.
140 Ibid, p. 55.
141 Osman Olcay, *Sèvres Anlasmasina doğru* (Ankara, 1981).
142 Lloyd George, *The Truth About the Peace Treaties* (London, 1938), Vol. 2. 143 Ibid, Vol. 2, pp. 1255ff.
144 Harry N. Howard, *op. cit.*, pp. 211-2, 231.
145 Maj. Gen. James G. Harbord, *Report of the American Military Mission to Armenia*, Senate Document No. 266 (1920), pp. 19, 24.
146 Seha Meray-Osman Olcay, *Osmanli Imparatorlugunun Çoküs Belgeleri* (Ankara, 1977), p. 74.

6. The War of Independence

1 Ataturk, *Nutuk* (Ankara, 1938), p. 6.
2 Kazim Karabekir, *Istiklal Harbimiz* (Istanbul, 1969), p. 25.
3 A. Rawlinson, *Adventures in the Near East* (New York, 1925).
4 Robert Dunn, *The World Alive* (New York).
5 AAEF-Levant 1918-29 (Arménie), Vol. 7, folio 99.
6 Kachaznuni, *op. cit.*, paragraphs 27, 28, 29, 30, 31.
7 Kasim Ener, *Cukurova Kurtulus Savasinda Adana Cephesi* (Ankara, 1970), PP~ 27,8.
8 AAEF-Levant 1918-29 (Arménie) Vol. 1, folio 244.
9 Ibid, Vol. 1, folio 245.
10 Ibid, Volume 0, folio 12.
11 Ibid, Vol. 2, folio 124.
12 Ibid, Vol. 2, folio 332.
13 Ibid, Vol. 6, folio 73.
14 Ibid, Vol. 6, folio 62.
15 Ibid, Vol. 7, folio 148.
16 Ibid, Vol. 7, folio 216.
17 Kazim Karabekir, *op. cit.*, p. 370.
18 Kasim Ener, *op. cit.*, Pp. 82-3.
19 Kazim Karabekir, *op. cit.*, p. 381.
20 AAEF-Levant 1918-29 (Arm6nie) Vol. 8, folio 91.
21 Ibid, Vol. 8, folio 180.
22 Ibid, Vol. 8, folio 187.

23 Ibid, Vol. 9, folio 10.

24 Ibid, Vol. 9, folio 36.

25 Ibid, Vol. 9, folio 65.

26 The Minutes of the Secret Session of TBMM (the Turkish Grand National Assembly) on 1 May 1920.

27 Ataturk, *op, cit.*, pp. 324-6.

28 Kasim Ener, *op. cit.*, pp. 176-7.

29 Ataturk, *op. cit.*, pp. 443-7.

30 Kasim Ener, *op. cit.*, pp. 284-7.

31 The unpublished Bristol Report may be found in the Manuscripts Section of the Library of Congress of the USA.

32 Arnold J. Toynbee, *The Western Question in Greece and Turkey* (New York, 1970), p. 284.

33 AAEF-Levant 1918-29, Vol. 1, folio 162 and 173.

34 Uras (1976), pp 717ff.

35 Joseph Grew, *Turbulent Era* (Boston, 1952), Vol. I, p. 483.

36 Seha Meray, *Lozan Baris Konferansi* (Ankara, 1973), Section I, Vol. 1, Book 1, pp. 184ff.

37 Uras (1976), quoting Hadissian, pp. 730-9.

38 Seha Meray, *op. cit.*, Section 1, Vol. 1, Book 2, p. 278.

39 Joseph Grew, *op. cit.*, Vol. 1, p. 531.

40 Doktor Riza Nur, *Hayat ve Hatiratim* (Istanbul, 1967), Vol. III, pp. 1062-3.

41 Kachaznuni, *op. cit.*, paragraph 35.

42 *Atatürk'un Milli Dis Politikasi* (Ankara, 1981), pp. 272-3.

Bibliography

Aghasi, *Zeitoun, traduction d'Archag Tchobanian*, Paris, 1897.

Aknouni, E., *Les Plaies du Caucase*, Geneva, 1905.

Allen, W.E.D., *Caucasian Battlefields*, Cambridge, 1953.

Ancel, Jacques, *Manuel Historique de la Question d'Orient*

Andonian, Aram, *Documents Officiels Concernant les Masacres Armeniens*, Paris, 1920.

Ani, Samuel d', *Tables chronologiques* in Brosset (below).

Arfa, Hassan, *The Kurds*, London, 1968.

Arikoglu, Damar, *Hatiralarim*, Istanbul, 1961

Ataturk, *Nutuk*, Ankara, 1938.

Atay, Falih Rifki, *Zeytindagi*, Istanbul, 1938.

Bayar, Celal, *Ben de yazdim*, Istanbul, 1965.

Bayur, Yusuf Hikmet, *Türk Inkilabi Tarihi*, 3 vols, Ankara, 1940-67.

Bliss, Rev. Edwin M., *Turkey and the Armenian Atrocities;* Philadelphia, 1896. Boudière, Georges, *Note sur la Campagne de Syrie-Cilicie.*

Boyajian, Dickran H., Armenia, *the case for a Forgotten Genocide*, New Jersey, 1972.

Brosset, M. F., *Collection d'Historiens Armeniens*, Amsterdam, 1979.

Burçak, Rifki Salim, *Türk-Rus-Ingiliz Münasebeitleri*, Istanbul, 1946.

Cemal Pasha, *Hatiralar*, Istanbul, 1959.

Constenson, Ludovic de, *Les Réformes en Turquie d'Asie*, Paris, 1913.

Courian, Ruppen, *Promartyrs de la Civilisation*, Yverdon, 1969.

Cuinet, Vital, *La Turquie d'Asie*, Paris, 1892.

Cursons, Viconte de, *La Rebellion Armenienne, son origine, son but,* Paris, 1895. Dadian, B., *La Sociéte Armenienne Contemporaine*, 1867.

Danismed, I. Hami, *Izahli Osmanli Tarihi Kronolojisi*, Istanbul, 1972.

Dedeyan, Gerard, *Histoire des Armeniens*, special edition, Toulouse, 1892.

Dixon-Johnson, C. F., *The Armenians*, Blackburn, 1916.

Dunn, Robert, *The World Alive*, New York.

Edip, Halide (Adivar), *The Turkish Ordeal*, London, 1928.

Eliot, Sir Charles, *Turkey in Europe*, Frank Cass, 1965.

Ener, Kasim, *Çukurova Kurtulus Savasinda Adana Cephesi*, Ankara, 1970.

Evans, Laurence, *U.S. Policy and the Partition of Turkey*, Baltimore, 1965.

Gabrieli, Francesco, *Mohammed and the Conquest of Islam.*

Gatteyrias, J. A. *L'Armenie et les Armeniens*, Paris, 1882.

Grousset, René, *Histoire de l'Armenie*, Paris, 1973.

Hamlin, Cyrus, *My Life and Times*, Boston, 1893.

Haste, Cate, *Keep the home fires burning*, London, 1977.

Hedin, Oden, *Bagdad, Babylon, Ninive*, Leipzig, 1918.

Herodotus, *The Histories*, Penguin Books, 1972.

Hocaoglu, Mehmet, *Tarihte Ermeni Mezalimi ve Ermeniler*, Istanbul, 1976.

Hogarth, David V., *A wondering scholar in the Levant*, New York, 1896.

Hovannisian, R. G., *Armenia on the road to Independence*, Los Angeles, 1967.

Howard, Harry N., *The King-Crane Commission*, Beirut, 1963.
Howard, Harry, *The Partition of Turkey*, New York, 1966.
Hrozny, Bedrick, *Histoire de l'Asie Anterieure*, Paris, 1947.
Jackh, Ernest, *The Rising Crescent*, New York, 1944.
Kachaznuni, Hovhannes, *Tasnaksutyun'un Artik Yapacagi Bir sey Yoktur* un- published Turkish translation.
Karabekir, Kazim, *Istiklal Harbimiz*, Istanbul, 1969.
Karpat, Kemal, *Ottoman Population Records*, 1978.
Kazemzade, Feruz, *Struggle for Transcaucasia*, New Haven, 1951.
Kedourie, Elie, *The Chatham House Version and other Middle Eastern Studies*, New York.
Khlebof, Twerdo, *Journal de Guerre*, 1919.
Koças, Sadi, *Tarih Boyunca Ermeniler ve Türk-Ermeni Iliskileri*, Ankara, 1967. Lang, David Marshall, *Armenia, Cradle of Civilisation*, London, 1980.
Lang, David Marshall, *The Armenians, a People in Exile*, London, 1981.
· Langer, William A., *The Diplomacy of Imperialism*.
Léart, Marcel, *La Question Armenienne a la Lumièire des Documents*, Paris, 1913.
Lepsius, Johannes, *l'Armenie et I'Europe*, Lausanne, 1896.
Lloyd George, D., *The Truth About Peace Treaties*, London, 1938.
Lynch, H. F. B., *Armenia, Travels and Studies*, Beirut, 1965.
Macler, Frédéric, *La Nation Armenienne, Son Passe, Ses Malheurs*, Paris, 1924.
Masterman, Lucy, *C.F.G. Masterman, a Biography*, London, 1939.
Matthew of Edessa, *Urfah Mateos'un Vekayinamesi ve Papaz Grigor'un zeyli*, Hrant D. Andreasyan, Ankara, 1962.
Mayewski, Gl., *Statistique des Provinces de Van et Bitlis*.
Mears, Elliot Grinnel, *Modern Turkey*, New York, 1924.
Meray, Seha, *Lozan Baris Konferansi*, Ankara, 1973.
Meray-Olcay (Seha-Osman), *Osmanli Imparatorlugunun Çöküs Belgeleri*, Ankara, 1977.
Missakian, J., *A Searchlight on the Armenian Question*, Boston, 1950.
Morgan, Jacques de, *Histoire du Peuple Arménien*, Paris, 1919.
Nalbandian, Louise, *The Armenian Revolutionary Movement*, Berkeley and Los Angeles, 1963.
Nazer, James, *The First Genocide of the 20th Century*, New York, 1968.
Nogales, Rafael de, *Four Years Beneath the Crescent*, New York, 1926.
Nur, Riza, *Hayat ve Hatiratim*, Istanbul, 1967.
Olcay, Osman, *Sevres Anlasmasina Dogru*, Ankara, 1981.
Oscanyan, C., *The Sultan and His People*, London, 1857.
Papazian, K. S., *Patriotism Perverted*, Boston, 1934.
Pastermadjian, H., *Histoire de I'Armenie*, Paris, 1949.
Pears, Edwin, *Forty Years in Constantinople*, London, 1916.
Ponsonby, Arthur, *Falsehood in War-Time*, London.
Powell, Alexander E., *The Struggle for Power in Muslim Asia*, New York, 1923.
Price, Claire, *The Rebirth of Turkey*, New York, 1923.

Price, Philips, *A History of Turkey*, London, 1956.

Rawlinson, A., *Adventures in the Near East*, New York, 1925.

Sabis, Ali Ihsan, *Harp Hatiralarim*, Ankara, 1951.

Sanjian, Avedis, K., *The Armenian Communities in Syria Under the Ottoman Empire*, Cambridge, Mass, 1965.

Saral, Ahmet Hulki, *Ermeni Meselesi*.

Shaw, S. J. and Shaw, G. K., *History of the Ottoman Empire and Modern Turkey*, Cambridge University Press, 1977.

Simsir, Bilal, *Malta Sürgunleri*, Istanbul, 1976.

Soviet Foreign Policy, Moscow, 1980.

Sykes, Sir Mark, *The Caliph's Last Heritage*, London, 1915.

Tarih Boyunca Ermeni Meselesi, Genelkurmay Yayini, 1979.

Toynbee, Arnold, *A Study in History*, Oxford University Press, 1963.

Toynbee, Arnold, *The Western Question in Greece and Turkey*, New York, 1970.

Toynbee, Arnold, *Armenian Atrocities, the Murder of a Nation*, New York, 1975.

Tozer, Fanshawe, H., *Turkish Armenia and Eastern Asia Minor*, London, 1881.

Turabian, Aram, *Les Volontaires Armeniens sous les Drapeaux Français*, Marseilles, 1917.

Uras, Esat, *Tarihte Ermeniler ve Ermeni Meselesi*, Istanbul, 1976.

Valyi, Felix, *Revolutions in Islam*, London, 1925.

Varandian, Mikael, *I'Armenie et la Question Arménienne*, Laval, 1917.

Walker, Christopher V., *Armenia, the Survival of a Nation*, London, 1980.

Weber, Frank G., *Eagles on the Crescent*, Cornell University Press, Ithaca.

Whitman, Sydney, *Turkish Memories*, London, 1914.

Williams, Rev. A. W., *Bleeding Armenia*, Publisher's Union, 1896.

Williams, Talcott, *Turkey, a World Problem of Today*, New York, 1922.

Xenophon, Anabase, *Garnier-Flammarion*, Paris, 1967.

Xenophon, *The Persian Expeditions*, Penguin Books, 1979.

Zara, Phillipe de, *Mustapha Kemal, Dictateur*, Paris, 1936.

Zeve, *Vani tanima ve tanitma cemiyeti yayini No. 2*, Istanbul, 1963.

Periodicals

The Armenian Review
Harp Tarihi Belgeleri Dergisi (Genelkurmay Yayini
International Journal of Middle East Studies
Turcica
Revue des Deux Mondes

320

B

C

G

H

I

V

226, 230-234, 239-
242,246,247, 251,
Tashnak Party, 119, 126, 153,
190,
Tayyar Pasha, Cafer, 240,
Tchalkouchian, Gr., 191,
Tevfik Pasha, 232, 233,
Terlemezian, Migirdich, 120,
130,
terrorists, 123, 126,
Thornton, Sir E., 117,
Tigran, 10, 16,
Timur, 14,
Tiridates III, 11,
Tophane Conference, 75, 76,
Tosun Pasha, 150,
Towards, N. N., 190,
Toynbee, Arnold, 2, 21, 39,
41-43, 87, 218-220,229,
Tozer, Henry, 36, 91,
Trabzon incidents, 149,
Tridat III, 24,
Trotter, Major, 90, 98, 100-
102, 108, 112, 114, 115
Turabian, Aram, 191,
Turco-Greek War, 110, 166,
240,
Turkish Army, 201, 217, 227,
245, 253, 268,
Turkish rule, 177, 178, 242,

U

Union and Progress Party,
233,
United States, 1,30-34, 39-42,
120, 219, 238, 240, 241,
anti-Turkish attitudes, 301,
302,
anti-Turkish propaganda, 36,
37,
public opinion in, 30, 34-37,
Urartu, 2,4,5,

Vahdettin, Sultan
'Mohammed VI), 37, 229,
232, 234,
Vahram V, 11, 22,
Vakaresko, Mademoiselle,
235,
Valyi, Felix, 27-30, 193,
Van revolts, 153, 154, 156,
160, 165, 197, 199, 200,
202, 203,
Vangenheim, Ambassador,
176, 182,
Varandian, Mikail, 61,
Vardapet, Vahan, 89, 94, 95,
Vazken I, 22,
Vehip Pasha, 228,
Velid, Khalif, 13,
Venizelos, M., 295,
Vienna, Congress of, 67,
Vincent, Sir Edgar, 156, 158,
Vorontsov, Prince, 51,
Vorontsov-Dachkov, 191,
Vram Chapouh, 11,

W

Walker, Christopher, 91,94,
95,
Weber, Frank G., 221,
Weizmann, Chaim, 241,
Wellington House, 40, 42,
Wheeler, M., 36,
White, Henry, 40,
White, Sir William, 130, 136,
Whitman, Sydney, 34, 35-38,
Wilhelm, Kaiser, 69, 175,
221,
Williams, A. A., 140,
Williams, Talcott, 29,
Wilson, Lieutenant, Colonel C.W.,
97, 111, 114, 115, 118,
Wilson, Woodrow,230, 241-
245, 268,

PUTNAM PUBLIC LIBRARY

3 3610 10117 4479

DISCARDED

956.62 Gurun   88032

The Armenian file.

PUTNAM PUBLIC LIBRARY
225 KENNEDY DRIVE
PUTNAM, CT 06260

GAYLORD MG